HUMAN RIGHTS AND THE WORLD'S MAJOR RELIGIONS

Human Rights and the World's Major Religions

William H. Brackney, Series Editor

Human Rights and the World's Major Religions
Volume 1: The Jewish Tradition
Peter J. Haas

Human Rights and the World's Major Religions
Volume 2: The Christian Tradition
William H. Brackney

Human Rights and the World's Major Religions
Volume 3: The Islamic Tradition
Muddathir 'Abd al-Rahim

Human Rights and the World's Major Religions
Volume 4: The Hindu Tradition
Harold Coward

Human Rights and the World's Major Religions
Volume 5: The Buddhist Tradition
Robert E. Florida

HUMAN RIGHTS
AND THE
WORLD'S MAJOR
RELIGIONS

VOLUME 2: THE CHRISTIAN TRADITION

I.C.C. LIBRARY

William H. Brackney

PRAEGER PERSPECTIVES

PRAEGER

Westport, Connecticut
London

Library of Congress Cataloging-in-Publication Data

Brackney, William H.
    Human rights and the world's major religions.
        p.   cm.
    Includes bibliographical references and index.
    Contents: v. 1. The Jewish tradition / Peter J. Haas—v. 2. The Christian tradition /
William H. Brackney—v. 3. The Islamic tradition / Muddathir Abd al-Rahim—v. 4.
The Hindu tradition / Harold Coward—v. 5. The Buddhist tradition / Robert E.
Florida.
        ISBN 0–275–98425–7 (set: alk. paper)—ISBN 0–275–98047–2 (v. 1: alk. paper)—
ISBN 0–313–30134–4 (v. 2: alk. paper)—ISBN 0–275–98045–6 (v. 3: alk. paper)—
ISBN 0–275–98381–1 (v. 4: alk. paper)—ISBN 0–313–31318–0 (v. 5: alk. paper)
        1. Human rights—Religious aspects.   I. Haas, Peter J. (Peter Jerome)
    BL65.H78H8595 2005
    201'.723—dc22   2003068987

British Library Cataloguing in Publication Data is available.

Library of Congress Catalog Card Number: 2003068987
ISBN: 0–275–98425–7 (set code)
            0–313–30134–4 (The Christian Tradition)
            0–313–31318–0 (The Buddhist Tradition)
            0–275–98381–1 (The Hindu Tradition)
            0–275–98045–6 (The Islamic Tradition)
            0–275–98047–2 (The Jewish Tradition)

First published in 2005

Praeger Publishers, 88 Post Road West, Westport, CT 06881
An imprint of Greenwood Publishing Group, Inc.
www.praeger.com

Printed in the United States of America

The paper used in this book complies with the
Permanent Paper Standard issued by the National
Information Standards Organization (Z39.48–1984).

10 9 8 7 6 5 4 3 2 1

Copyright Acknowledgment

The author and publisher gratefully acknowledge permission for use of the following material:

Excerpts from *The Power of the Poor in History: Selected Writings* by Gustavo Gutierrez. Translated
by Robert R. Barr. Maryknoll, NY: Orbis Books. 1983. Permission granted by Orbis Books.

This book is dedicated to
Erin Anne Brackney

In whom resides an activist Christian concern
for the rights and dignity of others.

CONTENTS

INTRODUCTION TO HUMAN RIGHTS AND THE WORLD'S MAJOR RELIGIONS

THIS BOOK IS THE SECOND OF A SERIES produced by Praeger Publishers titled Human Rights and the World's Major Religions. The purpose of the series is to define the meaning of human rights in the specific religious tradition and survey its breadth and development across time and cultures. Each author has crafted analytical chapters and selected appropriate primary source materials that illustrate their analyses. Additionally, these books are reference works that include biographical sections, extensive annotated bibliographies, a chronology, and an index. The religious traditions included in the series are Christianity, Buddhism, Judaism, Islam, and Hinduism.

In this volume, the Christian religious tradition is the focus. Because of the complexity of covering major Christian categories in one volume, the coverage first takes up theological foundations. Material from the Bible is surveyed, after which a discussion of Medieval, Enlightenment, and modern Christian theologians is given. Especially helpful is the breakout into major denominational traditions. Readers will find evangelicals, liberation theologians, and Hans Küng included. A second chapter chronicles "obstacles" to human rights in Christian thought and action, and this helps to objectify the treatment. The author displays his predisposition as a Baptist Christian by discussing religious liberty in a separate chapter. Finally a section on "social concerns" that form the bedrock of modern Christian discourse on human rights, precedes a key discussion of various Christian responses to United Nations declarations. This last chapter is brought to currency in 1998.

Part of the reference value to this series is the selection of illustrative primary sources that are noted throughout the analytical sections. Here one will find the Edict of Milan, the Rhode Island charter, *Pacem in terris*, and the United Nations Declaration of 1948, as well as Walter Rauschenbusch, Father John Ryan, Martin Luther, and more. Adjoining the sources is a biographical section and a comprehensive annotated bibliography; a chronology appears after the introduction, near the beginning of the book.

The author is well known for his work in the general field of post-Reformation Protestant thought. A historian and historical theologian by training, he completed his graduate work with distinction in history and religion at Temple University. He has taught at a wide variety of institutions, including Houghton College; Colgate Rochester Divinity School; The Eastern Baptist Theological Seminary, where he was vice president and dean; and McMaster University, where he was dean of the Faculty of Theology and principal of McMaster Divinity College. Since 2000, he has taught at Baylor University where he also serves as chair of the Department of Religion. Brackney has authored or edited more than fifteen books and more than sixty articles in professional journals. He has traveled in the international Christian community, lectured at institutions in Europe and South America, and engaged in formal dialogue with Jewish and Islamic thinkers. His special interests are the Free Church tradition, religious liberty and religious voluntarism, and the relationships between religion and politics.

We commend this volume to general readers in the area of human rights, historians of Christianity, and specialists who are in search of both a useful introduction and a collection of important illustrative documents.

William H. Brackney
Series Editor

FOREWORD

THE CONCEPT OF "HUMAN RIGHTS" features, paradoxically, as one of the most unitive yet most divisive terms in the contemporary world. On the one hand, especially since the promulgation of the Universal Declaration of Human Rights in 1948, it has become by design or default the common currency of the world, the expression of longings and hopes for deliverance from the scourges of war, oppression, poverty, and disease. On the other hand, it provokes heated and proliferating arguments: Do some rights take precedence over others—the right to free expression of political opinion, for instance, over the right to a secure home and job? And, *whose* rights matter most—for example, those of the individual or those of the community as a whole?

Once religion is acknowledged as a player on the scene, the debates become still more complicated. For one thing, to many observers, the concept of "human rights" belongs to the self-emancipatory project of Western post-Enlightenment, secular society and is thereby inherently antireligious in intent—almost as if the very concept of *human* rights were a denial of any valid *divine* right, not only of kings but the Deity as such. This perception can be owned equally by contemporary secularists and religious traditionalists, in praise and condemnation respectively. The argument, however, also becomes one *within* the sphere of religion itself. Particularly within its Western expressions, Christianity has broadly and progressively espoused the notion of human rights as consistent with belief in the Creator God as the source of human life and dignity, and with the gospel of liberation from sin and death into "the glorious freedom of the children of God" (Rom. 8:21). Indeed, not least through the efforts of such bodies as the World Council of Churches, Western Christianity made a significant contribution to the framing of the Universal Declaration of Human Rights itself. In part, from the seventeenth century onward, churches realized that their own integrity, health, and vitality were bound up with recognition of *religious freedom* as a cornerstone of all human rights. This recognition had grown most quickly among the Protestant churches. For a time until even as late as the end of the nineteenth century, this idea was resisted by the official teaching of the Roman Catholic Church, inheritor of the rigid version of the Augustinian doctrine that "error has no right." But a major, indeed revolutionary, breakthrough came with the Second Vatican Council in the 1960s. It is no accident that Pope John Paul II will probably be remembered, above all, for his championing of both religious and political freedom in Eastern Europe in the 1980s.

But the religious world as a whole is by no means entirely happy with the easy cohabitation of Christianity with the "Western liberal" notion of human rights. Indeed, increasing criticism of the whole formulation of the Universal Declaration is heard from within the Islamic world, which sees it as based upon assumptions and understandings alien to Muslim thought. The challenge to "the Christian West" comes not only from Islam. As those in Europe know full well, the Eastern Orthodox church, too, has unease with the "post-Enlightenment" West being seen as the seedbed of free-ranging individualism and romanticism. These disjunctions in basic understandings undoubtedly will provide the crucial context for much interreligious and intercultural dialogue in the coming decades. On all sides, there is need for fuller historical information and more careful reflection to promote genuine encounters rather than reactions to stereotypes.

It is a chief merit of this wide-ranging and highly informative book by William Brackney that it does not evade the difficult questions presented by and to the Christian tradition in the long history of thought and practice on human rights. Readers alike from within and outside the Christian tradition will find much to inform, and on occasion surprise, them. They will learn how many-textured is the Christian approach to a greater engagement with human rights conceptually, legislatively, and in social action. It is highly unusual to find, within the pages of a single volume, so much historical substance, theological and ethical analysis, and basic source material. For a long time to come, no-one who purports to pronounce in any way upon the Christian treatment of human rights will be able to afford to ignore this work. Especially important is the way in which Dr. Brackney sets this aspect of the Christian story within the context of the churches' social engagement. Superficial advocates (or critics) of human rights both within and outside the communities of faith frequently interpret the term individualistically. But the central and leading Christian protagonists for human rights have always been *social* thinkers and activists who have always been at least as concerned for the rights, freedom, and dignity of others as for their own.

It is also valuable that William Brackney in effect uncovers the question, Why do human rights matter? Or, what is the basis, the *ontology* even, of human rights? The collapse of purely utilitarian theories of ethics in recent times is in danger of leaving concern for human rights at the dubious mercy of the global market economy and to self-seeking political demagoguery, which may in turn actually cloak itself in high-sounding "religious" rhetoric. "Freedom" then becomes a vacuous shibboleth, understood in the narrowest sense of freedom of choice (such as even the demons presumably have), which is considerably less than the biblical concept of the *free responsiveness and free responsibility not in abstraction and individualistic isolation but with and for others and with and for God.* "For you were called to freedom . . . only do not use your freedom as an opportunity for self-indulgence, but through love become slaves [*sic*] to one another" (Gal. 5:13). In Christian understanding, *human rights* are to serve what is *rightly human*. They cannot simply be set down as an abstract code applying to humankind as a species, Homo sapiens, and as distinct from "animal rights." They are to be grounded in a knowledge of what, in the light of Christ, who is the beginning and end of humanity, is necessary for more truly human being. It is high time that Christian thinkers take up again the exploration of what Karl Barth called a "theanthropology," an understanding of the source, direction, and goal of human life and its structures, its possibilities and limitations under grace.

Such exploration is beyond the scope of this present work but underlines the book's importance. Dr. Brackney's work is an invaluable tool, not only in enlightening and informing in a notable way all who wish to study the legacy of the past and the immediate tasks in the present, but in encouraging Christians and others to explore further the resources of the traditions of faith in meeting the future challenges faced by human life on our planet. It is greatly welcomed and deserves widely to be read, in East and West alike.

Keith W. Clements
General Secretary
CONFERENCE OF EUROPEAN CHURCHES
GENEVA

ACKNOWLEDGMENTS

MY INTEREST IN THIS TOPIC BEGAN several years ago when I attended a meeting of the Baptist World Alliance Study Commission on Human Rights. As a Baptist Christian, I had heard much about the right to religious liberty, but I wanted exposure to the fuller agenda of human rights. My work with the Canadian Council of Churches and the Canadian Bible Society gave me opportunities for travel in the interest of the development and observation of human rights problems and prospects. Alicia Merritt, the editor at Greenwood Press for religion, gave me that opportunity when she invited me to edit the series Human Rights and the World's Major Religions and prepare the volume on the Christian tradition. I am profoundly grateful to her for the invitation and to the project for its transformative aspects.

I wish to express my appreciation to both individuals and libraries for their advice, support, and suggestions. Those who have provided special advice include Thorwald Lorenzen in Australia; James Wood in Virginia; Derek Davis and Marc Ellis at the J. M. Dawson Institute for Church State Studies at Baylor University; John Jonssen and Dan McGee in the Department of Religion at Baylor; Rhoda Howard and former colleagues in the Department of Religious Studies at McMaster University; and Archie Goldie, John Irwin, Louise Barber, Keith Clements, and Denton Lotz, my intellectual "friends" who have encouraged me at different points along the way. Several librarians have been more than helpful; so many have been suggestive of new directions to pursue:

Jeff Taylor, Phil Jones, Janet Sheets, Terri Jones, and John Robinson at Jones Library of Baylor University have fed my appetite for the minutest of details.

I am profoundly grateful to my graduate assistant for four years, Ms. Chung Yung Joyce Chan, for locating documents, preparing texts for inclusion, and passing along hundreds of bibliographic citations. Another doctoral student, Scott Houser, now serving in South Africa, has been most helpful as well. From time to time, undergraduate courses have opened new insights in my thinking and I'm grateful to the several years of classes at two institutions where I raised some of these issues for assessment.

Lastly, I wish to express my appreciation to Alicia Merritt, Suzanne Staszak-Silva, and a second generation of staff editors at Praeger Publishers who have patiently waited for and supported this project and the larger series in which it appears. Lewis Parker has been skillful, thorough, and supportive in his editorial preparation of the manuscript for publication. My son, Raphe, kindly typed the index.

INTRODUCTION |

T HE DISCUSSION OF HUMAN RIGHTS is a relatively recent occurrence. In fact, while "rights language" has been in vogue from the Enlightenment, most trace the current understanding and usage to the era of World War II. The rise of totalitarian dictatorships, torturous keeping of prisoners of war, refugees, militarism, and the ultimate use of nuclear weapons that annihilated hundreds of thousands of people called forth a concern for "human rights." This concern for human rights produced formulations of human rights, then declarations of concern by various bodies both government and moral, followed gradually by laws and councils that monitor human rights and, in some cases, punish violators of rights. Although it was conventional to think of the way persons treated each other to be a matter of national sovereignty, it has become a universal issue under international covenants and law. The United Nations has played the leading role in this development. Within the United Nations community, North American, and secondly European, voices have been leaders in articulating a concern for human rights.

The concept of human rights has evolved over time. Conceptually, human rights pertain to rights inherent in being human. Originally, these rights included life, liberty, security, freedom of religion, holding one's opinion, and the right of assembly. From the eighteenth to the twentieth century, these were considered in an individual sense. More latitude was added after 1950 as socialist countries spoke of economic and social rights such as work, food, housing, and so forth, and, in the 1960s, underdeveloped nations pressed their ideas of survival, self-determination, and participation. In the last two decades, the concept of human dignity has blossomed to include the quality of being human in its fullest sense and this has increased the possibilities of "human rights" endlessly. Finally, there is the connection that some make with the environment and nonhuman species. Here the language has shifted from "human rights" to "global ethics."

In the past fifty years, human rights have come to include several specific areas: prevention of genocide, traffic in persons, refugees, and displaced persons; rights of women and children, racial discrimination, antiapartheid, hostage-taking, torture, and cruel and inhumane punishment; and migrant workers, territorial asylum, criminal justice and offenders, older persons, persons with mental illness, national, ethnic or linguistic minorities, persons with disabilities, extreme poverty, and terrorism. As this agenda has grown, philosophers, politicians, ethicists, and religious specialists have debated what the foundation of "rights" is or should be.

One of the most fundamental issues, then, is whether human rights discourse is even appropriately connected with religion in general, let alone a particular religious tradition like Christianity. Many philosophers and secularists in the Enlightenment project have argued persuasively that natural law provides humanity with immutable rights. There is, therefore, no need to refer to any compelling moral code that has been produced in a specific religious tradition. One Canadian human rights authority has observed that "religion, like ethnicity, has become a discardable characteristic . . . religious belief is now a matter of individual choice."[1] Even for those who argue out of a religious context, there are so many moral codes growing out of specific cultures and traditions that deep divisions ensue over which code is authoritative. The multiplicity of religions thus illustrates that there is no single, universal, and compelling morality. Still others argue that because religion has been such an impediment to the achievement and practice of human rights, and in many ways it has contributed to an abuse of humanity, it is better left out of the discussion. Richard Rorty, a contemporary philosopher at Stanford University, encourages rights advocates to move from their own culture to a transcultural approach to validate "the cause of human rights." He thinks discussions about "rights foundationalism" are pointless. However, Christians in general seem to agree that even the most liberal theory of rights rests upon an understanding of human worth and dignity that is universal and inherent. Specialists in rights law like Michael J. Perry believe this inevitably leads to a quality of sacredness in metaphysical terms. Religious values in their broadest sense, satisfactorily define that sacredness.[2] To expand on that theme, as Max Stackhouse did two decades ago, human rights is a religious matter because of its claim about what is sacred, inviolable, and absolute in human affairs.[3] It thus becomes a legitimate task to relate human rights to religious and theological assertions, and in this case, Christianity in particular.

In general, one recognizes a second problem with connecting Christianity to human rights. History is clear that the advocacy of human rights as we understand it in modern discussion did not emerge from Christian teaching. Elements independent of each other are certainly present in Christian literature, but as a whole, Christianity had no category for human rights before the late nineteenth century. Rather, it came forth gradually in Enlightenment documents (influenced to be sure by religious ideas) and erupted in the international political community of the twentieth century. Its broad applicability now belongs properly to all humanity, not one religious or cultural tradition. In the face of this reality, Christian philosophers, theologians, and activists for human rights have *responded* to the declarations and issues from within their religious communities and dogma. This has often looked like ex post facto discourse, a rationalization or homologation of secular ideas to the language of religion. The most acceptable approaches seem to be those that argue for the universality of God over cultures and across history that assert all truth to belong to God (the Reformed tradition) and the careful tracing of seminal ideas like the dignity of humanity bound up with the *imago dei* from Creation (the Catholic tradition). In this way, we may proceed to treat human rights and Christianity.

The Christian religion is a complex religious tradition. Based ultimately on the life, teachings, and resurrection of Jesus of Nazareth, a first-century C.E. Jew, it initially centered in Palestine, Syria, and Egypt. Via apostolic propagation, the new religion spread north and west in the Roman Empire, reaching Spain and Britain by the end of its first half-century. Christian witness was also recorded in India and Mediterranean Africa by 100 C.E. Characterized by much diversity, an important attempt to build a common confession was made between the Councils of Nicea (325) and Chalcedon (451), but divergent positions continued in various parts of the Christian world, particularly on the doctrine of Christ and the polity of the church. For a thousand-year period following the fall of the Roman Empire, the Christian Church was the chief organizing institution in the West and the East, with a serious rift occurring in 1054 between the Eastern and Western church leaders. Rome continued as the Episcopal center of the West, as Constantinople became the principal center of the East. In the Middle Ages, Western Christianity spread to northern Europe and coastal Africa; Eastern Christianity traveled to Russia and interior Asia.

Following several attempts to reform the authoritarian nature of the papacy and bring about doctrinal changes, during the Age of Reform (1500–1600) the Western Church suffered widespread division generally referred to as Protestantism. Protestantism has many facets, illustrated in confessions that range from Lutheran to Reformed or from Calvinistic to the Anabaptists, the English Church, and smaller national movements across Europe. The Roman Catholic Church itself underwent major reform in response to the claims of Protestants and internal concerns. The Enlightenment had a profound influence upon Christianity, both positive and negative. The scholastic achievements of the seventeenth and eighteenth centuries produced a self-critical religious tradition, but many also felt Christianity lost its zeal and vitality during this period. The resultant responses in revivalism, romanticism, missionary expansion, and voluntarism reshaped Christianity into an even more racial-ethnically and geographically diverse religion. During the great century of missionary expansion (1800–1900), Christian groups evangelized India, China, Africa, Latin America, and the islands of the Pacific. Roman Catholicism grew in the same period as a result of immigration and evangelization, as did Eastern Orthodoxy to a lesser extent. The twentieth century was characterized on the one hand by greater cooperation in the ecumenical movement that brought together Protestants, and Catholics Eastern and Western and on the other hand by greater division by the evangelical factions. As of 2000, there were approximately one billion Christians located in virtually every country of the world.[4]

Christianity has thus differentiated itself divided into Catholic, Orthodox Catholic, Protestant, and highly individualized forms. History, theology, and polity vary greatly across the history of Christianity. The tradition is sacramental and yet confessional and experiential. Symbolism and aesthetics are important to Christians. Christian institutions constitute a major visible expression of the faith, including congrega-

tional, organizational, educational, health-care, administrative, missionary, and humanitarian forms. Beyond the person and enduring presence
of Jesus Christ, Christians share an extensive literary heritage, including
canonical works, extra-canonical writings, and the Jewish scriptures, as
well as a considerable quantity of interpretive doctrinal writings. From
its first century, Christianity has been subject to critical analysis and its
religious values have been adapted to numerous cultures. As one of the
great religions of the world, Christian thinkers and witness have inter-
acted with virtually every other religious tradition. Christians believe
that what validates and makes universal their monotheistic tradition is
their belief in the resurrection of Christ from a cruel Roman crucifixion,
its application to those who are his disciples "from every race and kind,"
and Christ's promise to establish his sovereignty and usher in eternal
life in the presence of God. The source of all value, morality, and dignity
lies in God as exemplified in Jesus Christ.

To survey and assess the understanding of a topic like human rights
in the Christian tradition is to take on a large assignment. One must
be content with describing the many responses to human rights across
centuries and traditions in current vogue. Fortunately, because Christianity has matured as a religious tradition in essentially a libertarian culture, it has become self-critical. Sincere, confessing Christians are
painfully aware of the abuses of human rights in their religious history.
No reputable biography or historical account can gloss over the realities.

The first task undertaken in chapter one of this work is to set forth
the Christian theological understanding of human rights. This of necessity involves assessing the biblical foundations in the New Testament,
as interpreted in light of the Old Testament. Then, the theological
evolution of the principles inherent in human rights from the Middle
Ages through the Age of Reform to the Enlightenment must be covered.
There are several key questions that all Christian theologians dealing in
this area of thought have paid heed to. In the modern era, we shall
survey the accomplishments of ecumenical Christian thinkers and then
those within the major confessional traditions that have worked on the
issues. These include Baptists, Lutherans, the Reformed Tradition, Roman Catholics, and Evangelicals.

The next two chapters deal with the actual record of human rights
experience in the Christian tradition. The obstacles to recognition of
human rights in the emerging Christian communities, the Medieval period, and throughout the course of modern Christian societies are self-

critically discussed. Attention is given to the patently obvious failure of Christian people to live up to their own standards or expectations. Sometimes, this behavior has been well rationalized with reference to scriptures or leading teachers or politicians. Other times, it has been the result of ignorance or lack of enlightenment. In the case of human rights language, culture has evolved to expose or elucidate certain concerns that were not as evident in early centuries of Christian life and thought. Inevitably, part of this discussion must address the ill treatment of persons within the Christian community holding divergent opinions, the crusades declared against "infidels," and denials of rights of free expression, education, and even religious liberty itself.

Following the discussion of "obstacles" the clear record of social concerns in the Christian community that forms the bedrock of modern human rights recognition is examined. It can be seen in its earliest development that the Christian community had a high regard for individual persons. Women, slaves, foreigners, persons of multiple races, and ethnic groups all found acceptance to a large degree in Christian congregations and, Christians believe, before God. Further, Christians have valued community, that is, collectives of not necessarily related people who constitute local congregations and larger associations of believers. Christians use metaphors like the "Body of Christ," "brotherhood," and "Kingdom of God/Christ" to express this unique social and theological relationship. Within this community, rules of conduct have been observed as well as maintaining an ethic of love toward one's neighbor from one generation to the next. And the overall example of the life, death, and resurrection of Jesus Christ, and belief in his continuing presence within his church, overarches all.

As most human rights theorists and Christian writers in particular agree, the basic and first human right is religious freedom. A separate treatment of religious liberty follows. The development of religious liberty as it pertains to individuals is assessed as well as the more communal aspects of later declarations.

Ultimately, the capstone of this treatment is the evolution of a united world political community that brought with it some foundational concurrence about individual, collective, and national relationships. Following World War I, a language of "human rights" was born, and Christian leaders and communions began to engage the dialogue. As the United Nations took shape, so also did the World Council of Churches, and significant changes came about in the Catholic and Orthodox Catholic communions. The agenda of human rights expanded, and, in the process, the discussion of a theological underpinning and the ethical implications for Christians increased and deepened. It is an important part of the story to trace not only the Christian influence upon the international political community's concern for human rights, but also the high priority that many churches and denominations of Christians now give to human rights. Chapter 5 is devoted to various Christian responses to United Nations declarations since 1948.

A valuable feature of this volume is the inclusion of resource materials. First are excerpted primary sources that illustrate the Christian engagement of human rights. Some of the documents selected demonstrate difficulties with rights, whereas others detail the steady evolution of declarations of human rights. Illustrations of social concerns, theological interpretations, and debates about human rights issues are included. In the following section, detailed biographical sketches are provided on over forty individuals of import who illustrate Christian involvement in human rights. An asterisk (*) has been affixed to the first mention of an individual who is featured in the biographical sketches. There is also a topical annotated bibliography that covers all of the chapters of the book. A useful chronology marking Christian events in human rights evolution appears in the beginning of this book, after the introduction.

In the last analysis, it is my position that human rights must be a part of Christian theological and ethical concern. There are, after all, as John K. Simmons at Western Illinois University has well pointed out, negative aspects of human rights equally bestowed upon all humanity. That is, to fail to respect human rights, he reminds us, "is to abuse the gift of freedom in everyone's nature. Treating people badly is to insult God in whose image they are made. Wronging another person can also harm those who love him because they share in his suffering."[5] Because of the New Testament principle of reciprocity ("What is done to the least of these my brothers, you do to me . . ."—Matt. 25:40) suggests that God himself is wronged by violations of human rights.

CHRONOLOGY |

First edition of *Yearbook of Human Rights*

1948   Universal Declaration of Human Rights issued by United Nations

1950   World Vision, International established

South African government passes Group Areas Act

1959   U.N. Declaration on the Rights of the Child

1961   Amnesty International founded

WCC issues "Statement on Religious Freedom" at New Delhi Assembly

1962   U.N. Declaration Against Race Discrimination

1963   Pope John issues encyclical *Pacem in terris*

1965   Vatican II issues *Dignitatis Humanae*

1966   The International Covenant on Economic, Social and Cultural Rights and the International Covenant on Civil and Political Rights published by the United Nations

Geneva Conference develops scale of human rights values

1967   U.N. Declaration on Territorial Asylum

1970   Lutheran World Federation approves Universal Declaration on Human Rights

1971   U.N. Declaration on the Rights of Mentally Retarded Persons

1973   Helsinki Conference on Security and Cooperation: Final Act (1975) included a section on human rights

1974   World Council of Churches human rights consultation at St. Poelten, Austria

1975   World Council of Churches Assembly at Nairobi broadens concept of human rights

U.N. Declaration on the Protection of All Persons from Being Subjected to Torture and Other Cruel, Inhuman, or Degrading Treatment or Punishment

U.N. Declaration on the Rights of Disabled Persons

1976   International U.N. Covenants take effect

1977   World Alliance of Reformed Churches publishes *Christian Declaration on Human Rights*

U.S. President James Earl Carter signs Human Rights Treaty

1979   Interconfessional Study Project on Theological Basis of Human Rights

Mother Theresa of Calcutta wins Nobel Prize for Peace

1985   U.N. Declaration on the Human Rights of Individuals Who Are Not Nationals of the Country in Which They Live

U.N. Declaration on the Basic Principles of Justice for Victims of Crime and Abuse of Power

1986   Bishop Desmond Tutu of South Africa awarded the Nobel Prize for Peace

1990   Hans Küng publishes *Global Responsibility*

1993   World's Parliament of Religions meets in Chicago and issues Declaration Toward a Global Ethic

1997   InterAction Council issues Universal Declaration on Human Responsibilities

1998   World Council Meeting at Morges, France

1999   Declaration on the Right and Responsibility of Individuals, Groups, and Organs of Society to Promote and Protect Universally Recognized Human Rights and Fundamental Freedoms

United Nations Decade of Human Rights Education begins

2002   Former U.S. president James Earl Carter receives Nobel Peace Prize for work in human rights

2003   Publication of a "Universal Declaration of Human Rights by the World's Religions" prepared by the Project on Religion and Human Rights, 1993–2002

Part I
Historical Development and Analysis

CHRISTIAN THEOLOGICAL FOUNDATIONS OF HUMAN RIGHTS

HAVING ESTABLISHED THE relevance of Christian thought to human rights discourse, Christian thinkers of varying kinds debate just how the theological foundations and elaboration of human rights are to be constructed. For many years, some argued that the very terminology of human rights was impious, that is, it was seen as an attack on the sovereignty of God. Typically, they referred to human *responsibilities* rather than human rights. Yet others have shown that human rights have their specific origins in political and humanistic circumstances and declarations rather than any universal religious or even ethical tradition. The challenges for Christian theologians, then, are how to connect human rights with a Christian view of reality and where the Christian faith and values can enhance the understanding and implementation of human rights. In addition, one theologian also believes Christians must critique the human rights tradition that has emerged in political and legal discourse in order to validate what belongs to God.[1] In the end, the most challenging aspect of this quest is to argue persuasively for Christianity as the universal moral basis of human rights, because human rights discourse without such a foundation is bankrupt and hollow. Christians believe, of course, that their religious perspective is ultimately comprehensive and valid, and thus establishing Christian values as the basis for human rights becomes universally applicable.

As theologians have shown, there are some basic premises that connect human rights discourse with Christian theology. A survey of history shows that a concern for universal human rights as such began in Christian societies. Documents such as the English Magna Charta, the Royal Oaths of the Nordic Kingdoms, the Edict of Nantes, the Virginia Declaration of Rights, the Declaration of Independence, and the French Declaration of the Rights of Man emerged from Christian cultures in an Enlightenment tradition. Integral to all of theses statements is the premise that human beings are born free and equal in dignity and rights. It is not difficult to find in classical Judeo-Christian thought the equivalent theological expressions. Specifically, primary among these is that all humans are children of God. Here one finds universality. The great Reformation principle of "justification by faith" before God established the inviolability of the person. The freedom called for in the declarations corresponds to freedom for Christians in the Body of Christ. But the painful reality of the history of Christian doctrine is that it did not directly give birth to a human rights tradition. Circumstances of brutality, coercion, oppression, and inhumanity did. Only when Christian theologians witnessed an emergence of rights discussions in the secular context of the twentieth century did they reexamine and recover their human rights foundations in scripture and tradition.

Christians believe that words of Jesus of Nazareth, in the context of the Old Testament or Hebrew scriptures, contain the most profound statements of all theological pronouncements in their tradition. For instance, Jesus spoke of freedom, by which he meant a freedom possessed by one's neighbor. In the teachings of Christ, discussions of equality took on new meanings, for they inevitably pointed to the weak, oppressed, and disadvantaged. Also, if Christianity is concerned with God's desire for the salvation of the world through the atonement of Christ, the universal community that Christians look forward to must include wholeness for all peoples—a "universal community of right" that Jesus and the apostles have referred to as the Kingdom of God. Christian theologians are convinced that "Christianity cannot stand outside the struggle for human rights because of its founder and its nature."[2]

THEOLOGICAL FOUNDATIONS IN THE BIBLE

SCRIPTURE IS FUNDAMENTAL to establishing Christian thought. Not only the New Testament literature pertaining to the life and teachings of Jesus of Nazareth and the apostolic era, but also the canon of Jewish literature that Christians refer to as the Old Testament, form the bedrock of Christian theology. In this way, Christian theology is an embellishment upon Jewish thought from the Second Temple or "Ioudaioist"[3] era. Any valid theological doctrine must grow out of a consistent reading and interpretation of Old and New Testaments.

A Christian understanding of human rights flows from the theological category, the "Works of God," and begins with creation. To assert that humans are born with certain qualities and rights is to engage the theology of creation. The discussion commences with the nature of God and God's creation in scripture. The relevant passage is Genesis 1:26–27; 31:

> Then God said, "Let us make humankind in our image, according to our likeness, and let them have dominion over the fish of the sea, and over the birds of the air, and over the cattle, and over the wild animals of the earth, and over every creeping thing that creeps upon the earth. So God created humankind in his image, in the image of God he created them. God saw everything that he had made and it was very good.

Christian theologians derive at least four meanings from this text. First, human beings are the superior part of God's creation. This is evident in the assessment "very good," which contrasts with the rest of the Creation that was said to be "good." Second, humans were given the opportunity to communicate with God. Third, humans were given dominion over the rest of animal life. Edmund Jacob, a leading Old Testament theologian at the University of Strasbourg, held this to be a kind of "lordly" function: lord over the animal kingdom. Or, as John Simmons observes, humans owe duties to others because of their natural equality as rational, purposive beings. Karl Barth also pointed out that the second half of verse 27, just as God is not alone in himself, God created male and female humans to live together in love and covenant. That covenant has hope and promise, fulfilled in Christ.[4]

To this initial passage are often added the words of Proverbs 20:27 that shed light upon human moral capacity: "The human spirit is the lamp of the Lord; how can we understand our own ways?" Here the allusions are to one who takes a lamp and moves about in the chambers of a house. In other words, there is a self-conscious spirit that God has given to humans that is able to reflect on problems and circumstances by searching out even the innermost thoughts of the most secret places. This is in order for humans to act morally. Many biblical commentators understand this capacity in light of Matthew 6:22: "The eye is the lamp of the body . . ." and 1 Corinthians 2:11: "For what human being knows what is truly human except the human spirit that is within?"

A second set of principles that Christian advocates of human rights derived from the Old Testament includes the universal right to be part of a nation and yet have mobility. In Deuteronomy 26:1–19, the heritage of Israel, whose ancestor was a "wandering Aramean," to become a distinct nation was recounted: "Today the Lord has accepted you as His own people, as he promised you." Upon their eventual enslavement in Egypt, God said, "Now I have heard the groaning of the Israelites, whom the Egyptians have enslaved, and I have remembered my covenant (Exod. 6:5). Related to these pronouncements about nationhood were denunciations of slavery and oppression. The classic passage telling of the burden to make bricks without straw (Exod. 5:6–9), resulting in Pharoah's command, "Let heavier work be laid upon them," defined the essence of oppression for Israel in Egypt. With respect to slavery, the deuteronomic historian recorded of the new Israelite principles: "If slaves run away from their owners and come to you for protection, do not send them back. . . . you are not to oppress them" (Deut. 23:15). Isaiah the prophet called for an end to oppression and slavery: "Loose the bonds of injustice and let the oppressed go free" (Isa. 58:6).

Many Christian interpreters see a formative understanding of justice in the Old Testament. Of judges in Israel, Moses commanded, "These men are to judge the people impartially. They are not to be unjust or show partiality in their judgments and they are not to accept bribes" (Deut. 16:18). Members of the Israelite community were not to show partiality against a poor person on trial, and foreigners were not to be mistreated "because you were aliens in the land of Egypt" (Exod. 23:9). Indeed, the Psalmist believed the underlying purpose of the councils of justice was "to defend the rights of the poor and the orphans" (Ps. 82: 3–5). Finally, it has been observed that Moses initiated a representative system of government for the Israelites in the Wilderness: "Choose some wise, understanding and experienced men from each tribe, and I will put them in charge of you." To the judges, his instructions read, "Judge everyone on the same basis, no matter who they are" (Deut. 1:9).[5]

Finally, the Old Testament prophets often call attention to a vision of glory and peace in the future of God's people. In Micah 4:1–8, the people say, "Come, let us go up to the mountain of the Lord, to the House of the God of Jacob; that he may teach us his ways and that we may walk in his paths" (Mic. 4:2). In this circumstance, "they shall beat their swords into plowshares, and their spears into pruning hooks; nation shall not lift up sword against nation, neither shall they learn war any more" (Mic. 4:3). Here, peace and nonviolence are obviously in view. Also in the prophetic tradition for some theologians is the restorative declaration in Isaiah 49:4: "Surely my cause is with the Lord, and my reward with my God." Here the term "cause" has been frequently translated as "right."

To summarize the Old Testament content supportive of human rights, the tradition of the books of Law reveal a covenant relationship between God and His people that implies a special relationship to God and responses that indicate generous action toward the powerless, including the widow, the poor and the stranger. The Proverbs indicate likewise a concern for the poor and powerless (Prov. 21:13) and the Psalms contain prayers of the poor (Ps. 40:17). Finally, the prophetic tradition contains the major theme of "doing justice," with God serving as the advocate for the powerless.[6]

To this Old Testament data can be added New Testament affirmations. The inherent value of individuals is passed to one's neighbors in Jesus' Great Commandment: "Love your neighbor as yourself" (Matt. 22:40). Likewise the Great Sermon contains the "golden rule": "Do for others what you would want them to do for you"(Matt. 7:12). Implied in the context of this passage is the integrity of claiming Jesus as Lord, because some come in sheep's clothing as false prophets. Those who are faithful followers were known by their fruits (Matt. 7:20), and rather than condemning others, they were to show mercy. They also exhibited a responsibility for others (Matt. 7:8–11). Elsewhere, Jesus promised a new quality of life to be universally enjoyed: "I have come that you might have life and have it more abundantly" (John 10:7). Additionally, Jesus said that "everyone who asks receives, and everyone who searches finds, and everyone who knocks, the door will be opened" (Matt. 7:8). Finally, for many, Jesus is seen as a "suffering Messiah" who in his incarnation, crucifixion, and death identified with the oppressed and became the "Man for others."[7]

In the New Testament freedom is an important dimension of human life. "Live as free people. . . . Respect everyone; love other believers, honor God and respect the Emperor" (1 Peter 2:11). Indeed, freedom is key to understanding rights in the theology of the New Testament. As Donel Murray points out, freedom is a Trinitarian matter. Jesus Christ, the Son of God, has set all humans free (Gal. 5:1). The Spirit in his very presence, gives freedom (2 Cor. 3:17). The Father, source of all freedom, has loved humans first: "In this is love: not that we loved God but that he loved us and sent his Son to be the atoning sacrifice for our sins" (1 John 4:10). Jesus championed the poor, the meek, and the merciful, those who mourn, those who were persecuted, those on the fringes of his society (Matt. 5:3–10).

Pauline thought also does much to undergird universal human rights. In Titus 3:4–6, Paul reminds his friend that the kindness and love of God our Savior for mankind "were revealed . . . through his own compassion he saved us." Moreover, the concept of the "righteousness of God," whereby God has established his righteousness outside the Torah, applies to Jew and pagan alike who have faith in Jesus Christ. This righteousness is subsumed in divine love and the will of God that all men should obtain salvation. Another way of putting it is that God wills justice for everyone, including justice for the sinner. Finally, it is important to point out that the Great Commandment to love God and to love one's neighbor, knows no limits to its applicability. Love, therefore, is best expressed in justice and righteousness, or as some Christian theologians argue, through universal recognition of human rights and dignity.[8]

The New Testament also clearly established other principles of human rights, Christians declare. For instance, there is the right of assembly: "Not neglecting to meet together, as is the habit of some, but encouraging one another all the more . . ." (Heb. 10:25). From the example of Jesus and others, Christians opposed torture and inhumane treatment. The author of Peter reminded his readers in the first century that Jesus' example passed to the rest: "When he was abused, he did not return abuse; when he suffered, he did not threaten; but he entrusted himself to the one who judges justly. He himself bore our sins in his body on the cross, so that, free from sins, we might live for righteousness; by his wounds you have been healed" (1 Pet. 2:24).

Josef Blank, a New Testament professor at the University of Saarland, has also pointed out the relevance of the concept of "philanthropia." In Acts 27, Julius the centurion, who was charged with delivering Paul to the imperial tribunal in Rome, displayed a humane attitude. Similarly, the Malta inhabitants rescued Paul and provided refuge when he was shipwrecked (Acts 28:2). Perhaps the leading data is in Titus 3:4–6 where God's love and kindness toward mankind along with God's compassion, provides our inheritance of eternal life as well as a powerful example to the early church. This sense of philanthropia mirrors contemporary New Testament–era ideals of compassion as found in Philo and Hellenistic writers who reveal *humanitas*.[9]

FURTHER THEOLOGICAL DEVELOPMENT

MAX STACKHOUSE, a Christian ethicist at Andover Newton Theological School and Princeton Seminary, has provided a useful synthesis of how Christian thought came to be interwoven with issues of human rights. Early Christians interfaced their Hebrew and Greek understandings of community, morality, and social institutions with writers like Plato, Aristotle, and the Stoics. They brought forth universalistic views about moral law and human nature. During the medieval period, a common understanding in the Catholic tradition emerged in support of a universal moral law that governed all human relations and was mediated through the Church. This "public theology" was further defined among the scholastic debates. In the Middle Ages, beginning with the twelfth century, it was possible to be a lord or *dominus* of one's relevant moral world, or property. For Thomas Aquinas, God was thought to be the center of the universe and he gave to humans binding law. Humans therefore owed God duties as their ultimate sovereign. Helping along the process of identifying this universal Christian (and Western) morality were the ecumenical church councils that took into account the whole body of people in Christian society and dared to speak for both the state and the church. This raised the question of whether claims about universal principals were decided by an appeal to some objective authority, like the church, or shaped out of a dialogue that was reported "out of the conciliar tradition." The conciliar tradition, often speaking through or in tandem with the papal office, was the dominant authority.[10]

Later in the Reformation period, Stackhouse identified three important streams that have had influence in Western moral and cultural development: evangelical Calvinism, imperial Calvinism, and Free Church Calvinism, all of which constitute a "Reformed" tradition. Lutherans, radical reformers, and Catholics are found among evangelical

Calvinists and exhibit a dogmatic focus that accents revelation and a kingdom of God on earth. Polemics have been its mainstay. Imperial Calvinism, which has manifested itself as "elitist, repressive, dogmatic, and theocratic," comprises Puritans, apartheid Dutch Calvinists, and some Scottish thinkers, to mention some examples. Obedience for imperial Calvinists has been of higher value than liberty. The third group, Free Church Calvinists, has operated with an appreciation for "covenant," whereby people enter into agreements with God and each other to establish sociality, recognize morality, and bond together in a community of pluralism. Universal moral reality is discerned in this community in keeping with its basically Calvinistic perspective. The body politic, synonymous with the ecclesial community, has the right and responsibility under God to establish a moral regime and to create institutions of accountability. The Free Church Calvinists became the dominant form in the West. Pluralist democracy in a Christian republic by the nineteenth century, then, became the forum of public Christian theology.[11]

Stackhouse also argued that Thomas Hobbes, John Locke, and John Stuart Mill successfully critiqued the prevailing Calvinistic synthesis as they observed it in English Protestantism. Hobbes argued that human rights are civil rights, constructed by human will for the benefit of the body politic. His objective was to liberate humanity from theological norms. Locke, similarly was shocked at the contentiousness of the Cromwellian Puritan regime in which his father served, and he opted for a tolerance and pluralism that was compelling without the need of revelation. Locke believed there is a natural basis for moral law that transcends arbitrary political authority and endless religious strife. Truth for him came through experience and opinions, to which natural philosophy could be a reliable guide. In Locke's theory, God is detached in the sense that he gave the law for human benefit, not to dominate them. Fellow creatures become equals and moral relations exist between persons. Each person thus has self worth, dignity, one's own person. Duty comes to mean what is due another person. While Locke did not define "rights" as such, his work came to be determinative. Finally, Mill critiqued the Calvinistic traditions by arguing that the theological system was a threat to spontaneity and feeling. Mill built his approach upon a psycho-ethical foundation in which laws were to be judged by their capacity to produce pleasure or inhibit pain. As the eighteenth century evolved to the nineteenth, Liberals and Calvinists came to value private property, one's body, family, work, the university, and religious expression, to name major categories. The cultural lodgment of this synthesis was found in England and even more in the history of American legal and moral traditions. The human rights discussion of the twentieth century is cradled in this heritage, and even more to the point, Christian theologians have constructed their responses within the same boundaries.[12]

As Christian theologians have tackled the issue of human rights, two problems have surfaced that illustrate the complexity of the theological task. First is the question of the sovereignty of God, or the matter of "God's rights," and the impact of human sinfulness. Can one speak of human rights without reference to God? Christian theologians are clear that rights cannot be understood to emerge from some "essential humanity" or a materialistic process of self-deliverance. Rather, if one understands God in the fullest biblical sense, God is concerned and involved in the totality of creation and its needs, and this becomes liberating. Before God (coram Deo) the pursuit of human rights poses a sacred obligation, and when humans fail, they have an impact upon a larger picture of all of God's creation. Individuals, it is stated, must claim their rights and protect them in order to fulfill duties or be faithful to God. For instance, Albert Gelin theorizes that in the biblical narrative of the orders of creation, animals may have been symbolic of evil and thus man was created to conquer evil, just as God conquers evil.[13] Such metaphorical interpretations seem strange, however, to modern thinkers who have a more ecologically sensitive understanding of the stewardship given to humans. But, the point of connectedness with all of Creation remains. In a similar vein, no one Christian group can claim sole ownership of human rights advocacy. For the ecumenical Christian, the issue of human rights belongs surely to no one sect or church but to the entire Body of Christ.[14] Human rights discussions are ecumenical by nature. For many theologians, human rights are but the application of divine rights, derived from the nature, creative act, and purposes of God and entrusted to the stewardship of the universal church.[15]

A second and related question that emerges is, To what extent does exercising human rights violate the rights of God? Do humans enjoy rights at all if God is sovereign in the fullest sense of that term? The Swiss theologian, Emil Brunner,* preferred to discuss human rights as a matter of justice, wherein the civic order was to imitate the divine order.[16] Similarly, Jürgen Moltmann* in his early writings wrote of "covenant responsibilities," but was never clear about God's rights.[17] Albert Knudsen at Boston University long ago argued that God must be understood as a moral being as well with respect to his creation. For him, this implied that God's creatures have rights over against God as well as duties toward him. Knudsen held that human freedom demanded such.[18] Catholic, Lutheran, and Reformed theologians disagree vehemently on this matter, as their approaches would suggest. In the end, the notion of claiming rights against God seems preposterous to many theologians, first because God is no threat to personal welfare, and second because the profound impacts of human selfishness and sinfulness have combined to create a general moral weakness and a real vulnerability for all humans. God remains the dominant and unequal participant in the relationship.

A second pressing concern is the question of who is claiming/articulating human rights. Robert and Alice Fraser Evans, two American Presbyterian educator-activists, have helpfully pointed out that there are at least three perspectives on rights. Those in the First World emphasize individual rights such as freedom of speech, religion, and the right to assemble. Security, property, and due process in law are likewise relevant. The foundational right in this tradition is to be free. When members of the First World community observe denials of these freedoms by authoritarian regimes, morality is outraged. As some have observed, there can be a tendency toward an individualistic liberalism than can be destructive of Christian ideals of community. In contrast, however, is the perception from the Second World. Comprising the Marxist worldview, in those nations rights include work, material security, health, education, and housing. In the Second World, individual freedom always takes its place behind social solidarity and social needs. The Communist Manifesto was for generations the practical statement of rights in social context for the Second World. Here, a problematic result can be a collectivism that destroys human personality.[19] Finally, there is a Third World perspective. In the Southern Hemisphere, the stress is upon survival and liberation. Beginning in 1981, representatives meeting at Cancun, Mexico, called attention to the violation of workers, unjust use and distribution of natural resources, and the effects of war and cultural corruption on food supplies, shelter, health, and education.[20] Needless to say, these multiple perspectives have greatly complicated the theological task of Christians in engaging the human rights language. Ecumenical discussion and consensus of a truly global kind have become absolutely essential in creating a usable Christian theology of human rights.

As the debates and discussions over the validity of human rights have moved ahead, much interest in framing the issues in an ethical context has been expressed. For many, what extends forth from the biblical foundation is the need for a universal ethic, which has not yet emerged among Christians. Prominent Christian ethicists like James M. Gustafson, formerly at Yale and the University of Chicago, caution that there is no universally recognized normative concept of inviolable rights and there is no objectivity to human nature. He, like most ethicists, is caught in the choice between the sacredness of the rights of an individual and the question of benefits for society as a whole.[21] But the question of universality remains a tantalizing one. One important voice in the community of theologian/ethicists has asserted that "enormous progress could be achieved for the human race if all the great religions . . . were to lend their support to such common fundamental ethical demands, so that they become something like the basic pillars of a fundamental world ethic."[22]

So far, then, the Christian community at large has been left with an unfinished theological foundation. What has advanced the Christian ownership of human rights is the consensus reached in ecumenical discussions. The first stage has been the development within the confessional traditions of human rights discourse that is compatible with a given confession. Lutherans, the Reformed tradition, Baptists, and Roman Catholics have made substantial theological contributions. Later, especially in the World Council of Churches and the united evangelical movements, an operating consensus was reached that is a sufficient rationale for human rights advocacy and activism. This has essentially been a First World discussion. But, in the past three decades, Liberation theology has influenced the denominational traditions, the World Council, and the evangelical communities. The discussion now turns to examine individual Christian denominations.

WITHIN SPECIFIC CONFESSIONAL TRADITIONS

MAINSTREAM U.S. AND British Baptists have invested much in their contribution to a theological formation of human rights. Baptists can legitimately claim four centuries of concern for human rights. The Baptist position on human rights reflects a typical First World definition of human rights, with its emphasis upon individual rights in an enlightened society. Their case starts with religious liberty as the foundation of all other human rights and the key to growth in categories of human rights. First, rights are grounded in the mission of the gospel "to preach the gospel to the poor, heal the broken-hearted, and deliverance to the captives." Often using the language of liberation theologians, Baptists are responsive to the Old Testament prophetic calls for justice (cf. Mic. 6:8). Many Baptists then affirm humanity created in the image of God, which implies inalienable and inviolable rights of full humanity. The *imago dei* is pushed further to an exalted creation order that is "less than God, but greater than the angels" and "made for freedom not slavery." The goal of human rights discussion among Baptists is a free conscience, a limited state, and a free and democratic society. In the twentieth century, Baptists have pursued the thinking of Southern Baptist theologian Edgar Y. Mullins, who posited the individual competency of the soul before God and the rights and privileges derived from that competency. Much of the theological and philosophic case that Baptists make is built upon the writings of Locke and their own champions of religious liberty, Thomas Helwys* and Roger Williams* of the seventeenth century.[23] Williams, for instance, wrote in the preface to his 1643 work, *The Bloudy Tenent of Persecution for Cause of Conscience*, "It is the will and command of God that, since the coming of his son, the Lord Jesus, a permission of the most paganish, Jewish, Turkish, or anti-Christian consciences and worships be granted to all men in all nations and countries."[24] The Baptist Joint Committee on Public Affairs (BJC), a Baptist advocacy group in Washington, D.C., since 1939, lists the following concerns for human rights: nondiscrimination, world peace, conscientious objection, world hunger, the right to an education, the right to employment, nonproliferation of nuclear arms, and the rights of displaced persons. Likewise, the Baptist World Alliance (BWA), which was originally organized in 1905 to promote religious liberty, maintains a Study Commission on Human Rights that continues to address responses to reported violations of human rights, mainly religious liberty.

One thoughtful Baptist theologian, Thorwald Lorenzen of Europe and later of Australia, has at least two concerns from a Baptist perspective. First, there is the matter of ontology. When rights activists and theologians talk of all human beings being born free and equal in dignity and human rights, "What is the source of their rights or from whence are rights derived ontologically?" he asks. Postmodernists and persons outside the religious traditions frequently argue for some undefined universal moral basis. Since there is no consensus about such a universal theory, the core of human rights soon becomes empty. Or, perhaps it is grounded in the sense of *humanum*, which has never been satisfactorily plumbed. It therefore becomes the task of the religions of the world to affirm that it is God who endows humanity with human qualities and rights.[25] Lorenzen is concerned for the *universal* nature of human rights, and in so doing, he picks up a contemporary Lutheran contribution. Again, postmodern thinkers dismiss universality in light of situational and relative rights. Various non-Western nations also argue that there can be no universal understanding as long as individualistic approaches define the West and communitarian and socialist ideas define other nations. Moreover, the highly categorized interests of nationalism pose yet another kind of threat to universality. Here again, the Christian theologian reminds the world community, "God is the creator of heaven and earth" and the "all-encompassing reality and the ground of all that is, that is seen and unseen."[26]

Lutheran theologians have introduced the doctrine of the church as a foundation of human rights. First, the community of Christ is a gift to which all Christians have equal access. Second, the church is an institution in society and needs to be governed by human rights principles. This includes allocation of resources and personnel. Further, encouragement of social change is a part of the church's mission as well as empowerment. Examples include the civil rights movement in the United States and the antiapartheid crusades in South Africa. Finally, the church serves as an agent of communication and a mediator between other social institutions. The dissemination of information through Christian networks is a powerful force in support of human rights.[27] However, the church as a foundation for human rights has limitations. Does a distinctively Christian formulation for human rights lead inevitably to an elitist position? The theologian must ask, What about those outside the Body of Christ?[28]

Another Lutheran concern in the discussion of human rights is "universality." Wolfgang Huber at the University of Heidelberg reminds his church that human rights advocates must be careful not to identify their definitions of human rights with prevailing conditions in a given historical or social context. That inevitably leads to invalidation. Moreover, the codification of human rights in international law has validated human rights as universal. The theological task, therefore, is to connect God's desire for the salvation of the world, a theology of hope in the Kingdom of God, with human rights.[29]

Although Dietrich Bonhoeffer* died before the major thrusts of human rights discourse occurred, his theological understanding and ethics have enjoyed a revival in the Lutheran tradition and beyond. Bonhoeffer began his career in the early 1930s against a backdrop of the rise of national socialism in Germany. As a university lecturer and pastor, he was appalled at the seeming takeover of the Lutheran Church hierarchy. He became part of the "confessing church" that opposed the Nazis. Bonhoeffer also found the treatment of Jews in Germany unacceptable, particularly with the Jewish evacuation of Berlin. A distant accomplice in a plot against Hitler, Bonhoeffer was imprisoned and ultimately executed with others in his Christian circle. Before his capture and during his incarceration, however, he created an enduring legacy that ethicists and human rights advocates have rediscovered in the late twentieth century. To those who reject human rights discourse because it seems to be driven by secular models, Bonhoeffer's ideas are seen as a call for a Christological basis for all ethics, a biblically based human rights. Taking John 19:5 ("Behold the man . . ."), Bonhoeffer emphasized real human beings who encounter suffering and oppression, rather than some idealized form of "humanity."[30] He further stressed the importance of penultimate experience, that is, the things before "last things." While the gospel is ultimate, the things of this life matter a great deal and form a preparatory stage for the coming of Christ. Finally, Bonhoeffer was strong in his assertion of natural rights and the importance of duties before responsibilities. "God always gave, before he demanded," he wrote.[31] As Michael Westmoreland-White at Simmons University has observed, Bonhoeffer's ethics spoke both to Christian believers out of a strong biblical basis and to the non-Christian world with integrity, and thus avoided the "two realms" problem of other ethicists.[32]

The Reformed theological tradition has, over a lengthy evolution, made an important contribution to a theology of human rights. From John Calvin forward, four principles have guided the Reformed perspective: the sovereignty of God, the totality of God's work in creation, the sinfulness of humanity, and the redemptive grace of God in Christ. Translated into contemporary Reformed discourse, theologians point out that rather than "rights of mankind," God possesses a right or claim

upon human beings. God and humans are bound to each other by covenant and this covenant has taken concrete shape in the history of
salvation and liberation.[33] God's concern is for all of his creation, human
and nonhuman, the totality of life in the natural order. Yet, human
beings have exhibited inhumane and evil behavior toward each other
and this is recognized as sin, even within the Christian churches. The
Reformed tradition maintains a strong doctrine of the grace of God as
revealed in Christ, who witnesses to the fullness of God's intention in
humanity, complete with dignity and communion among each other and
with God.[34]

Brunner, a professor of theology at the University of Zurich and later
Princeton Theological Seminary, was a leading Reformed theologian
during the period when the United Nations developed its human rights
ideology. In the 1947 Gifford Lectures at the University of St. Andrews,
he held that natural laws, from the Christian point of view, are not
entities in themselves, but belong to the sphere of contingent relative
being. They are created by God as static, stable, dependable traits of a
God-created universe.[35] Further, he articulated his understanding that
all men are created by God equally in his image and they all share in
an original dignity of person conferred by God. Perhaps most importantly, Brunner cautioned that a Christian idea of rights has reference
exclusively to humans and never to God. "Man has no rights over
against God, being his creature and property," he wrote, he lives entirely
from God's grace and mercy."[36] In the final analysis, all rights are limited
by the imperative of love. Brunner's position on human rights was to
influence an entire generation not only of Reformed thinkers, but also
of many other Christian theologians as well.

Perhaps the most articulate case for human rights of the past quarter
century in the Reformed tradition has been made by Moltmann. Writing
from a foundation as a former German prisoner of war in England, Moltmann has identified with suffering people. He sees the need to join the
radical narrative of scripture with a radical witness of Christian praxis.
The result is an unbroken line of solidarity from the cross to those
currently oppressed. Basic to Moltmann's ethics is the idea of promise,
meaning God's promise to humanity through the death and resurrection
of Jesus Christ. He does not come to human rights through legal declarations, rather through God's right or claim on human beings and
human beings' rule over the earth, their future, and their dignity. Nor
does he base his claims upon natural law, as for instance Roman Cath-

olics have, because a Christian doctrine of natural law adds nothing to natural law and misses the main point that any rights of humanity are a reflection of the right of God.[37]

Moltmann agrees with other Christian theologians that human rights proceed from what it means to say that humans are created in God's image. But Moltmann means something much different from traditional formulations by his understanding of the "image of God." The primary meaning of the *imago dei* is humanity in its relationship with both human and nonhuman creation. Fellowship and covenant demand a human responsibility for others that manifests itself in a respect for the dignity of others universally and by acting in favor of the right of one's neighbor. Human beings have inalienable and indivisible rights and duties toward each other and for God; part of the responsibility is the liberation of those from whom rights have been withheld. Understanding fully the scope of human rights is a process that will be fully realized in the Kingdom of God.

Inspired by the neo-Marxist Ernest Bloch and Barth, Moltmann thus speaks of a theology of hope whereby he means not merely an otherworldly notion but a transformation of human society in the present, because the church is a constant disturbance in society. It is the task of the church to call society to realize righteousness, freedom, and human dignity. Three acts of God inform the task of theology for Moltmann: the creation of man and woman in God's image, the incarnation of God in Christ, and the coming Kingdom of God as the consummation of history. God, therefore, has an unmistakable claim on human lives. Yet, in a broader sense, Moltmann believes that all of life is to mirror God's character, qualities like freedom, community, and self-determination. He uses the terminology of political theology to signal that every Christian theology ought to have political consciousness. While theology springs from the church, of necessity it has social and political functions. Specifically, it must respond to "vicious circles of death" that include poverty, coercion, racial and cultural alienation, industrial pollution of nature, and nihilism.

Similar to earlier Reformed approaches to ethics, Moltmann thinks highly of the notion of covenant. As God liberated the Hebrews from bondage in Egypt, so God intends to liberate people from oppression in contemporary society. There are four basic elements to the image of God as a foundation of human rights. First is the "relational" in which respect for freedom of conscience is the foundation. Second is the notion that God ordained the state for humans; that is, the purpose of government is to ensure democratic relationships: separation of powers, time limits on office holding, self-rule, and participatory democracy. In a "communal" category, the social side of freedom is in focus where individual states have human duties" to ensure that others observe a universal sense of fairness and avoid extreme expressions of individualism. Human rights can only be realized in a universal community. And finally he writes of the "ecological" category where he stresses that what man's "dominion" over creation implies is respect for the "nonhuman" parts of creation. This specifically involves the environment, work, shelter, economic possessions, shelter, and so forth. His 1989 treatise, *Creating a Just Future*, concentrated on this theme. It is abundantly clear in Moltmann's theology that humans have a responsibility to those who come after them. The weakest links in the chain of humanity are children and the yet to be born. "A breach of contract between generations," he wrote, "could prove fatal for mankind." In more recent published work, Moltmann has drawn upon the idea of "shalom" as peace with God and with other human beings.[38]

Moltmann and other Christian theologians have suggested that the next generation of discussions and agreements on human rights must move toward social rights or "rights of the human race" and the right to protection from mass annihilation. Too much of human rights discourse has used the language of individualism. At fault here has been the liberal tradition of the West that stressed individual rights over against political rule. Rather, one should understand that social equality is the desired ideal and this is only achievable in the solidarity of human beings with one another. Not just human dignity of persons is involved, but human sociality is also at stake, which is as important to being human as personhood is. In the shadow of Hiroshima, Japan, and the arms race, Moltmann reminds the church that national foreign policies have been predicated upon rivalry with other nations. This must change in the future and be based on the survival of humanity, a worldwide domestic policy to ensure the humanness of all, the mutual promotion of life and security for all. It is, in the last analysis, not a matter of human rights, but the right of the human race to survive.[39] In his Reformed theological tradition, Moltmann thus expresses his continuing affirmation of the sovereignty of God and the unity of creation.

In the end, Moltmann has been prepared to move theoretical theological discussions of human rights toward ethics. He expects Christian churches, congregations, and ecumenical organizations to act and ad-vocate. First, they must represent the unassailable dignity of human be-ings and their indivisible unity. Second, Christians are called to restore particular human rights that have been neglected, denied, or repressed. Third, he believes Christians must overcome their natural egoism of individual social and human rights expressions over nature and other classes of people in the present and for future generations. Finally, this may mean that Christians must stand up for dignity of humanity against inhumanity, even if it entails suffering and great sacrifice.[40]

Roman Catholics have a long heritage of addressing human rights concerns theologically. Since the medieval theologians, "human rights" have been part of "natural law." God in his sovereignty has created the law of creation that is inherent in the very nature of things. All creation is subject to this law. Thomas Aquinas (1225–1249) defined natural law as the participation of eternal law in rational creatures, and he listed the categories of existence, self-preservation, family, education, society, and religion. Other Scholastics like Gratian (fl.1140–1175), found evi-dences of it in the Ten Commandments and the Gospels. Natural law, then, in the dogma of the church, came to mean the ordered wisdom of God as human reason received it. Wrong, therefore, is done against God, not against other persons, and the purpose of civil law has been to protect specific rights between persons implied in natural law. Civil law protects rights such as life, worship, property, labor, speech, assem-bly, and reputation. To put it in succinct terms, in historic Catholic teaching, humans owe God obedience to his law because he is their creator and rightly superior lawmaker. Likewise they owe obedience to civil laws in respect to each other.

The biblical term *imago dei* has been at the heart of Roman Catholic thinking since the early medieval period, and it continues to provide a foundation for human rights understanding. What is involved in the *imago dei* from the contribution of Augustine and Aquinas, for instance, is that the relevant being and activity of God are regarded as that of a pure spirit loving and knowing itself. Human beings alone in all creation have that same capacity to know and to love. Aquinas was careful to assert that the matephor *imago dei* involves both an "exemplar" and an "image," and the image is always distinct from the exmplar. Modern Catholic writers have demonstrated that this enables humans to think in a relational sense. God freely initiates and maintains relationships with humans. In the same way, humans create relationships with each other. Guiding these relationships are the basic rights of each human to be oneself, live out one's destinies, and with respect to God, to grow more like God. Claiming rights—human rights—therefore involves exercising those freedoms in light of the awareness that others will enjoy those freedoms as well.[41]

As David J. Hollenbach at Boston College observes, Roman Catholic thinking about human rights changed dramatically under the pontificate of John XXIII (Angelo Giuseppe Roncalli*). Several contextual factors were part of a long-term shift, including the establishment of the United Nations, which suggested a pluralistic world order; the establishment of the World Council of Churches, which staked out a Christian response to matters of world order; and the formation of organizations like the International Committee of Jurists, Amnesty International, and World Vision. To these catalysts must of course be added the genuine commitment of John XXIII toward religious liberty and human rights. After 1963, the church built its case upon human dignity, linking the individual libertarian ideals of the West with social participation and economic bases of socialism regimes, very much attuned to the voices of the Southern Hemisphere. John XXIII's major encyclical, *Pacem in Terris* (discussed in Chapter 5) focused upon all the U.N.-declared rights, plus bodily integrity, food, clothing, shelter, rest, medical care, life, and the support needed to maintain those rights.[42]

An important outgrowth of the Roman Catholic tradition is the mostly Latin American theological movement known as "liberation theology," which began in the 1960s. Its writers have provided the Christian community with a compelling theological approach to human rights. Liberation theology has roots in liberal Catholic thought propounded by philosopher-theologians like Jacques Maritain* in early twentieth-century France who blended Thomistic theology with modern democratic idealism. Peruvian Gustavo Gutierrez,* one of the early and leading liberationists, has stressed the importance of understanding history and theology from the perspective of the poor. Likewise Enrique Dussel* and Leonardo Boff* have followed the path set by Gutierrez. This new approach made a formal debut in 1968 at the Second Catholic Bishops Conference in Medellin, Colombia, which was called to interpret Vatican II for the Latin American context.

Instead of seeing scripture and tradition as a closed canon, liberation theologians view scripture as an open narrative wherein God has revealed himself and continues to do so. His revelation is not through powerful institutions, but through a church of the poor.[43] Yahweh intervenes in history to establish justice and right. The ultimate manifestation of God is in Christ who is the liberator: God become poor (Isa. 61:1–2; Luke 4:16–21). The Lord's Supper, for instance, receives a new interpretation, that of a communion with the poor in history. Evangelization is not winning converts to an institution, but pure liberation that goes to the root of injustice and exploitation. These qualities stand against slavery and humiliation of the poor. The Great Commandment comes to be understood in terms of the poor as its object. The ultimate goal for Gutierrez is a church that becomes the "social appropriation of the gospel"[44] and its messenger. Instead of a church built from within, the church needs to be rebuilt from below. The poor actually become the people of God, millions that there are. To this Jan Sobrino, a Jesuit Liberation theologian, has added that crucified people, that is the oppressed and their martyrs, become the modern equivalent of Yahweh's "suffering servant." Like the servant, the crucified people are despised and rejected; everything has been taken from them, even human dignity.[45] This kind of project has huge implications for human rights. In Latin America, it is an urgent human rights agenda.

Pablo Richard at the National University of Costa Rica adds to the meaning of liberation theology that, in critiquing the Christendom model of understanding human rights, one moves inevitably to a new understanding of theology. Defending the lives of indigenous peoples is both a new hermeneutic and strategy for the church in Latin America. Just as Christendom destroyed the lives of indigenous peoples five centuries ago, it must now engage in saving these peoples' lives as ethnic groups, as races. It means saving their physical lives, their lands, their labor, their health, their homes, their culture and their religion. Nothing less than the credibility of God is at stake. Those church leaders who have taken up this challenge for indigenous peoples have often met with violence.

What are the rights of the poor, as liberation theologians see it? Among its agenda are protection against persecution for being a "subversive Christian"; the right of the poor to exist and think; and the right to be free from hunger and economic exploitation, exile, imprisonment, and the threat of death. Liberal theology and social thought assume a society model in which social equality exists and human rights are somehow derived from that equality. In the Latin American context and elsewhere, social equality does not exist. Therefore, the program of human rights must begin in the experience of a world of poverty. But, this is not an easy prospect for those devoted to theological liberation. Bishop Leonidas Proano of Ecuador, the so-called Indians' bishop, died in 1988 in defense of indigenous peoples, and doubtless many other Christians have become martyrs as well.[46]

The liberation theology movement also had profound effects in the struggle for human rights in South Africa. Called in that region "contextual theology," it took account not only of race and class exploitation, but also the interaction of non-Christian traditions, notably Islam and African religions. As reflected in the "Kairos Document of 1985," a more militant theology developed where confrontation of evil takes precedence over reconciliation. Signers of the document agreed that the typical otherworldly theology of conflict resolution in Reformed theology was inadequate against apartheid. Only after repentance and dismantling of evil structures could reconciliation occur. Christians were called upon to unseat tyrants, eliminate oppression, and establish just government structures. In this way human rights would be recognized.[47]

An intriguing contribution to a Christian theology of human rights has come from the dialogue produced between the Reformed community and liberation theologians. Daniel Vidal, a theologian at the Evangelical Seminary in Madrid, has joined European colleagues in suggesting a "Christological Approach" that blends the work of Christ with new concepts of freedom. This position argues that God revealed himself in Jesus Christ as the objective reality of freedom for the "new man," and as a result, human rights are established as an expression of human liberation. Basing their position on 2 Corinthians 5:19, Vidal and others find a covenant of liberation and reconciliation through Christ. Jesus Christ has established communion with God the Father for humanity, and through Christ a person is freed to be a child of God and given the opportunity to liberate every other creature for communion with God the Creator, Savior, and Redeemer.[48]

One of the most provocative voices to emerge from the Roman Catholic community of theologians in the past century has been Hans Küng.* Küng a theologian at Tübingen, Germany, developed an ecumenical approach to contemporary theological issues and began to question certain dogmas of the church. Eventually he lost his license to teach as a Roman Catholic, but has continued as an "ecumenical theologian." To the contemporary discussions of "rights," Küng has added the need of the great religions of the world to develop a universal ethic. He has asked the all-important question, Why should anyone observe human rights? He persuasively points out that one of the results of historical criticism is that fixed moral/ethical solutions to human problems seem to come less from transcendent commandments than the results of social processes. He has observed that nonreligious people as well have a need to observe human rights. He also notes that the problems that humans encounter require earthly solutions. "Whether as Jews, Christians, Muslims, or as members of an Indian, Chinese, or Japanese religion, human beings are themselves responsible for the concrete fashioning of their morality."[49] They cannot always rely on a higher authority because of the autonomy they exercise in their world. Furthermore, one now has to take into account scientific methodology and empirical data in order to make ethical, valid decisions and establish ethical norms. Pre-scientific perceptions of ethical norms are too simplistic for the technological complexities of everyday life in the twenty-first century. Küng's answer to these dilemmas is to construct a new role for the religions of the world, to arrive at a universal world ethic. He refers to a "primal ground" that Christians and others call God, but what in all religions amounts to a kind of theonomy or "higher transcendent law." This theonomy produces in human beings the guarantee of human autonomy, and that includes the right not to be part of any religious tradition at all. Religions, Küng believes, can speak with more authority than individuals because they carry the oldest, strongest, and most urgent desires of mankind. Religions have the capability to shape the totality of human life and to be tested over time.[50]

The obvious difficulty in Küng's position is the lack of unity among the world's great religions. Each has a different locus of authority and in many cases, differing ethics. In fact, there are some spectacular differences, and in the case of Christianity, there are elements of finality and absoluteness. Küng proposes to meet this difficulty by asserting that a unity of the world religions is not necessary; rather one should think of a unity in diversity. He urges that each religion be accepted as a legitimate path to salvation in itself. "What we need," he writes, "and what I hope for, is peace between the religions; because without peace between religions there will be no peace between nations!"[51] He finds several basic ethical imperatives in common among the Semitic religions and the mystical religions of the Far East. These include: not killing the innocent, not lying or breaking promises; a ban on adultery and fornication; and the commandment "Thou shalt do good."[52] Küng summarizes this overall common religious ethic as "true humanity—*humanitas.*" Hu-

manitas requires that humans should behave humanely toward other fellow human beings. It is the minimum demand of all religions. For him, the declaration from the World Conference of Religions for Peace adopted at Kyoto, Japan, in 1970 demonstrated what the concrete universal religious ethic could be.[53] One finds in the approach of Küng a cutting-edge Christian interpretation not only of human rights, but of Christian theology in general.

Rounding out the development of Christian thinking about human rights is the Evangelical tradition. Here one is confronted with an array of theological development from a conservative confessionalism to a charismatic or Pentecostal appreciation for experience. Evangelicals are found in all segments of traditional denominationalism, as well as in independently organized new sects and parachurch organizations. What all evangelicals have in common is a priority upon the authority of scripture, the lordship of Christ, personal conversion, and a strong sense of Christian witness and mission. When evangelicals approach the issues of human rights, they do so through these lenses. As John R. W. Stott, an evangelical Anglican rector at London's All Soul's Church, has warned, however, "Christians often cringe when the conversation turns to human rights." It is essentially a conflict model of discussion from a biblical perspective.

One of the earliest evangelical theologians to respond to human rights issues was Carl F. H. Henry. Henry taught at Fuller Theological Seminary, Northern Baptist Seminary, and The Eastern Baptist Theological Seminary and also served as editor of *Christianity Today*. His influence among evangelicals was significant and his work won respect among non-evangelicals as well. Over the course of his long career, Henry's approach to human rights issues paralleled both the history of U.N. declarations and the broadening of evangelicalism. In the early part of his writing, he was critical of the U.N. discussion because it ignored the whole question of the ultimate source of human rights. "International politics has no established legal authority," he believed. "Christians must insist on divine sanction for political authority in institutions."[54] Henry was slow to acknowledge the value of liberation theology, finally admitting that the God of scripture consistently identifies with the poor and oppressed. Evangelical Christianity focuses the problem of universal humanity in a larger context of reconciliation between man and God, and this was an absolute in Henry's position.[55]

As his thought matured, Henry began to explore various foundations of "rights." Modern psychology fell short because it did not account for the problem of sin, which he defined as a disposition of the heart grounded in inherited factors. Philosophical formulations like discussions of "humanness" were pretentious frauds because nothing was at the core. Human rights cannot be derived from positive law or human experience because of the limitations of both, he wrote. Further secular evolutionary theories could guarantee neither universal nor enduring human rights. Nor could they define norms for human rights. The problem as Henry saw it was that both lacked revelational criteria to distinguish the divine from the demonic in social transformation. The answer must be found in a sovereign supernatural deity and a transcendent ethics that obligates all mankind. Given his frequent references to American political documents, Henry was also troubled by the notion that all men were created equal was considered a biblical precept per se.[56]

Ultimately, Henry joined other theologians in positing his case for human rights and responsibilities in the *imago dei*. The legitimacy of inviolable human rights turns on God's creation of all humans in God's image. Henry was willing to concede with earlier theologians that man is finite and bears the image of God only in certain respects, but through personality man is the finite counterpart of the mind that conceived him. The whole conception of human rights becomes tenuous for Henry unless it is grounded in man's primal right that Henry understands as the freedom from being stripped of his divinely stipulated dignity.[57] All other rights are derived from this basic right and involve the principle of reciprocity. For Henry, this answered the all-important question of what makes rights right. Justice, a related theological concept, resides in the God of justice and justification.[58] Gradually, Henry came to affirm human rights for persons of alternative lifestyles as well as the full equality of women as a biblical precept.[59] In his great theological treatise, he urged Christians to take seriously their political duty, because human rights are important not only in man's sight, but in God's eyes as well. If Christians concentrate only on moral and spiritual freedom to the exclusion of legal freedoms, they diminish the love of neighbor.[60] Henry thus brought the issue of human rights into clear focus for the Evangelical community.

A second important evangelical thinker in the second half of the twentieth century is Ronald J. Sider. A Canadian Mennonite by upbringing and trained as an historical theologian, Sider plunged into the areas of ethics and economics with his provocative book, *Rich Christians* in *An Age of Hunger* (1977). Increasingly, Sider and his colleagues, Jim Wallis of *Sojourners Magazine*, Tom Sine of World Concern, and Vinay Samuel and Christopher Sugden of the Oxford Center for Mission Studies, seem to have taken a cue from liberation theologians. Sider was convinced that "the rich may prosper for a time but eventually God will destroy them; the poor on the other hand, God will exalt," and "as the people of God become coworkers in this task of liberation, revealed principles on justice in society will shape their thought and action."[61] Regarding private property, Sider sounded a Christian socialist note when he asserted, "Since God is the only absolute power, our right to acquire and use property is definitely limited. The human right to the resources necessary to earn a just living overrides any notion of absolute private ownership."[62]

Working out of the ethics of human rights rather than pure theology, Sider cited world hunger as the grossest violation of human rights: "One billion people have stunted bodies or damaged brains because of inadequate food." He inveighed harshly against the wealth of the North American and European communities who rationalize their affluence at the expense of the poor. He attacked structural evil, as had Walter Rauschenbusch* seventy-five years before, and he proposed everything from a graduated tithe to communal living as measures the Christian community could take to address the dire needs of the starving world. Sider's ecclesiological focus was that "as the new people of God, the church should be a new society incarnating biblical principles on justice in society through its common life. He was convinced that as a transformed community, the church may have some power of moral suasion upon government to legislate more justly. Sider's theological and ethical influence reached a high watermark in 1973 when he convened a workshop in Chicago of prominent young Evangelicals to reflect on social concerns. What they produced was the Chicago Declaration of Social Concern, which confessed to evangelical complicity in racial discrimination, materialism, economic injustice, and race and sex discrimination. Out of that event came the organization Evangelicals for Social Action, which has carried a significant constituency of American Evangelicals oriented to human rights issues and categories. Overall, Sider and his evangelical cohorts argued for a theology of development by which people gain greater control over themselves, their environment and their future in order to realize the full potential of life that God has made possible.[63] A theology of development implies social change in which Christians change their own ways of stewardship and respond to the cries of the oppressed.

Within the last two decades, Stott has become an important voice on human rights issues. An Anglican priest and chaplain to the queen, Stott is well traveled and instigated the TEAR Fund among other organizations to carry forth his evangelical social action agenda. Stott has demonstrated a keen, though biased awareness of human rights advocacy and political history and wants to begin at another point than secular declarations in the United Nations context. He is particularly bothered by the approach of many to violations of human rights, without a necessary moral compass. To this challenge, Stott asserts that the origin of human rights is Creation, and rather than tracking either the Catholic or World Council pathways, he cites the eighteenth-century Deist Thomas Paine as an authority.[64] Concerned about the factor of human sinfulness, Stott has proposed what he considers three "biblical" ideas summarizing the divine purpose for human life and from which human rights must proceed: dignity, equality, and responsibility.

Possessing dignity, for Stott, stems from human creation by God and involves one's relationship to God, relations with one's fellow humans, and relations to the earth. He has clearly stated, "Our value depends on God's view of us and relationship to us."[65] He writes that good gifts of the Creator have been spoiled by human selfishness and this must be corrected in the quality of equality. Rather than there being one dominant community over others in the Bible, Stott thinks that no community may violate the rights of another and that God shows special favor upon the weak and vulnerable. He bases his position on the saga of Job, who proclaimed the unified creation of all (Job 31:13–15), and Paul's comments about masters and slaves such as, "There is no favoritism with God."(Eph. 6:9). Finally, he sets aside the discussion of human "rights" as an assertion of rights over against another. Instead, Stott has built his case for human responsibilities. Citing Christopher Wright's idea of a universal declaration of human responsibilities in scripture,[66] he argues that it is the Christian's responsibility to secure the rights of others. This may mean foregoing one's own rights in the "law of love." Stott is adamant that "we are our brother's keepers" and one has a duty to serve the poor and defend the powerless. In this regard, the Christian community should set the example for other communities. Here, like Sider, Stott's ecclesiology comes into view, as he thinks of the local church as a sign of God's rule where human dignity and equality are invariably recognized and "in which there is no favoritism, partiality, or discrimination and where humans can be free as God made them."[67]

FROM RIGHTS TO RESPONSIBILITIES

IN THE LAST two decades, led in part by Evangelicals, the path of human rights activity has moved from understanding and affirming the importance of human rights declarations to theologically articulating human rights as human responsibilities. In a significant way this has occurred because, in the ecumenical community of Christians on the one hand, there is no consensus about a universal ethic. Moral imperatives are not easily obtained. In the evangelical communities, on the other hand, for some the terminology of "rights" seems to offend the doctrine of God. A group of prominent former world leaders collectively known as the InterAction Council, for instance, has produced the Universal Declaration of Human Responsibilities, which draws upon the thinking of Küng, who has argued in this context for the necessity of a universal ethic that can be derived from all of the world's religions, particularly Judaism, Christianity, and Islam. The declaration holds that persons of goodwill everywhere want to be treated humanely, that is with respect to human dignity, rights, and differing qualities. Closely tied to this initial principle is the entitlement to the benefits of the Golden Rule: "What you do not wish to be done to yourself, do not do to others."[68] Egoism is a main theme of the writers as it is promotive of selfishness, class thinking, racism, nationalism, and sexism. Rather than the traditional "Thou shalt not kill" of the Judeo-Christian usage, "Have respect for life" is used. Respect for the earth and the responsible use of power are affirmed. Article 15 goes well beyond traditional religious freedom, as it asserts the representatives of religions have a special responsibility to avoid expressions of prejudice and acts of discrimination toward those of different beliefs. Further, religious leaders are challenged not to incite religious wars, but to foster tolerance and respect for all peoples.[69] In such declarations, Christian principles are evident, but only as they harmonize with other ethical norms of other religions.

A SUMMARY OF CHRISTIAN THEOLOGICAL REFLECTION

CHRISTIAN THEOLOGIANS SEEM to have agreed that human rights issues belong in the forum of theological reflection. It is unacceptable that human beings could be expected to uphold moral standards without reference to a Supreme Being. Indeed, the secular expressions, such as those in the U.N. context, are hollow without a metaphysical core. Further, Christian theologians are compelled to answer the silence of scripture in the use of human rights language by pointing to the ethical codes, teachings of Jesus, and community standards in the apostolic churches that parallel modern human rights statements and categories. Finally, historical theologians have uncovered a Christian influence upon many "secular" documents and declarations: the Act of Toleration, the Declaration of Independence, and even the U.N. Declaration on Human Rights.

Liberation theologians have had a profound influence upon mainstream Western theologians. Identification with the world's poor and oppressed has moved from reinterpretation of biblical passages and theological reflection to the basis of human rights activism. Responses to apartheid as well as the "developmentalism" of Evangelicals in addressing hunger, religious freedom, women's rights, and peace all reflect the liberationist approach.

Finally, in the 1990s Christian theologians turned to a discussion of human rights as human responsibilities. Here one reads the evangelical discourse on divine creation and parenthood and on the laws of love and brotherhood. One also sees a more activistic role among Christian leaders in alleviating the effects of violated human rights as part of Christian stewardship of morality and resources. Important theologians such as Kung have recognized the emptiness of human rights without religious values, while at the same time practically recognizing religious differentiation among the world's peoples. Rather than overarching imperatives, their mode is to bind humanity under God to specific responsibilities that reflect the person and will of God. This type of "extended Christian theology" seems likely to engage only a minority of Christians, however, because of a sense of the loss of theological particularity that most Christians desire to maintain.

Christian theologians for the most part live within the bounds of some form of confessional tradition. This is true as well of those who represent their confessional traditions at the table of ecumenical dialogue. After nearly a half century, the ecumenical Christian community has decided that there are basically three foundations for advocating human rights: the *imago dei*, the atonement, and the Great Commandment. In a confessional statement reaffirmed in 1998, the World Council of Churches asserted that Christian involvement in human rights stems from "the emphasis of the gospel on the value of all human beings in the sight of God, on the atoning and redeeming work of Christ, that has given to the human person true dignity, on love as a motive for action, and on love for one's neighbor as the practical expression of an active faith in Christ."[70]

In the end, as Moltmann aptly stated, "The task of Christian theology is not that of trying to present once more what thousands of experts, lawyers, legislators, and diplomats in the United Nations have already accomplished." Rather, these theological foundations build upon two millennia of Christian thought and ethics to define more fully God's provision for and claim upon humanity's dignity and its rule over the earth and its future.[71]

ORGANIZED CHRISTIANITY AND OBSTACLES TO HUMAN RIGHTS

S OUTH AFRICAN ANGLICAN Archbishop Desmond Tutu*
has written, "We must hang our heads in shame, when we
survey the gory and shameful history of the Church of Christ."[1] Despite
its early recognition of Judaic teachings, plus Christological and apostolic affirmations of human dignity and community, the record of organized Christianity has presented serious obstacles to what would later
be referred to as "human rights." Self-critically, this chapter will examine
the record and comment upon the contexts as well.

Hans Küng has observed that each of the Christian traditions have
chapters of violating human rights that they would like to silence. He
is correct, painfully so. Early Christian history is replete with instances
of Christians punishing each other and denying rights to coreligionists.
Christianity was far from a unified religious tradition at its origins, and
it can be demonstrated that several sometimes-competitive versions existed in tandem with each other. In the apostolic writings of Paul, one
reads, "If any one among you is preaching to you a gospel contrary to
that which we preached to you, let him be accursed" (Gal. 1:8). Among
the earliest were Gnosticism and those who followed Marcion (c.175).
As Walter Nigg at the University of Zurich has shown, the "outsider"
evolved into the "heretic." Heretics were not pagans, but Christians who
held alternative Christian views intensely. Heretics were often precur-
sors of new ideas.[2] Unfortunately, the dominant thinkers and schools
often labeled such creativity negatively and took pains to ostracize or

even silence dissent. The earliest Christian "heretic" was perhaps Priscillian, who was executed in 385 for dissent. Another early example of ill treatment of diverse opinion was the British monk Pelagius, who was so vilified by Augustine that virtually no original material of his writing survives. Heresy often became a matter of conscience where those so accused felt the only alternative with integrity was to give their lives for their positions. They took solace from the New Testament advice, "All who desire to live a godly life in Christ Jesus will be persecuted" (2 Tim. 3:12).

Irenaeus, bishop of Lyon, was the first "heresiologist" or categorizer of heretical ideas. In his book, *Against Heresies* (190), his intention was "not only to show the beast, but to wound it from all sides."[3] Gnosticism was his first enemy to the mainstream tradition and he prayed that those who were caught up in it "would not linger in the pit which they have dug for themselves."[4] He so interpreted scripture as to negate any other interpretation. In so doing he relied upon a growing tradition, and, as some historians have seen him, he was the first great theologian of tradition in the history of Christianity. He associated the dominant tradition with Rome and bluntly proclaimed, "Every church must agree with Rome because of its special precedence." Other writers followed in the train of Irenaeus, including Hippolytus and Epiphanius. The result was that, by about the year 250, both the personalities and the literature of Christianity were destroyed, except for the fragments that survive in the refutations. However, to their historical chagrin, the heresiologists did not destroy the tendency toward heresy.

Intolerance to alternative ideas continued in the Nicene era. In the year 319, Bishop Alexander of Alexandria laid out his doctrine of Christ, which tied together the oneness of each member of the Godhead in a trinitarian formula. His presbyter Arius, a gifted writer and theologian, however, taught that "there was a time when Christ was not," a serious deviation from the received tradition. Arius counted among his friends and supporters many bishops in the East and women in particular. The new Emperor Constantine saw the Arian controversy as a major schismatic possibility, and he convened a council of bishops at Nicea to resolve the doctrinal controversy and other pressing matters. The result was a resounding definition of "orthodoxy" that sent a signal throughout the Christian world and formed the first of the great creeds. Arius himself was banished from his church and with the help of an able, vain, and ambitious Athanasius, a slander campaign ensued against all followers of Arian doctrine. The pendulum swung back in the next three decades against Athanasius, who was banished into exile. Finally, in 451 at the Council of Chalcedon, the meaning of the doctrine of the person of Christ was authoritatively determined in the church and a standard for evaluation of heresy and subsequent discipline were determined.

Another important denial of status and free expression in the fifth century was made by the British monk and theologian, Pelagius. In about 405, he dissented from the commonly held position of Augustine on the doctrine of grace. Following another "heretical" thinker, Celestius, Pelagius developed different views of original sin and baptism. In 413, Jerome, writing from Palestine, warned against Pelagius's teaching. Two years later, Pelagius was tried for heresy at the Synod of Diospolis, but he was acquitted. Augustine, however, renewed his attacks and Pelagius wrote one of his most important works, *In Defense of Free Will*. The Councils at Milevus and Carthage in 416 condemned him for these positions. At length, Pelagius was expelled from Jerusalem, then from Palestine, and his followers and all of his writings were likewise banned. "Pelagianism," which placed stress upon freedom of the will and denied original sin, was widely condemned across the church. Only through the heavily biased rejoinders in the writings of St. Augustine is Pelagius even remembered at all.

The crusades of the eleventh through the fourteenth centuries confront the Christian historian with circumstances illustrative of little appreciation for human life, property, and racial and ethnic integrity. Also evident was aggressive abuse of religious power and distortion of doctrine for the purposes of organizational and personal gain. Mainstream Western (Roman Catholic) appreciation for Islam was minimal and extremely hostile. In 1144 when the city of Edessa fell to Imad ad-Din Zanghi, the Turkish Islamic emir of Mosul and Aleppo, Pope Eugenius III labeled the interlopers "pagans" and "enemies of the cross of Christ." Among the "sins" of Muslims were killing Christians, scattering and trampling of saints' relics, and, in general, creating "danger for the Church of God and for the whole of Christendom."[5] A pattern of religious enmity was thus set in place for centuries to come between Christians and Muslims that would create untold opportunities of human rights denials.

At the foundation of the crusades were three premises. First, the "just war" idea was based on the intention of the participants. That is, if a warrior faced conflict in a battle and thought that his actions were expressive of a love for God and neighbor, his cause was considered "just."

Second, violence was not considered inherently evil. This included physical injury and homicide. Third, it was assumed that the will of Christ could be identified with a particular system or organized political unit, like the Western church. The agents of Christ in what historian Jonathan Riley-Smith at the University of London calls the "political Christ" were Christian emperors, kings, bishops, and popes.[6] The words of Christ, taken directly from the gospels, seemed to authorize rulers to take action: "If any man will come after me, let him deny himself, take up his cross and follow me" (Luke 14:27); "Every one who has left house or brethren or sisters or father or mother or wife or children or fields, for my name's sake, shall receive a hundredfold and will inherit eternal life" (Matt. 19:29); "Those who want to save their life will lose it and those who lose their life for my sake, will save it" (Luke 9:24).

As for the crusades themselves, the record is vivid. The First Crusade, which Pope Urban II announced in 1095, resulted in a series of Latin kingdoms set up in the conquered holy lands. Once the armies reached the East, the conquerors followed the principle that the conquerors ruled the territories and determined the liturgical rite. This produced a religious conquest by Latin Christianity not only over the Muslims, but also over Eastern Christianity as well. In the ensuing years, a stronger rationale for crusading was developed with contributions from Peter the Venerable and Gratian's compilation of canon law, *Decretum*. Heresy, it was argued, could be suppressed by force. As one historian put it, "War need not be sinful, could be just, and could be authorized by God, and on God's behalf, the pope."[7]

When reports of the fall of Edessa in 1144 reached Europe, a Second Crusade, fired up by Bernard of Clairvaux, was proclaimed. It resulted in military reversals, treachery, and mistreatment of crusaders. Witnesses wrote of greed and violence that seemed to be the result of God withdrawing his favor upon the enterprise, or so it was rationalized. The fall of Jerusalem in 1187 led to a Third Crusade that produced stunning tales of royal daring of Richard the Lion Heart, Philip of France, and Frederick I of Germany. Small territorial gains were achieved in Palestine, while the leaders quarreled covetously in Europe among themselves. Significant territorial gains were made but the recapture of Jerusalem in the twelfth century eluded the crusaders. The Fourth Crusade (1202–1204) demonstrated conflict between Christian armies of France and Venice and actually focused upon difficulties in Hungary. The indebtedness to Venetian shipbuilders and too few crusaders led to a diverted plan to attack and plunder the riches of Constantinople. A ruthless systematic destruction of the city occurred in 1204, looting the greatest storehouse of relics in Christendom. The result was that Baldwin of Flanders, a Roman Catholic, would occupy the seat of Eastern Christianity thereafter. A "Children's Crusade" was launched in 1212 that resulted in its participants reaching Italy where many were abducted by the local populace and held as servants or slaves. Others were said to have reached the coast "where they were tricked by seamen and ships masters and carried off into far-distant places."[8] Many were sold into slavery in Muslim lands. The Fifth, Sixth, Seventh, and Eighth Crusades brought more intrigue than accomplishment, and the overall attempt to recover the Holy Lands finally ended in 1270.

The Christian crusading mindset continued, however, as Pope Innocent III focused on the suppression of doctrinal heresy in communities in the Alps where pockets of Cathari supported by mercenaries maintained a dualistic theology, well beyond the confessions of orthodoxy. During the thirteenth century, the Cathars developed a type of neo-Manichaeistic theology, renouncing the world, trinitarian thought, and the Roman hierarchy. In 1208, a papal legate in southwestern France was assassinated, and this prompted Pope Innocent III to proclaim a crusade against a heresy that was, in his mind, worse than Islam. The Albigensian Crusade across the thirteenth century in intervals of forty days each, involved a bloody series of campaigns against pockets of heretics, led by Cistercians and Dominican Friars. At the head of the papal armies was Simon of Montfort who was barbarous in pursuit of Cathars and who wreaked death and destruction upon countless innocent citizens. The end of the Albigensian Crusade led to the disposition of conquered lands among new lords, the establishment of an endowment for a university, and an ongoing inquisition to reveal the continuing heresy that military conquest did not extirpate.

A dark chapter of Christian intolerance and denial of rights emerged in the thirteenth century. Known collectively as the Inquisition, it left an indelible stain on the Christian tradition. During the so-called High Middle Ages, the number of heretics seemed to swell to a peak. The church sought to deal with this outbreak by hunting down those suspected of holding unorthodox opinions, and using violence against them to silence their voices as well as to discourage others. Hohenstaufen emperor Frederick II (1194–1250) took up the cause in assistance of the church and issued the Decree on Heretics. The church imitated his brutal and ruthless tactics. After 1230, the popes determined to hold regular inquiries and to stage trials if necessary. The inquisitors were drawn from the Dominican order and to a lesser degree from among the Franciscans. The underlying Christian rationalization for this kind of activity was the Genesis story where, after the Fall, God became the first inquisitor, holding Adam and Eve guilty in a secret trial without witnesses. The greatest of the Grand Inquisitors was the Spaniard Tomás de Torquemada (1420–1498), who was obsessed with the purification of the church. The course of events was gruesome: local persons were queried to obtain evidence, after which a trial was organized under the direction of a member of the Orders. If the testimony proved unsatisfactory, torture was applied and severe penalties were meted out that ranged from dehumanizing public penance and cruel torture to banishment or death. Those sentenced to death were typically burned at the stake. As one writer has observed, the real harm that the Inquisition inflicted on religion was the linkage of religion with fearful coercion. Confidence in the idea of a Christian humanity was shaken.[9]

In many ways, the crusading mentality continued in the settlement of the Americas. The Spanish and Portuguese governments, with the knowledge and support of the Catholic Church, sent explorers, friars, adventurers, and scoundrels to Central and South America to claim territory and what gold they could find for their respective sovereigns. Many of these "conquistadors" were fresh from the religious conquests against the Moors and elsewhere on duty for the Catholic faith. Native American peoples were slaughtered or quickly subjugated to the conquering Christian powers. As Darcy Ribeiro has observed, "Spaniards and Portuguese performed their feats in the name of Christendom, trying to believe that they were fulfilling a sacred destiny of freeing the Indians from idolatry and heresy in order to save at least their souls for eternal life. They wore their bodies out with exemplary efficiency."[10] The conquest, as Enrique Dussel has asserted, was "a European Christian act."[11]

The underlying principles of the enslavement of the American Indians involved Aristotle's doctrine of natural slavery and medieval notions about the forceful conversion of the heathen. As it worked in practical experience, the officials of the church read a declaration known as the "Requierimiento," which in part, and in Spanish, informed the Indians that their lands had been donated to the Spanish kings: "We shall take you and your wives and children, and shall make slaves of them, and as such, shall sell and dispose of them, as your Highnesses may command;

and we shall take away your goods and shall do all the harm and damage that we can, as to vassals that do not obey."[12] To avoid this catastrophe, the Indians became slaves and accepted baptism, often without instruction. Bartolomé Las Casas,* seen as an advocate of the religious rights of the Indians, held out that Indians were rational men and deserved to be instructed in the faith. More common were the mass "conversions" and baptisms totaling over four million persons between 1524 and 1536. The record was a Franciscan report of fifteen thousand baptisms in one day at Xochimilco, Mexico.

In the growing debate over the enforcement of Christianity upon American native peoples, the high point came in the Great Debate at Valladolid 1550–1551. Juan Gines de Sepulveda took the position that wars against the Indians were just and constituted a necessary stage in their evangelization. Sepulveda drew heavily upon the Laws of the Burgos (1513) that provided for humane but harsh treatment of the Indians with good intent toward their Christianization. He wrote that the Indians had no skills toward political culture and were inferior beings whose status warranted enslavement. He favored the encomienda system as the means toward their inculturalization as Christians. Las Casas's essential position was the contrary: "Our Christian relation is suitable for and may be adapted to all the nations of the world, and all alike may receive it; and no one may be deprived of his liberty, nor may he be enslaved on the excuse that he is natural slave."[13] Pope Paul III, like his predecessors, vacillated on the direction of the church's evangelical thrusts, ruling in 1537 in *Sublimis Deus* that Indians were by no means to be deprived of their liberty or possession of their property, nor should they be enslaved, all the while allowing their Spanish and Portuguese sovereigns to use force to continue in cooperation with members of Christian Orders. The result of the Valladolid Debate was the ruling of King Philip of Spain in 1573 that underscored the instruction of the Indians, and under their acceptance of the Holy Faith, their enjoyment of civil and economic pursuits. If "pacification" failed to bring the Indians to Christianity, the use of force, "doing as little harm as possible," was authorized.

In actual experience, the term "reduction" is used to describe the process by which indigenous Americans were "reduced" to inferior status. This was a political, economic, and, importantly, religious total reordering of Indian life. The Crown and the church agreed that scattered Indian settlements had to be relocated into convenient and controlled villages or settlements. The first instructions for Indian reduction were laid down in 1503 and followed by the famous "Burgos Laws" of 1512. As conquistadors militarily subdued the tribes, the Dominicans, Franciscans, and Jesuits followed with organizing indigenous peoples for Christianization. Indian settlements were set up on a strict pastoral care plan with walled communities and dawn-to-dusk religious and educational activities, followed by economic assignments. Although the orders and missionaries constantly reported that their efforts were beneficial to the Indian populations, the Indian culture and their population numbers were radically "reduced." Generally, studies of architecture and written reports seem to indicate that Franciscan missions were more humane and religiously dominated than those administered by the Society of Jesus.[14] In each case, by the seventeenth century, the Catholic priest or member of an order was the facilitator and manager of the reduction of the indigenous peoples.

African slavery would follow closely the subjugation of Indian peoples in the Catholic dominions of Central and South America. It would become deeply imbedded, racial, and theologically sanctioned. In 1434 a papal bull gave Portuguese King Alphonso the right to enslave heathen peoples. As noted earlier, the Indians of the Caribbean were the first eligible subjects for enslavement. Eventually a search for a more suitable work force took place and the black slave trade commenced. By means of the *asiento*, a permit that the Portuguese monarchy granted monopolistic companies, Portuguese traders became the leaders in the African slave trade and most of their slaves went to Central and South America. It is not overstating the case to assert that the church became the breeding ground of racial slavery both by theology and example through the practices of the clergy. One of the fascinating results of the institution of slavery in Latin America was the creation of the "Black Code," which was essentially intended to define relationships between slaves and royal subjects. Not only did the code establish an elaborate racial caste system that saw slaves as chattels without rights, but also article one actually targeted Protestants and Jews as "enemies of the very name Christian."[15] The underlying purpose of the code, which lasted until 1848, was to uphold the discipline of the Catholic, Apostolic, and Roman Church. The code led to a permanent assumption of blacks as inferior, engaging in sorcery, uneducable, and prone to rebellion.[16]

The various forms of "Protestantism" in the Reformation provided a new adversary within the Christian religious tradition that led to gross abuses of human rights. Protestants perpetrated some of these abuses upon other groups. For instance, an elderly Martin Luther fanned anti-Semitic fires by writing a tract, *Von ben Juden und ihren Lugen* (*On the Jews and Their Lies*) (1543), in which he urged that Jews be deported to a territory of their own where they would be confined to agricultural pursuits and their synagogues burned. Further, he supported violent means to put down the Peasant's Revolt in 1524–1525 and silence Anabaptists whom he referred to as *schwermer* (fanatics), particularly those at Muenster. In 1530 and again in 1536, Luther and Melancthon signed memoranda that supported brutal suppression of Anabaptists as blasphemers.[17] And Luther was not alone in advocating violence toward the religious rights of others. The firebrand Thomas Muntzer wrote to Count Ernst von Mansfield in 1525 about the persecution of Anabaptists, "If you do not take care of this matter, I will proclaim to all the world that all brethren should confidently dare their blood, as against the Turks. You will be prosecuted and exterminated."[18] Huldrych Zwingli, the illustrious preacher of the Reformed faith in Zurich, agreed with the use of the sword in the case of religious tyrants, warning, "Should you fail to become righteous . . . you will be trampled under foot."[19] John Calvin and the Geneva City Council had common cause with Catholic authorities that Michael Servetus was guilty of heretical teaching in his denial of the trinity and infant baptism, two charges potentially punishable by death. Calvin was the first preferer of charges, the expert witness at the trial, and he played a role in choosing the mode of execution of the illustrious theologian/scientist.[20] Servetus was burned at the stake.

Christian abuses of other Christians also took shape between Protestants and Catholics in Europe. Huldrych Zwingli's experience with the Catholic forces of Emperor Charles V well illustrated the point. Between 1529 and 1531 the Zwinglian Reformation was rapidly spreading through the cantons of northern Switzerland and this was hurried on by the interests of Phillip of Hesse and others who favored a Protestant Union among Basel, Bern, Zurich, Strassbourg, and certain German territories. A powerful bloc would have been formed that not only would have united Protestant territories, but blocked the main trade and religious routes from southern Catholic Europe to the Habsburg dominions in Austria. Further, a war of words flared up with Catholic priests defaming Protestants as "heretical soul-thieves" and "soul-murderers," whereas the Protestants used names like "flesh-sellers, blood-suckers, mass-men, image-slaves, money-guzzlers and idolaters" to characterize Catholics.[21]

At length, the papally sanctioned armies of Charles V amassed at Kappel to stop the advance of Zwinglianism, and the forces of Zurich, with Zwingli at their head, met their match in defense of their territory and the overlordship of the Roman faith. The Battle of Kappel ended in the solution *cuis regio, eius religio*, but not before Zwingli, the heroic Reformer was killed, his remains quartered and burned with a mixture of dung to demonstrate the intensity of feeling against him as an "arch-heretic" and to prevent his remains from becoming relics.

Perhaps the most extensive catalogs of Christian abuse of human rights in the Reformation era came from among the Anabaptists. The often published *Martyrs' Mirror: The Story of Fifteen Centuries of Christian Martyrdom from the Time of Christ to A.D. 1660* (1660, 1685, 1950), edited by Thieleman J. van Braght, conveys over thirteen hundred stories of persecution, imprisonment, physical torture, and martyrdom, mostly executed by political accomplices under the aegis of establishment leaders of the church. The case of Peter Gerrits, Peter Joris, Peter Lydecker, and Johanna Mels in 1536 was typical. These four individuals were found guilty of Anabaptist views and practices, upon which decision the burgomeister at Zierichsee imprisoned them for seven weeks, after which they were placed upon the rack and tortured, then publicly beheaded. After execution, their bodies were burned and their heads placed on stakes at the city gates. Similarly, the well-known theologian, Balthasar Hubmaier* was long imprisoned and burned at the stake, and his wife was mercifully drowned by authorities in Vienna.[22] A similar accounting is found in *The Chronicle of the Hutterian Brethren* (1581), which focuses particularly upon that persecuted sect from Moravia. The *Chronicle* recounts one instance in 1605 of abuse and torture from military authorities with the support of Catholic leaders:

> The towns of Tyrnau and Skalitz surrendered, and so did many Hungarian lords, on some of whose estates our brothers were living. The enemy drew closer and closer, and the burning, murdering, and pillaging began. The church had to undergo great privation and terror and untold anguish of heart, such as they had never heard of or suffered before. It began when the enemy made a night raid on Sabbatisch on May 3. Through God's providence our people had fled into the woods, but two brothers who were still in the house were horribly tortured. One in particular was dreadfully burned and racked, and his tongue was torn from the back of his throat, then both were hacked to dearth. . . . Three brothers and a sister

were overtaken by the enemy and killed, and three others were carried off as prisoners.[23]

English Christianity made a significantly negative contribution to the suppression of human rights. As King Henry VIII moved the church in England away from Roman domination, he also caused the dismemberment of hundreds of religious communities, destroyed monastic properties, and filled the royal treasury with funds from the sale of church lands. His daughter Mary, better known as "Bloody Mary," was responsible for the execution or imprisonment of hundreds and the expulsion of the Marian exiles (1553–1558). John Foxe's *Book of Martyrs* (1563) recounted the stories of those who suffered through the troubled times. Some relief was felt during the reign of Elizabeth I, but her archbishops suppressed Puritanism and vigorously enforced the *Book of Common Prayer*. In the Stuart era, James I and his son Charles I promulgated laws in protection of the Church of England that made it virtually impossible for dissenters and Roman Catholics legally to worship or propagate their beliefs.[24] The Court of the High Commission was reinvigorated to deal with dissent and new oaths were written to ensure the divine right of the monarchy and the established church. It is estimated that fifty thousand people left England between 1625 and 1650 to seek religious asylum, a direct result of the ecclesiastical despotism of Archbishop William Laud. Some accommodation was made for special groups during the Puritan Commonwealth, and it is clear that Oliver Cromwell himself held a tolerant position toward both the sects and Catholics, even though negative circumstances like the Royalist Plot of 1654 produced anxiety about increased toleration. The twin punctuation marks of the Protectorate that spelled intolerance were the Blasphemy Act of 1648 and its 1650 successor. This legislation, as W. K. Jordan has observed, provided a fair indication of the repressive discipline that Protestant orthodoxy, specifically the Presbyterians and Independents, were willing to apply against radical dissent.[25] Following the Protectorate, the Restoration called forth the Clarendon Code, whereby in five statutes members of municipal bodies had to take oaths of allegiance, all clergy had to consent to the *Book of Common Prayer*, persons over sixteen years old attending a nonconformist service were to be fined, and clergy were forbidden to return to a town they previously served to conduct nonconformist services.[26]

A modicum of religious peace was achieved in the Act of Toleration, passed by Parliament in 1689. That piece of legislation, normally seen as a concession to religious liberty, may also be interpreted as a limited but continuing attempt on the part of an established church to control religious expression in England and its colonies. The Act specifically acknowledged the value of "scrupulous consciences in the exercise of religion" as an "effectual means to unite their Majesties' Protestant subjects in interest and affection." The rollback of four major pieces of legislation from the reign of Elizabeth I through Charles II to allow for freedom of dissenter worship, *under the specific condition* of an oath and profession of faith, continued the dominant role of the Church of England in partnership with the Crown in determining legitimate Christian expression and identity. The declaration of fidelity specifically identified the Roman Catholic action of excommunication and foreign interference by an ecclesiastical authority as abhorrent to being true and faithful subjects of William and Mary. In tandem, the prescribed profession of faith affirmed only a trinitarian formula and the divine inspiration of the Holy Scriptures of the Old and New Testaments as the essence of Christian belief. The three beneficiaries of the Act were popish recusants, Protestant nonconformists, and Quakers.[27] Still in force were Sunday laws, and outside the law were Unitarians, Jews, and persons holding no religious persuasion.[28]

The situation of religious intolerance continued on a separate plane among the English Colonies in North America. In the initial colonization of Virginia (1607), strict laws protected the position of the Church of England. Hints in early records of discrimination against those of Anabaptist persuasion exist. Virginia became a royal colony and governors like Sir William Berkeley in the mid-seventeenth century, continued to enforce vigorously the religious uniformity laws. In Maryland, Catholic forces clashed with Puritan settlers. In New England, the Congregationalist Standing Order proved as redoubtable a force as the Church of England in its suppression of Anabaptists, antinomians, Quakers, and Seekers. All were banished from the Massachusetts Bay Colony. Tax laws benefited the established parishes well into the nineteenth century, and until the later eighteenth century, dissenters were not allowed to attend the existing colleges. An especially offensive instance of a denial of human rights occurred in the witchcraft scare in Salem, Massachusetts, in 1692–1693. Following spurious reports of demon possession in the household of the Rev. Samuel Parris, colony leaders, including the respected Increase Mather and his son, Cotton

Mather, held investigations to discover "spectral evidence" of demon presence on women's (and some accompanying men's) bodies. The resulting trials produced twenty-seven convictions, twelve female executions, six male executions, and one man's being pressed to death. The shock of such behavior based upon a literal reading of the Christian scriptures, delivered a severe blow to defenders of the invisible world, to use one historian's words.[29]

A lesser-recalled chapter in religious intolerance took place as a result of the imperial playoff of colonies in northern North America in the Treaty of Utrecht (1713). Great Britain, victorious in the War of the Spanish Succession, received most of France's colonies in North America, except for Cape Breton and some islands off Newfoundland. For a time, the British tolerated and subjugated Acadian settlers in the Annapolis Valley of Nova Scotia by requiring a loyalty oath, but in 1755, the government under Lt. Governor Charles Lawrence took new decisive steps. All Acadians were rounded up at key sites, notably Grand Pre along the Minas Basin, and forcibly evicted from their homes and property. Houses, villages, and churches were burned. Partly for political and also for religious reasons, twenty-two hundred Roman Catholic refugees were displaced among the lower colonies, in France or the outer islands with no regard for their long-term assimilation. Some were left on islands in the harsh Bay of Fundy to starve. Later in 1760, the British government reopened the Acadian lands for resale and Protestant New Englanders moved in and recolonized the region as Nova Scotia. Parishes of Congregationalists, Anglicans, and Baptists predominated where once a Roman Catholic community had flourished. A poem, "Evangeline," by Henry Wadsworth Longfellow, later romanticized the plight of the Acadians, who have become a symbol of genocide and religious intolerance in the Canadian heritage.

Historians of the slavery system have recorded the role Christian culture played in the racial subjugation of non-Caucasians. Biblical interpretation that reached back to Noah and his sons clearly made a case for blackness being a punishment for sin. Black people lived in Africa and were perceived to be living in subhuman, barbarous conditions. The perceived superiority of European Christian culture to African and Middle Eastern cultures had deep religious undertones. Some West Central Africans believed that Catholics had a kingdom of slaves under the earth or sea and that when black people died, the whites kept them chained under the earth. Not only did Christian merchants manage the slave trade, but also priests in Angola were known to be trading in slaves. It would appear that neither Catholic nor Protestant slave traders had any religious sensitivity as they captured native peoples and transported them to the Americas. Exported slaves were branded as proofs of ownership and baptism. As one historian points out, it was a peculiar irony that only Christians could be sold and they could be sold only to Christians.[30] As Winthrop Jordan at the University of California—Berkeley observed, "To be Christian was to be civilized, rather than barbarous, English rather than African, white rather than black. The term "Christian" itself proved to have remarkable elasticity, for by the end of the seventeenth century it was being used to define a species of slavery which had altogether lost any connection with explicit religious difference."[31] With the sanction of Christian leaders, then, persons of color were pressed into a permanent servitude in which they lost their freedom and humanity forever. When one cogent case for the cruelty of perpetual slavery reached the Vatican, steps were taken that would have denounced the practices, but the existing trade was deemed "expedient" because of the great need for Negroes in America.[32] An instance of supreme irony when missionary evangelists threatened West Africans with either having their hair burned off or joining their ancestors in hell, the West Africans preferred to join their relatives in hell.

Once Africans were enslaved, Christian leaders found rationalizations for the continuation of the "peculiar institution." Methodist, Presbyterian, and Baptist ministers in the American South wrote a strong proslavery argument. As the debate between Baptist university president and moral philosopher Francis Wayland (a northern Baptist) and Richard Fuller, an illustrious Southern Baptist pastor, showed, southerners were indignant about the abolitionist attack upon their peculiar institution and economic system. They refused to take full responsibility for slavery, arguing its preexistence in antiquity as well as the Americas. Further, they said, slavery was benevolent in that it actually improved the lot of those enslaved from their heathen and brutish African backgrounds. They much emphasized that Jesus and the Apostle Paul recognized slavery and did not command (at least as far as scripture was concerned) its termination. As Fuller put it, "If slavery was sanctioned in the Old, and permitted in the New Testament, it is not a sin; and he who says it is, will answer to God whom he affronts, and not to me."[33]

As historian William G. McLoughlin, formerly at Brown University, has shown, the missionary experience of Protestants with the Cherokee people in the period 1799–1839 was closely akin to the slave experience.[34] From George Washington to Andrew Jackson it was the policy of the U.S. government to assimilate Indians into American (Caucasian) culture, making them ultimately citizens and dividing their lands among the survivors and redistributing the rest to new settlers. Missionaries— Moravian, Presbyterian, Methodist, Congregationalist, and Baptist— took the assignment to help assimilate the Indians. In so doing, the missions essentially destroyed the native cultures, supported relocation, and even assisted in the establishment of the reservation system. Racial inferiority of the Indian peoples was assumed, especially by the southern missionaries. When in 1827–1828 "White Path's Rebellion" occurred, many of the missionaries claimed ignorance of why the Cherokees resented the missionary efforts and declared their sovereignty.

By 1832, the majority of the denominations with missionaries to the Cherokees had withdrawn from supporting resistance to the government's removal strategy. They confined their work to preaching and teaching school. Uniformly, they advocated signing a treaty and moving to western lands. Denominational missionaries were in truth agents of the War Department and received large subsidies for their labors. Many of the individual missionaries were frustrated with the removal idea, but their boards dictated their actions. In the end as one writer put it, "Blood was thicker than water, ethnocentrism was stronger than righteousness."[35]

The evolution of American Christianity in the nineteenth century brought forth more chapters in the denial of human rights. In the religio-political arena, one of the first examples of one Christian faction denying rights to another was the Antimasonic movement of the 1820s. Following the abduction and possible murder of a stonemason who exposed secrets of the upstate New York Masonic order, a widespread contagion of antagonism toward Freemasonry broke out and targeted the "extirpation" of all lodges from their communities. A large part of the Antimasonic movement was evangelical in church membership and temperament. The crusade they launched in 1827 New York and that reached a peak in the presidential election of 1832, called upon members of lodges to renounce their vows and publicly declare against secret societies. Revival techniques were held across a region called the "Infected District," and numbers of innocent fraternal members were publicly humiliated or disfellowshipped from their churches and associations. The Antimasonic Party that emerged as a bridge between the first and second American political party systems was the beginning of the linkage between religious convictions and political activism. Historian Alice Felt Tyler characterized it as a "denial of democratic principles."

Like the Antimasons, the "Know Nothing Movement," propelled by an intense anti-Catholic feeling, displayed anti-Christian attitudes from Protestants toward Catholics. The antagonism had its direct roots in the emigration of significant numbers of Europeans to the United States in the first decades of the century. The largest group was the Irish. Protestants expressed chagrin over the failure of Europeans to take care of their food and labor problems and saw the influence of the Irish in the American job market as entirely negative. Moreover, in 1827 Pope Leo XII issued a jubilee calling for renewed interest in Catholicism the world over, and this emboldened priests to seek new converts. This, coupled with the plan to Americanize the church, created the opportunity for Protestants to organize. In 1831, the New York Protestant Association was formed followed by four others in major cities in the Northeast. A low point of the crusade was reached in 1834 when the Ursuline Convent School and adjacent buildings in Charlestown, Massachusetts, were burned to the ground by an angry mob. Similar scenes were repeated in Philadelphia and New York. Ultimately, the movement achieved political recognition as an alternative Protestant Party that ran Millard Fillmore as a candidate for president in 1854. The crusade produced a raft of vitriolic anti-Catholic literature that survived long after its era.[36]

A stark example of a particularly damaging contemporary instance of violation of human rights in the name of Christianity occurred in the residential educational institutions in Canada from about 1880 to 1969. Between 1871 and 1877, seven treaties were signed between the Dominion of Canada and various First Nations tribes of northwestern Ontario and the Prairie territories that called for schooling. Particularly a component of the Indian Act of 1876, "Indians" were defined as a separate social group and the government gave approval to a cooperative program whereby government funds and oversight in cooperation with church groups would administer residential schools for Indians. The Christian denominations included Roman Catholic, Anglican, Presbyterian, and Methodist. Continual budget reductions in government grants led to reliance upon congregational support as a form of missionary endeavor. One of the stated purposes of the program came to be the evangelization of the Indian children, assuming that Indians were morally weak and they should be assisted to become "good Christians." As historian J. R. Miller has shown, a grand program of cultural assimilation took place with the resulting loss of any appreciation for aboriginal language or culture.[37] Denominational competition was so fierce to secure students that financial inducements were made to parents and priests. Once on campus, children were subjected to harsh living conditions, inadequate food, hard labor, abusive treatment, and sexual improprieties. Once discovered through expose testimonies of aboriginal alumni, the residential school problem resulted in a billion dollar legal campaign against the surviving denominations across Canada, as well as a human rights fiasco.[38]

Roman Catholic hegemony in Latin America led historically to two types of abusive behavior in the Christian community over four centuries. First, the influence of Erasmian humanism in the Latin American church was of great concern to the Papacy, as well as to colonizing powers, Spain and Portugal. In the latter half of the sixteenth century, the Spanish Inquisition was established throughout South America and this resulted in a deep Counter Reformation movement throughout the colonies. Social castes mirrored Aristotelian/Thomistic theologies and Protestantism of any kind was anathema. A collective anti-Protestant and antiforeigner mentality pervaded the Spanish colonies. Conflicts also developed between the advocates of humanism among the Franciscans and Dominicans on the one hand and the secular clergy on the other. Ultimately, the bishops and advocates of Counter Reformation won the struggle.

As late as 1810, violent reactions to perceived Protestant thinking was meted out to Catholic reformers. Miguel Hidalgo and Jose Maria Morelos, promoters of Mexican independence, were condemned and executed as Lutheran heretics. Charges were made against the heresies of the Enlightenment and particularly against "tolerationism." Banning of books and persecution of clandestine readers increased during the period of Bourbon reforms in Spain and its colonies as well as Pompal's reforms in Brazil.

The tide of intra-Christian religious persecution turned dramatically, however, with the Age of Revolution that commenced in 1808. Across the region from Mexico to Chile, the forces of liberal government produced new republics. In some cases, the Catholic Church and its religious orders allied themselves with change, but in others, there was resistance to religious toleration, secular education, and political reform.

Although the overall tide was inevitable, later in the century, there were still stiff reactions to liberalization and modernization processes. In Bolivia, for instance, a pioneer Protestant missionary from Canada, Archibald Reekie, was stoned outside his house in Cochabamba by Catholic priest-inspired mobs in 1907. In 1949, eight missionaries and local Baptist leaders were killed in a church-instigated melee at Merk 'Amaya, near Oruro. Another center of persecution of Protestants was Colombia. Throughout the 1940s and 1950s repression of liberal sectors was bloody, with eighty-five thousand dead in the uprising of 1958 that included freemasons, freethinkers, leaders of mutual societies, and Protestant leaders. In addition, 270 Protestant schools were closed and sixty chapels destroyed. Jean-Pierre Bastian has noted the proliferation of anti-Protestant hymns and sermons, threats, insults, house searches, and interference in religious activities in what has been described as much as a religious motive as political, where the Catholic Church joined forces with conservative regimes.[39]

The missionary context in the Far East provided an often neglected instance of questionable human rights activity in the Christian community. Until the late 1830s, the Chinese government kept Western trading and religious interests under close control, limiting presence to thirteen factories in Canton. The British, however, were not satisfied with the restrictions and an Anglo-Chinese war ensued between 1839 and 1842. The chief commodity of the British trade was opium and the Chinese went to war to halt the trade. China was defeated, a new treaty opining five more ports was concluded, and the opium trade increased. Records show that Christian missionaries were accomplices in this trade by using vessels carrying the opium for transport and by translating in the Chinese ports. The Chinese came to naturally associate the evils of opium with Christian missions, given the high profile of missionaries like Robert Morrison and Carl Gutzlaff in trading circles.

The historian of Christianity is forced to acknowledge that nations in twentieth-century Europe that were predominantly Christian and operated under influences of major churches were perpetrators of serious human rights denials. Nazi Germany stands at the top of the list as an evolved and perverse use of Lutheran thinking and misappropriation of Catholic resources. There is little doubt that ideologues in the Hitler regime used Luther's writings extensively, most vividly his late-in-life diatribes against the Jews. In 1937, after a study of the Society of Jesus, the German SS advised that Jesuits had used brilliant operational methods in achieving the Catholic Church's power politics. Particularly adept in gathering information and managing the ideological struggle, Jesuits supposedly knew before anyone else where attacks or countermeasures would occur, and they maintained a widespread net of contacts and sources of information.[40] The Gestapo was encouraged to emulate the Jesuits.

One can also recount the violent history of Christianity in Ireland since the seventeenth century. Ireland, long a stronghold of Roman Catholicism, was changed materially by the influx of large numbers of Protestants—Presbyterians and Anglicans—who settled in the Ulster counties of the north in particular. In the nineteenth century, with the support of the Catholic Church, a home rule movement led to the establishment of a Republic of Ireland in the south that was predominantly Catholic. In the north a continuing British "statelet," Northern Ireland, became predominantly Protestant. Across the twentieth century, Catholic religious forces have sponsored a campaign for a united Ireland and focused upon an overthrow of the Ulster government. Displays of violence pitting Protestantism against popery have erupted with regularity and seemingly within the Catholic aegis of just war. Likewise, Presbyterians with a theologically fundamentalist temperament have staged demonstrations on public holidays against the Catholic community and in league with the Orange Order that openly celebrates Irish Protestant history. Meanwhile, guerilla organizations, like the Irish Republican Army and Sein Fein, bomb buildings and automobiles and conduct assassinations in order to nurture the nationalist south's objective in ousting British (and Protestant) rule. Repeated attempts at a negotiated peace by outside interests have failed as the competing Christian religious differences continue to be a determining factor.[41]

In the South African context, yet another chapter of a major Christian group being part of human rights denial took place. The discovery of diamonds in 1867 and gold in 1886 plunged the Transvaal region and all of South Africa into the global economy and the politics of industrializing Europe. An already divided culture between Dutch and British interests found itself dealing with urbanization, competing ideologies, pluralization, and racial conflicts. The strongest force in the Christian community as the twentieth century dawned, was the Afrikaner influence as represented in the Dutch Reformed Church (NGK), Hervormde Kerk (HGK), Gereformeerde Kerk (GK), the Dutch Reformed Missionary Church (NGSK), and the Dutch Reformed Church in Africa (NGKA), the last two of which were segregated for Coloureds and Africans. These churches provided a religious value system for the State of South Africa as it encountered challenges of modernity in the next eight decades. The predominant church bodies became associated with the dominant political party and a massive program of social engineering.

Reflecting ideological trends in Europe, mostly conservative in the Dutch context, a theological/ideological tradition emerged in South Africa that can be described as self-determinative, patriarchal, and neo-Calvinistic. Against the modernist teachings of evolution and science, a strong doctrine of God's sovereignty in creation was promulgated. Church leaders like F.J.M. Potgieter, H. G. Stoker, and J. D. Vorster published titles like "Holding the Course in Crisis" (1935–1941) that defended traditional values against social pluralization and a breakdown in moral values. The perceived that "black peril," which resulted from blacks flocking to cities, coupled with the "poor whites" problem constituted a huge poverty issue economically. The government's response, in tandem with the churches, was to support segregation of blacks from poor whites so that whites could enjoy healthy suburbs in which to raise Christian families. Two leading characteristics of the apartheid system thus emerged with complete sanction of the Reformed churches: group areas or settlements and white supremacy. In the election of 1948, the leading Afrikaner National Party was swept overwhelmingly into power and legislation that deepened apartheid became law. "Voortrekkers," guarding against race mixture that they thought militated against the Word of God, thus preserved a pure Christian race through legislation like the Prohibition of Mixed Marriages Act (1949), the Group Areas Act (1950), and the Immorality Act (1957). As one historical theologian has put it, a "Kuyperian neo-Calvinism" from the Netherlands was grafted to a nationalist political agenda.[42] One of the most striking actions taken in church context was the rejection in 1951 of the Universal Declaration of Human Rights in the Transvaal Synod of the NGK. Although the churches adopted missionary strategies from church planting to Bible translations, apartheid policies continued in the established churches well into the 1990s when the system was brought down politically.

Later in the twentieth century, the breakup of Yugoslavia revealed just how brutal the torture and dislocation of two Christian groups, the Orthodox and the Catholics, could be against each other. Hundreds of thousands of Serbs and Croats were killed silently and buried in mass unmarked graves or forcibly removed from their homelands, not to speak of Serbian aggression against Muslim Bosnians. Few would discount the essentially religious undertones of that civil war. As one recent historian commented, "Religious symbols and customs, though often only cultivated in vague and residual forms, have become part of the national heritage and as such help to delineate ethnic boundaries."[43] Paul Mojzes, a Balkan specialist at Stockton College in New Jersey, has argued that religious symbols as emblems serve like clan totems and create tribal distinctions. They sacralize the nation and demonize its enemies, reducing complex realities of society and politics to a simple distinction between good and evil.[44] Behind the separate ministates of the late twentieth century were "millets" created during the period of the former Ottoman Empire with deep local religious identities. The Ottomans ruled the Balkan region through the smaller units and provided oversight to deter destructive intramural fighting. However, once a coerced political unity collapsed in the 1990s, groups with militant Christian identities lined up against each other to gain supremacy.

Christian behavior antagonistic to human rights was not confined to Christian nations and ethnic groups clashing politically and militarily against each other in the latter half of the twentieth century. An example of oppression within an important part of the Christian family occurred as Roman Catholic theologians began to participate in ecumenical discussions involving the World Council of Churches, formed in 1948. Especially after 1950, the Vatican watched very closely the attendance at ecumenical meetings and publications of prominent theologians like Yves Congar, Henri Lubac, Karl Rahner, John Courtney Murray,* and Küng. Mistrust of motives and an overall concern for the purity of church dogma led to censure of several prominent theologians and the removal of others from their teaching chairs.[45]

The record of Christian individuals and associations in abuse of human rights is clear. Insofar as the religious teachings of the faith are concerned, it has been sometimes attributable to misinterpretation of the core values, like the Crusades, whereas in other instances it has been a matter of overzealous behavior, as with the Inquisition or colonial evangelization or the burning of Michael Servetus in Calvin's Geneva. In a few cases, it reflects a deliberate attempt to use Christian ideals for unworthy political or social objectives. Examples of this are the apartheid system in South Africa and the genocide in Ireland and the former

Yugoslavia. The doctrines of human freedom and depravity in the Christian theological tradition explain (but do not excuse) this type of interpretation and behavior, which so completely militate against the values that Jesus Christ taught and that have characterized Christian experience in its most humane development.

3

RELIGIOUS LIBERTY—THE CORNERSTONE OF HUMAN RIGHTS

I N THE CONTEXT OF HISTORIC Western Christianity, religious liberty is the first recognized human right. Because of the nature of religious claims, from it all other rights are defined. The terminology of religious liberty provides important variations that must not be neglected. Christian writers speak of religious liberty as the opportunity to express one's religious beliefs and values without prevention or coercion. The vocabulary of religious liberty is an important element in definition; various related terms provide differing shades of what freedom can mean. The term "religious freedom" usually designates the emergence of uncoerced and open religious practices in a context where liberty has been inhibited in some fashion. These practices include holding and articulating one's beliefs without penalty or interference, freedom of worship, freedom to propagate one's religious beliefs, freedom to educate one's children in the faith of the parents, and freedom to build religious institutions and manage them. "Religious toleration" is a quite different concept, wherein it is recognized that some dominant personality (like a king or magistrate) or an institution has allowed limited freedom according to defined boundaries. Thus by permission, a category of persons or a group may enjoy limited free expression of religion, usually for a period of time. Finally, some writers, notably Roger Williams, also wrote of "soul freedom," by which he meant "the absolute duty of the civil state to set free the soules of all men" from "hireling ministries" and established churches.[1] Because "religious liberty" is a relatively recent Enlightenment concept, most historians find more evidences of toleration in earlier periods of Christian history than true religious freedom.

Contemporary writers have demonstrated the highly individualistic nature of religious liberty discussions in Western platforms. Often, these are at variance with other cultures, notably those in the East, the socialist countries before 1990, and even places like Canada where community rights are a dominant motif. This has in part been resolved by theologians like Jesuit David Hollenbach in the Catholic tradition. He argues in favor of understanding religious liberty, coupled with freedom of expression, as participation in the public life of society. The common good of the society is thus enhanced as people express their religious beliefs in public without interference. Religious liberty makes that possible. While religious liberty begins with individuals, it certainly has group applications and community benefits.[2]

EARLY CHRISTIAN DEVELOPMENTS

PERHAPS THE FIRST move with respect to the Christian community toward religious rights was seen in the Edict of Milan, 313. This proclamation of Constantine and Licinius provided "Christians and others full authority to observe the religion that each preferred . . . that no one whatsoever should be denied the opportunity to give his heart to the observance of the Christian religion." The edict further provided compensation for confiscated properties, notably churches where Christians assembled. This was, of course, not a Christian act, per se, because it also guaranteed other religions the same privileges of freedom of worship, "for the sake of peace of our times" and of course "Divine favor" upon their rule.[3] In the third century of their history, then, Christians had a model of religious freedom and property rights upon which to draw.

The Age of Reform proved to be a mixed blessing for religious toleration among Christians. The struggles between Catholics and Protestants having been laid to rest, separate kingdoms in Europe emerged to pursue their own courses with respect to religious diversity. As W. K. Jordan at Harvard observed some years ago, "The reformers like the Church from which they had parted, cared nothing for freedom. They cared only for truth."[4] Under a regionally defined confessionalism, Protestants sought to remove the presence of dissenters from their territory.

It became a matter of defining truth as the magisterial reformers, Luther, Calvin, Zwingli, and others saw it.

Among the first Christians of the Reformation era to call for religious freedom were the Anabaptists. From their beginnings in Zurich, Switzerland, in 1525, these Bible-oriented, antiestablishmentarians suffered persecution for their religious beliefs and practices. Some were banished, others were imprisoned, and hundreds were executed over the next century. Beginning with their stance on infant baptism, Anabaptists opposed coercion of belief. Pilgram Marpeck, a South German Anabaptist, thought that infant baptism forced people into the kingdom of God. Another early statement of faith declared a parody on the Great Commission, "Go into all the world, teach all nations; however, him who refuses to accept or believe your teaching you are to catch, torture, yes, strangle until he believes." Yet another famous Anabaptist theologian, Hubmaier, opined in his tract, *On Heretics and Those Who Burn Them*, "Now it appears to anyone, even to a blind person, that the law for the burning of heretics is an invention of the devil. Truth is unkillable."[5] Later in Anabaptist development, Menno Simons adopted a typical theology of martyrdom toward his persecutors: "Take heed, awake, be converted, so that the innocent blood of the pious children of God which calls for vengeance in heaven may no more be found on your hands forever."[6] Among all of the Reformers, the Anabaptists struck a clear path for religious liberty.

It would be in the English context that an important stream of religious toleration would flow. The English national church had been well-defined by the reforms of Henry VIII who attempted in every way to maintain the Catholic character of the church in his realm. The church was coterminus with the realm, and reformers like Thomas Cromwell and Thomas Cranmer were clear about the powers of the magistrate, who was set by God for the "defense of the good and godly, and to chasten and punish the wicked." Magistrates were likewise given the responsibility to destroy the Kingdom of Anti-Christ and all false doctrine and to punish false prophets.[7] Papists, Anabaptists, and sectarians were those who were targeted to conform to the established church's doctrine and pattern of worship. The pursuit of dissenters under Henry and Edward was mild compared to the situation under "Bloody Mary" during 1558–1563. Under Mary, no distinction was made between inward and outward conformity. During the "Elizabethan Settlement," the Act of Uniformity continued unabated: although the human conscience in essence was free, public exercise of any but the established religion was not tolerated. Yet, repression of dissent under Elizabeth was restrained and mild in order to portray a practically benevolent government posture. The Catholic problem vexed the Crown more than Protestants, but it must be noted that anti-Catholic fines were rarely collected and no Catholic was executed for an eleven-year period 1577–1588. In most cases, Puritans who kept their peace and limited their "missionary impulses" were left virtually alone. So, Englishmen were left not with a clear theoretical construct of religious toleration in Reformed England, but with a practical sense of what toleration could be.

As Puritans became more influential in the later Elizabethan period, it became obvious that they were far less tolerant than the Anglicans. Their sense of authority was rooted squarely in scripture as the Word of God, and heresy was not to be tolerated in any measure. The model church was that of Geneva and the civil powers were to execute the religious values of the kingdom. In fact, the church was superior to the state, and the church had the right to censure the magistracy. Puritans believed in an individual's ability to receive revelation from God and act according to one's conscience. But, this was offset by the Puritan's desire for uniformity of doctrine. Consequently, under Puritan auspices, the conscience was inviolable but there was no discussion of freedom. It would be the Separatists who contributed directly to religious toleration by the very act of their separation. Their Congregationalist views of the church ended a unified and Catholic church and raised the question of whether differing forms of Christianity could and should coexist. Over time, the Separatists proved their case and the door to toleration was opened wide. A voluntary church, as Robert Browne taught, was inconsistent with religious repression.

It was Anabaptists in England that focused the issue more sharply. In the mid-1570s, groups of Anabaptists, probably from Flanders, were apprehended and brought to trial under heresy laws. Many of them were eventually released, but two, Pieters and Terwoort, refused to recant and were executed in a moment of Elizabeth's need to prove her orthodoxy. Both men condemned religious persecution and suffered that fate. Their views and their examples were not lost on the next generation of dissenters whose views grew out of actual experience.

The next generation belonged to the Baptists. This stalwart group of nonconformists led the way in calling for unrestricted religious freedom in the early seventeenth century. They were witnesses of persecution and understood the meaning of the Anabaptists Pieters and Terwoort and the writings of Browne and others. One of the two earliest Baptist thinkers, Thomas Helwys* of Nottinghamshire (fl. 1606–1612), wrote what has called the finest, fullest treatment of religious liberty in the English language. In his book, *A Short Declaration of the Mistery of Iniquity*, he warned that persecution does not lead to conformity and that "the king is a mortal man and hath not authority over the consciences of his subjects." Helwys went on to state a case for complete religious toleration: "Let them be heretics, Turks, Jews, or whatsoever, it appertains not to the earthly power to punish them in the least measure." Seven decades later, the Calvinistic branch of Baptists stated in their second confession of faith, "God alone is Lord of the Conscience, and hath left it free from the Doctrines and Commandments of men which are in any thing contrary to his Word, or not contained in it."[8] Baptists continued to press this case into the eighteenth century in England and in North America and were the pioneers in the further development of the concept of religious toleration.

During the colonial period in English North America, several additional important steps were taken in various parts of the Christian community toward religious toleration. The first broadly conceived statement on religious toleration is to be found in colonial Maryland in the 1649 Act of Toleration. Maryland, a colony founded in 1632 largely to give solace to Roman Catholics in Stuart England, soon became a battleground between the Catholic settlement at St. Mary's City and a Puritan town at Providence (later Annapolis). Cecilius Calvert,* Second Lord Baltimore, attempted to create a harmonious solution by having the colonial Assembly pass an "Act Concerning Religion" that protected Protestants from Catholic proprietors and Catholics from rising Puritan sentiments. The act went far in prohibiting the "troubling, molesting, and discountenancing" of persons for religious sentiments. Unfortunately, the Act of Toleration was repudiated under a Puritan Assembly in the colony in 1654.[9]

A second bold experiment occurred in the establishment of Rhode Island Colony. Here, Roger Williams and a group of dissenters had fled from the establishment Congregational communities of Massachusetts Bay and, having struck peace with the Indians, planted a colony in Narragansett Country. Williams and his cohorts practiced a high degree of respect for various religious opinions, including those of the indigenous people.

More than Williams, in the long run, it was John Clarke* of Newport who led the successful campaign for religious freedom in the Colony of Rhode Island. His congregation at Newport was a model of toleration, supportive of Jews and Quakers in the community as early as 1658. In 1652, Clarke published *Ill Newes from New England,* a book that contained factual accounts of religious persecution in Massachusetts and surrounding communities. His response to religious persecution included a challenge to prove such authority from the scriptures, the law of the Golden Rule, and the belief that forced worship produces only hypocrites before God. Clarke spent twelve years in London preparing the political way for a "lively experiment" to be embodied in the charter that King Charles II granted in 1663. The document read in part, "Noe person within the sayd colony, at any time hereafter, shall bee in any wise molested, punished, disquieted, or called in question, for any differences in opinione in matters of religion."[10] Clarke's contribution was assured by his friend Williams, who offered his grateful thanks for Clarke's grand motive "giving liberty to all men's spirits in spiritual matters."

Different from the essentially Baptist position in Rhode Island was that of William Penn* and the Quakers. Penn's position on religious toleration was close to that of the Puritans. He wrote about liberty of conscience as an absolute freedom, but he limited his application of the freedom to practicing Christians, particularly, though not exclusively Protestants. Fundamental to his understanding was also freedom of worship. Because Quakers had suffered persecution from authorities through their early history, Penn defined persecution as any attempt to force uniformity in belief or practice. "I abhor two principles in religion and pity them that own them," he wrote. "The first is obedience to authority, without conviction; the other is destroying them that differ from me for God's sake."[11] Persecution was wrong, he believed, because it violated the prerogatives of God. He also saw it as usurping the capability to judge truth and error. Moreover, it overthrew Christ's religion by irreligious acts and it was contradictive of human nature and reason. Finally, persecution was antithetical to the law of love in the New Testament and it had failed to produce the peace that peacemakers work for. It was through this lens that he viewed religious freedom in his 1670 tract, *The Great Case of Liberty of Conscience, Once More Briefly Debated and Defended by the Authority of Reason, Scripture and Antiquity* that he wrote in Newgate Prison.

Toleration for Penn, as Mary Dunn argued some years ago, served the practical end of uniting England as a Protestant nation against Rome. He believed that in the place of an established church, the government had a responsibility to promote practical and general religion because "moral uniformity is requisite to preserve the peace."[12] This was the thesis of *An Address to Protestants of All Persuasions, More Especially the Magistracy and Clergy, for the Promotion of Virtue and Charity* (1679). He included knowledge that "God is . . . that the way of God is a way of purity, Patience, Meekness etc. . . . , that God was manifested extraordinarily in the flesh, and that he gave his life for the world."[13] Governments would do well to promote such religious values, Penn thought, to encourage virtue, to confirm the restoration of the monarchy, and to ensure itself of good citizens and statesmen. He was unable apparently to fathom a separate sphere of authority for the church from the state and he seemed not to understand the difference between a sin and a civil offense.[14] In this regard, he was hardly distinct from the Church of England, particularly the Latitudinarian party that embraced morality over orthodoxy.

The Act of Toleration of 1689 was directed at scrupulous consciences among certain dissenters. It specifically rescinded eleven acts passed during the reigns of Elizabeth I and Charles II that required conformity to the established church. Pains, penalties, and prosecution in an ecclesiastical court were no longer the fate of those who swore allegiance to William and Mary, renouncing Roman Catholic authority in particular and, in a second oath, declaring their faith in the God as Father, Son, and Holy Spirit and the divine inspiration of the canonical scriptures. Sabbatarian worship was excluded in favor of the Lord's Day and places of nonconformist worship were to be registered with the local bishop. The act benefited Congregationalists, Presbyterians, and Baptists. Suspicion of Quakers was finally allayed and a second "toleration" act was passed in 1696 in which a declaration in lieu of an oath sufficed. While Quaker worship was not further specified, their juridical practices were thus legitimated. From this point onward, Protestantism in England expanded and "dissent" became an officially sanctioned category of Christianity that eventually included Unitarians and Methodists. The politicization of dissent as a result of toleration was institutionalized in the Three Dissenting Denominations and the Dissenting Deputies.

The English context was not alone in witnessing an advance toward religious toleration within the Christian community. Following the bloody religious wars in France from 1562 to 1576, which reached a peak in the 1572 St. Bartholomew's Day Massacre, newly crowned King Henry IV looked for the opportunity to protect the religious rights of his Huguenot countrymen. At length and over the protests of Catholics and the Vatican, he issued the Edict of Nantes in spring 1598. The declaration, hailed as "the first written promise to grant specific religious freedoms to a persecuted minority," restored the Catholic faith to all the regions that were inclined toward Catholicism and permitted those of the Reformed (Protestant) religion to live and abide in kingdoms and countries belonging to France "without being annoyed, molested, or compelled contrary to their consciences." Protestants were allowed to practice their faith in their homes and villages, to instruct their children, and to publish books in Protestant cities. Finally, Protestant students were to be admitted to universities, colleges, and schools, and hospitals, retreats, and public charities were opened to Protestants.[15] Unfortunately for the long-term French context, Louis XIV, grandson of Henry IV, revoked the edict in 1685.

Religious toleration was to be only a temporary benchmark in the evolution of human rights, however. As the French Protestant Rabaut de Saint Etienne put it, toleration "implies an idea of compassion that degrades man. I demand equal freedom for all. . . . Man, whatever his religious belief, has the right of enjoying all the sacred privileges that belong to mankind."[16] Here was a sure harbinger of complete religious freedom: in the French Revolution, religious liberty would be largely set aside in favor of an increasingly secular approach to statecraft, as outlined in the Declaration of the Rights of Man.

The American revolutionary context witnessed the next important stages in the development of religious liberty. Two Baptist clergymen, Isaac Backus* and John Leland,* stand out as the promoters of the ideal of separation of church and state, an important eighteenth-century corollary to religious liberty. Backus fought the Standing Order Congregationalist Church authorities in Massachusetts over recognition of ministers, taxation for support of established churches and toleration for certain sects. He then turned to the Continental Congress in 1774 to make a case for disestablishment. Leland wrote in opposition to taxation, military exemptions, legislative chaplains, and Sunday mail service. Leland was close to both Thomas Jefferson and James Madison in the crucial period of forming a bill of rights. Neither thought toleration adequate. Both were willing to build a "wall" to keep the state out of the churchly sphere, while assuming that it was quite legitimate for religious interests to influence government policy.[17] The result was the influential phraseology in the U.S. Bill of Rights, "Congress shall make no law respecting an establishment of religion, or prohibiting the free exercise thereof."

The Christian community continued to carry its struggle for religious liberty in its missionary efforts during the nineteenth century. Baptists provide an important case history. Operating with a theology that demanded a religiously open climate for evangelism, Baptist missionaries often confronted governments and cultures that attempted to thwart or bar their interference in the prevailing religious circumstances. William Carey, who was beleaguered by discriminatory regulations of the British East India Company, along with influential friends lobbied Parliament for a more tolerant circumstance in the company's revised charter of 1813. In Burma, for instance, Adoniram Judson,* under the support of the American Baptist community, in 1819 presented the emperor of the Golden Presence at the Court of Ava a petition for religious toleration to preach and make converts among the empire.[18] Judson was an educational product of Congregationalist schools in the United States and represented the ideals of American Baptists. Within two decades, Burma enjoyed a vibrant Christian community.

The story of religious freedom prompted by Christians in China and Japan is similar. In treaties concluded with China in 1842 and 1858–1860, Christian missionaries from numerous sending denominations and countries, Catholic, Orthodox, and Protestant, won religious toleration for both Chinese Christians and missionaries, the right to place officers in Peking, and importantly, the privilege to travel in the interior.[19] Japan, long insulated from Western culture, opened to missionary activity as a result of the 1853–1854 expedition of Commodore Matthew C. Perry, the diplomatic mission of Townshend Harris, and the language interpreter ministry of Samuel Wells Williams. Religious toleration flowed from political treaties with the Japanese government that allowed a full range of Christian churches to be planted, including a "Church of the Twenty-Six Martyrs."[20]

Finally, in Europe, the stronghold of Lutheranism, Baptist missionary and church planter Johann G. Oncken was frequently brought before magistrates on account of his preaching. In one instance, Oncken was asked to list all of his preachers and then all of his members. His reply was, "Every Baptist is a missionary!" His work, along with Julius Koebner's, opened the door for a reluctant acceptance of libertarian Baptist witness in Reformation Europe. Baptists, Methodists, Socinians, and other dissenters across Europe came to enjoy toleration from Germany to Poland by the 1880s. Likewise, in Britain the movement toward religious voluntarism captured the attention of dissenters in England, Scotland, and Wales. The British Anti-State Church Association (1844), renamed in 1853 the Society for the Liberation of the Church from State Patronage and Control, sought to end all connections between government and the Church of England. No public worship had received government subsidies since 1824; the national education legislation of the 1870s prevented support for the church's educational facilities; and the Church of England was substantially reorganized in 1919. State churches were superseded and/or abolished in Scotland (1847), Ireland (1871), and Wales (1915), thus achieving a "free trade in religion" in Britain.

THE GOLDEN AGE OF RELIGIOUS LIBERTY DECLARATIONS

IT HAS BEEN observed that religious freedom, once the child of skepticism, is now the child of faith. The movement of this basic human right into ecclesiastical discourse has been a most important development. The half-century beginning in 1945 will be remembered as the golden age of religious liberty declarations. The dominant declaration was of course the United Nations Universal Declaration of Human Rights, much influenced by Christian thinkers, to be followed by the World Council of Churches' Declaration on Religious Liberty and the Declaration on Religious Freedom of Vatican II. Together, these declarations and the support given them by various parts of the Christian community, achieve a substantial contribution to the recognition of the human right of religious freedom for the modern Christian tradition. The declarations and statements also profile a conciliar tradition in dealing with human rights issues.

In the background of the Universal Declaration of Human Rights are several important statements. First was President Franklin Roosevelt's "Four Freedoms" speech that he delivered as the State of the Union address in 1944. Among Roosevelt's "four freedoms" was the "freedom of every person to worship God in his own way, everywhere in the world." At least one denominational group, the Baptists in the United

States, had gone on record by defining religious liberty in its joint statement, "An American Baptist Bill of Rights." This proclamation from the American evangelical community may well have chafed the Roosevelt administration, for it blocked a clear course to an administration objective, namely appointing a U.S. ambassador to the Vatican. The document was filled with libertarian language like "Free Churches in a Free State," "anti-paternalism," "full liberty in religious concernments," and "separation of church and state."[21] Yet, it was not directly for Baptist thinking that a foundation was laid for a world order based upon religious liberty.

What was directly influential upon the development of an international consensus on religious liberty as a human right was the ecumenical Christian community's concern for missionary security and freedom. The Oxford Life and Work Conference of 1937 and the Madras Missionary Conference of 1938 both addressed this issue. During World War II, concern continued and was voiced to both the United States and Great Britain, centers of most missionary activity.

In 1946, the Commission of the Churches on International Affairs (CCIA) led in contacts with international agencies, particularly the United Nations, "for the encouragement of respect for, and observance of, human rights and fundamental freedoms, special attention being given to the problem of religious liberty."[22] In the context of the United Nations, O. Frederick Nolde,* first officer of the CCIA, adopted as his first objective to ensure that the international standards being set were compatible with a Christian conception of man and society. In particular, it was essential that the proposed "Bill of Human Rights" did not commence from a point where it appeared that governments granted human rights, but that it would be clear that humans inherently possessed rights by virtue of their being. This he accomplished by being present for every meeting, offering proposed phraseology, and closely shadowing the key leaders like Eleanor Roosevelt* and Charles Malik.*

Article 18 of the United Nations Universal Declaration of Human Rights reads, "Everyone has the right to freedom of thought, conscience and religion; this right includes freedom to change his religion or belief, and freedom, either alone or in community with others and in public or private, to manifest his religion or belief in teaching, practice, worship, and observance." It is known that Nolde, a Lutheran seminary professor from Philadelphia, Pennsylvania, had as much as anyone to do with the particular wording of the important phrase, "freedom to change his religion or belief." Of further relevance was a concession made to Marxist governments to include "belief" as a synonym for "religion." The heart of the article guaranteed Christians, for instance, the right to hold their views, to propagate them, and to exercise them in worship. This language of course extended to all other religious traditions as well. Carefully, as Mrs. Roosevelt and Malik would later observe, there was no bias toward any particular belief; instead it was structured as a completely unabridged statement.

The Universal Declaration in the U.N. context laid the foundation for a fuller statement on religious liberty from individual religious traditions. Christians responded in several ways, exhibiting their great diversity, over the next twenty years. First came the discussion in the newly formed World Council of Churches, reflecting what one writer has called a new "conciliarism."[23] This body represented Protestants from around the globe and Orthodox Christians. Roman Catholics were not involved directly, but did have input from the sidelines. In preparation for the first meeting of the WCC in Amsterdam in 1948, the CCIA sent letters of inquiry to church leaders in many countries to determine their desires for identifying the essential elements of religious freedom as well as their potential support for them. That survey informed the drafting of the WCC Declaration on Religious Liberty, hailed as a landmark in its field.

Specifically, what emerged from the debates and surveys of the new World Council of Churches was a fuller Christian exposition of what religious liberty should mean. The title of the declaration focused upon the concept of liberty rather than a doctrine of humanity. There was obvious dependence upon three hundred years of Protestant conceptualization in the drafting process. The theological rationale began with the Pauline doctrine that Christ has set people free (Gal. 5:1). This expanded to contain terminology in the Reformed tradition, "the nature and destiny of man," and terminology about creation, redemption, calling, and man's activities in family, state, and culture. Reaching across centuries of antiestablishment and denial of human rights in various forms of discrimination, the document categorically referred to religious liberty without reference to race, color, sex, language, or religion.

There were four areas of specificity in the WCC Declaration on Religious Liberty. First was the right to determine one's faith and creed. Here was a focus upon freedom of access to information. Second was the right to express one's beliefs in worship, teaching, practice, and proclamation for relationships in the political and social spheres. This discussion was directed specifically at attempts to limit free expression in communication. The writers did exempt parents, who must have the right to control what their children are taught, and legitimate boundaries set to protect order and welfare and the freedom of others.

The third and fourth rights claimed in the essentially Protestant declaration pertain to the rights of associations parallel to those claimed for individuals. Much influenced by the International Missionary Council, the members of the WCC felt obliged to work to guarantee the right of missionary organizations to collect funds, hold property, send personnel beyond national borders, and receive financial support from whatever sources. The assumption was that the Christian community had great diversity in its outreach and this diversity needed to be assured of opportunities and support. While not the direct focus of the World Council Declaration on Religious Liberty, these same rights sought for the Christian community were valid for non-Christian religious organizations and associations as well.

A second important stage in the evolution of World Council of Churches' thinking on religious liberty took shape in the 1950s and culminated in the Statement on Religious Liberty of 1961. Christian leaders were aware of changed circumstances for the worse, where, in several nations like China and the Soviet republics, religious liberty was being openly challenged. Refugees were flooding from communist nations to the West and the chasm between the rich and the poor peoples of the world was receiving new attention. Additionally, issues of race relations dominated the U.S. sociopolitical agenda. For the first time, the Assembly meeting at New Delhi in 1961 was held in a developing nation and on the program were reports targeting concerns of struggling minorities and nations. The Assembly body determined to redouble its efforts in support of religious liberty, but actually only reaffirmed earlier language in this regard.[24]

Other changes that pertained to the emphasis previously placed upon religious liberty occurred in the World Council in the decade of the sixties. First, at a significant meeting in Odessa, USSR, in 1964, the rights of atheists entered the mainstream of religious liberty. This finally created a commitment in the Christian community to total religious freedom. Second, the secretariat was thereafter able to spend its energy influencing trouble spots around the world in which Christians and others faced deprivation of religious liberty. Third, in part due to both criticism from conservative Christians and lack of adequate funding, the international witness of the World Council of Churches in the area of religious liberty was refocused in the seventies to national and local work. The WCC thus became a clearinghouse or "switching station" for religious liberty. Moreover, the Commission of the Churches on International Affairs (CCIA) turned to international peace and security, disarmament, refugees, and dependent peoples on its agenda.

The worldwide shift toward emphasizing religious liberty in the Christian community had a profound impact upon Roman Catholics as well as Protestants. Catholic observers and advisors watched the U.N. discussions and played a role behind the scenes in the World Council of Churches. Gradually, by the late 1950s, Catholic scholars and leaders prepared their response to the issues.

For a variety of reasons, the Catholic tradition has only recently in its history arrived at a position affirming religious freedom. In 1832, for instance, Pope Gregory XVI described liberty of conscience as "false and absurd," a "mad principle." He attached it to other errors including liberty of the press, which he described as an execrable liberty that can never inspire sufficient horror. His successor, Pius IX, included it in his Syllabus of Errors. And as late as the 1950s, a Jesuit priest, John Courtney Murray, was silenced for questioning the authority of church tradition. All of that negative tradition began to change with John XXIII (Angelo Giuseppe Roncalli*) in 1963, who in *Pacem in terris* asserted, "Man has a natural right to freedom of speech and publication." The pope held further that humans had a right to worship God in accordance with the dictates of their own conscience and to profess religion in both public and private.[25]

Under the progressive leadership of John XXIII and later Paul VI, Vatican II spoke to the all-important issue of religious liberty in *Dignitatis humanae*, issued in 1965. This important new direction came after centuries of denunciations of political statements like the 1789 Declaration of the Rights of Man on the basis of their growing out of humanism and individualist bases. As late as 1862, the church denounced religious freedom as contrary to official church dogma in the Syllabus of Errors. In contrast, the Declaration on Religious Freedom (1965), spoke to secular society, declaring that the highest value that both the church and society are called upon to protect is the personal and social free exercise of religion.[26] The ratifying Vatican II statement said, "The Vatican Council declares that man has a right to religious freedom. The nature of this freedom is that all men should be exempt from all constraint exercised by individuals, social groups, or any human power, so that no one is forced to act against his conscience in a religious matter or prevented from acting according to his conscience." Included along with this powerful declaration, as Charles Wackenheim has shown, is a mass of argumentation and texts that reach back to the fourth century and the Catholic Church's role as the teacher of truth.[27]

In assessing the Vatican II declaration, one first realizes that it is the only part of the conciliar matter that is addressed to the entire world. It recognizes the flow of human thought and energy, largely in the twentieth century, in its preface: "A sense of the dignity of the human person has been impressing itself more and more deeply on the consciousness of contemporary man."[28] The church is now directed at those within its religious tradition and those without. The statement claims freedoms for Catholic Christians and, with this declaration, the same for everyone else. Indeed, as early as 1964, Pope Paul VI had prepared for this eventuality in appointing a Secretariat for non-Christian Religions headed by Paolo Cardinal Marella. Fruitful contact was established between Catholics and Hindus, Moslems, and Jews. The result of this initiative was to be seen in the Vatican II Declaration on the Relationship of the Church to non-Christian Religions (1965).

Imbedded in the rationale of the declaration was an affirmation of human freedom as contained in the Word of God and the Fathers of the Church. The theological core of the Catholic understanding of religious freedom was Christological. It drew its power first from the Great Commission in Matthew 28:19–20 and Mark 16:16. Seemingly, there should be no boundaries or hindrances upon Christians to proclaim the good news, nor upon any other free expression of religious values. It is to be remembered that the disciple is bound by a grave obligation to Christ his master, faithfully to proclaim the gospel and vigorously to defend it, while at the same time acting lovingly, prudently, and patiently in dealing with those in error or ignorance. This Christological motif was extended as God requires mankind to respond to him in spirit and truth, as truth reaches its height in Jesus Christ. Jesus aroused faith in persons, he did not coerce them. Finally, true freedom was seen as being achieved in the work of redemption through Christ, which came ultimately through his example as a servant and one who was accountable in part to civil authorities. Further, there was a developed argument from the dignity of the human person that lead to limitations being placed upon governments and institutions not to violate individual freedoms. Persons were defined as being endowed with reason and free will and thus the capability to bear responsibility for their actions and decisions. Divine law was given the premier place among human obligations and nothing should inhibit every human from responding to the divine law as it is mediated through human conscience.

The Vatican II declaration specifically claimed freedoms for the Catholic Church that apply to all churches and associations. The church is to be free from interference in its ministry and the conduct of its witness and relationship to its members. This includes especially the training of ministers, communications among church structures and personnel, and the erection of buildings and holding property with religious intent. Likewise, the family is a concern in the declaration. Parents enjoy the rights of educating their children according to the beliefs of the parents and the church is guaranteed the right to maintain religious instruction.

Very strong language is used in the Vatican document regarding government repression of religion. Different from the medieval concept of the religious responsibilities of the state, the state becomes the guarantor of religious freedom for its citizens. Negatively, this means that the state is to create no repressive means nor is it to deny a group the right to practice its religion through giving favored status to one religious body or expression. Positively, it is incumbent upon the government to create conditions favorable to the fostering of religious life and so that people may profit by the moral qualities of justice and peace.[29] Underlying much of the development of religious expectations and the state are familiar Protestant and Enlightenment principles of separation of church and state, equality before the law, and common welfare.

SUMMARY

IN SUMMARY OF all that can be observed about religious liberty from a Christian perspective, four fundamental points must be made. First, religious freedom as a right of persons to immunity from external coercion is not formally enunciated in revealed Christian scripture. Second, through narratives and first-century teachings, from a Christian perspective, religious liberty has roots conceptually in revelation. Christian theologians have derived from scripture the bases of religious freedom and organized and embellished that data to form dogma. Third, a primary assumption in the Christian articulation of religious freedom is that the right to receive religious truth, whether truth or error, allows for the ultimate disappearance of error and acceptance of truth. Fourth, an important part of the case for religious freedom germinates in the painful experiences of religious persecution. In every case, where an important declaration of religious freedom has been made, it is preceded by a history of persecution and denials of human rights.

There are further points to be made. The noted ecumenical scholar and director of the WCC Commission on Faith and Order, Lukas Vischer, in 1966 observed from within the World Council community that there was likely no exhaustive, comprehensive case to be made that all of the churches would accept. He noted to the Catholic community that religious freedom must involve the relations of church and state; relations among the churches themselves, missions and new churches; international organization; and some recognition of separated churches. Ultimately, he cautioned that the world was crying out for a more stable order and the churches together needed to provide a broader basis for mutual relationships.[30] He was accurate in his assessments.

Finally, many others have recognized that religious liberty cannot depend upon the content of religious beliefs. Religious freedom pertains to persons as the subjects of the freedom. This entails persons as individuals and in association. The Christian community now universally declares that the foundation of the right to religious freedom lies within the dignity of every human being. It is part of the constitutive elements of the human being that men are intelligent and free by nature, and, hence, naturally privileged to bear responsibility in every sphere. Norms of sincerity and truth are involved and these can only be recognized and exercised in freedom.[31]

The ecumenical Christian community has continued to revise earlier well-worn definitions of religious liberty. For instance, in the late twentieth century, it came to be universally recognized that religious liberty is a civil right, ratified out of motives for the common welfare. This now involves assumptions of religious pluralism, interdependence of political communities, and greater sensitivity of human beings in religious matters. In the area of human rights, religious liberty will continue to be a fruitful topic of discussion and policy formation.

4

THE SOCIAL CONCERNS OF CHRISTIANITY

BEGINNING IN THE SEVENTEENTH century, Christians of varying denominations developed social concerns, that is concerns, for more than individual salvation, as part of their interpretation of the Gospel. Many became aware of structural and communal needs with solutions often based in communities. These early "concerns" would presage the later response to an agenda of recognizing human rights. Social concerns are a far cry from recognition of human rights, but in the course of Christian history, social concerns form a background for human rights.

Roman Catholic tradition has recognized the church's responsibility to address social concerns for centuries. As early as the fifth century, bishops were required by church law to spend a portion of diocesan funds to assist the poor through the "hospitum." Medieval bishops divided their responsibilities among the poor, strangers, and the sick and disabled. Homes or hostels for the poor were endowed and these evolved into "hospitals" of various types. Throughout Western Christendom by the fourteenth century, the church maintained hospitals for special groups like Jews and generally for the poor. With the advent of the mendicant orders like Franciscans, Dominicans, Carmelites, and Augustinians, friars traveled from urban center to urban center to respond to the new social conditions. In the 1200s, yet another movement alongside the mendicants emerged, the beguines and beghards, lay fraternities who worked in various social ministries. Later, as these were regularized, sodalities and associations took up Christian work among those with special needs. During the Reformation, some of the new denominations, notably the Anglicans and Lutherans, carried on in welfare ministries through brotherhoods and sisterhoods.

The movement that religious historians refer to as "Pietism" may be the rootage of modern Christian social concern. Pietism had its origins in Lutheran and Reformed post-Reformation Protestantism. Many pastors and leaders in Germany and Reformed countries came to feel that the orthodoxy resultant from the reform movements of the early sixteenth century had lapsed into staleness and uninspiring intellectualism. Their response was to seek ways to activate the gospel and involve all Christians in "heartfelt" or experiential Christianity. Pastors and educators like Philip J. Spener and Auguste H. Franke reorganized their congregations to allow for reflection groups of study and prayer and they encouraged laity to become in involved in practical work like care for the sick and aged, child care, homes for orphans, and missionary work overseas. The congregational strategies these early Pietists developed soon became blueprints for denominational renewal in churches like the Evangelical Lutheran Church and the Reformed Church. At Halle in Germany, a university was reorganized to include training ministers on Pietist models. When Pietist missionary pastors went abroad, they took account of the social as well as the spiritual needs of those committed to their care and established schools, orphanages, hospitals, and welfare programs.

As Christians emigrated to the Americas, among their first social concerns were aboriginal peoples. Spanish, English, and French missionaries approached the challenge with differing ways and means. The Spanish, for instance, relied on the Franciscans and Jesuits to order and maintain their mission stations. Franciscans led in the establishment of missions that walled in communities of agriculture and learning for those who voluntarily entered the mission. Franciscans refused to learn the native languages, insisting instead on language instruction in Spanish and to a limited degree Latin. In contrast, Jesuits, focused upon advance work in remote regions like northern Mexico and in small encampments, learned native languages, and codified what they observed and heard. Those who submitted to life in the mission compound were cared for and learned a new livelihood in the encomienda system that lasted until the late eighteenth century in Peru, Mexico, and the American Southwest. If one accepts the enforcement of a colonial Christian society, there were socially constructive elements of benefit to the Indian populations in New Spain, such as agricultural and industrial skills, encouragement for a family structure, and a stable food supply.

The French colonial missions were similar to those in New Spain, though less numerous and highly developed. The orders active in New France were primarily the Jesuits, then the Recollets, Sulpicians, and several women's and lay orders that were the result of the religious revival in France in the first half of the seventeenth century. The Jesuits concentrated on the far outposts associated with the fur trade, like those located at Huronia on the St. Lawrence and Ste.-Marie at Midland Bay. After an initial period of despising Indian religious traditions, Jesuit priests turned to an aggressive form of evangelization that also opposed the liquor traffic among the traders and Indians and the immorality that was rampant between the traders and Indian women. The religious communities provided spiritual instruction, rudimentary medical care, and hospitality for aboriginal peoples. In the large villages like Trois Rivieres, Quebec, Montreal, and Tadoussac, various institutions evolved that served modest numbers of Indians during the colonial period.

In the English context, specific steps were taken with government sanction to minister to the aboriginal populations. New England became the first focal point for Indian "missionary concern" and this began in the early years of Massachusetts Bay. Early governors of the Colony had been dismissive of negotiating with the Indians for land claims, although the 1629 instructions to the planters conveyed this necessity. Roger Williams, an Anglican-become-Puritan, arrived in Salem, Massachusetts, in 1631 and almost immediately became an advocate for Indian rights to the land. Early in his New World experience, he declined to become a party to "anti-Christian conversions" from "one false worship to another." He preferred "to wait upon God and His holy season."[1] Williams further evinced a deepened cultural appreciation of Indian peoples with his 1643 book, *A Key into the Language of the Natives in that Part of America, called New England.*[2] Following his banishment from Massachusetts Bay in 1636, he sensitively negotiated a land deed to his Rhode Island settlement, treating the Narragansetts and Wampanoags as respected equals.

In 1649, the English Parliament passed an act establishing the New England Company, whose objectives were in part to bring about the conversion of the Indian peoples of New England. The most impressive result of the Company was the work of John Eliot, missionary to the

Algonkian Indians of northern and western New England. Eliot produced a Bible in the language and, along the way to its publication in 1663, advocated special care and treatment of the process of Indian conversion. Eliot, Daniel Gookin, and Thomas Mayhew were instrumental in the 1660s in conversion of Indians and boasted of no less than fourteen "Praying Indian towns" with about 4,000 residents across New England. Harvard College, under the auspices of Congregational ministers, began an Indian school in its first generation, and what became Dartmouth College commenced as a school for Indians. Later in the century, the Church of England created the Society for the Propagation of the Gospel (SPG), which focused particularly upon the Indians. Thomas Bray was the chief architect of the SPG in its attempts to ensure that the Church of England would predominate in the American colonies.

In the Middle Colonies, William Penn led in creating treaties with the Delawares that were founded upon respect for their culture and land claims. As long as Quakers were the predominant group in the colony, harmonious relations remained intact. The Moravians, in particular, became the centerpiece of compassionate outreach to aboriginal peoples. Arriving in Georgia in 1735 and in Pennsylvania in 1740, they established missions to the Indians at the beginning of their work. Orphanages in the Pietist tradition existed in Savannah, Georgia, and Nazareth, Pennsylvania. In the hinterlands of Ohio Country, a major Indian mission was set up at Gnaddenhutten that visitors called a model community.

The colonial experience provided a positive foundation for social concern for the Indians. New York City denominations in 1796 cooperated in a mission outreach to the Six Nations of the Niagara Frontier, which saw evangelization and aboriginal churches on both sides of the border well after the War of 1812. As the great national missionary organizations took shape in the first decades of the nineteenth century, Indian missions were included in the plans for the American Board of Commissioners for Foreign Missions, the General Missionary Convention of the Baptist Denomination, and the American Home Mission Society. All followed a pattern of erecting schools and churches for the spiritual and economic development of the various tribes. As the focus upon missions to aboriginal peoples waned in view of the reservation system and permanent assignment of denominations to tribes, a new area of concern took shape.

Perhaps the most pressing issue for eighteenth-century Christians with a social conscience was the institution of slavery. Quakers in Pennsylvania led the way in addressing the problem. Quaker writers and activists led the way in the Philadelphia area yearly meetings. Anthony Benezet* and John Woolman* found slave-keeping among the Friends incompatible with their principles, and Woolman penned *Considerations on the Keeping of* Negroes in 1754, a tract that was widely read. Benezet followed Woolman in attacking the slave trade. Reports of oppressive treatment abounded in the colonies and the Friends had developed a deeper moral consciousness over treatment of Indians in the Shawnee War of 1756–1758. At the yearly meetings of 1755 and 1758, the Friends agreed to abolish slavery and called upon their colleagues to be consistent with their religious principles and manumit their slaves. The next decade saw scores of slaves freed and monthly meetings set up exclusively of Negroes organized.[3] Others, including Baptists, also made public declarations: "Slavery is a violent deprivation of the rights of nature, and inconsistent with a republican government," Virginia ministers voted in 1789. They pledged to take "every legal measure" to extirpate the "horrid evil" from the land.[4]

Prominent American Quakers also took note of other areas of human need. Thomas Eddy,* an urbane New York Quaker, made large sums of money in the tobacco trade and turned to philanthropy and social reform. Having been incarcerated during the revolutionary era, he knew well the need for prison reform and the rights of prisoners. In conjunction with Philip Schuyler, Eddy worked through the Philadelphia Society for Alleviating the Miseries of Public Prisons and later the New York Legislature to reduce the number of capital crimes and cruel treatment. He advocated sanitary, humane conditions, single cells, education for prisoners, and religious instruction. Eddy was among the first to favor abolition of capital punishment. Other Friends followed Eddy's work with programs for city dispensaries, humane care for mental patients, and the prevention of pauperism. Poor laws and penal codes in most northeastern cities and states followed this broad effort of Quakers.[5]

The Christian witness in missionary context often demonstrated progressive thinking about matters of human freedom, dignity, and rights. Against the horrid tales of slave-catching and trading in Africa, there are the instances of colonies in Liberia and Sierra Leone that American Christians set up as model Christian communities for freed Negroes from America. This was largely the effort of the local colonization groups and later the American Colonization Society, formed by Christian individuals in 1817. In India, missionaries confronted three practices that were grossly inhumane: murder of female children, burning of widows with their deceased husbands, and drowning of elderly people. William Carey, Baptist missionary to Bengal, reported the burning of 10,000 women annually with their husbands. Carey, in response, led a successful campaign to outlaw the practice in British territories.[6]

John Wesley and the Methodist movement in England, Wales, and the United States made important contributions to Christian social activism. Early in his ministry, he preached to classes of poor people historically outside the established church, like miners and industrial workers. One of Wesley's leading concerns was slavery. He read with appreciation Benezet's work denouncing the slave trade and quoted from it liberally in his *Thoughts Upon Slavery*, published in 1774. He appealed more to natural law rather than scripture, because he likely thought the real perpetrators would not respond to theological arguments. Rather, Wesley appealed to justice, mercy, and truth and concluded slavery was wrong. He carefully mingled Judge Blackstone's legal understanding of natural law with the idea of *imago dei* and a soteriological angle. Slavery was thus dehumanizing, it was contrary to a spirit of brotherhood under God, and an end to slavery, in Wesley's mind, would further exhibit God's redemption and liberation as he had acted in allowing the return of Jewish exiles from Babylon.[7] In the last twenty-five years of Wesley's life, he added other social concern themes to his tract-writing, notably smuggling, traffic in spirituous liquors, and the evils of the industrial system, including exploitation of women and children in factories.

In both the British and early American contexts, Methodists exhibited genuine concern for various social and political realties. For instance, Methodists in the northern United States early responded to antislavery initiatives. A conscience group within the M. E. Church, the Wesleyan Methodist Connection, bolted in 1843 and under the leadership of Orange Scott and Luther Lee, pursued an antislavery agenda. Another schism, the Methodist Protestants, organized in the 1820s around greater lay participation in the church, exhibited a characteristicly democratic flavor in their new structure.

In response to a preponderance of historiography extolling the rise of the Social Gospel movement, evangelical historians have pointed out that the real concern for social issues and human rights was a product of the evangelical awakenings of the 1830s–1850s. Donald Dayton, for instance, argued persuasively that the original reforming influence in American religion was evangelicalism. He points out that antislavery, feminism, civil disobedience to bring about social change, temperance, and a sensitivity for the poor were all part of the pre-Civil War heritage of Evangelicals. His heroes and heroines are Jonathan Blanchard, Charles G. Finney, Theodore Weld, Orange Scott, Phoebe Palmer, and Catherine Booth, to mention a few.[8] These preachers and lawyers stood against powerful institutional forces and held their ground to bring about the first great concerted concern for human rights. Other historians have demonstrated this tendency toward evangelical techniques inherent in other reform movements, notably the Antimasonic Crusade that began as a religious movement but was snatched away by designing politicians.[9] What happened to Evangelicalism to create a radical departure from its reforming roots? Dayton argued that a combination of factors, including Finney's revival techniques that stressed individual conversion, the placement of theological barriers against the rest of the Christian world, and the achievements of the Civil War in obliterating slavery, were contributing factors. Other factors included the evolution of a pre-millennial eschatology that sought to remove Evangelicals from the world, and the adoption of Princeton theology and its interpretation of Old Calvinism as the dominant theological expression of Evangelicals. As Dayton argues, "The great heritage of Evangelicals social witness was buried and largely forgotten.[10] One of the long-lasting remains of that heritage is found in its literature, with titles like Finney's *Lectures on Revivals of Religion* (1868), Theodore Weld's *Slavery As It Is* (1839), B. T. Roberts' *Ordaining Women* (1891), and W. T. Stead's *If Christ Came to Chicago* (1894).

Numerous authors have shown that the grand effort of the Second Great Awakening, insofar as social concern was evident, was the crusade against slavery. Here, many elements of the Christian faith were evident. The roots of the antislavery crusade began in the social conscience of New England and blossomed in the Burned-over District of western New York and the Western Reserve in Ohio. In these regions a special emphasis upon the perfectability of human society led to a focus upon obvious social ills, notably slavery. Ministers of all the Protestant groups could be found in the ultraistic emphases that led eventually by the 1830s to organized antislavery. Finney, the great lawyer-become-evangelist and later college president at Oberlin, led the religious fervor of the 1820s and 1830s into focused social reform. Others followed like

William Lloyd Garrison, Jonathan Blanchard, William H. Brisbane, and Arthur and Lewis Tappan, two laymen whose philanthropy made possible mass meetings, publications, and political strategies. When the American Antislavery Society was formed in 1833, it was patterned after the great national Christian voluntary associations for missions, education, and publication. By the 1840s, the religious basis had been transformed into political activism in the formation of the Liberty Party that was composed of substantial numbers of evangelical Christians. Quakers, Congregationalists, Presbyterians, and Baptists maintained the Underground Railroad, a line of refugee hostels stretching from the Upper South to the Canadian border, defying enforcement of fugitive slave laws. During the Civil War, the antislavery energies were redirected into Christian service agencies like the U.S. Christian Commission that ministered to troops and the needs of freed slaves. Finally, during Reconstruction, those who had fought the war against slavery gave generously to various denominational missions to educate the freedmen and establish their citizenship.

Next to antislavery, the crusade to secure recognition and rights for women was foremost in the antebellum period. Among Quakers, there was an early recognition of women receiving "spiritual revelation" pertinent to the meeting. The Hicksite Quakers moved the farthest in recognition of women, placing no barriers before female leadership within the meeting. Among the outstanding women leaders in the antislavery crusade were Sarah and Angelina Grimke* of South Carolina and later Massachusetts. Likewise, Lucretia Mott was a significant abolitionist leader in Philadelphia. The temperance movement gave rise to its coterie of female leaders, notably Elizabeth Cady Stanton. A high watermark in the evolution of women's rights came at a small chapel of the Wesleyan Methodists in Seneca Falls, New York. On July 19–20, 1848, over one hundred persons met in the meetinghouse of this antislavery Methodist sect. They passed a Declaration of Sentiments that imitated the Declaration of Independence, save for their substitution of "man" for "King George," and the addition of various deprivations that women had suffered. The document, authored by Lucretia and James Mott and Stanton, was laced with references to Judaeo-Christian themes and reflected the religious orientation of its authors.

A second avenue that many women followed to increase their opportunities opened in the missionary enterprise. In this regard, the wives of Adoniram Judson, Ann, Sarah, and Emily, provided a significant set

of role models for young Christian women. These stalwart women missionary pioneers were people of courage, tenacity, scholarship, and literary attainment. Their careers opened paths of service by the 1870s at
home and abroad for women missionaries. Further, this led to women's
mission organizations for women to manage as administrators. Joan Jacobs Brumberg at Cornell University has shown that this created a "fem-
ine internationale" that surely enhanced the recognition of women's
rights in the Christian community and beyond.[11]

Christians before the Civil War were also involved in campaigns to
limit the consumption of alcohol. Well back into the eighteenth century, Protestant Christian ministers had decried the excessive use of
spirits. John Wesley, in his ethical instructions to Methodists, enjoined
abstinence from the sale and use of intoxicating beverages. Likewise,
Quakers like Benjamin Rush of Philadelphia appeared before the General Assembly of the Presbyterian Church in 1811 to make a plea for
temperance because of its political effects. Following the War of 1812,
the number of victims of excessive drinking seemed to be on the rise
and clergy moved to address the problem. It was not only a sin for the
drunkard, but also for those who stood idly by to watch others slip into
abuse. The crusade often focused on the family and the abuse that alcoholics perpetrated upon wives and children.

Influential clergy were drawn into the temperance movement. Lyman
Beecher of Boston led the campaign within the ranks of New England
Congregational clergy. In 1826, yet another national voluntary reform
organization was started, the American Society for the Promotion of
Temperance. At Chase's Tavern in Baltimore, Maryland, a new phase
of the movement began in 1840 with the Washingtonian Movement.
A small group of drinkers committed themselves to total abstinence from
all alcoholic beverages and within five years, the campaign spread
through the country. Numerous evangelists, like Jacob Knapp of New
York, and abolitionists, like William Lloyd Garrison,* joined the revival
against drink. Eventually, clergy carried the temperance crusade to London, England, where in 1846 the World's Temperance Convention was
held. The attention given to abstinence in the Christian community
had much to do with the passage of laws limiting, if not abolishing,
alcohol consumption in many communities.

Given the amount of military engagement in the first decades of U.S.
history, it is not surprising to find that Christian groups began to organize for peace. Quakers of course opposed armed conflict with Britain

during the War for Independence. Benezet published an important pamphlet, *Thoughts on the Nature of War* in 1776 just as the Declaration of Independence was issued. In 1809, a Presbyterian merchant in New York likewise issued *The Mediator's Kingdom Not of This World* (1809), which argued from the Sermon on the Mount a radical nonresistant position. The formation of alliances in Europe among Christian monarchies did much to foster the notion that war was no solution to international conflicts. With the War of 1812, both Congregationalists and Unitarians in New England joined the chorus for peace. Famed Unitarian preacher William Ellery Channing helped to organize the Massachusetts Peace Society in his home in 1815. William Ladd, a wealthy farmer in Maine, wrote numerous articles urging a national organization for peace because he felt "he owed it to God and my fellow creatures to do something to hasten the glorious era when men shall learn war no more."[12] The result of his labors was a partnership with David L. Dodge of New York to form the American Peace Society in 1828.

It has been noted that the peace movement in conjunction with the antislavery movement kept the crusade against slavery relatively nonviolent for three decades. Even Garrison, ardent defender of abolitionism, agreed to a Declaration of Principles of a Non-Resistance Society. Perhaps the biggest challenge to peace advocates of the antebellum era was the War with Mexico, which drew forth eloquent expressions of peace laced with poetic allusions from the pens of Theodore Parker, Horace Greeley, and John Greenleaf Whittier. The hero of the climactic moment of the peace crusade was Elihu Burritt, who launched the issue of peace onto the international Christian agenda with the formation of the League of International Brotherhood in 1846.

In Britain, benevolent and evangelical purposes characterized the early nineteenth-century Christian scene as a "golden age of voluntary religious association."[13] A typology of these organizations demonstrates they promoted renewal, increased cooperation, social and religious critique, and empowerment, and they expanded Christian services. For the purposes in this study, many also corrected or alleviated human rights abuses.[14] For instance, there were the National Society for Educating the Poor (1811), Society for the Abolition of Capital Punishment (1828), the Society for the Extinction of the Slave Trade (1840), the Homes for the Aged Poor (1869), and the National Association for the Care of the Feeble-minded (1895), among hundreds of others.[15] Collectively, these were known as the "Age of Societies" and the "Evangelical United

Front." Persons from all the denominations freely mingled in the various activities and concerns.

At about the same time, Anglican Christians experimented with various forms of Christian socialism. F. D. Maurice and Charles Kingsley attempted to realize the Kingdom of God by creating socialist societies and a Workingman's College. These efforts failed in large part because they were promoted by middle-class advocates and because much of the working classes were Roman Catholic. The Salvation Army made striking gains in reaching the urban poorer classes in the last quarter of the century, and all denominations competed for the children of working-class folk in the Sunday School movement.

Similarly, Robert Baird, a well-traveled American observer who wrote the first full analysis of religion in the United States, described his native country in 1843 as a place with a "desire to do good" where the voluntary principle was "the grand and only alternative." There were major national societies with religious origins and/or control that worked at building churches, home missions, schools, colleges and universities, publishing, temperance, beneficent causes, and abolishing existing evils. For Baird, this was the natural outworking of the principle of religious liberty.[16] Not only did each of the mainstream denominations and the Roman Catholic Church participate in the voluntary empire, but interdenominational national and regional bodies also emerged to pursue their social concern objectives.

The American Civil War released a huge amount of moral energy into emancipation of slaves. In many ways it was an end to the social concerns of the first half of the nineteenth century, using up both personnel and momentum. Many of the Protestant churches were split into regional factions and this caused a temporary setback for social concerns. During the era of Reconstruction and later in the rise of big business, it appeared that churches were actually in concert with the forces of urbanization and industrialization that took hold in Western Europe and North America. However, the problems of housing, child labor, exploitation of workers, and immigration caught the attention of a new generation of concerned Christian activists. Quakers were a lone witness on peace, Indians, and race relations, building programs and efforts through the Lake Mohonk Mountain House Retreat Center that opened in 1870. These conferences influenced politicians, government workers, educators, missionaries, and clergy to create an awareness of social problems in the United States and abroad.

In the United States, social reform in the last two decades of the nineteenth century was inextricably connected with Christian witness. According to its historians, the "social gospel movement," as it has been labeled, was a mostly American phenomenon that grew out of several concerns and a specific cultural context.[17] Chief among the social concerns were urbanization and industrialization, coupled with which were changing patterns of theological discourse and social thought. Immigration and the commercial development of cities created a rise in the demand for housing, with concomitant needs for sanitation, education, and law enforcement. The labor problem shared in America and Europe produced renewed interest in socialistic experiments that captivated many social theorists. Economic changes also produced challenges. Following the Civil War, America's major urban centers emerged with an enormous accumulation of capital and a deprived working class. Machines created a new form of dehumanized laborers, inadequate wages, unsafe working conditions, and exploitation of women and children in the workforce, all characterizing the scene in most factories. Socialist ideas and rhetoric could be found to varying degrees in organized labor, but in general, Protestant and Catholic clergy rejected socialism as a non-Christian solution to obvious problems. Socialism assumed that transformation could occur through social groups and systems; Protestants in particular stressed the transformation of individual character. But, before old revivalistic forms could be brought to bear, Protestantism itself underwent serious adjustments, for instance new acceptance of biblical criticism and openness to evolutionary hypotheses that seemed to undermine the authority of scripture. Moreover, the application of the new social sciences to theological disciplines, notably church history and historical theology, eroded confidence in institutions and dogmatic formulae of human sinfulness and a pessimistic worldview.

A bevy of new Protestant voices began to meet the challenges of the labor issue in particular. England's Frederick Maurice and Charles Kingsley applied the principles of socialism in England and had many devotees in the United States. Newman Smyth at Center Church, New Haven, Connecticut, urged a candid consideration of the problems of labor. Washington Gladden, pastor of First Congregational Church in Columbus, Ohio, wrote of "applied Christianity," whereby he argued that the problems associated with the laboring classes could only be met by bringing more of the laborers into the churches, previously controlled by capitalist and employing classes. Gladden urged a new receptivity and interpretation for the Christian law, "Thou shalt love thy neighbor as thyself." He saw the Kingdom of God as both spiritual and temporal; its chief aspect should be a socially awakened church. He became an advocate of labor and called upon corporations to practice Christian ethical principles. He led his denomination in adopting stances on exploitation of laborers, redistribution of wealth, and mistreatment of black Americans. Other voices, like Josiah Strong, chimed in with warnings that sin had to be accounted for in any new human approach to social problems. Richard Ely, professor at Johns Hopkins University and founder of the American Institute of Christian Sociology, criticized Christian orthodoxy as being unconcerned about the social aspects of Christianity and urged theologians to reread the gospels. The Reverend Edward Everett Hale of Boston thought the churches had accommodated a "medieval" view exclusively directed at the salvation of souls. Salvation came to be redefined as "positive righteousness in all the earth" and the Kingdom of God became the "righteous rule of God in human affairs."[18] In this period, the Episcopal Church founded three organizations to meet the labor crisis—the Church Association for the Advancement of the Interests of Labor, the Society for Christian Socialists, and the Christian Social Union—plus sisterhoods like those in England to work among the poor.[19] The last half of the century was not lacking in Christian reforming impulses on either side of the Atlantic.

Rauschenbusch, a professor of church history at Baptist-related Rochester New York Theological Seminary, proved to be the prophet and saint of the social gospel movement. Rauschenbusch had learned first-hand the exigencies of life in the city during his pastorate in New York's Lower East Side. As a student in Germany, he was exposed to new approaches to dogma and Christian experience. In his tenure as a seminary professor, he developed a full-blown exposition of the social gospel in four major books. Rather than stressing an individualistic theology of salvation, Rauschenbusch wrote instead of the "Kingdom of God." That conceptualization, he thought, was at the heart of Jesus' message. "My sole desire," he wrote, "has been to summon the Christian passion for justice and the Christian powers of love and mercy to do their share in redeeming our social order from its inherent wrongs."[20] Rauschenbusch also stressed the prophetic nature of social concern, as found in the Old Testament and in the words of Jesus. Much interested in spirituality, he wrote a compendium of prayers for use in church worship that stressed social gospel activism and the triumph of the Kingdom. As he matured,

Rauschenbusch openly critiqued capitalism as an unregenerate form of economic organization and he laid out a specific agenda for social reform. He insisted upon social justice and economic democracy as "minimum requirements" upon which a new social order should be constructed. Every worker was entitled to ownership of property, he wrote. In the end, Rauschenbusch came to think of himself as a "Christian socialist," an epithet not lost on his many critics in the evangelical circles.

In the United States, the social gospel movement triumphed among mainline Protestant churches. Various voluntary organizations sprang up in the new century to study and address social problems, like the need for fresh-air activities for inner-city children, or to advocate the rights of women. Next, the various denominations started commissions, boards, and committees to institutionalize their social concern. Presbyterians formed a Department of Church and Labor in 1903; the Congregational churches took similar action before 1905. Broadening their social activism agenda, Episcopalians formed in 1919 the Church League for Industrial Democracy as well as departments for World Relief, Community Action, and Health and Welfare Services. Methodists formed the Federation for Social Service in Washington, D.C., in 1905, and with the blessing of Rauschenbusch himself in 1913, the newly formed Northern Baptist Convention formed a primary Board of Christian Social Concern. Perhaps the greatest organizational achievement of the social gospel movement was its marriage to the federation movement to establish in 1908 the Federal Council of Churches of Christ. It soon became "the virtual keeper of the social gospel." At its founding, the member bodies adopted a statement creed that came to be known as the "social creed of the churches," and the following year, the executive council created the Commission on the Church and Social Service.[21]

In the Canadian context, the social gospel movement moved much more closely in tandem with aspirations of socialism. In the 1930s, severe climatic circumstances in the Prairies led to low agricultural productivity, high unemployment, draining of community resources, and a seemingly entrenched poverty class. Methodists led the articulation of a radical social Christian witness, and, given the spread of Methodist congregations among the depressed regions, the denomination's influence was large. One of the most important contributions that social gospellers made was the creation of a language of reform that rejected capitalism, yet held on to Christian values. "Prairie Radicalism" emerged among angry farmers who fought monopoly capitalist interests in wheat markets. Matched by a series of economic cooperatives in Nova Scotia, a Cooperative Commonwealth Federation (CCF) was formed in 1933. Social gospel theologians like Gregory Vlastos and R.B.Y. Scott lent their perspectives to the movement and organized their own associations, notably the Fellowship for a Christian Social Order, which influenced the Protestant Churches, and the League for Social Reconstruction, which imitated the British Fabian Society. The political movement made headway into the 1940s but then lost steam to the Liberal Party, which adopted many of its reforms with a more mainstream agenda. Canadian social gospel advocates artfully addressed the critiques of Reinhold Niebuhr that the social gospel neglected the factor of human sinfulness by arguing persuasively that the sin of the world was essentially social and pervasive. They also avoided the Rauschenbuschian notion that the Kingdom of God would be established in human society. In keeping with Canadian communitarian ideals, Canadian theologians asserted that the Gospel summoned Christians to understand love as an expression of mutuality rather than in competitive or exploitative terms.[22] Eventually, however, as prosperity resumed in the postwar economy, the CCF evolved into the New Democrat Party, which carried forth a modified socialist agenda among Canadian political choices, and the organizational aspects of the social gospel movement, like the Fellowship for a Christian Social Order, declined.

A special note should be made in the Canadian context about Catholic support of the social gospel. In general, Canadian Catholics followed the rejection of socialist movements that Pope Pius IX made in his 1931 encyclical, *Quadragesimo Anno*. Two years later, the CCF was denounced as part of a movement that could undermine world order. In Quebec particularly, bishops condemned all forms of social Christianity because of socialist opposition to large corporations in the province and the platform of the party in support of a strong federal government. The issue of a unified Canada over against an independent Quebec rose to prominence. The one region where extensive Catholic support was manifest in the socialist dimensions of Christian activism was on Cape Breton Island, where Catholics in large numbers did support the CCF and the Catholic Bishop did not interfere. Miners and workers have continued to elect CCF and later New Democrat candidates to Parliament, including Father Andrew Hogan, the first priest ever elected to Parliament. Following the trend, in later decades Catholic workers and intellectuals organized themselves as Politises Chretiens, an association that aimed in the 1970s to mingle Marxist socialism with Catholic faith perspectives.[23]

In the United States, during the decades of the thirties and forties, Christian denominations offered a variety of responses to human rights issues. Overall, the movement was toward greater recognition of human rights. Responses were often dictated on the basis of regional location, particularly on matters of race. Lynchings and executions that were rampant across the South often drew little attention in the formal church communities. But at the national level, and among Northern associations, strong denunciations of brutality were made. In 1919, the Presbyterians spoke out against lynching, and by the mid-thirties, the Unitarians, Church of the Brethren, Reformed Church, Episcopalians, Congregationalists, Northern Baptists, and Methodists all passed resolutions against lynching. Likewise the Federal Council of Churches produced numerous useful editorials condemning the practice.[24]

But, the matter of racial harmony and equality was another matter. Here the lines were drawn very deeply. Following World War I, anti-Semitic voices among the denominations were heard. Examples abound of racial segregation policies being ratified among Southern churches. Robert Miller, an American religious historian claimed, "many Southern Baptists defended Negro segregation in the mid-twentieth century as fervently as they did Negro slavery in the mid-nineteenth."[25] Southern Methodist bishops opposed reunion for many years because of the Negro issue. On the positive side of the ledger, there is much to commend. The Federal Council of Churches organized a Commission on the Church and Race Relations in 1921. The Methodist Episcopal Church in the North produced an official statement on race relations that called for an end to public discrimination in hotels. Congregationalists pledged themselves to complete citizenship for Negroes and Northern Baptists denounced racial superiority and stated that race prejudice was the greatest hindrance to the Kingdom of God on earth. They even advocated boycotting restaurants. The Presbyterians, both North and South, led all other denominations in liberal attitudes toward the Negro.[26] Lutherans, their historian indicates, addressed racial issues through statement that provided information and guidance, major examples of which came forward in 1957 and 1964. By 1974, the American Lutheran Church had identified racism with sin and action was needed because the Prayer of the Church condemns us. Civil disobedience was a viable option. In the 1970s and 1980s, the church pushed further its agenda toward Native Americans, Hispanics, and other minorities with organizations like the Lutheran Human Relations Association.[27]

Leading the march toward recognition of "human rights," various Protestant groups manifested a stance toward peace during the many wars of the twentieth century. The Episcopal Church and several Baptist groups formally established "peace fellowships" that educated conscientious objectors and launched formal protests against military action, notably the Vietnam War.[28] Some parishes came to be refuge places of asylum in response to militarism in Central America. Other denominations supported overall peace initiatives through the National Council of Churches.

In the twentieth century, Roman Catholic thinking began to take account of the social dimensions of Christianity. Pope Leo XIII, heavily influenced by Thomistic understanding of natural law, deeply distrusted rampant democracy and the liberal tradition that grew out of the Enlightenment. In his major encyclical, *Rerum Novarum* (1891), he affirmed an individual's right to private property and laws of nature that promoted peace and tranquil living together. Beyond that, the Vatican wrote favorably of just wages and contracts between employers and workers. In the same era, John Ryan,* a prominent ethicist and social reformer in the United States, closely parallel to Walter Rauschenbusch among Protestants, was advocating economic justice. He authored an influential pamphlet, *Social Reconstruction: A General Review of the Problems and Survey of Remedies* (1919), that contained a detailed set of principles for minimum-wage legislation, an age limit for child labor, a defense of the right to organize, and proposals for public housing and a national employment service. Ryan's thought had a profound effect upon the National Catholic Welfare Conference against stiff opposition from industrial leaders in the United States. Eventually, the Vatican affirmed the work of the Council, and indirectly Ryan's new directions, by offering it as a model to other countries with emerging industrial economies.[29]

In the following pontificate of Pius XI, who in his 1931 encyclical, *Quadragesimo Anno* (QA), changed directions and pushed the Catholic Church to support a Christian social order that integrated economic rights with civil and social concerns. Justice and the common good were foundational to the Vatican, whose position was actually written by Oswald von Nell-Breuning. Pius imitated Mussolini's attempt at an economic corporate model and had praise for Austria's new constitution of 1934. *Quadragesimo Anno* also introduced the notion of "subsidiarity" (assigning greater and higher associations to the tasks that can be performed by subordinate associations) and favored an expanded role of a state in regulating private property. Real social transformation was hinted at in QA. The giant step that Catholic leaders took in the early twentieth century was a firm understanding of "the common good of all."[30]

On a practical level, no record of social concern and human rights in the Catholic tradition exceeds that of Mother Teresa (Agnes Gonxha Bojaxhiu*) of Calcutta. Her observations of poverty and abject hopelessness in Indian cities in the 1940s led to the formation of the Missionary Sisters. Under her able leadership, the Sisters opened schools, hospice centers, and homes for the care of desperate people. Popes and politicians recognized her selfless work, sanctioned her efforts, and recognized her personal achievements.

Two mainstream Christian groups deserve special attention for their social activism in the twentieth century. The Society of Friends, maintaining a liberal-philosophic approach to human needs and social justice, were at the vanguard of peace initiatives during World War I and II with programs to train and defend conscientious objectors. In 1917, this evolved into the American Friends Service Committee, an international training and relief organization. Following World War II, Friends supported demonstrations against nuclear testing in Nevada and New Mexico, and in 1958, sponsored a sailing ship, the *Golden Rule*, to visit Eniwetok Atoll, site of U.S. Pacific nuclear testing. A Peace Institute was commenced at Lake Mohonk in New York in 1961. In the 1960s, Quakers made their presence felt in church building projects in Mississippi and behind the leadership of Bayard Rustin,* opposed the Vietnam War, and coordinated race relations efforts across the United States.

Similarly in the evangelical vein, the Salvation Army developed a serious social ministry agenda in the later nineteenth and early twentieth centuries that included work in the southern states among Negroes during Reconstruction, rescue homes for women, an antilynching campaign, General William Booth's "In Darkest England" crusade for the urban poor of London, cheap food and shelter depots, and industrial salvage wagons in northeastern U.S. cities. In the 1980s and 1990s, the Army took a charitable position on homosexuality and extensive programs to prevent AIDS and minister to its victims.[31] In a thoughtful theological statement approved in 1988, the Army affirmed two fundamental principles undergirding its social ministries: first, that God established the value of human beings by creating a special place for them in his kingdom, and second, that humans have a social ministry that is redemptive. There is a responsibility of God's people to care for other human beings.[32]

The resurgence of theological conservatism in Western Protestantism after World War II caused advocates of social concerns to make their cases more cautiously. In the United States, a preoccupation with communism led legislators like Senator Joseph McCarthy to conduct witchhunts for anyone who appeared inclined toward non-capitalistic thinking. Open attacks upon the National Council of Churches in the United States and the newly created World Council of Churches ensued among fundamentalists like Bible Presbyterian pastor Carl MacIntyre in the United States and Ian Paisley in Ireland. Only in the 1970s did a return of social activism occur with the rise of a new generation of evangelicals who blended a biblically centered social activism with conservative evangelical doctrines. Centered at Fuller Theological Seminary, Wheaton College, and The Eastern Baptist Theological Seminary, these leaders initiated a new spate of voluntary associations, now dubbed "parachurch" groups to meet concerns like abortion, the rights of women, capital punishment, and economic justice. Episcopalians, United Methodists, Mennonites, Presbyterians, and the United Church of Christ all took leads in the new recognition of social implications of the gospel.

Among evangelicals, the Lausanne movement became a focal point for fusion of evangelical theology with themes of social witness. Carrying both the endorsement of Billy Graham and John R. W. Stott, who wrote the fundamental principles, the Lausanne Committee for World Evangelization commenced in 1974 as an evangelistic endeavor with a social consciousness. In 1989, the social dimensions of the Lausanne movement were sharpened at Manila where "Lausanne II" was achieved in which language of a "Whole Gospel for a Whole World" is used frequently to refer to the responsibility of evangelical Christians for the economic and social contexts of the cultures they wish to reach with the gospel.[33] Gradually, a new infrastructure of evangelical supra-organizations supplanted the leadership of the older councils of churches; this happened most dramatically across three decades in Canada with the emergence of the Evangelical Fellowship of Canada boldly outdistancing the Canadian Council of Churches, since the 1940s an ecumenical voice for human rights and social concern.

Elsewhere, notably in the United States, the formal structures of evangelicalism have been less inclined to assume socially concerned positions. This has led to clusters of evangelicals who call for social action. One of the most far-reaching of these was World Vision International. Founded in 1950, World Vision's mission has been "to follow Jesus Christ in working with the poor and oppressed to promote human transformation, seek justice, and bear witness to the good news of the Kingdom of God." By the 1990s, this expansive relief organization had adopted the language of development and identification with poor and oppressed peoples in a context of a theology of creation and stewardship. It ranks as the largest relief agency in the world.

As more of a social conscience developed among evangelicals, the possibilities of greater concerted efforts emerged. In 1973, historical theologian and activist Ronald Sider convened a group of evangelicals in Chicago to consider a possible evangelical response to a series of social, economic issues. The result was the Chicago Declaration, which fifty-three people signed. From that gathering, the organization Evangelicals for Social Action emerged and, later, another focused on the right-to-life position, "Just Life." Another well-publicized example of "evangelical social change" is Habitat for Humanity International. Founded in 1976 by Millard Fuller,* Habitat has built and rehabilitated more than 125,000 houses for families in need worldwide. Two of its strongest advocates are former President Jimmy Carter* and First Lady Rosalyn Carter, who have organized several "Jimmy Carter Work Projects" in urban areas for Habitat. By the 1980s, it became fashionable for evangelical gatherings to include moderate human rights concerns to their statements and declarations. The Lausanne Committee on World Evangelization typified this in its Manila Manifesto where the signatories affirmed classic evangelical doctrines of human sinfulness, a high Christology and evangelism, and also the gospel as "good news for the poor, destitute, suffering or oppressed." Connecting inseparably "good news" and "good works," the Manifesto stated, "We are to preach and teach, minister to the sick, feed the hungry, care for prisoners, help the disadvantaged and the handicapped, and deliver the oppressed."[34]

Finally, an important epicenter of Christian social concern has developed in modern Britain among mainline Christians. This has often taken a similar shape to contemporary developments in the United

States. Industrial missions, particularly to those in cities wrecked by World War II, were prevalent in the late 1940s. Initiatives of the Christian community have often paralleled the political party in power, such as after the election of 1924 when Labour came to power and Archbishop William Temple presided over a Conference on Christian Politics, Economics and Citizenship.[35] Under the umbrella of the British Council of Churches, the dilemma posed by modern warfare led to a considerable opposition to nuclear weapons. This body also fostered concern for a more just economic order and studied the effects of colonialism and apartheid in South Africa. In more recent decades, the churches in Britain have become sensitive to the rights of women and much work has been done by denominations in interpreting and implementing the Race Relations Act of 1965 and the legislation of 1976 that created a Commission for Racial Equality. In general, the ecumenicity of British Christianity has led to an increased social awareness and activism for both denominations and local congregations. Organizationally illustrative of this has been the founding of OXFAM (Oxford Famine Relief Committee, 1943), Christian Aid (1945), Christian Action (1948), and CAFOD (Catholic Fund for Overseas Development, 1961).[36] By the turn of a new millennium, it was universally acceptable among all but the most retrenched fundamentalist groups of Western Christians that the nature of the Christian gospel carried a social concern as well as a focus upon individual salvation.

CHRISTIAN RESPONSES TO THE UNITED NATIONS DECLARATIONS

BACKGROUND TO THE UNIVERSAL DECLARATION

THE ESTABLISHMENT OF THE United Nations forever changed the sensitivity and priority of social witness and human rights in the Christian tradition. Formed in 1945, the United Nations set the standards and pace for recognition of human rights. Churches and Christian organizations found themselves often unwittingly in a respondent mode to debates and pronouncements of the world organization. Structurally the Christian community imitated the bureaus and strategies of the United Nations.

First, an overview of the evolution of human rights concerns that led up to the Universal Declaration of 1948 is in order. An important facet in this development was the initial involvement of Christian thinkers and leaders to precursor structures and formal discussions within what became the United Nations. Administratively speaking, the taproot to human rights discussion was American Secretary of State Cordell Hull's 1943 creation of an Economic and Social Council that would address the subject. As part of his planned postwar foreign policy agenda, Hull was concerned about human rights, but unsure about whether it was a political, social, or cultural issue. At the security conference at Dumbarton Oaks in early 1944, it became apparent that the United States favored an organization that had subsidiary commissions, one of which should address human rights. Among those organizations outside the government that responded to these initiatives was the Federal Council of Churches of Christ.

Given the appearance of totalitarian government regimes around the globe in the 1930s, plus the circulation of details in the context of the League of Nations and the Christian community's engagement of issues in the Life and Work Movement,[1] it is not surprising that some denominations considered the implications of certain human rights for world order. Baptists in the United States in 1939 moved boldly across regional, theological, and racial lines to express an important position on religious liberty and related concerns. Northern Baptists, with a long heritage of religious liberty, led Southern and National (black) Baptists in making a pronouncement on liberty. Called the American Baptist Bill of Rights, the writers stressed spirituality over establishments of religion, the competency of the human soul in religion, free churches in a free state, and opposition to paternalism and special favors being granted to any state. Of particular concern was the possibility, proffered in the Roosevelt administration, of U.S. diplomatic recognition of the Vatican State. Baptists, to the contrary, opposed all forms of intermixing politics and religious matters. Whether the "Bill of Rights" actually influenced public policy is yet to be determined. It did reflect the opinion of over eight million members in the U.S. evangelical community.

Many posit the ideological beginnings of articulating a need for recognition of human rights in the Committee on Human Rights of the Commission to Study the Organization of Peace, which prepared documentation as early as 1939. In a 1942 speech to B'nai B'rith, Winston Churchill spoke of "the time when this world's struggle ends with the enthronement of human rights."[2] Of high significance was the "Four Freedoms" speech of U.S. president Franklin D. Roosevelt. In January 1944, Roosevelt built his State of the Union speech around "Four Freedoms": freedom of speech and expression, freedom of worship, freedom from want, and freedom from fear. This led to joint presentations on human rights being prepared among the Federal Council of Churches of Christ and the interdenominational Foreign Missions Conference. Their Joint Statement on Religious Liberty was presented to world leaders, including President Roosevelt in 1944. Later, as the war concluded, long-cherished plans went into full swing.

When the new Commission on Human Rights came into structural being, its mandate contained forceful language in protection of minorities and prevention of discrimination. At Hunter College in New York in 1946, a central Commission on Human Rights got underway with the wise leadership of Eleanor Roosevelt. Those who are credited with giving shape to the new Commission included Charles Malik (Lebanon), Carlos Romulos (Philippines), Rene Cassin (France), P. C. Chang (China), Trygvie Lie (Norway), and John Humphrey (Canada). The commission was accountable to the Economic and Social Council (ECOSOC) and thence to the General Assembly.[3]

The first large task of the Commission on Human Rights was the preparation of the Declaration of Human Rights. A drafting committee of three, Eleanor Roosevelt, Malik, and Chang, prepared the initial version, with revisions and additions provided by five additional members and John Humphrey,* who worked on the outline article by article and was the principal writer. In May 1948, responses from governments were taken into consideration, and in December the commission passed the declaration without a dissenting vote. Two days later, the General Assembly of the United Nations added its approval. A comparison with the U.S. Constitution, the English Bill of Rights, and the French Declaration on the Rights of Man demonstrates seven positively stated rights: life, liberty and security of persons; recognition of persons before the law; freedom of movement; nationality; freedom of thought and conscience; freedom of assembly and association; and participation in one's government. Likewise, there were three common prohibitions: slavery, torture, and arbitrary arrest and detention. Two areas of distinctly Christian wording were turned aside, one by Malik that would have guaranteed the right to life from the time of conception and the other a Roman Catholic proposal that called for inclusion of a reference to deity. To the latter idea, the commission responded that persons are born with rights rather than endowed with them by nature or a creator.[4]

From its origins, the world political body essentially acts in three ways with respect to human rights: *declarations* that elaborate basic principles, *conventions* that push the declarations into international law through treaties that nations ratify; and *guidelines* that present procedures for implementation.[5] Eight major declarations have emerged from the U.N. General Assembly or its commissions in 1948–1998: the Universal Declaration of Human Rights (1948); Declaration of the Rights of the Child (1959); Declaration of the Elimination of All Forms of Racial Discrimination (1963); Declaration on the Elimination of Discrimination Against Women and the Declaration on Territorial Asylum (1967); Declaration on Protection of All Persons from Being Subjected to Torture, and Other Cruel, Inhuman or Degrading Treatment or Punishment (1975); Declaration on the Right of Peoples to Peace (1984); Declaration on the Right to Development (1986). In addition, as part of U.N. Conferences in Istanbul and Rome, respectively, declarations on the right to housing (1996) and food (1996) were established. Conventions on these same topics have generally followed with ratification often taking many years, notably those approved in 1966, the Covenant on Economic, Social and Cultural Rights, and the Covenant on Civil and Political Rights, that took effect in 1976. Another notable event was the Helsinki Conference on Security and Cooperation that produced as part of its "Final Act," a paper, "The Respect of Human Rights and Fundamental Freedoms."

Another important tool the United Nations uses is "conferencing" certain key issues and concerns. Between 1968 and 1996, fourteen of these events have been staged: International Conference on Human Rights in Teheran (1968); World Conference on the Environment in Stockholm (1972); United Nations Population Conference in Bucharest (1974); World Food Conference in Rome (1974); First World Conference on Women in Mexico City (1975), followed by a Second World Conference on Women in Copenhagen (1980) and a Third World Conference on Women in Nairobi (1985); World Summit for Children in New York (1990); International Conference on the Environment and Development (also known as the Earth Summit) (1992); the World Conference on Human Rights in Vienna (1993); International Conference on Population and Development in Cairo (1994); World Summit on Social Development in Copenhagen (1995); the Fourth World Conference on Women in Beijing (1995); and Habitat II in Istanbul (1996). These conferences have focused the human rights agenda and generated widespread discussion and action in religious communities. Of crucial importance in 1968 was the recognition of the International Year of Human Rights. Generally speaking, the history of United Nations dealing with human rights has moved through five stages: quest for human rights, 1947–1954; promotion of human rights ideals, 1955–1966; non-aligned nation's initiatives and standard-setting, 1967–1979; nation-specific activities, 1980–1986; institutional adjustments, 1986–present.[6]

Christian witness has often been present throughout the formal U.N. processes. For instance, in the preparation of the Universal Declaration on Human Rights, leading Christian thinkers had direct input in the text formation. Malik, a Lebanese Orthodox believer, had definite religious convictions about the need to protect human rights. What constituted the humanity of man more than anything else, he believed, was an inward freedom that was absolutely inviolable. He had an appreciation for human sinfulness, thus there was an ongoing need for statutes and declarations. But, he believed that "in this life we can have a foretaste of what it means to live in the spirit . . . a life of the just in the koinonia of the church, the humble life of faith working through love." He further held that "the Holy Spirit was working through the Church of Jesus Christ, in whom all fullness dwells." His excitement in 1947 and later was often expressed in presentations to various Christian groups: "Responsible political humanity is now for the first time addressing mankind through the United Nations and saying, 'These are your rights to which you are entitled by nature—rise and claim them!' "[7]

Three other Christian leaders had important influence in the drafting of the Universal Declaration. First was Monsignor Angelo Giuseppi Roncalli, later to be Pope John XXIII, who was present in the deliberations as papal nuncio in Paris. He was a close advisor to Rene Cassin. Second was O. Frederick Nolde, a Lutheran professor from Philadelphia who represented the Federal Council of Churches in the United States and enjoyed access to Secretary of State Edward Stettinius and Judge Joseph M. Proskauer, the representative of the American Jewish Committee. Nolde also published an article, "Possible Functions of the Commission on Human Rights" in *The Annals of the American Academy of Political and Social Science* in January 1946 that publicly laid out an agenda for the proposed United Nations division. While an ardent Christian witness, Nolde reminded the Christian community that it was not the task of the United Nations to accomplish what was essentially a matter of religious conviction.[8] Finally, Mrs. Roosevelt herself hailed the declaration as "a moral and spiritual milestone that reflected the "true spirit of Christianity."[9]

THE CHRISTIAN COMMUNITY RESPONDS FORMALLY

FORMAL CHRISTIAN RESPONSES to United Nations declarations and conventions have varied greatly. Some have quickly embraced the principles of human rights whereas others have tried to translate the ideas inherent in human rights into theological premises with biblical foundations. Still others have stoutly opposed the entire human rights project.

It was strategic that the World Council of Churches was formed following World War II amidst a background of the formation of the United Nations. As history would have it, because the nature of human rights requires the broadest possible religious community, the World Council of Churches became the leading forum for Christian responses to human rights dialogue and initiative. For those church traditions that are members of the WCC, it is the primary forum for their assertions on human rights. These include Presbyterians, Methodists, United Church of Christ/United Reformed Church, Anglicans/Episcopalians, Disciples of Christ, the Orthodox Catholics, and since 1961, official observer status for the Roman Catholic Church.[10]

As the United Nations debated and ratified its charter on human rights, the international ecumenical Christian community took up the issue of religious liberty as its initial foray into human rights advocacy. The first step was the formation of the Commission of the Churches on International Affairs (CCIA), which was organized at Cambridge, England, in 1946, otherwise referred to as the "Cambridge Conference." The CCIA had educational and advocacy functions, selecting problem areas and questions around the world upon which it might focus. It was a major catalyst in formulating the religious liberty provisions in the Universal Declaration of Human Rights in 1948. Much of the survey work that defined the requirements of religious liberty was conducted by the CCIA. Also, the CCIA investigated possible collaboration with the Roman Catholic Church, given its particular diplomatic strategies and the overall matter of religious liberty. In preparation for the World Council of Churches assemblies at Amsterdam, New Delhi, and Evanston, Illinois, the CCIA was heavily involved in setting the agenda and staffing the areas of international affairs. Thirteen years after its formation, when the WCC adopted a sequel Statement on Religious Liberty (1961), the CCIA was a major catalyst. One of the outstanding achievements of the CCIA was the acceptance of the "right of atheists to be atheists" in response to the position of the USSR in 1964. In its pursuit of human rights violations from Spain and Italy to Vietnam and the advocacy of equal rights to propagate one's faith, the WCC underscored its commitment to human rights without discrimination.[11] The CCIA continued its work, largely focusing upon service as a source of stimulus and knowledge for various national councils, ecumenical fellowships, and

Christian groups. The most important contribution of CCIA, its development and advocacy of religious liberty declarations, was discussed previously in chapter 3.

At the conclusion of the Second World War, with hostilities impending in Europe and the Far East, the CCIA developed an agenda in the area of international pace and security. In 1949, it sponsored a symposium, "The Ideological Conflict and International Tensions Involved in It." The Symposium prompted the executive committee of the World Council of Churches to address the police action in Korea, and it emphasized the need for negotiation and conciliation. Similarly, the matter of a divided Germany was addressed in the Council's Committee on Christian Responsibility for European Co-operation. Delegates of CCIA visited both Korea and Germany to generate better understanding between the militant parties. Representations were also made to Indo-China, Egypt, Hungary, Cuba, Laos, Vietnam, Cyprus, Angola, and Mozambique. Disarmament, refugees, and dependent peoples, as well as advice on economic and social development to various bureaus of the United Nations, rounded out a very energetic program for the CCIA in its first two decades.

Further definition of and advocacy for human rights was seen on a slow and steady basis in the assemblies and consultations that occurred from 1961 to 1975. New Delhi witnessed attention upon developing nations and religious liberty, as discussed above. At Uppsala in 1968, the twentieth anniversary of the Universal Declaration of Human Rights was recognized, and delegates pressed violence in Africa and Armenian/Jewish conflicts as specific concerns of human rights. A wider perspective on human rights was opened in the passage of the statement Protection of Individuals and Groups in the Political World, also prepared by the delegates. Following Uppsala, a significant meeting within the World Council of Churches community was convened as "The Human Rights Consultation" at St. Poeltan, Austria, in October 1974. This was actually an outgrowth of the United Nations Consultation on Human Rights at Teheran in 1968. The principal outcome of the St. Poeltan meeting was to broaden permanently the concept of human rights. The "analysis" that came forward listed six well-defined areas: a fundamental right to live; the right to enjoy and preserve one's cultural identity; the right to take part in decision making within their societies; the right to hold differing opinions; a right to personal dignity; and a freedom of choice with respect to religion. Importantly, delegates from Eastern Europe in a socialist context who participated in the St. Poeltan meetings argued against a purely humanistic interpretation of rights, asserting instead that such rights belonged to God alone. The delegates produced *Human Rights and Christian Responsibility* (1974).

Over a two-decade period, the WCC has taken its human rights agenda very seriously. At Nairobi in 1975, the WCC Assembly agreed that religious liberty was inseparable from other human rights and a consensus was reached in the international Christian community on the content of human rights. Resulting from the Central Committee meeting in Jamaica in 1979, delegates further held that the primary responsibility for human rights action was to be in the regional, national, and local church organizations. Methodologically, about a dozen strategic initiatives were taken during this period under WCC auspices: workshops and training programs, dialogue encounters, assistance to victims, delegations to critical areas, government intervention, testimony in international forums, development of international standards of assessments, advocacy and prophetic roles, and sharing of resources and expertise between regions. Out of all of this work have emerged fourteen priority concerns: rights of women; rights of uprooted people; colonialism and self-determination; rights of indigenous peoples; elimination of discrimination; economic and social justice; torture and the death penalty; rights of children; impunity for crimes; ecological rights; information technology; erosion of power and the authority of the state; promotion of peace; and religious freedom.[12]

In the years 1994 to 1998 regional consultations were held that produced a series of updates and new challenges for the WCC. In general, the discussion of human rights was universalized, involving broader definitions and participation. A general international consultation, reaching back to St. Poeltan in 1974, was held at Morges, Switzerland, in June 1998 to receive these findings. It was entitled "Human Rights and the Churches: The New Challenges" and was spearheaded by CCIA. The importance of St. Poeltan was that representatives of the Third World were present and a new agenda was set. From Latin America they heard that greater attention should be given to the struggle against poverty and efforts in education and coordination needed to be increased. Meetings in Asia and the Pacific region produced a concern for racial/ethnic strife, inhumane treatment, environmental hazards, and use of military force to suppress the struggle for independence. Human rights awareness in general was not yet mature. Delegates from the Middle East listed concerns of inter-religious dialogue, lack of democratic process, and marginalized groups. European meetings developed a list of priorities that included globalization of the economies, growing ethno-nationalism, vulnerable groups, threats to religious freedom, and environmental concerns. From Africa came voices advocating concerns of health, political stability, justice, and increasing national indebtedness. Overall, religious freedom remained internationally the top priority.[13]

The Roman Catholic Church, representing the majority of Christians in the world, has made slow, but steady progress in its response to the human rights agenda. Ultimately, what the Catholic magisterium meant by the terminology, "rights of man," is that all men are endowed with a rational soul and created in the image of God and share the same nature and the same origin. All are redeemed by Christ and enjoy the same calling and divine destiny. "Their fundamental equality must, therefore, be increasingly acknowledged." This is the essence of the argument in statements like *Pacem in Terris* (1963).[14]

The beginning, then, of a theological case for human rights in the Catholic tradition, is the dignity of the individual, rooted in the *imago dei*. In Catholic tradition, the "individual" must be understood in relation to other individuals. As Aquinas put it, "The goods of creation are meant to be shared by all."[15] Although hints of a position favorable to human rights can be seen earlier, the "watershed" of human rights consideration is found in the pontificate of John XXIII (1958–1963). In 1961, for instance, he affirmed in *Mater et Magistra* that Catholic social thought was rooted in the dignity and rights of the human person. On October 11, 1962, he convened Vatican II, the first ecumenical council in almost a century, and he placed an implicit human rights concern on its table. As Richard Evans Brown has pointed out, Vatican II signaled two shifts in regard to Catholic social teaching: the juridical, hierarchical definition of church was displaced by more attention to biblical and symbolic images, and the theological context of the church came to be the kingdom of God.[16]

Catholic theologians, with the encouragement of John XXIII, began to write of "socialization," meaning the network of relationships that connect individuals. In *Pacem in Terris*, the pope spoke of natural law imprinted in human hearts that exhibits a list of human rights: right to life; a worthy standard of living; right to work; rights pertaining to moral and cultural values; freedom of worship; right to associations; immigration rights; political rights; and economic rights, including private property. He was also sensitive to women who possessed the right to adequate working conditions: "Women rightly demand both in domestic and public life the rights and duties which belong to them as human persons."[17]

At the death of John XXIII, Pope Paul VI carried forth much of the same agenda. In Vatican II sessions through 1965, far-reaching reforms took shape as Paul VI moved the church even further along the continuum of recognizing human rights. In *Gaudium et Spes* (1965), the church acknowledged global interdependence, with a new openness to several economic models. Its view of man was existential, using generic terms like "mankind" and "human family" that emphasized historical continuity. A dialogue was set in place between the church and modern society, specifically the human sciences.[18] Finally, in human rights terms, the capstone of Vatican II was laid in the Declaration on Religious Freedom, promulgated at the last WCC session in December 1965. *Dignitatis Humanae*, "On the Right of Persons and Communities to Social and Civil Freedom in Matters Religious," set forth the necessity of religious freedom to maintain relationships of peace and harmony within the whole of mankind.[19]

Paul's greater attention to social concerns and human rights continued after Vatican II concluded. In two further encyclicals, *Populorum Progressio* (1967) and *Octogesima Adveniens* (1971), Paul advocated a greater role for the congregations to address poverty and the right of justice in poorer nations. Like his predecessor, Paul moved away from dogmatic announcements of church doctrine to language of "social teachings" that reached to biblical precedents. His preferential option was definitely for the poor and his overarching concern was to assert the most basic human right of all, namely that God destined the earth with all that it contains for the use of all men and nations, in such a way that created things in fair share should accrue to all men under the leadership of justice with charity as a companion.[20] A fair assessment is that Paul VI took the United Nations very seriously in its human rights leadership.

Behind the personal lead of Polish-bred pontiff, John Paul II, the Roman Catholic community forged ahead in the last two decades of the twentieth century in its affirmation of human rights. Former theological professor Karol Wojtyla* was able to critique both Marxism and the West as he arrived at several theological positions unique to the church in the 1980s. *Redemptor Hominis*, issued in 1979, built a theological basis for understanding human rights as derived from an individual's relationship to Christ. He was critical of contemporary consumer culture and reached back to the strides made by the United Nations for its efforts conducive to the definition and establishment of man's objective and inviolable rights.[21] In his second encyclical, *Dives in Misericordia* (1980), he pointed out the connection between mercy and human dignity, based upon a reading of the parable of the Prodigal Son. In 1981, he issued *Laborum Exercens*, in which he noted the international importance of work, "a heritage shared by all." Parts of the "right to work" were just remuneration, suitable employment, organization of the labor process to respect persons, and the right to organize collectively. John Paul II highlighted the importance of solidarity with the poor in *Sollicitudo Rei Socialis* (1987). In that statement he pointed out the stagnation of developing nations and the poverty of the arms race, preferring an option of Christian charity and solidarity. Texts like Luke 16:19–31 in that encyclical allowed the hungry, the homeless, those lacking health care, and those without hope to become the "beggars lying at the gate." Unlike his 1987 pronouncement that did not use rights language, in 1991 in his encyclical, *Centesimus Annus*, John Paul II powerfully affirmed human rights in the aftermath of the fall of Marxism in Eastern Europe. He was personally concerned that free market directions should be kept in tandem with the tendency toward state intervention in the economies.

Scholars and ethicists in the church have pointed out three areas where the church has a human rights concern: non-Catholics, that is members of other faiths or unchurched persons; members of the church; and priests and other members employed by the church. Since Vatican II, the church has become less arrogant, more open to ecumenical and interfaith dialogue, cooperative in burial of non-Catholics in Catholic cemeteries, and sharing in the interests of Christian unity. Within the church, there has been greater involvement of laity, yet there is still exclusion of women from ordination. Among priests and employees, salaries and benefits have increased and senates of priests have been organized, but certain prohibitions remain such as celibacy, opposition to organization of collective bargaining, intolerance for homosexual behavior, and arbitrary assignments of personnel by bishops. It has been pointed out in The Pastoral Constitution on the Church in the Modern World, a promulgation of Vatican II, that a deeper concern for "freedom of faith" (actually terminology for Freedom of Opinion) found expression. Freedom of faith pertains to expression within a faith community against the conservative forces in the church who want the right to discipline unacceptable beliefs and behavior by separation or expulsion from the community.[22]

Formal steps have been made at varying levels in the church to address human rights issues. For instance, the Canon Law Society of America expressed their convictions about free speech and assembly, among other rights, in 1969. In the 1970s, synods issued documents defining justice in the world (1971), the Fundamental Rights and Obligations of the Faithful (1971), and a Declaration of Christian Freedoms at a symposium at Catholic University of America in 1968.

INDIVIDUAL PROTESTANT RESPONSES

JOHN CALVIN, IN his *Institutes of the Christian Religion* (1536), wrote a section on the theology of revolution, and given their position as a religious minority over the centuries, Calvinists have been sensitive to at least the need for religious freedom. For modern Christians in the Reformed or Calvinistic/Zwinglian traditions, a theological approach to human rights has begun with a recognition of the sovereignty of God over all creation: "The earth is the Lord's and all that is in it" (Ps. 24:1). Modern Reformed theologians, while much supportive of affirmations of human rights, are also cautious to recognize that no human declaration can be equated with Christian faith. Rather, declarations can be instruments of God to advance God's purposes toward the fullness of life.[23] Much progress has been made in the Reformed community in support of human rights. Beginning in 1936, the Presbyterian Church in the USA (PCUSA) explicitly noted the centrality of human rights in fourteen principles that place human rights over property rights, economic justice, children's rights, and living conditions. In 1942, the PCUSA called for the framing of an enduring peace and in 1950 for full religious freedom. In 1944, the church noted that anti-Semitism could not survive where true Christianity exists. Following World War II, the PCUSA joined the ecumenical movement in urging the United Nations to formulate an international bill of rights, protection for women and minorities, and prevention of all forms of discrimination. When the United Nations made its Declaration on Human Rights in 1948, the General Assembly stated, "The Declaration of Human Rights holds immense promise for the welfare of all mankind."[24]

Likewise, the Congregational movement placed a value on social concerns from its history in the later nineteenth and early twentieth centuries. During the twenties and the Great Depression, Congregationalists held tenaciously to pacifism, a minimum wage, unemployment insurance, and racial justice. Many were more comfortable with a modified socialism than rampant capitalism.[25] During World War II and after, much of the former energy of Congregationalism that was part of the social gospel movement was directed at realizing union with the General Convention of Christian Churches, and later negotiating a union with the Evangelical and Reformed Church. The new United Church of Christ (UCC) focused its efforts through ecumenical organizations and was active in peace and justice concerns and racial desegregation. The advancement of women's concerns and more recently the recognition of gay/lesbian rights have provided a broad agenda for discussion in the UCC. Ultimately the merger that created the United Church of Christ 1957–1961 facilitated interest in an even larger Reformed discussion of human rights. A similar union took place in Britain in 1972, creating the United Reformed Church (URC), which also contributed to international engagement.

The great branches of the Reformed family in the United States joined forces in 1970 at the international level. When the General Council of the World Alliance of Reformed Churches (WARC) met in Nairobi, Kenya, that year, they quickly turned to the issue of human rights. Among other contemporary crises, Czechoslovakia had just been invaded and on every continent there were startling violations of human rights. Representing a major Christian theological family than included North America, Britain, and Europe, the WARC authorized a study titled "The Theological Basis of Human Rights and the Liberation of Human Beings," led by the eminent theologian, Jürgen Moltmann of the University of Tübingen. Six years later, The WARC meeting in London issued the paper, "A Christian Declaration on Human Rights." That document, plus eleven other papers, was published in German and English as *A Christian Declaration on Human Rights: Theological Studies of the World Alliance of Reformed* Churches, edited by Allen O. Miller. Twenty-one theologians from six continents participated. The Moltmann-inspired "Declaration" put forward several important principles: the basis of fundamental human rights is God's right to the human being; emphasis needs to be placed upon a holistic and interdependent understanding of human rights; a Christian understanding of human rights necessarily involves the free grace of God and the idea of rec-onciliation.[26]

Like their Reformed brethren, Lutherans worldwide began to take seriously the challenges of human rights in the wake of the Universal Declaration. In 1947, for instance, the delegates to the First General Assembly of the Lutheran World Federation (LWF) looked approvingly at the international awareness of human rights. Meeting in the Lutheran city of Uppsala, Sweden, Lutheran delegates urged a statement at the Fourth Assembly of the World Council of Churches in 1968 that pre-supposed the protection of human dignity and the full equality of races and nations, religions, and ideologies as a common goal of the com-munity of nations. Two years later at Evian, France, the LWF General Assembly approved a search for ways and means of studying the Uni-versal Declaration of Human Rights to the end that the member churches would apply the declaration in their respective national lives. Seven years after its meeting in Evian, the Lutheran World Federation again took up the issue of the church's response to human rights, in part because of the increase in violations of human rights on a global scale. These included unlawful imprisonment and loss of freedom; degrading and torturous treatment; and discrimination on the basis of sex, religion, and political conviction.

Lutheran scholars have categorized rights in three areas: rights to free-dom and protection; rights of equality; and rights concerning partici-pation. Lutheran theology provides a cogent set of responses. First, there is a concern for all men living under the "worldly regiment of God." Second, the right to be free is not ultimately a gift of government or society, but lies appropriately in God's justification of sinners. Men re-ceive a dignity and position over which they have no control because God has granted it through justification. Equality stems from being made in the image of God, and through Christ, this position is restored in redemption. In the church, all men are called to be brothers and sisters. Human rights to participation are derived from one's longing to be part of a greater humanity through an active life in the human environment. Baptism gives access to a fellowship that implies spiritual multiplicity: "There is neither Jew nor Greek, neither bond nor free, neither male nor female; for you are all one in Christ Jesus." (Gal. 3:28). Although the Christian's position in the community of saints cannot be transferred directly to civil society, it can provide a model, Lutherans believe. By analogy, what Christians teach about the koinonia of a congregation may apply to the area of worldly human rights. In the end, Lutheran scholars hold that worldly law is sustained by reason, and Christian experience teaches faith, hope, and love. Christians must also recognize that the Kingdom of God is believed to draw near in this world.

The 1977 consultation also reminded Christians of time-honored Lutheran positions. As Luther taught it, the church must always be reforming, self-critical. Christians must not leave government alone to manage society, because God has called Christian leaders to coresponsibility. Of high importance is the value of the Word of God in serving as a standard and sharpening the critique. Furthermore, the limitations of the church in its imperfections and failures must be recognized, that is, the factor of sinfulness. Finally, Lutherans recognize the importance of participating in the ecumenical movement where "Churches and Christians can give each other mutual support both in recognizing their own failures and limitations and also in mapping out their specific possibilities ands opportunities."[27]

In recognition of the growing complexity of human rights issues, the 1977 Lutheran Consultation agreed to give priority to the arms race, for human rights cannot be pursued except where peace is a precondition, and also to the ecological problems of pollution, technological development, energy, urbanization, and industrialization. The churches of Africa were a particular focus.

Methodist Christians, particularly in the United States and Great Britain, have taken firm stands on human rights and, as discussed earlier, this has derived from their founder, the Reverend John Wesley. They were active, for instance, in temperance and peace initiatives. Their creed became the foundation among mainline Protestants in the Federal Council of Churches of Christ in the United States. The "Books of Discipline" in the twentieth century have carried a full affirmation of social concerns and human rights. In the newly formed church of 1939, the Board of Christian Social Concern became a permanent feature of American Methodists, from which denominational position statements on various human rights issues have been made.

Since 1968, when the United Methodist Church took shape, the denomination has regularly participated in ecumenical work for human rights, as well as carried its own agenda in its General Board of Church and Society. For contemporary United Methodists, human dignity is the wellspring of all human rights. "It encompasses all gifts of talent, and grace, life and beauty, wisdom and discernment that are all endowed by God on every person. Dignity is inherent, indivisible, and inalienable in very person including the communities they found." Denying human rights, according to the 1998 statement of the bishops, is a desecration of God's commandments, "because to deny and violate human rights is to tarnish this dignity and diminish God's image in persons."[28] Methodists have a wide variety of emphases in their human rights program, including "empowerment and capacity-building" based upon the theological concept of a "beloved community," the elimination of hunger, and the eradication of poverty, which they derive from the Banquet Story in Luke 14:13. They also maintain a firm commitment to resolving conflicts through peaceful means and addressing violence and justice through "communities and alliances of hope."[29] Needless to say, with its Church Center for the United Nations in New York City, Methodists are among the most ardent supporters of the United Nations and its declarations on various forms of human rights.

Baptists consider themselves in the forefront of human rights advocacy because of their long-standing position favoring religious freedom. Their spokesmen take pride in predating many of the U.N. positions on religious liberty and human rights. Beginning with Thomas Helwys in seventeenth-century England through the campaign for separation of church and state in the eighteenth-century United States and the nineteenth-century missionary advance, mainstream Baptists have advocated total religious freedom for all persons, regardless of religious preference or an absence of one. British Baptists following the trend of religious voluntarism of the mid-nineteenth century, identified with the Liberal Party and the Liberation Society that sought disestablishment of the Church of England. Baptists in the United States have taken up the cause of religious liberty as a particular cultural responsibility to developing nations and against repressive political regimes. A high watermark of Baptists came in the issuance in 1939 of the American Baptist Bill of Rights, which captured three centuries of ideology and called for an end to totalitarian governments. The statement jointly approved by the Northern Baptist Convention, the Southern Baptist Convention, and the National Baptist Convention, declared that "Baptists condemn any compulsion in religion or constraint of the free consideration of the claims of religion. We stand for a civil state, with full liberty in religious concernments."[30] A decade later the Council of the Baptist Union of

Great Britain and Ireland approved a statement on the doctrine of the church that stressed the "Crown rights of the Redeemer" and spiritual freedom characteristic of the Baptists since the seventeenth century.[31]

Although no organization speaks for local congregations legislatively, Baptists who participate in the Baptist World Alliance (BWA) have expressed their voice on matters of religious liberty. In 1905 when the BWA was founded, one of its charter purposes was the promotion of religious liberty. At the Seventh World Congress in Copenhagen in 1947, the Commission on Religious Liberty was authorized and four resolutions were adopted that signaled a human rights agenda: international relations, race relations, the Jews, and displaced persons. That World Congress also denounced lynchings, race extermination, unfair employment practices, and denials of political rights. In 1950, the World Congress urged all nations to support the United Nations Declaration on Human Rights. It also gave its assent to the United Nations Convention on Genocide. Support, for religious liberty continued in the discussions and manifestos of the Alliance through the fifties and sixties, culminating in the Tokyo affirmations of world peace, stewardship and survival on earth, and economic justice. The Commission on Religious Liberty evolved into a Commission on Freedom, Justice, and Peace, and by the late 1980s, a Commission on Human Rights. Boldly, the Toronto Congress in 1980 declared, "Every major doctrine is related to human rights, beginning with the biblical revelation of God." The Alliance has been proactive in the last two decades with visits to areas where human rights are under attack, and various pronouncements of concern for political prisoners and oppressed peoples.[32]

An often-overlooked response to the human rights statements of the past half-century came from the African American community of Christians in the United States and parallels in Africa. It is not by historical accident that the ministerial career of Martin Luther King, Jr.,* commenced in Montgomery, Alabama, in the first generation of human rights declarations. He became a visible symbol of Christian opposition to oppression of persons of color. While not involved directly in formal human rights discussions, King stressed the solidarity of the human family and the need of "self" to be fulfilled in the self of others. He further postulated theologically that the worth of an individual is in one's relatedness to God.[33] Eventually, the human rights agenda for King and others in the civil rights movement focused upon racial discrimination and later on poverty and peace/justice concerns. This took on an institutional dimension in the formation of the Southern Christian Leadership Conference (SCLC) in the southern United States, led by King and Ralph Abernathy, both Baptist ministers. In his last sermon, preached in Memphis, Tennessee, in 1968, King stressed the urgency of focusing the energies of the "human rights revolution" on "bringing the colored peoples of the world out of their long years of poverty, hurt and neglect."[34] To pinpoint the force of human rights advocacy upon desegregation in the United States was a central objective in his crusade for equal rights. While King's approach was dismissed by advocates of gradualism in the largest black Baptist denomination, the National Baptist Convention in the USA, King and Brooklyn, New York, pastor Gardner C. Taylor had brought into being a new coalition, the Progressive National Baptist Convention. This new Christian denomination articulated ecumenism and a declared civil and human rights activism that outlived the martyred King. Foundational to these advocacy channels was the emergence of black theology, a movement that has been described as "unreservedly identified with the goals of the oppressed and seeks to interpret the divine character of the struggle for liberation."[35] Insofar as its human rights concerns, thinkers in the black theology tradition have continuously spoken out in favor of racial equality, peace and justice, fair housing, and educational reforms. Among the outstanding black thinkers and activists from the 1950s to the 1980s were Albert B. Cleage, Jr., Mordecai Johnson, Joseph R. Washington, Jr., and James Cone. Several black theologians, like Deotis Roberts and Howard Thurman, have exhibited dependencies upon previous experiences in Africa and Asia, notably pursuing the thought of Mahatma Gandhi.[36]

The black theology movement in the United States in the 1960s had a direct bearing upon the antiapartheid struggle in South Africa. As far back as 1912, the African National Congress offered a colored voice of opposition to apartheid legislation and programs. In the 1920s, a Methodist minister, Zaccheus Mahabene, as president of the ANC argued that the universal acknowledgement of Christ as Lord would break down racial barriers. He and others in the African National Congress were careful to avoid making antiapartheid an antiwhite campaign, instead seeking a more substantive evangelical theological basis for human rights. In the 1960s, the equivalent of black theology in the United States came forth as the Black Consciousness Movement (BCM). Many of its younger adherents, like Allan Boesak, were imprisoned, and others were murdered or assassinated. New leadership in South Africa became enamored of black American heroes like Booker T. Washington, W.E.B. Du Bois, and Martin Luther King, Jr. With the support of the World Council of Churches "Programme to Combat Racism," worldwide attention was drawn to South African Students Organization (SASO) and the African Nation Congress's renewed efforts. Gradually, the stress upon liberation among the black theology–inspired African Initiated Churches and the parachurch prophetic organizations like Christian Institute, led to changes in leadership among the mainline denominations, such as the rise of Desmond Tutu to archbishop of Capetown and Manas Buthelezi becoming a Lutheran bishop. Strong responses in affirmation of human rights were made to the Group Areas Act (1950), the Defiance Campaign of the 1950s, and the Sharpeville Shooting (1960). A high price was paid for this advocacy, with more than five thousand protestors being killed in an attempt by police and the army to silence the liberation movement between 1985 and 1989.[37]

Closely related to the black theology movement in South Africa was the development of the "Kairos Document." After decades of church responses to apartheid that seemed timid and compromising, a collection of many black and some white pastors, theologians, and laymen from various denominational perspectives met in Johannesburg and later Soweto, to address the deepening crisis of apartheid. The crisis was created by the worsening oppression of the government and the inability of the churches to address the situation. Led by theologians like Albert Nolan, the writers critiqued "state theology" as idolatrous and obsessed with communism and law and order. The churches had emphasized justice, nonviolence and reconciliation, but had missed the important point that there could be no reconciliation without justice and no justice without reform. Instead, the Kairos signatories made it clear that God and Christians need to identify with the oppressed and a stand must be taken against tyranny. Prophetic theology reads the signs of the times, they wrote, and Christians may need to resort to civil disobedience in order to be a true moral guide in their society. The Kairos Document eventually caught the attention of theologians and activists worldwide because of its leading-edge biblical orientation. More than one hundred Evangelicals and churchmen alike adopted a covenantal relationship with those in South Africa and eventually brought to bear a powerful witness on the situation.[38]

One might also note the response of collectives of Christian communities worldwide to the United Nations declarations and conventions.[39] In Britain, for instance, in the 1970s, the Church of England joined with the British Council of Churches in identifying with oppressed peoples in Africa and Latin America. Resolutions against oil sanctions came from the Methodist Church in 1979. Among other issues the churches faced together were Polish independence, Iranian return to militant Islam, the prison tortures in Chile and martyrdoms in Uganda, and finally the Falklands War and nuclear disarmament.[40] Elsewhere in Europe, French Christians in 1978 created Action des Chretiens pour l'Abolition de la Torture, which uses prayer and advocacy to stand against brutal treatment of prisoners; in Hungary, the Evangelical Lutheran Church declared its opposition to an individualistic interpretation of the gospel in interpreting human rights; and in the former Soviet Union several groups started funds or legal aid programs to assert human rights. On the continent of Africa, new Christian churches have addressed human rights, as represented at the 1977 meeting of the Pan African Conference of Third World Theologians and the All Africa Conference of Churches, which launched a theological study of the biblical basis of human rights. Of particular interest in Africa has been the valiant struggle of South African leaders like Desmond Tutu, Allan Boesak, and Steve Biko to recognize the "dignity of all men" in the 1980s.

In 1981, the Christian Conference of Asia declared its interest in the plight of those denied human rights and held subsequent meetings to define and advocate human rights. Concern for human rights violations on a massive scale was raised in India in 1975–1977 when the government of Indira Gandhi suspended constitutional rights. A decade later, a national conference on "The Emerging Church of the Poor" was held in India. Similar gatherings have occurred in Indonesia, Sri Lanka, and Kerala, India. Examples also abound of justice and peace commissions and advocacy group formation in the Philippines, Korea, Hong Kong, and Taiwan. Leaders of the Catholic Church in Asia have been at the forefront of the human rights recognition. Perhaps no other region of the world has produced the substantive theological and theo-political interpretations of human rights that have come from Latin America. Beginning in the 1960s, Catholic groups articulated a concern for human rights that produced Episcopal conferences at Medellin, Colombia, in 1968 and Puebla, Mexico, in 1979. Brazilian bishops produced a regional Universal Declaration of Human Rights in 1973 that was followed by a major international campaign of information sharing. This had telling impact upon authoritarian governments in Chile, El Salvador, Panama, Nicaragua, and Peru, to mention major troubled nations. Martyrdoms, threats of violence against advocates, and repressions of human rights have typically followed in the wake of stances that the church has taken. Liberation theology has accompanied a drive for human rights in a region where human rights are not just a fixture of foreign policy, but "a matter of life, death, and our confessing life," to quote Methodist Bishop Mortimer Arias.[41] In total, efforts across the nations of the world within Christian communities have included assemblies, prisoner advocacy, commissions for justice and peace, educational publications in many languages, church intercession with authorities, legal assistance, public demonstrations, strikes, and monitoring of troubled situations and political processes.

Not all of the Christian responses to human rights declarations and conventions have occurred exclusively within Christian boundaries. There have been other forums of Christian reflection. One is the Jacob Blaustein Institute for the Advancement of Human Rights of the American Jewish Institute. The institute has sponsored several colloquia relevant to Christians and involving prominent Christian participants, the first of which was at McGill University in Montreal, Quebec, in 1974. The papers of this colloquium were published as *Essays on Human Rights: Contemporary Issues and Perspectives* (1978) and included a paper by Daniel Patrick Moynihan. Columbia University cooperated with the institute in 1982 in a second colloquium focused upon religion and human rights. These were published under the title, *Religion and Human Rights*. The third colloquium under the direction of Leonard Swidler and Temple University was held at Haverford College in Philadelphia, November 1985. Its publication was *Religious Liberty and Human Rights in Nations and in Religions* (1986).

Two other forums in which Christians have been active since the 1950s have been the InterAction Council and the World's Parliament of Religions. The InterAction Council was founded in 1983 by Takeo Fukuda, former prime minister of Japan. His notion was to gather heads of state to reflect on world problems and potential solutions. Initially, about thirty leaders gathered annually to work on peace and security, the global economy, and population and the environment. In 1987, the council met in Rome to engage religious leaders on the topics. On a second track, Hans Küng's book, *Global Responsibility* (1990) spawned a new interest in creating a global ethic and this took specific shape at the World's Parliament of Religions in 1993. The Declaration Toward a Global Ethic was signed by over six thousand representatives and affirmed the conviction that all men and women have a responsibility for a better world order. The 1948 Universal Declaration was specifically mentioned, and the categories of human rights, freedom, justice, peace, and the preservation of the earth were given priority.[42]

In 1995, former German chancellor Helmut Schmidt became active in the InterAction Council and sought the advice of Christian ecumenical theologian Küng in relating human values to the world's great religions. Schmidt was influenced in his awareness of religion's role by his friendship with former Egyptian president Anwar Sādāt who challenged him with the "Abrahamic ecumene," a belief in the common origins of Judaism, Islam, and Christianity as a vision for peace. Küng brought to the InterAction Council the questions of moral standards for all humanity and peace-building possibilities among the world's religions. In 1996 and 1997, drafts emerged from Council study committees of ethical standards and a religious consensus that included nonviolence, toleration, truthfulness, and partnership became the key words in agreements. Humane treatment of every human being and what is known among Christians as the "Golden Rule" were overarching theological constructs. Küng's book, *A Global Ethic for Global Politics and Economics* (1997), became a leading resource toward the preparation of The Universal Declaration of Human Responsibilities issued by the InterAction Council in September 1997.[43]

A final comment about data for the Christian community in the area of human rights: Several Christian denominations and the World Council of Churches maintain databases about violations of human rights and government/private sector work that could impinge upon human rights. Over the past four decades, they have become universally reliant upon two nonreligious organizations, Amnesty International (AI) and Human Rights Watch (HRW). Amnesty International began in 1961 as "Appeal for Amnesty" in response to incarceration for prisoners of conscience. In the 1970s, AI was expanded to monitor the entire human rights agenda. The organization, based in London, regularly reports on the state of human rights worldwide. It accepts no government funds and is accountable to an international council. Similarly, Human Rights Watch, founded in 1978 and based in New York, maintains offices on every continent. A smaller constituency, HRW identifies human rights problems and seeks dialogue with governments and exerts pressure through institutions and agencies for transformation. Oftentimes, it is the foci and strategies that are developed in AI and HRW that set the pace for Christian activism, also supplying statistical and narrative details concerning human rights.

Related to the implications of the World's Parliament of Religions is the Project on Religion and Human Rights, which convened in 1993. On the fiftieth anniversary of the original Universal Declaration of Human Rights, representatives of several religious traditions produced a draft of a "Universal Declaration of Human Rights by the World's Religions." Subsequently, the draft has been circulated for responses among representatives of the religious traditions, including Christians, and it was published in 2003. It remains to be seen how Christian thinkers at large will address its provisions.[44]

SUMMARY

THERE IS NO doubt that the United Nations' action toward the production of a Universal Declaration of Human Rights and subsequent conventions and declarations set the pace for international awareness of human rights. Equally, there is little doubt that there was important Christian influence, both historically and in the actual preparation, upon the declaration. In the next half-century, the ecumenical Christian community, followed by the Roman Catholic church, individual communions, and lastly the evangelical movement responded to this initiative. Responses varied from outright support for the U.N. declaration to further theological reflection and, among many Christians, a program of relief from oppression and identification with those whose rights have been curtailed or denied.

As noted at the beginning of this chapter, over the past fifty years some Christians have opposed the struggle for human rights. Evangelical Christians, for instance, have at least three problems with the United Nations approach to human rights. First, they are unsure that human rights are supported in the Old and New Testament scriptures. Second, God is not universally recognized as the ultimate source of human rights, and particularly there appears to some to be an unclear relationship between the work of Christ and human rights. Some groups embrace human rights in a limited fashion, for instance avowing religious liberty while not practicing toleration of diverse opinions in their own ranks. Further, some American Christians have viewed the United Nations as an inferior body to their own national interests and dismiss its declarations and oppose ratification of its conventions. Finally, there are many Christians of a confessional, liturgical, or mystical type who disavow any type of activism, preferring either an individualistic understanding of their faith or holding that a sovereign God will act justly without any interference from human facilitation.

THE FUTURE OF CHRISTIANITY AND HUMAN RIGHTS

CHRISTIAN INVOLVEMENT IN AND advocacy of human rights face some real challenges in the present era. The first is what Louis Henkin at Columbia University referred to as "disappointed expectations." In 1948, there was a widespread assumption that there would soon develop a consensus on the definition and implementation of human rights. No such consensus has yet been reached after a half century. Henkin also observed that most participants in the early history of the Universal Declaration assumed that governments would give high priority to human rights and submit to methods of scrutiny. This has not happened, even in the liberal democracies. And finally, an altruistic attitude toward the promotion, protection, and impartial implementation and adjudication of human rights was assumed. This has not been the case. If the history of the antiapartheid struggle in South Africa is any example, the international community has been very timid to address human rights issues.[1]

THE CHALLENGE OF RELIGION

RELIGION ITSELF HAS been more often a deterrent than a blessing to the human rights struggle. As James E. Wood at Baylor University has pointed out, "The very particularity of religion did not make for tolerance or the recognition of religious human rights outside of one's own religious tradition."[2] Rather, religion was the root cause of division, discord, conflicts, and bloody wars between tribes, communities, and nations. Although each of the world religions in the modern era has asserted some form of tolerance and willingness to engage in dialogue for the sake of humanity, the "finality" of all religions remains a serious stumbling block[3] to a foundation for human rights in religion in general of any particular religious tradition. Another difficulty that religion in itself raises is that of complexity. Differences between religious traditions, the theistic types and the ethical types for instance, can "thicken" the religious factor as Martin Marty at the University of Chicago has put it.[4] Religious experience, when connected to race, culture, language, or national identity, as so easily has been the case in human history, is decidedly complex.

CHALLENGES SPECIFIC TO CHRISTIANS

UNIQUE TO THE Christian community are also several factors. There is, for instance, no enduring Christian consensus about the theological foundations of human rights. A significant thrust of Christianity is its character as a revealed religion, placing greater stress upon divine enablement than human autonomy and initiative. Writers from St. Paul to Augustine in the first five centuries stressed the ultimate fulfillment of the Christian gospel in the coming Kingdom of God. This was carried forth in the Christian medieval synthesis and, to a large extent, in various streams of the Reformations. Later, Evangelicals assumed this perspective as well. According to this perspective, problems identified with human violence, deprivation, discrimination, and so forth would be ultimately resolved by God in the eschatological kingdom. The "disparity of understandings," the debate over whether human "rights" is a valid Christian issue, remains a thorny prospect.[5] Those in the larger Reformed tradition continue to argue that human rights discourse devalues the sovereignty of God and seeks to empower humans over against God. Theologians working in the Christian tradition often find themselves on the margins of their churches and thus they seek broader constituencies to work within. While the accomplishments of theologians like Küng and Moltmann have been widely recognized, their primary impact has been in dialogue with non-Christian traditions like the World's Parliament of Religions (1993) and the InterAction Council. This has sparked limited interest among Roman Catholics, mainline Protestants, or Evangelicals and finds almost no institutional identification.

A second problem somewhat unique to Christians is the increased secularization of Christian societies. Secularization has been a long, slow process that began to show real results in the last quarter of the twentieth century. A secular culture, writes A. J. Conyers at Baylor University, is one where means take precedence over ends and thus the role of religion is diminished.[6] The United States has been described in the last quarter century as "post-denominational" and largely "post-Christian." In Canada with the creation of the Canadian Charter of Rights and separation from the British political system, under former Prime Minister Pierre Elliot Trudeau, "pluralism" and "multiculturalism" became the watchwords, with Christian groups clamoring to find their place of influence in the new social context. In some dramatic transformations, Canadian churches have been silent, bruised, or unsuccessful in advocating "Christian" responses to child abuse in schools operated by the churches, abortion rights (including the assassination of medical doctors), and recognition of gay marriages. Similar trends are seen in Western Europe where establishment churches have plummeted in membership, significant portions of the populations are unattached to a church, and the influx of immigrant groups professing allegiance to other world religions is significant.

One of the results of secularization has been the increasing reluctance among many Christians to include human rights as a religious concern. In exchange for secular society's gift of religious freedom, many Christians have conceded human rights to the political sphere where civil law and treaties define and enforce "rights." John Witte at Emory University has argued that over the past four decades that there has been a noticeable "deprecation" of religious rights, which he attributes in part to agnosticism and apathy and in part to a re-prioritization of rights so that religious rights have moved to the bottom of an "honor roll of superior rights."[7] Other rights concerning poverty, imprisonment, refugees, and crimes against women have all taken notice ahead of religious rights and as well an awareness of the religious bases of rights discourse. One of the most serious results of this "deprecation" has been an exaggeration of the role of the state as a protector of rights. The U.N. community has divided rights into civil and political; social; cultural and economic; and environmental and developmental categories and disconnected the entire discussion from its historic religious foundations.

The response of the Christian community has been to attempt to recover a Christian foundation, while becoming bewildered at the array of new categories of rights. It is a very daunting task indeed to expect that any Christian community or organization will mount a cogent and persuasive case for each category of rights anytime soon.

In addition to the secularization issues, the localization of Christianity that some refer to as the "postmodern" phenomenon has not been an asset to human rights advocacy. Christian local congregations tend to focus on local and regional concerns over global matters. Support for basic human rights can be expressed in "out of the cold" programs to provide shelter for homeless persons in frigid cities of the North, meals programs for indigent and elderly persons, chaplaincy programs in prisons, and housing projects for the poor. The near bankruptcy of the U.S. National Council of Churches in 1999–2000 demonstrates graphically the lessening of interest and support for ecumenical, national, and human rights concerns. More recently, U.S. military involvement in Iraq (2003) has prompted conservative American Christians to wonder why funds are being spent to improve human rights and social needs in Iraq while the needs of the unemployed and others in the United States go unmet. Overall, the amount of funds raised for work beyond the local congregation has plummeted and numerous Christian charities are facing severe deficits.

Another problem is the politicization of human rights in general and particular. In the first decade after the Universal Declaration, there was heightened awareness of the mortal imperatives associated with human rights. In the West, there was a virtual "rights revolution" that focused in the United States on civil rights. Beyond North America beginning in the 1960s, human rights became captive to larger political alignments and antagonisms: between East and West or between capitalist and socialist nations. Ironically, the liberal Western powers have been reluctant to ratify conventions pertaining to human rights and Eastern bloc nations did just the opposite. When the United Nations community proposed establishing a high commissioner for human rights in the 1960s, the socialist states saw it as a possible intrusion into their national life and rejected the notion. To date, there is no universally accepted law or agency that enforces human rights. The theological debates and church advocacy of human rights in the Christian communities has thus become a particularistic moral voice in the shadows of internal national objectives and geopolitics.

Related to the politicization process is the universalizing tendency of human rights. In the immediate postwar discussions, the support for human rights was an outgrowth of Christian cultures. Although not exclusively Christian in their outlooks, the very writers of the Universal Declaration were largely Christian in orientation. Buttressing the political/legal/philosophical discourse about "rights" was the newly created World Council of Churches and its full embrace of human rights, notably religious liberty. Later, the Orthodox and Roman Catholic communions added their numerical and moral strength to the discussions. Again, however, in the 1960s a variety of new voices that reflected much broader religious traditions and the ideals of Marxist socialism entered the forum and universalized the meaning of human rights engagement. This was symbolized in the substitution of "belief" for "religion" in the statements on religious liberty. In a very real sense, Christian leadership in the development of human rights discourse lost important ground to a more universal ideological base for human rights.

Over the past fifty years, there has been a noticeable lack of unity among Christian bodies about any form of activism, particularly human rights. With the formation of advocacy organizations like Amnesty International and Human Rights Watch (discussed earlier), which have as their raison d'etre universal human rights, the energy that is generated in their work far overshadows what Christian organizations with multiple objectives can produce. Added to these organizations are the numerous humanitarian associations like the International Red Cross, which raises funds to meet human needs and often reports on human rights concerns. Implicitly, the Christian community has transferred human rights to that arena and out of direct responsibility and sometimes awareness of the Christian denominations. Moreover, among the more conservative wings of the Christian family, some quietly believe that human rights are promoted by Marxist writers and belong more to the political arena than to the churches. There is a significant body of Christian reactionaries in the United States who want the United States to sever ties with the United Nations, and this has dampened Christian engagement of human rights.

Many Christian writers bemoan the "strange death of liberal Protestant Christianity."[8] The historic churches of the social gospel and ecumenical type have fallen on tough times financially and human rights and social activism have been adversely affected. The poor financial investment returns experienced in the U.S. mainline denominations in the late 1990s have led to huge cuts in program funds and staff. The

American Baptists, Disciples of Christ, United Methodists, Presbyterians, and Episcopal Church exemplify this trend. Social concern has largely been relegated to local congregational and community activities rather than global ethical concerns. The National Council of Churches in the United States, which represents many of these denominations nationally, came near bankruptcy in the late 1990s, and even after reorganization has hardly recovered its previous agenda. In one member denomination, the listing of churches not wishing to be identified with ecumenical Christianity has increased over the past decade.[9] Similarly the Canadian Council of Churches faced severe cutbacks and reduction of denominational support in the 1990s that has been eclipsed by the Evangelical Fellowship of Canada.

Clearly the leading loci of human rights thinking and advocacy adjacent to or within the Christian community are in North America, Europe, and Latin America. As discussed previously in chapter 1, these regions represent differing emphases, ranging from individualism to collectivism to oppressed peoples, respectively. In North America, human rights is directly related to American and Canadian foreign policies. In Europe, there is a growing Eurocentrism that is highly focused upon Eastern Europe and Russia and its satellite nations, with some reference to Africa and its former colonial ties. The Latin American situation has settled down considerably from the ferment of the 1960s through the 1980s. Large amounts of Protestant and particularly Pentecostal influences are seen in the Christian communities of Brazil, Argentina, Bolivia, Chile, and in the Central American republics of Nicaragua and El Salvador. The needs of these historically Christian cultures differ widely, and those concerned for the definition and protection of human rights represent a wide spectrum of Christian opinion. The Roman Catholic Church is addressing many of the circumstances in more sympathetic ways than in the pre-Vatican II era. There is still concern within the Latin American community for human rights abuses that reflect historic antagonisms between Catholics and Protestants ("Evangelicals").

THE SHIFTING GEOPOLITICS OF CHRISTIANITY AND HUMAN RIGHTS

ANOTHER REALITY AMONG Christians is that the growing edge of Christian culture worldwide has either been surpassed by geopolitical circumstances or is still in a missionary or minority stage. In China, for instance, the influence of Christianity came to a virtual standstill in 1949–1953 as Maoist revolutionary forces assumed control of the country. Christian institutions were closed, property confiscated, and indigenous as well as foreign Christians often brutally treated. Any advocacy for human rights within China was silenced, if it had ever been strong. In the years since more openness to the West has occurred, Chinese Christian churches have reemerged, and cooperative Christian endeavors have developed, such as the Amity Foundation. They are all under a carefully controlled government policy known as the "Three Self Movement," itself promotive of a "post-Christian era." Human rights abuses in China have become a concern in the West, where Christians rely upon government leaders to negotiate individual circumstances and place human rights in the larger frame of economic reference.

Similarly in Africa, where colonial powers worked hand in glove with missionary bodies like in Liberia, Sierra Leone, Zaire, or Angola in the past, great setbacks have been suffered in the influence of Christians upon the cultures. Christianity is more often than not associated with Western industrial interests and exploitative economics. Even in Eastern Europe where Christianity has been present for over two millennia, establishment and evangelical forms of Christianity frequently clash, with resulting gross violations of religious liberty and personal security. Serbia, Bulgaria, and Turkey are examples. Christian witness, without accompanying American or NATO military presence, has been relatively limited in addressing human rights concerns in concert with other religious traditions. Here, nations in the Middle East and northern Africa offer prime Muslim examples. All too often, Christian witness is perceived to place a higher priority on religious evangelization or proselytism than upon addressing human rights. Thus, Christianity becomes a competitive religious tradition, unwanted in the region.

A word about American Christian leadership in human rights advocacy is appropriate. Since World War II, concern for human rights has been a minor political platform associated with Democratic Party incumbency. While Democrat Harry Truman supported Mrs. Roosevelt in her leadership of human rights issues in the formation of the United Nations, Republican Dwight Eisenhower as president de-emphasized human rights and the U.N. agenda. The Kennedy-Johnson years were burdened by Southeast Asian concerns and the march toward universal civil rights in the United States, only to be followed by the Nixon and Ford imperialistic presidencies and again a disinclination toward the United Nations. During the seventies, the World Council of Churches came under bitter attack among American Christians. Democratic President Jimmy Carter ushered in a new era of defining American foreign policy by reference to human rights concerns, proffering an international treaty that has not yet been ratified. He was clear in his connection of human rights with his Christian experience. There was strong opposition, however, to Carter's advocacy of human rights from U.S. corporate interests. The Ronald Reagan Republican years (1980–1988) took unexpected turns toward the Western capitalist liberation of Eastern Europe, only to be followed by a petroleum-driven national interests policy under Republican George H. W. Bush and fiscally conservative Democrat William J. Clinton (1992–2000). Somewhat surprisingly, President George W. Bush, a Republican who enjoys the ardent support of conservative Christians, has offset his affirmation of American political and industrial supremacy by a commitment to helping to assuage the health crises in Africa. Thus far, however, he has steadfastly refused to press for ratification of human rights or environmental treaties in the interests of national economic and military security. His administration has an objective to privatize religious concerns, including much of the human rights agenda.

The point of the political connection of statecraft and Christian concern for human rights in the United States is that conservative Christians in America have triumphed electorally in the last two decades, taken over several religious denominational structures, operated through new para-church bodies, and redefined the political landscape to conform to their limited social agenda. This conservative resurgence has set aside or blunted the recognition of women globally, slowed efforts to transform poverty in developing nations, and used military force to exert its national interests. American church bodies have not followed through with the bold commitments of the mid-twentieth century, preferring rather to either redefine human rights into evangelical social concern or retreat from a global ethic and humanitarian ideals. Groups that have their origins in the discourse of religious liberty, the Baptists for instance, have surprisingly joined the chorus of conservative evangelicalism taking a dim view of ecumenism and human rights advocacy.

FUTURE PROSPECTS

THE BEST PROSPECTS for a meaningful engagement of human rights issues in the Christian context continues to lie in the ecumenical arena. Two realities mandate this connection. First, *humanitas* is best expressed in the fullest involvement of the entire Christian community. In a world of multiple religious traditions, plus increasing secularism, the Christian community must recover its universally human scope. The first step that the Christian community must take is toward its own unification. Organic union is not the objective, because a proper doctrine of the Spirit requires diversity. But serious cooperation is called for. Then, Christians must take seriously other world religious traditions, starting with Judaism and Islam, the so-called "Abrahamic ecumene." No one denomination has the resources, including Catholic, Protestant or Orthodox, and it is simply impractical to launch serious forays into human rights from individual confessions. The halting trend toward organic unions and greater cooperation plus the diminishing support for the World Council bode poorly for concerted action.

Another serious matter confronting the Christian community is the dichotomy between theology and ethics. This has been driven in large part by the evangelical tradition that insists upon avoiding the language of human rights per se, while developing ethical concerns with a new vocabulary. Evangelicals, confessional churches, and Christian voluntary associations should agree on the validity of human rights discourse and common responses that are authentically Christian. Here, what is likely required is a new comprehensive doctrine of the church that is both local in manifestation yet global in mission. It will have to include all those who claim "Christ as Saviour and Lord."

The most promising efforts in Christian engagement of human rights lie in the Roman Catholic and United Methodist approaches. Vatican II and its aftermath have laid a challenging prospect for human rights in at least two ways. First, Catholics are encouraged to attend to non-Christians and engage in ecumenical dialogue. They, like other Christians, have determined that "the increasing presence of multiple faiths in secular societies makes religious isolation impossible and interfaith encounters inevitable."[10] It is simply unacceptable for Christians not to take into account non-Christians. Second, Catholic theologians continue to develop clear, biblical bases for understanding human rights. Their strongest footing is found in the *imago dei* and *humanitas* dogmas.

The church has been able to avoid what Martin Marty has called the "highly non-committal, low conviction, 'tolerant' forms of faith."[11] The sheer numbers of Catholics and the global spread of the church make its statements on human rights exceedingly important to the Christian community.

Of all the Protestant communions, the United Methodists, based in the United States, have the broadest and most energetic program for addressing human rights. At their base, Methodists have affirmed the work of the United Nations. They are the only denomination to have a major "church center" in New York at the United Nations. Their theological basis, derived from founder John Wesley, is published in their 2000 *Book of Discipline* as part of the "Social Principles." These state in part, "We commit ourselves as a Church to the achievement of a world community that is a fellowship of persons who honestly love one another. We pledge ourselves to seek the meaning of the gospel in all issues that divide people and threaten the growth of world community."[12] The implementation of this ideal involves work in the United States through the General Board of Church and Society, which has programs for most major regions around the world and many emerging and flashpoint issues. The regional foci provide a kind of monitor for problems and needs, whereas issues like peace with justice, poverty, international criminal court, disarmament, labor and the workforce, humanitarian aid, HIV/AIDS, indigenous peoples, refugees, development, terrorism, and the environment specify action. Closely tied to the United Nations, the church promotes United Nations Sunday each year and responds directly to the U.N. Security Council's agenda. From time to time position statements are issued under the authority of the bishops and formal letters are sent to various heads of state about the church's concerns. In 2003, for example, a letter was sent to the U.S. secretary of state citing human rights violations and a churchwide resolution was passed on "Globalization and Its Impact on Human Dignity and Human Rights." Carrying forth with its heritage of domestic social concerns that often mirror human rights issues, the Methodist Church in the United States has formally listed twenty-one issues on its agenda, including children, women, racial justice, immigration, housing, hate crimes, disabilities, population, and genetics. Debt relief and poverty were major foci in 2003, relating to international political and economic summits.

The Roman Catholic and United Methodist cases display exemplary Christian responses to contemporary human rights agenda. They represent, however, a small contribution of a religious tradition that has from its inception been aware of the needs of humanity. Incarnational theology lies at the heart of Christianity. Members of this very diverse religious tradition hopefully will once again sense the urgency of global needs and lay aside their internal differences to address in unity what commenced in religious discourse concerning human rights.

As a contemporary Christian statesman has observed, the Christian faith is driven toward an ultimate victory of goodness, truth, compassion, and love, against their ghastly counterparts.[13] The struggle for justice, peace and equity—basic human rights—is inherent in what it means to be Christian.

Part II
Human Rights
Resources in the
Christian Tradition

Sources Illustrative of Human Rights in the Christian Tradition

Public Recognition of Christianity

Roman Emperor Constantine's biographers recount the story of his religious conversion to Christianity through a dream on the eve of a major battle. His success prompted him to reverse the persecution policy of the empire against the Christians. Rather than recognizing Christianity as the state religion, he and his co-emperor, Licinius, gave official toleration to Christians and others. The Edict of Milan was the first declaration for religious toleration in the history of Christianity.

The Edict of Milan

When I, Constantine Augustus, as well as I, Licinius Augustus, fortunately met near Mediolanurn (Milan), and were considering everything that pertained to the public welfare and security, we thought, among other things which we saw would be for the good of many, those regulations pertaining to the reverence of the Divinity ought certainly to be made first, so that we might grant to the Christians and others full authority to observe that religion which each preferred; whence any divinity whatsoever in the seat of the heavens may be propitious and kindly disposed to us and all who are placed under our rule. And thus by this wholesome counsel and most upright provision we thought to arrange that no one whatsoever should be denied the opportunity to give his heart to the observance of the Christian religion, of that religion which he should think best for himself, so that the Supreme Deity (to whose worship we freely yield our hearts) may show in all things His usual favor and benevolence. Therefore your worship should know that it has pleased us to remove all conditions whatsoever, which were in the rescripts formerly given to you officially, concerning the Christians and now any one who wishes to observe Christian religion may do so freely and openly, without molestation. We thought it fit to commend these things most fully to your care that you may know that we have given to those Christians free and unrestricted opportunity of religious worship. When you see that this has been granted to them by us, your Worship will know that we have also conceded to other religions the right of open and free observance of their worship for the sake of peace of our times, that each one may have the free opportunity to worship as he pleases; this regulation is made that we may not seem to detract from any dignity or any religion. Moreover, in the case of the Christians especially we esteemed it best to order that if it happens anyone heretofore has bought from our treasury from anyone whatsoever, those places where they were previously accustomed to assemble, concerning which a certain decree had been made and a letter sent to you officially, the same shall be restored to Christians without payment or any claim of recompense and without any kind of fraud or deception. Those moreover, who have obtained the same by gift, are likewise to return them at once to the Christians. Besides, both those who have purchased and those who have secured them by gift, are to appeal to the vicar if they seek any recompense from our bounty, that they may be cared for through our clemency. All this property ought to be delivered at once to the community of the Christians through your intercession, and without delay. And since these Christians are known to have possessed not only those places in which they were accustomed to assemble, but also other property, namely the churches, belonging to them as a corporation and not as individuals, all these things which we have included under the above law, you will order to be restored, without any hesitation or controversy at all, to these Christians, that is to say to the corporations and their conventicles: providing of course, that the above arrangements be followed so that those who return the same without payment, as we have said, may be for an indemnity from our bounty. In all these circumstances you ought to tender your most efficacious intervention to the community of the Christians, that our command may be carried into effect as quickly as possible, whereby, moreover, through our clemency, public order may be secured. Let this be done so that, as we have said above, Divine favor towards us, which, under the most important circumstances we have already experienced may, for all time, preserve and prosper our successes together with the good of the state. Moreover in order that the statement of this decree of our good will may come to the notice of all, this rescript, published by your decree, shall be announced everywhere and brought to the knowledge of all, so that the decree of this, our benevolence, cannot be concealed.

SOURCE: Lactantius, *De Mort. Pers.*, Chapter 48, ed. O. F. Fritzshe, in *Translations and Reprints from the Original Sources of European History* (Philadelphia: University of Pennsylvania Press, 1897), 28–30.

THE CALLING OF A CRUSADE

POPE URBAN II assembled a collection of French nobility at Clermont and proclaimed a holy crusade to recover the holy places of Christendom from the Muslims. He also expressed concern for the plight of the Eastern Church. The result was an outpouring of support, men, and arms for the First Crusade. The pope promised a plenary indulgence and laid restrictions on clergy and married men.

DEUS VOLT!

Bishop Urban, servant of the servants of God, to all the faithful waiting in Flanders, both rulers and subjects: greetings, grace, and apostolic blessing. We know you have already heard from the testimony of many that the frenzy of the barbarians has devastated the churches of God in the east, and has even, shame to say, seized into slavery the holy city of Christ, Jerusalem. Grieving in pious contemplation of this disaster, we visited France and strongly urged the princes and people of that land to work for the liberation of the Eastern Church.

At the Council of Auvergne, we enjoined on them this undertaking for the remission of all their sins, and appointed our dear Adhemar, bishop of LePuy, as leader of the journey on our behalf, so that whoever should set out on such a journey should obey his orders as if they were our own. If God calls any of you to this task, know that the bishop will set out, with the aid of God, on 15 August, the feast of the Assumption of the Blessed Virgin. . . .

We have heard that some of you desire to go to Jerusalem, because you know that this would greatly please us. Know then, that anyone who sets out on that journey, not out of lust for worldly advantage but only for the salvation of his soul and for the liberation of the Church, is remitted in entirety all penance for his sins, if he has made a true and perfect act of confession. This is because he has dedicated his person and his wealth to the love of God and his neighbor.

But we will not allow priests and monks to go there without the permission of their bishop or abbot. Furthermore, bishops should ensure that parishioners are not left without priests. Attention must be paid also to young married men, to make certain that they do not rashly undertake such a journey without the agreement of their wives. May Almighty God strengthen you in his love and fear and bring you free from all sins and errors to the contemplation of perfect charity and true piety. . . .

A real commotion arose through all the regions of France, so that if anyone earnestly wished to flow God with pure heart and mind, and wanted to bear the cross faithfully after him, he would hasten to take the road to the Holy Sepulchre. For Pope Urban II began to deliver eloquent sermons and to preach, saying that if anyone wished to save his soul, he should not hesitate to undertake with humble spirit the way of the Lord, and if he did not have a great deal of money, divine mercy would provide for him. For the lord pope said, "Brothers, you must suffer many things in the name of Christ, wretchedness, poverty, nakedness, persecution, need, sickness, hunger, thirst and other things of this kind, just as the Lord says to his disciples: "You must suffer many things in my name."

When news of this sermon had spread throughout all the regions of France, the French, hearing such words, straightaway began to sew crosses over their right shoulders, saying that they would all as one follow in the footsteps of Christ, by whom they had been redeemed from the power of hell. And they left their homes straightaway.

The great warrior Bohemund of Taranto, who was besieging Amalfi, hearing that an immense army of French Christians was on its way to the Lord's Sepulchre began to inquire carefully as to what weapons this army was carrying, what sign they bore on Christ's journey, and what battle-cry they called out in the fight.

He was told respectively: 'They carry weapons suited for war, they bear the cross of Christ on their right shoulder or between the shoulders; and with one voice they cry out the words" God wills it, God wills it, God wills it!"

Source: Rosalind M. T. Hill, trans. and ed., *Gesta Francorum et aliorum Hierosolymitanorum* (London: T. Nelson, 1962).

Martin Luther's Attitude Toward the Jews

Martin Luther, long celebrated as the heroic figure of the Age of Reform, exhibited deeply negative attitudes about certain ethnic groups. In later life, he wrote tracts that conveyed anti-Semitism. His prose would haunt his memory, for under the Nazi regime in the 1930s many of his violent recommendations were carried out.

The Jews and Their Lies

If they were not so stone-blind, their own vile external life would indeed convince them of the true nature of their penitence. For it abounds with witchcraft, conjuring signs, figures, and the tetragrammaton of the name, that is, with idolatry, envy, and conceit. Moreover, they are nothing but thieves, and robbers who daily eat no morsel and wear no thread of clothing which they have not stolen, and pilfered by means of their accursed usury. Thus they live from day to day, together with wife and child, by theft and robbery, as arch-thieves and robbers, in the most impenitent security. For a usurer is an arch thief and a robber who should rightly be hanged on the gallows seven times higher than other thieves. . . . Now behold what a fine, thick fat lie they pronounce when they say that they are held captive by us. Jerusalem was destroyed over fourteen hundred years ago, and at that time we Christians were harassed and persecuted by the Jews throughout the world for about three hundred years, as we said earlier. We might well complain that during that time they held us Christians captive and killed us, which is the plain truth. Furthermore, we do not know to the present day which devil brought them into our country. We surely did not bring them from Jerusalem. . . .

In addition, no one is holding them here now. The country and the roads are open for them to proceed to their land whenever they wish. If they did so, we would be glad to present gifts to them on the occasion; it would be good riddance. For they are a heavy burden, a plague, a pestilence, a sheer misfortune for our country. . . .

What shall we Christians do with this rejected and condemned people, the Jews? Since they live among us, we dare not tolerate their conduct, now that we are aware of their lying and reviling and blaspheming. If we do, we become sharers in their lies, cursing, and blasphemy. Thus we cannot extinguish the unquenchable fire of divine wrath, of which the prophets speak, nor can we convert the Jews. With prayer and the fear of God we must practice a sharp mercy to see whether we might save at least a few from the glowing flames. We dare not avenge ourselves. Vengeance a thousand times worse than we could wish them already has them by the throat. I give you my sincere advice:

First, to set fire to their synagogues or schools and to bury and cover with dirt whatever will not burn, so that no man will ever again see a cinder of them. This is to be done in honor of our Lord and of Christendom, so that God might see we are Christians, and do not condone or knowingly tolerate such public lying, cursing, and blaspheming of his Son and of his Christians. . . .[1]

Second, I advise that their houses also be razed and destroyed. For they pursue in them the same aims as in their synagogues. Instead they might be lodged under a roof or in a barn, like the gypsies. This will bring home to them the fact that they are not masters in our country, as they boast, but that they are living in exile and captivity, as they incessantly wail and lament about us before God.

Third, I advise that all their prayer books and Talmudic writings, in which such idolatry, lies, cursing, and blasphemy are taught, be taken from them.

Fourth, I advise that their rabbis be forbidden to teach henceforth on pain of loss of life and limb. For they have justly forfeited the right to such an office by holding the poor Jews captive with the sayings of Moses. . . .

Fifth, I advise that safe-conduct on the highways be abolished completely for the Jews. For they have no business in the countryside, since they are not lords, officials, tradesmen, or the like. Let them stay at home. . . .

Sixth, I advise that usury be prohibited to them, and that all cash and treasure of silver and gold be taken from them and put aside for safe-keeping. The reason for such a measure is that, as said above, they have no other means of earning a livelihood than usury, and by it they have stolen and robbed from us all they possess. Such money should be used in no other way than the following: Whenever a Jew is sincerely converted, he should be handed one hundred, two hundred, or three hundred florins, as personal circumstances may suggest. With this he could set himself up in some occupation for the support of his poor wife and children, and the maintenance of the old or feeble. For such evil gains are cursed if they are not put to use with God's blessing in a good and worthy cause.

Seventh, I recommend putting a flail, an ax, a hoe, a spade, a distaff, or a spindle into the hands of young strong Jews and Jewesses and letting them earn their bread in the sweat of their brow, as was imposed on the children of Adam (Gen. 3:19). For it is not fitting that they should let us accused Goyim toil in the sweat of our faces while they, the holy people, idle away their time behind the stove, feasting and farting, and on top of all that, boasting blasphemously of their lordship over the Christians by means of our sweat. No, one should toss out these lazy rogues by the seat of their pants.

And you, my dear gentlemen and friends who are pastors and preachers, I wish to remind you very faithfully of your official duty, so that you too may warn your parishioners concerning their eternal harm, as you know how to do—namely, that they be on their guard against the Jews and avoid them as far as possible. They should not curse them or harm their persons, however. For the Jews have cursed and harmed themselves more than enough by cursing the Man Jesus of Nazareth, Mary's son, which they unfortunately have been doing for over fourteen hundred years. Let the government deal with them in this respect, as I have suggested. But whether the government acts or not, let everyone at least be guided by his own conscience and form for himself a definition or image of a Jew.

May Christ, our dear Lord, convert them mercifully and preserve us steadfastly and immovably in the knowledge of him, which is eternal life.

Source: Martin Luther, *On The Jews and Their Lies*, (1543), trans. Martin H. Bertram, in *Luther's Works*, Vol. 47, ed. Franklin Sherman (Philadelphia: Fortress Press, 1971), 242; 268–272.

RELIGIOUS TOLERATION AND HERETICS

BALTHASAR HUBMAIER BEGAN his career within the Catholic tradition as a theologian at the University of Ingolstadt and later in Regensburg as a priest. He moved to Anabaptist ideas, including believer's baptism and religious liberty. Highly persecuted, he was executed for his beliefs. His treatise on the punishment of heresy is one of the most far-reaching of the Age of Reform.

THE TREATMENT OF HERETICS

Article 1

Heretics are those who wantonly resist the Holy Scripture. The first of them was the devil, who spoke to Eve: "By no means will you die." (Gen. 3:4) Together with his followers.

Article 2

Likewise are those persons heretics who blind the Scripture, and who exposit it otherwise than the Holy Spirit demands, such as [interpreting] "a wife" as a prebend, "pasturing" as ruling, "a stone" as the rock, "church" as Rome, who proclaim this everywhere and force us to believe such nonsense.

Article 3

Those who are such should be overcome with holy instruction, not contentiously but gently, even though the Holy Scripture also includes wrath.

Article 4

But the wrath of Scripture is truly a spiritual flame and a loving zeal, which burns only with the Word of God.

Article 5

Should they not yield to words of authority or gospel reasons, then avoid them and let them go on to rant and rage (Titus 3:10) so that those who are filthy may become yet more filthy. (Rev. 22:11)

Article 6

The law which condemns heretics to [execution by] fire is based upon Zion in blood and Jerusalem in wickedness.

Article 7

Therefore they are taken away with sighs, so that the righteousness of God (for whose judgment they are held) will either convert them or harden them, so that the blind will [continue to] lead the blind [Matt. 15:14] and always both the seducers and the seduced descend further into iniquity.

Article 8

That is just what Christ intended when he said, "Let both grow up together until the harvest, lest in gathering the tares you tear up the wheat together with it." [Matt. 13:29f.] "There must be divisions so that the trustworthy among you may be manifest." (1 Cor. 11:19)

Article 9

Who, even though they resist, are not to be destroyed until Christ will say to the reapers; "Gather the tares first and bind them in bundles to be burned." (Matt. 13:30)

Article 10

The result of these words will not be negligence but a struggle as we combat without interruption, not against human beings, but against their godless teachings.

Article 11

Negligent bishops are to blame that there are divisions. "For while people were sleeping, the enemies came." (Matt. 13:25)

Article 12

Again: "Blessed [is] the man who stands watch before the bridal chamber" (Prov. 8:34), and neither sleeps "nor sits in the seat of mockers." (Psalm 1:1)

Article 13

It follows now that the inquisitors are the greatest heretics of all, because counter to the teaching and example of Jesus they condemn heretics to fire; and before it is time they pull up the wheat together with the tares.

Article 14

For Christ did not come to slaughter, kill, burn, but so that those who live should live yet more abundantly. (John 10:10)

Article 15

Yea, we should pray and hope for repentance as long as a person lives in this misery.

Article 16

But a Turk or a heretic cannot be overcome by our doing, neither by sword nor by fire, but alone with patience and supplication, whereby we patiently await divine judgment.

Article 17

If we act otherwise God will consider our sword as chaff and our fire mockery. (Job 41:19)

Article 18

The entire Dominican order (to which our black and white bird Anthonius belongs) has fallen away from gospel teaching even more miserably in that it is thus far only from that order that the heretical inquisitors have come.

Article 19

If they knew of whose spirit they are, they would not so shamelessly distort the Word of God or so often shout: "Into the fire! Into the fire!" (Luke 9:54)

Article 20

Nor is it an excuse for them (as they babble) that they turn the godless over to the secular authority, for whoever in this way turns someone over is even more guilty of sin. (John 19:11)

Article 21

Every Christian has a sword [to use] against the godless, namely the [sword of the] Word of God (Eph. 6:17f), but not a sword against the evildoers.

Article 22

It is fitting that secular authority puts to death the wicked (Rom. 13: 4) who cause bodily harm to the defenseless. But the unbeliever should be harmed by no one should he not be willing to change and should he forsake the gospel.

Article 23

Christ said the same thing clearly: "Do not fear those who kill the body but are unable to kill the soul." (Matt. 10:28)

Article 24

The authorities judge the evildoers but not the godless, who can harm neither body nor should but rather are useful, so that as is known God can make good out of evil.

Article 25

For faith which flows from the wellspring of the gospel lives only in the presence of testing; the rougher the test, the greater is the faith.

Article 26

But since not everyone has been taught the gospel, bishops are not less at fault than the common people: the former in that they have not taken care to have a better shepherd, the latter in that they have not fulfilled their function.

Article 27

When one blind person leads another, they both fall into the pit together according to the righteous judgment of God. (Matt. 15:14)

Article 28

Therefore to burn heretics appears to be confessing Christ (Titus 1:16), but indeed it is to deny him and is to be more abominable than Jehoiakim, the king of Judah. (Jer. 36)

Article 29

If to burn heretics is such a great evil, how much greater will be the evil, to burn to ashes the genuine proclaimers of the Word of God, without having convinced them, without having debated the truth with them.

Article 30

The greatest deception of the people is the kind of zeal for God which is invested without Scripture in the interest of the salvation of souls, the honor of the church, love for the truth, good intentions, usages or custom, episcopal decrees, and the indications of reason, all of which have seen begged from the light of nature. Theses are lethal errors, when they are not led and directed according to Scripture.

Article 31

A person should not presume, misled by the masks of his intention, to do anything better or surer than what God said with his own mouth.

Article 32

Those who count on their own good intentions and believe that they are doing the better are like Uzzah and Peter. Jesus named the latter Satan (Matt. 16:23); the former was destroyed miserably. (2 Kings 36)

Article 33

Thus Elnathan, Delaiah, and Gemariah acted wisely when they contradicted Jehoiakim, king of Judah, as he threw Jeremiah's book into the fire. (Jer. 36:25)

Article 34

The fact that after the book was burned Baruch wrote another better one on the basis of oral dictation by Jeremiah (Jer. 36:28) is God's righteous punishment for the improper burning. Thus it shall proceed so that on those who fear the frost, a cold snow will fall. (Job 6:16)

Article 35

We do not, however, hold that it is unchristian to burn books of error and irreverence, as in the deed testified to in the Acts of the Apostles (19:19). To burn innocent paper is a trifle, but to demonstrate what is error and to prove the same with Scripture is an art.

Article 36

Now it appears to anyone, even to a blind person, that the law [which provides] for the burning of heretics is an invention of the devil. Truth is Unkillable.

SOURCE: Balthasar Hubmaier, *On Heretics and Those Who Burn Them*, in *The Writings of Balthasar Hubmaier*, trans. George Diuguid Davidson (Goshen, IN: Mennonite Historical Library, 1939), 25–35.

MENNO SIMONS ON RELIGIOUS FREEDOM

A LATER, MORE fully developed idea of religious toleration appeared in the writings of Menno Simons, a Dutch Catholic priest turned Anabaptist. Simons addressed his case to various classes of people: rulers, magistrates, the aristocracy, and common persons. He also categorized the various forms of brutal and inhumane punishment and torture that Anabaptists experienced.

APPEAL FOR TOLERATION

Take heed, ye illustrious, noble, and reverend sirs. Take heed, ye who enforce the laws in the country against whom it is that your cruel, bloody sword is sometimes sharpened and drawn. I tell you in Christ Jesus that we seek nothing but what we have urged here, as you may clearly see by many, namely, that there is not a false syllable nor deceitful word heard from our mouths or found in us. But we are forced and led by you to the sword, to fire, and to water, as poor, innocent sheep to the slaughter.

And if you should point me to the abominable actions of the corrupt sects, and say that you must therefore oppose baptism by the sword in order that such ungodly doings may be checked and hindered, then I would reply, as follows. Christian baptism is not a corrupt sect. It is the Word of God. Secondly, the holy, Christian baptism does not cause mutiny nor shameful actions, but false teachers and false prophets do, those who boast themselves to be baptized Christians and yet before God are not that. Thirdly, there is nothing under heaven at which I am more amazed and alarmed than I am at the wicked nature of the false, corrupt sects. They frighten me more than death, for I know that all men must die. Heb. 9:27. They frighten me more than the tyrannical sword, for if they take my body, then there is nothing more that they can do. Matt. 10:28. They frighten me more than Satan, for in Christ he is vanquished for me. But if the terrible doctrine of the corrupt sects is found in me, then I would verily be lost already; eternal woe would be to my poor soul. Therefore I would rather die the death (the omniscient One knows) that to eat, drink, to have fellowship or conversation which such, if I knew that they would not be helped by my conversation or admonition. For it is emphatically forbidden in the Word of Christ to keep the company of such. Matt. 7:15; I Cor. 5:11; II Thess. 3:14; Phil. 3. And by the grace of god, I do firmly confess that they are not in the house of the Lord, in the church of the living God, and in the body of Jesus Christ.

Therefore I say, if you find in me or in my teachings which is the Word of God, or among those who are taught by me or by my colleagues any thievery, murder, perjury, sedition, rebellion, or any other criminal act, as were and are found among the corrupt sects—then punish all of us. We would be deserving of punishment if this were the case. I repeat, if we are disobedient to God in regard to religious matters, we are willing to be instructed and corrected by the Word of God, for we seek diligently to do and fulfill His most holy will. Or if we are disobedient to the emperor in matters to which he is called and ordained of God, I say matters to which he is called, then we will willingly submit to such punishment as you may see fit to inflict upon us. But if we sincerely fear and seek our Lord and God, as I trust we do, and if we are obedient unto the emperor in temporal matters as we should be according to the Word of God (Matt. 22:21; Rom. 13:7; I Pet. 2:1; Titus 3:1), and if then we have to suffer and be persecuted and crucified for the sake of the truth of the Lord, then we should consider that the disciple is not above his Master nor the servant above his lord. If they have called the master of the house Beelzebub, how much more shall they call them of his household. Matt. 10:24, 25.

Yet you should know and acknowledge, O dear noble, illustrious lords, ye judges and officers of the law, that as often as you take, condemn, and put to the sword such people, that you thrust your tyrannical word into the blessed flesh of the Lord Jesus Christ, that you break the bones of His holy body, for they are flesh of His flesh and bone of His bone. Eph. 5: 30. They are His chosen, beloved brethren and sisters, who are together with Him, born from above of one Father. John 1:13. They are His dearly beloved children who are born of the seed of His holy Word. They are His spotless, holy, and pure bride whom He in His great love has wed.

Why? Because they have by the operation of their faith and led by the holy Spirit heartily committed themselves to the service of our beloved Lord Jesus Christ. They do not live any more according to their lusts but in conformity to the will of God alone as indicated in His holy, blessed Word. They would rather surrender everything which they possess and suffer envy, slander, scourging, persecution, agony, famine, thirst, nakedness, cold, heat, poverty, imprisonment, banishment, water, fire, and sword, or any other punishment than to forsake the Gospel of grace and the confession of God and be separated from the love which is in Christ Jesus. Rom 8:35. But they are averse to the vain doctrine and commandments of men. . . .

All the priests and monks, clerics and Baal-priests who seek and respect nothing but their gluttonous, greedy, and foul belly, and their avaricious, pompous flesh, these do nothing but vilify, slander, lie, and accuse. The judges and magistrates who seek to live off the bloody labor of the miserable take them and deliver them into the hands of the tyrants that they may be in good graces with the rulers, as the prophet says. Mic. 7. What the prince desires the judge declares in order that he may do him further service. The lords and keepers of the law are generally after nothing but favor and friendship of their prince to whom they are sworn—after authority and good wages, sought with great avarice. These are they who torture, banish, confiscate, and murder, as the prophet says, Her princes within her are roaring lions; her judges are evening wolves; they gnaw at the bones till the morrow. Zeph. 3:3. . . .

O beloved lords and judges of the land, observe how all the righteous, the prophets, Christ Jesus Himself, together with His holy apostles and servants have been treated from the beginning. And to this day you mistreat similarly those who in purity of heart seek the truth and life eternal. We must run the risk. If you do not fear God, and do not sheathe your murderous sword against Christ Jesus and against His holy church, then we esteem it better to fall into the hands of worldly princes and judges, than to fall into the hands of God. Dan. 6:13. I repeat, take heed, awake, and be converted, so that the innocent blood of the pious children of God which calls for vengeance in heaven may no more be found on your hands forever.

Take heed, also, ye wise and learned ones! Ye common people likewise! For such a people are they, and such is their doctrine and faith whom you daily ridicule and mock as fools, whom you slander as heretics and deceivers, whom you take and deliver and murder in your hearts as thieves, murderers, and criminals. Yet God's word shall never be broken.

SOURCE: Menno Simons, "Christian Baptism: An Explanation of Christian Baptism in Water as Derived from the Word of God," *The Complete Works of Menno Simons*, Vol. 2 (Elkhart, IN: John F. Funk and Brothers, 1871), 228.

RELIGIOUS TOLERATION IN FRANCE

AFTER DECADES OF Catholic-Protestant wars, Henry of Navarre,* a Huguenot, ascended the throne in France. Determined to bring an end to hostilities and recognize the rights of his fellow Protestants, Henry issued the Edict of Nantes in 1598. This declaration of toleration for a minority group was one of the most far-reaching steps in the history of Christianity.

THE EDICT OF NANTES

Henry, by the grace of God king of France and of Navarre, to all to whom these presents come, greeting:

Among the benefits which it has pleased God to heap upon us, the most signal and precious is his granting us the strength and ability to withstand the fearful disorders and troubles which prevailed on our advent in this kingdom. The realm was so torn by innumerable factions and sects that the most legitimate of all the parties was fewest in numbers. God has given us the strength to stand out against this storm; we have finally surmounted the waves and made our port of safety —peace for our state. For which his be the glory all in all, and ours a free recognition of his grace in making use of our instrumentality in the good work. . . . We implore and await from the Divine Goodness the same protection and favor which he has ever granted to this kingdom from the beginning. . . .

We have, by this perpetual and irrevocable edict, established and proclaimed and do establish and proclaim:

I. First, that the recollection of everything done by one party or the other between March 1585, and our accession to the crown, and during all the preceding period of troubles, remain obliterated and forgotten, as if no such things had ever happened. . . .

III. We ordain that the Catholic Apostolic and Roman religion shall be restored and reestablished in all places and localities of this our kingdom and countries subject to our sway, where the exercise of the same has been interrupted, in order that it may be peaceably and freely exercised, without any trouble or hindrance; forbidding very expressly all persons, of whatsoever estate, quality or condition, from troubling, molesting, or disturbing ecclesiastics in celebration of divine service, in the enjoyment or collection of tithes, fruits, or revenues of their benefices, and all other rights and dues belonging to them; and that all those who during the troubles have taken possession and peaceable enjoyment of such rights, liberties, and sureties as they had before they were deprived of them. . . .

VI. And in order to leave no occasion for troubles or differences between our subjects, we have permitted, and herewith permit, those of the said religion called Reformed to live and abide in all the cities ans places of this our kingdom and countries of our sway, without being annoyed, molested, or compelled to do anything in the matter of religion contrary to their consciences, . . . upon condition that they comport themselves in other respects according to that which is contained in this our present edict.

VII. It is permitted to all lords, gentlemen, and other persons making profession of the said religion called Reform, holding the right of high justice (or a certain feudal tenure), to exercise the said religion in their houses. . . .

IX. We also permit those of the said religion to make and continue the exercise of the same in all villages and places of our dominion where it was established by them and publicly enjoyed several and divers times in the year 1597, up to the end of the month of August, notwithstanding all decrees and judgments to the contrary. . . .

XIII. We very expressly forbid to all those of the said religion its exercise, either in respect to ministry, regulation, discipline, or the public instruction of children, or otherwise, in this our kingdom and lands of our dominion, otherwise than in the places permitted and granted by the present edict.

XIV. It is forbidden as well to perform any function of the said religion in our court or retinue, or in our lands and territories beyond the mountains, or in our city of Paris, or within five leagues of the said city. . . .

XVIII. We also forbid all our subjects, of whatever quality and condition, from carrying off by force or persuasion, against the will of their parents, the children of said religion, in order to cause them to be baptized or confirmed in the Catholic Apostolic and Roman Church; the same is forbidden to those of the said religion called Reformed, upon penalty of being punished with special severity. . . .

XXI. Books concerning the said religion called Reformed may not be printed and publicly sold, except in cities and places where the public exercise of the said religion is permitted.

XXII. We ordain that there shall be no difference or distinction made in respect to the said religion, in receiving subjects to be instructed in universities, colleges, and schools; and in receiving the sick and poor into hospitals, retreats, and public charities.

SOURCE: Quoted in Noel B. Gerson, *The Edict of Nantes* (New York: Grosset and Dunlap, 1969), 149–151.

THOMAS HELWYS ON RELIGIOUS LIBERTY

UNDER THE YOKE of oppression of King James I, hundreds of refugees left England for the continent. Among them was Thomas Helwys, a Baptist lawyer who settled temporarily at Amsterdam. At length, about 1612, Helwys decided to return to England where he helped to organize a Baptist congregation near London. His book, *A Short Declaration of the Mistery of Iniquity* (1612), has been called the "finest and fullest defense of total religious liberty in the English language." It would be influential for generations to come.

THE MISTERY OF INIQUITY

Hear, O King, and despise not the counsel of the poor, and let their complaints come before thee.

The king is a mortal man and not God, therefore has no power over the immortal souls of his subjects, to make laws and ordinances for them, and to set spiritual lords over them.

If the king has authority to make spiritual lords and laws, then he is an immortal God and not a mortal man.

O king, be not seduced by deceivers to sin against God whom you ought to obey, nor against your poor subjects who ought and will obey you in all things with body, life and goods, or else let their lives be taken from the earth.

God save the king. . . .

We still pray our lord the king that we may be free from suspect, for having any thoughts of provoking evil against them of the Romish religion, in regard of their profession, if they are true and faithful subjects to the king. For we do freely profess that our lord the king has no more power over their consciences than over ours, and that is none at all. For our lord the king is but an earthly king, and he has no authority as a king but in earthly causes. And if the king's people be obedient and true subjects, obeying all human laws made by the king, our lord the king can require no more. For men's religion to God is between God and themselves. The king shall not answer for it. Nether may the king be judge between God and man. Let them be heretics, Turks, Jews, or whatsoever, it appertains not to the earthly power to punish them in the least measure. This is made evident to our lord the king by the scriptures.

SOURCE: Thomas Helwys, *A Short Declaration of the Mistery of Iniquity* (London: 1612).

COLONIAL TOLERATION

GEORGE CALVERT AND his heirs, the Lords Baltimore, were close friends of Stuart monarchs James I and Charles I. George, who converted to Catholicism, applied for a colonial patent in the 1620s and was granted a site in Newfoundland that proved to be unworkable for his purposes. He requested another location and was given the region to the north of Virginia. His son, Cecil actually settled the colony, naming it in honor of Queen Henrietta Maria, a practicing Catholic. After only a short period, strife broke out in the colony between Catholic and Protestant settlers. Wisely, Calvert wrote a law of toleration, which the Maryland House of Assembly subsequently passed, that placed penalties for discrimination of various kinds according to religion. It was the first law of its kind in English North America.

MARYLAND ACT CONCERNING RELIGION
1649

Forasmuch as in a well governed and Xpian Comon Weath matters concerning Relgion and the honor of God ought in the first place to bee taken, into serious consideracôn and endeavoured to bee settled. Be it therefore ordered and enacted by the Right Hoble Cecilius Lord Baron of Baltemore absolute Lord and Proprietary of this Province with the advise and consent of this Generall Assembly. That whatsoever pson or psons within this Province and the Islands thereunto belonging shall from henceforth blaspheme God, that is Curse him, or deny our Saviour Jesus Christ to bee the sonne of God, or shall deny the holy Trinity the ffather sonne and holy Ghost, or the Godhead of any of the said Three psons of the Trinity or the Vnity of the Godhead, or shall use or utter any reproachfull Speeches, words or language concerning the said Holy Trinity, or any of the said three psons thereof, shalbe punished with death and confiscaton or forfeiture of all his or her lands and goods to the Lord Proprietary and his heires, And bee it also Enacted by the Authority and with the advise and assent aforesaid. That whatsoever pson or psons shall from henceforth use or utter any reproachfull words or Speeches concerning the blessed Virgin Mary the Mother of our Savior or the holy Apostles or Evangelists or any of them shall in such case for the first offence forfeit to the said Lord Proprietary and his heirs Lords and Proprietaries of this Province the sume of ffive pound Sterling or the value thereof to be Levyed on the goods and chattells of every such pson soe offending.

And be it also further Enacted by the same authority advise and assent that whatsoever pson or psons shall from henceforth vppon any occasion of Offence or otherwise in a reproachful manner or Way declare call or denominate any pson or psons whatsoever inhabiting residing traffiqueing trading or comerceing within this Province or within any the Ports, Harbors, Creeks or Havens to the same belonging an heritick, Scismatick, Idolator, puritan, Independent, Prespiterian, popish prest, Jesuite, Jesuited papist, Lutheran, Calvenist, Anabapist, Brownist, Antinomian, Barrowist, Roundhead, Sepatist, or any other name or terme in a reproachfull manner relating to matter of Religion shall for every such Offence forfeit and loose the some of tenne shillings sterling or the value thereof to bee levied on the goods and chattells of every such Offender and Offenders.

And whereas the inforceing of the conscience in matters of Religion hath frequently fallen out to be of dangerous Consequence in those commonwealthes where it hath been practised, And for the more quiett and peaceable governemt. of this Province, and the better to pserve mutuall Love and amity amongst the Inhabitants thereof. Be it Therefore also by the Lo: Proprietary with the advise and consent of this Assembly Ordeyned & enacted (except as in this psent Act is before Declared and sett forth) that noe person or psons whatsoever within this Province, or the Islands, Ports, Harbors, Creekes, or havens thereunto belonging professing to believe in Jesus Christ, shall from henceforth bee any waies troubled, Molested or discountenanced for or in respect of his or her religion nor in the free exercise thereof within this Province or the Islands thereunto belonging nor any way compelled to the beleife or exercise of any other Religion against his or her consent, soe as they be not unfaithfull to the Lord Proprietary, or molest or conspire against the civill Governemt. (p. 50)

SOURCE: Maryland Archives I: 244–247, cited in *The Founders' Constitution*, Vol. 5: Amendments I–XII, eds. Philip B. Kurland and Ralph Lerner (Chicago: University of Chicago Press, 1987), 49–50, selection 5.

THE RHODE ISLAND CHARTER

THE COLONY OF Rhode Island was founded in 1638/1639 by Roger Williams and religious dissidents from Massachusetts Bay Colony. Williams and his cohort, John Clarke of Newport, led the colony in a policy of religious toleration and equitable treatment of the Indian tribes. In 1663 Clarke finally obtained a permanent charter for Rhode Island that contained the first English national recognition of religious toleration. The key phraseology "enjoyment . . . of matters of religious concernments" belongs to Clarke.

RELIGIOUS TOLERATION IN RHODE ISLAND

. . . [A]nd because some of the people and inhabitants of the same colonie cannot, in their private opinions, conform to the publique exercise of religion, according to the litturgy, formes, and ceremonies of the

Church of England, or take or subscribe the oaths and articles made and established in their behalf; and for that the same, by reason of the remote distances of those places will (as we hope) bee noe breach of the unitie and uniformitie established in this nation . . . doe hereby . . . ordeyne that noe person within the sayd colonie, at any time hereafter, shall bee in any wise molested, punished, disquieted, or called in question, for any differences in opinione in matters of religion . . . but that all and everye person and persons may . . . freely and fullye have and enjoy his and theire own judgments and consciences in matters of religious concernments . . . they behaving themselves peaceably and quietly, and not using this libertie to lycentiousnesse and profanesse, nor to the civill injurye or outward disturbance of others. . . .

SOURCE: Cited in Anson Phelps Stokes, *Church and State in the United States: Historical Development and Contemporary Problems of Religious Freedom Under the Constitution*, vol. I (New York: Harper and Brothers, 1964), 205.

THE ENGLISH ACT OF TOLERATION

AFTER OVER A century of religious turmoil and reversals of the Protestant/Catholic debate, James II abdicated the throne and Parliament passed the Bill of Rights and Succession. William of Orange and Mary, the Protestant daughter of Charles II, ascended the throne. One of the first pieces of legislation Parliament sent to them was the Act of Toleration. It was a major achievement in English culture and became the foundation of similar acts of the future.

AN ACT FOR EXEMPTING THEIR MAJESTIES' PROTESTANT SUBJECTS DISSENTING FROM THE CHURCH OF ENGLAND FROM THE PENALTIES OF CERTAIN LAWS

Forasmuch as some ease to scrupulous consciences in the exercise of religion may be an effectual means to unite their Majesties' Protestant subjects in interest and affection, be it enacted . . . that neither the statute made in the three and twentieth year of the reign of the late Queen Elizabeth entitled, *An Act to retain the queen's Majesty's subjects in their due obedience* nor the statute made in the twenty-ninth year of the said queen entitled, *An act for the more speedy and due execution of certain branches of the statute* made in the three and twentieth year of the queen's Majesty's reign, viz., the aforesaid Act, nor that branch or clause of a statute made in the first year of the reign of the said queen entitled, *An Act for the uniformity of common prayer and service in the Church and administration of the sacraments*, whereby all persons having no lawful or reasonable excuse to be absent are required to resort to their parish church or chapel or some usual place where the common prayer shall be used, upon pain of punishment by the censures of the Church and also upon pain that every person so offending shall forfeit for every such offence twelve pence, nor the statute made in the third year of the reign of the late King James the First entitled, *An Act for the better discovering and repressing popish recusants*, nor that other statute made in the same year entitled, *An Act to prevent and avoid dangers which may grow by popish recusants*, nor any other law or statute of this realm made against papists or popish recusants, except the statute made in the five and twentieth year of King Charles the Second entitled, *An Act for preventing dangers which may happen from popish recusants*, and except also the statute made in the thirtieth year of the said King Charles the Second entitled, *An Act for the more effectual preserving the king's person and government by disabling papists from sitting in either House of Parliament*, shall construed to extend to any person or persons dissenting from the Church of England that shall take the oaths mentioned in a statute made this present Parliament entitled, *An Act for removing and preventing all questions and disputes concerning the assembling and sitting of this present parliament*, and shall make and subscribe the declaration mentioned in a statute made in thirtieth year of the reign of King Charles the Second entitled, *An Act to prevent papists from sitting in either House of Parliament*, which oaths and declaration the justices of peace at the general sessions of the peace to be held for the county or place where such person shall live are hereby required to tender and administer to such persons as shall offer themselves to take, make and subscribe the same, and thereof to keep a register. . . .

III. And be it further enacted . . . that all and every person and persons shall as aforesaid take the said oaths, and make and subscribe the declaration aforesaid, shall not be liable to any pains, penalties or forfeitures mentioned in an Act made in the five and thirtieth year of the reign of the late Queen Elizabeth entitled, *An Act to retain the queen's Majesty's subjects in their due obedience*, nor in an Act made in the two and twentieth year of the reign of the late King Charles the Second entitled, *An Act to prevent and suppress seditious conventicles*; nor shall any of the said persons be prosecuted in any ecclesiastical court for or by reason of the nonconforming to the Church of England.

IV. Provided always, and be it enacted . . . that if any assembly of persons dissenting from the Church of England shall be had in any place for religious worship with the doors locked, barred or bolted during any time of such meeting together, all and every person or persons that shall come to and be at such meeting shall not receive any benefit from this law, but be liable to all the pains and penalties of all the aforesaid laws recited in this Act for such their meeting, notwithstanding his taking the oaths and his making and subscribing the declaration aforesaid; provided always, that nothing herein contained shall be construed to exempt any of the persons aforesaid from paying of tithes or other parochial duties, or any other duties to the church or minister, nor from any prosecution in any ecclesiastical court or elsewhere for the same. . . .

VII. And whereas some dissenting Protestants scruple the baptizing of infants, be it enacted . . . that every person in pretended Holy Orders, or pretending to Holy Orders, or preacher or teacher, that shall subscribe the aforesaid articles of religion except before excepted, and also except part of the seven and twentieth article touching infant baptism, and shall take the said oaths and make and subscribe the declaration aforesaid in manner aforesaid, every such person shall enjoy all the privileges, benefits and advantages which any other dissenting minister as aforesaid might have or enjoy by virtue of this Act. . . .

X. And whereas there are certain other persons, dissenters from the Church of England, who scruple the taking of any oath, be it enacted . . . that every such person shall make and subscribe the aforesaid declaration and also this declaration of fidelity following, viz.,

I, A. B., do sincerely promise and solemnly declare before God and the world that I will be true and faithful to King William and Queen Mary, and I do solemnly profess and declare that I do from my heart abhor, detest and renounce as impious and heretical that damnable doctrine and position that princes excommunicated or deprived by the Pope or any authority of the see of Rome may be deposed or murthered by their subjects or any other whatsoever, and I do declare that no foreign prince, person, prelate, state or potentate hath or ought to have any power, jurisdiction, superiority, pre-eminence or authority, ecclesiastical or spiritual, within this realm.

And shall subscribe a profession of their Christian belief in these words,

I, A. B., profess faith in God the Father, and in Jesus Christ his Eternal Son, the true God, and in the Holy Spirit, one God blessed for evermore, and do acknowledge the Holy Scriptures of the Old and New Testament to be given by divine inspiration.

And every such person that shall make and subscribe the two declarations and profession aforesaid, being thereunto required, shall be exempted from all the pains and penalties of all and every the aforementioned statutes made against popish recusants or Protestant nonconformists, and also from the penalties of an Act made in the fifth year of the reign of the late Queen Elizabeth entitled, *An Act for the assurance of the queen's royal power over all estates and subjects within her dominions*, for or by reason of such persons not taking or refusing to take the oath mentioned in the said Act, and also from the penalties of an Act made in the thirteenth and fourteenth years of the reign of King Charles the Second entitled, *An Act for preventing mischiefs that may arise by certain persons called Quakers refusing to take lawful oaths*, and enjoy all other the benefits, privileges and advantages under the like limitations, provisos and conditions which any other dissenters shall or ought to enjoy by virtue of this Act. . . .

XIII. Provided always, and it is the true intent and meaning of this Act, that all the laws made and provided for the frequenting of divine service on the Lord's Day, commonly called Sunday, shall be still in force and executed against all persons that offend against the said laws, except such persons come to some congregation or assembly of religious worship allowed or permitted by this Act.

XIV. Provided always, and be it further enacted . . . that neither this Act nor any clause, article or thing herein contained shall extend or be construed to extend to give any ease, benefit or advantage to any papist or popish recusant whatsoever, or any person that shall deny in his preaching or writing the doctrine of the Blessed Trinity as it is declared in the aforesaid articles of religion. . . .

XVI. Provided always, that no congregation or assembly for religious worship shall be permitted or allowed by this Act until the place of such meeting shall be certified to the bishop of the diocese, or to the archdeacon of that archdeaconry, or to the justices of the peace at the general or quarter-sessions of the peace for the county, city or place in which such meeting shall be held, and registered in the said bishop's or archdeacon's court respectively, or recorded as the said general or quarter-sessions. . . .

SOURCE: Andrew Browning, ed., *English Historical Documents, 1660–1714* (New York: Oxford University Press, 1953), 400–403.

THE RELIEF OF QUAKERS, 1696

WITH THE PASSAGE of the Act of Toleration in 1689, it was recognized that Quakers still suffered various forms of discrimination, including a rejection of their position against oath taking. Their right to make a declaration instead of taking an oath was recognized in the Quaker Relief Act of 1696.

AN ACT THAT THE SOLEMN AFFIRMATION AND DECLARATION OF THE PEOPLE CALLED QUAKERS SHALL BE ACCEPTED INSTEAD OF AN OATH IN THE USUAL FORM

Whereas divers dissenters commonly called Quakers, refusing to take an oath in courts of justice and other places, are frequently imprisoned and their estates sequestered by process of contempt issuing out of such courts, to the ruin of themselves and families, for remedy thereof, be it enacted . . . that from and after the fourth day of May which shall be in the year of our Lord one thousand six hundred ninety-six every Quaker within this kingdom of England, dominion of Wales or town of Berwick-upon-Tweed who shall be required upon any lawful occasion to take an oath in any case where by law an oath is required shall instead of the usual form be permitted to make his or her solemn affirmation or declaration in these words following, viz.,

I, A. B., do declare in the presence of Almighty God, the witness of the truth of what I say, which said solemn affirmation or declaration shall be adjudged and taken, and is hereby enacted and declared, to be of the same force and effect to all intents and purposes in all courts of justice and other places where by law an oath is required. . . .

II. And be it further enacted . . . that if any Quaker making such solemn affirmation or declaration shall be lawfully convicted wilfully, falsely and corruptly to have affirmed or declared any matter or thing which, if the same had been in the usual form, would have amounted to wilful and corrupt perjury, every such Quaker so offending shall incur the same penalties and forfeitures as by the laws and statutes of this realm are engaged against persons convicted of willful and corrupt perjury. . . .

V. Provided, and be it enacted, that no Quaker or reputed Quaker shall by virtue of this Act be qualified or permitted to give evidence in any criminal causes, or serve on any juries, or bear any office or place of profit in the government, anything in this Act contained to the contrary in any wise notwithstanding. . . .

SOURCE: Andrew Browning, ed., *English Historical Documents, 1660–1714* (New York: Oxford University Press, 1953), 404.

QUAKERS AND EARLY AMERICAN ANTISLAVERY

ANTHONY BENEZET, A Quaker merchant from London and later Philadelphia, wrote a tract in 1748 that heavily influenced the Society of Friends with respect to the evils of slaveholding. A decade later, the Philadelphia Yearly Meeting took a strong stand against slaveholding. Later John Wesley read Benezet's work and expressed appreciation for his position.

OBSERVATIONS ON THE INSLAVING, IMPORTING AND PURCHASING OF NEGROES

It is thought that the English transport annually near Fifty Thousand of those Unhappy Creatures, and the other European Nations together about Two Hundred Thousand more. . . .

Let but any one reflect that each Individual of the number had some tender attachment which was broken by this cruel Separation; some Parent or Wife, who had not even the Opportunity of mingling tears in a parting Embrace; or perhaps some Infant whom his Labour was to feed and Vigilance protect; or let any consider what it is to lose a Child, a Husband or any dear Relation and then let them say what they must think of those who are engaged in, or encourage such a Trade. By the fore mentioned Accounts it appears, how by various perfidious and cruel Methods the unhappy Negroes are enslaved, and that mostly, by the procurement of those called Christians, and violently rent from the tenderest Ties of Nature, to toil in hard Labour, often without sufficient Supplies of Food, and under hard Taskmasters, and this mostly to uphold the Luxury or Covetousness of proud, selfish Men, without any hope of ever seeing again their native Land; or an end to their Miseries. Oh ye cruel Taskmasters! Ye hard-hearted Oppressors, will not God hear their cry? And what shall ye do, when God riseth up, and when he visiteth; what will ye answer him? Did not he that made you, make them? And did not one fashion you in the Womb?

Hitherto I have considered the Trade as inconsistent with the Gospel of Christ, as contrary to natural Justice, and the common feelings of Humanity, and productive of infinite calamities to many Thousand Families, nay to many nations and consequently offensive to God the Father of all Mankind. Yet it must be allowed, there are some well-minded Persons, into whose Hands some of the Negroes have fallen, either by inheritance, Executorship, or even some perhaps purely from Charitable Motives, who rather desire to manage wisely for their good, than to make Gain by their Labour; these I truly sympathize with, for considering the general situation of those unhappy people, they have indeed a difficult Path to tread.

I might next consider the Trade as it is destructive of the Welfare of human Society, and inconsistent with the Peace and Prosperity of a Country, as by it the number of natural Enemies must be increased, and the Place of those taken up who would be its support and security. Or I might shew from innumerable examples, how it introduces Idleness, discourages Marriage, corrupts the Youth and ruins and debauches Morals. I might likewise expose the weakness of those Arguments, which are commonly advanced in Order to vindicate the Purchasers, such as their being Slaves in their own Country, and therefore may be to us, or that they are made acquainted with Christianity in lieu of their Liberty, or that the last Purchaser will use them better than they formerly were: But not to

mention, that these are only vain pretenses, that the true motive of encouraging the Trade is selfish Avarice: to say nothing of the weakness of
the Argument: That because others do ill, we may do so too; or the
absurdity of recommending the Christian Religion by Injustice and disregard to the Rights and Liberties of Mankind, or the Encouragement
that every new Purchaser gives to a Trade altogether unjust and iniquitous. What is always said, will I hope be sufficient to prevent any consid-
erate Christian from being, in any Degree defiled with a Gain so full of
Horrors, and so palpably inconsistent with the gospel of our blessed Lord
and Saviour Jesus Christ which breaths nothing but love and Good will
to all Men of every Nation, Kindred, Tongue and People. Under the
Mosaic Law Man-stealing was the only Theft punishable by Death: It is
thus expressed in Exodus Chap. 21:16. *He that stealeth a Man and selleth
him, or if he be found in his hand he shall surely be put to death.*

SOURCE: Anthony Benezet, *Observations on the Inslaving, importing and purchasing
of Negroes; With some Advice thereon, extracted from the Epistle of the Yearly-Meeting
of the People called Quakers, held at London in the Year 1748* (Germantown: Christopher Sower, 1760), 8–11.

ADVICE FROM THE YEARLY MEETING, 1758

We fervently warn all in possession with us, that they be careful to
avoid being any Way concerned in reaping the unrighteous profit arising
from that iniquitous Practice of stealing in Negroes and other Slaves;
whereby in the original Purchase one Man selleth another, as he doth
the Beasts that perishes, without any better Pretention to a Property in
him, than that of superior Force: in direct violation of the Gospel-Rule
which reacheth every one to do as they would be done by, and to do
good unto All; being the Reverse of that covetous Disposition, which
furnishes Encouragement to those ignorant People to perpetuate their
savage Wars, in order to supply the Demands of this most unnatural Traf-
fick, whereby great Numbers of Mankind, free by Nature, are subjected
to inextricable Bondage; and which hath often been observed, to fill their
Possessors, with Haughtiness, Tyranny, Luxury and Barbarity, corrupting
the Minds, and debating the Morals of their Children, to the unspeakable
Prejudice of Religion and Virtue, and the Exclusion of that holy Spirit

of universal Love, Meekness and Charity, which is the unchangeable Nature & the Glory of true Christianity. We therefore can do no less than, with the greatest Earnestness, to impress it upon Friends everywhere, that they endeavour to keep their Hands clear of this unrighteous Gain of Oppression.

SOURCE: Extract from the *Epistle of the Yearly Meeting of the People called Quakers, held at London in the Year 1758* (London: 1758).

THE RIGHTS OF WOMEN

ON JULY 19–20, 1848, more than one hundred persons met at the Wesleyan Methodist Chapel in Seneca Falls, New York, and approved the Declaration of Sentiments and several resolutions. The language was Christian and the leaders represented a cross section of upstate New York Protestantism. Beyond the list of abuses women had suffered at the hands of men, there was a series of a dozen resolutions passed, including one that required women to seek the elective franchise. The declaration refers to inherent rights that each woman possesses from her creator.

DECLARATION OF SENTIMENTS

When, in the course of human events, it becomes necessary for one portion of the family of man to assume among the people of the earth a position different from that which they have hitherto occupied, but one to which the laws of nature and of nature's God entitle them, a decent respect to the opinions of mankind requires that they should declare the causes that impel them to such a course.

We hold these truths to be self-evident: that all men and women are created equal; that they are endowed by their Creator with certain inalienable rights; that among these are life, liberty, and the pursuit of happiness; that to secure these rights governments are instituted, deriving their just powers from the consent of the governed. Whenever any form of government becomes destructive of these ends, it is the right of those who suffer from it to refuse allegiance to it, and to insist upon the institution of a new government, laying its foundation on such principles, and organizing its powers in such form, as to them shall seem most likely to affect their safety and happiness. Prudence indeed, will dictate that governments long established should not be changed for light and transient causes; and accordingly all experience hath shown that mankind are more disposed to suffer, while evils are sufferable, than to right themselves by abolishing the forms to which they were accustomed. But when a long train of abuses and usurpations, pursuing invariably the same object evinces a design to reduce them under absolute despotism, it is their duty to throw off such government, and to provide new guards for their future security. Such has been the patient sufferance of the women under this government, and such is now the necessity which constrains them to demand the equal station to which they are entitled.

The history of mankind is a history of repeated injuries and usurpations on the part of man toward woman, having in direct object the establishment of an absolute tyranny over her. To prove this, let facts be submitted to a candid world.

He has never permitted her to exercise her inalienable right to the elective franchise.

He has compelled her to submit to laws, in the formation of which she had no voice.

He has withheld from her rights which are given to the most ignorant and degraded men—both natives and foreigners.

Having deprived her of this first right of a citizen, the elective franchise, thereby leaving her without representation in the halls of legislation, he has oppressed her on all sides.

He has made her, if married, in the eye of the law, civilly dead.

He has taken from her all right in property, even to the wages she earns.

He has made her, morally, an irresponsible being, as she can commit many crimes with impunity, provided they be done in the presence of her husband. In the covenant of marriage, she is compelled to promise obedience to her husband, he becoming, to all intents and purposes, her master—the law giving him power to deprive her of her liberty, and to administer chastisement.

He has so framed the laws of divorce, as to what shall be the proper causes, and in case of separation, to whom the guardianship of the children shall be given, as to be wholly regardless of the happiness of women—the law, in all cases, going upon a false supposition of the supremacy of man, and giving all power into his hands.

After depriving her of all rights as a married woman, if single, and the owner of property, he has taxed her to support a government which recognizes her only when her property can be made profitable to it.

He has monopolized nearly all the profitable employments, and from those she is permitted to follow, she receives but a scanty remuneration. He closes against her all the avenues to wealth and distinction which he considers most honorable to himself. As a teacher of theology, medicine, or law, she is not known.

He has denied her the facilities for obtaining a thorough education, all colleges being closed against her.

He allows her in Church, as well as State, but a subordinate position, claiming Apostolic authority for her exclusion from the ministry, and, with some exceptions, from any public participation in the affairs of the Church.

He has created a false public sentiment by giving to the world a different code of morals for men and women, by which moral delinquencies which exclude women from society, are not only tolerated, but deemed of little account in man.

He has usurped the prerogative of Jehovah himself, claiming it as his right to assign for her a sphere of action, when that belongs to her conscience and to her God.

He has endeavored, in every way that he could, to destroy her confidence in her own powers, to lessen her self-respect, and to make her willing to lead a dependent and abject life.

Now, in view of this entire disfranchisement of one-half the people of this country, their social and religious degradation—in view of the unjust laws above mentioned, and because women do feel themselves aggrieved, oppressed, and fraudulently deprived of their most sacred rights, we insist that they have immediate admission to all the rights and privileges which belong to them as citizens of the United States.

In entering upon the great work before us, we anticipate no small amount of misconception, misrepresentation, and ridicule; but we shall use every instrumentality within our power to effect our object. We shall employ agents, circulate tracts, petition the State and National legislatures, and endeavor to enlist the pulpit and the press in our behalf. We hope this Convention will be followed by a series of Conventions embracing every part of the country.

SOURCE: Elizabeth Cady Stanton, Susan B. Anthony, and Matilda Joslyn Gage, eds., *History of Woman Suffrage*, vol. 1 (New York: Fowler and Wells, 1881), 70–71.

JOHN IRELAND ON RACIAL DISCRIMINATION

EACH YEAR ON January 1, Emancipation Day was celebrated in the American black community. In 1891, against a background of the "Jim Crow era," Catholic Archbishop John Ireland of St. Paul, Minnesota, took the occasion to declare one of the most liberal positions in the history of American Catholicism on race relations.

AN AMERICAN CATHOLIC SPEAKS OUT

The Christian religion emphasized the brotherhood of man, the value of the soul, charity to the weak and the oppressed. Slavery was the denial of Christian principles and Christian virtues. It was the denial of the freedom of the Gospel, which found access to the soul of the slave, only as the master permitted or ordained. Let us on this emancipation day thank God for the blessings of Christianity. The spirit of Christian freedom is today poured out upon the nations of the earth. The mighty social wave which is now lifting upward upon its crest the masses of the people of all lands, is but another manifestation of the same heavenly spirit.

Let us do our full duty. There is work for us. I have said that slavery has been abolished in America; the trail of the serpent, however, still marks the ground. We do not accord to our black brothers all the rights and privileges of freedom and of a common humanity. They are the victims of an unreasoning and unjustifiable ostracism. They may live, provided they live away from us, as a separate and inferior race, with whom close contact is pollution. It looks as if we had grudgingly granted them emancipation, as if we fain still would be the masters, and hold them in servitude.

What do I claim for the black man? That which I claim for the white man, neither more or less. I would blot out the color line. White men have their estrangements. They separate on lines of wealth, or intelligence, of culture, of ancestry. . . . But let there be no barrier against mere color. . . .

Men are all of the same race, sprung from the one father and the one mother. Ethnology and Holy Writ give the same testimony. The subdivisions of race are but the accidental deviations from the parent stock, which revert to the same model as easily with the length of years as they diverted from it. The notion that God by special interposition marked off the subdivisions of the human family, and set upon each one an indelible seal of permanence is the dream of ignorance or bigotry. . . .

We are the victims of foolish prejudice, and the sooner we free ourselves from it, the sooner shall we grow to true manhood. Is it to our honor that we persecute men because of the social conditions of their fathers? It is not so long ago since the proudest peoples of Europe were immersed in barbarism. It is not to our honor that we punish men for the satisfaction of our own pride. Why, the fact that the Negro was once our slave should compel us to treat him liberality, to compensate him if possible for wrong done, and obliterate in mutual forebearance and favor the sad memories of years gone by.

The Negro problem is upon us, and there is no solution for it, peaceful and permanent, than to grant to our fellow citizens practical and effective equality with white citizens. It is not possible to keep up a wall of separation between whites and blacks, and the attempt to do this is a declaration of continuous war. Simple common sense dictates the solution. The Negroes are among us to the number of eight millions; they will here remain: we must accept the situation and abide by the consequences, whatever pride or taste may dictate.

I would break down all barriers. Let the Negro be our equal before the law. There are States where the violation in the Negro of the most sacred right secured impunity before the law. In many states the law forbids marriage between black and white—in this manner fomenting immorality and putting injury no less upon the white whom it pretends to elevate as upon the black for whose degradation it has no care.

Let the Negro be our equal in the enjoyment of all the political rights of the citizen. The constitution grants him those rights: let us be loyal to the Constitution. If the education of the Negro does not fit him to be a voter, and an office holder, let us for his sake and our own, hurry to enlighten him.

I would open to the Negro all industrial and professional avenues—the test for his advance being his ability, but never his color. I would in all public gatherings, and in all public resorts, in gall and hotels, treat the black man as I treat the white. I might shun the vulgar man, whatever his color, but the gentleman, whatever his color, I would not dare push away from me. . . .

I claim the right I grant to others—and my door is open to men of all colors, and no one should blame me. Social equality is a matter of taste; the granting of it largely depends on our elevation above the prejudice, and the identification of minds and hearts with the precepts and the counsels of the gospel.

SOURCE: Joseph N. Moody, ed., "Archbishop John Ireland: No Barrier Against Color," in *Church and Society: Catholic Social and Political Thought and Movements 1789–1950* (New York: Arts, Inc., 1953), 887–889.

Nazi Religious Policies and German Christians

THE INTERACTION OF National Socialism with Christianity in Germany during the period 1925–1945 is replete with abuses both of Christian ethics and Christians themselves. The inability of church leaders to successfully challenge the Nazis, at sometimes even appearing to be complicit with their aims, is a mark of the era. By 1933, a "confessing church" emerged behind the leadership of pastors like Martin Niemoeller, true to the gospel and the principles of the Reformation. In the face of overwhelming atrocities committed by the government, the church was forced eventually to confess, on behalf of the nation, the abuses to human life under the Hitler regime. The first selection asserts Hitler's policy of "religious freedom" for the Protestant and Catholic Churches. The second selection illustrates how the information-gathering strategies of the Society of Jesus were misappropriated by the Nazis. The third selection recovers a "confessing church" that organized itself as an "Emergency Alliance" against interference by the state, whereas the fourth selection is a confession of the Old Prussian Church and a public condemnation of the Final Solution.

HITLER'S POLICY OF TOLERATION, 1933

The national government regards the two Christian confessions as the most important factors for the preservation of our national culture. It will

honour the treaties concluded between them and the provincial governments. Their rights will not be infringed. It does, however, hope and trust
that the work for the national and moral renewal of our nation, which
the government has taken upon it, will for its part be given like approval.
Its attitude to all the other confessions will be that of objective justice.

The national government will guarantee the Christian confessions their
due influence in school and educational matters. It is concerned to foster
a frank and harmonious relationship between church and state. The fight
against a materialistic view of the world and for the creation of a genuine
national community is as much in the interests of the German nation as
those of our Christian faith.

Likewise the government of the Reich, which regards Christianity as
the unshakeable foundation of our national life and morality, regards the
fostering and the extension of the friendly relations to the Holy See as a
matter of the greatest importance.

The rights of the churches will not be restricted, nor will their relationship to the state be changed.

SOURCE: *Kirchliches Jahrbuch* (Gütersloh: C. Bertelsmann, 1933), 13.

THE SS AND THE JESUITS, 1937

As the fighting corps of the Vatican, the Jesuit order, with its multi-
farious contacts, the outstanding training of its members, and its brilliant
operational methods, is one of the most important instruments of the
Church's power politics.

This body of men, organized along strictly hierarchical lines, combines
the tasks of defense against opponents, positive attack on the enemy and
the gathering of information for the Vatican.

Its great successes in gathering information, which above all else maintains the regard in which the Jesuit order is held at the Vatican, are due
mainly to the fact that to the onlooker the work of gathering information
appears quite secondary to the role assigned it in the ideological struggle.
By means of the ideological struggle and the specialist knowledge of the
Society of Jesus which subserves it the Jesuits have created such a widespread net of contacts that sources of information are automatically available to them.

On the other hand their brilliant information service enables the Jesuits to know before anyone else where attacks or countermeasures are to be expected and hence they are also in the best position for a successful conduct of the Church's attacks and counter-measures.

For almost four hundred years this method of combining an information service with a troop to defend the propagate its ideology has been successfully tested by the Jesuits.

Source: Friedrich Zipfel, *Kirchenkampf in Deutschland* (Berlin: DeGruyter, 1965), 423.

LETTER OF MARTIN NIEMOELLER, 1933

On the day after the General Synod six General Superintendents were dismissed from office and retired without any sort of explanation. Since this time there has been widespread confusion, perplexity, and deep unrest among the congregations in and around Berlin. This state of affairs is aggravated by stormy goings-on in some congregations. Church organizations, for example, which do not want to lend their wholehearted support to the 'Faith Movement of German Christians' are forbidden the use of rooms in the church house on the instructions of the congregation's church council. In other instances, specific measures have been taken against individual pastors at the behest of the 'Faith Movement' in their respective congregations, the goal being 'disciplinary removal.' Characteristically, the church 'leaders' and authorities have capitulated to these endeavours, since the people now demand that the promise given in the election campaign should now be kept.

These events have given rise to a shameful faint-heartedness among many ministerial brethren; although serious-minded men, some have gone over to the 'German Christians' against their own better judgment, knowing that what they did was contrary to their ordination vow and was a violation of their consciences.

Because of this distress we have called into being an 'Emergency Alliance' of pastors who have given over one another their word in a written declaration that they will be bound in their preaching by Holy Scripture and the Reformation confessions alone (hence no bond or any other 'spiritual' authority) and that they will alleviate the distress of those brethren who have to suffer for this to the best of their ability.

Support has been solicited privately by trusted individuals; as a result the whole membership of the Young Reformers Movement has not yet been reached. At the moment about 1,300 have signed, not counting Westphalia which already had its own fraternity. Members of the Young Reformers Movement who wish to join an alliance of this nature are cordially invited to request from me the engagement to membership.

Our aim must be to have an alliance like this in every provincial church and every province; that these alliances should stand by one another (otherwise one province will be 'cleaned up' after the other); and that members of the alliance actively set about building up the Christian congregation within their sphere of influence (mobilization of the laity).

I am well aware that this alliance will neither redeem the church nor shake the world; but I am equally aware that we owe it to the Lord of the church and to the brethren to do what we can; in these days a prudent retreat to the role of a mere spectator amounts to betrayal, for those under stress have no assurance of our brotherly solidarity. So let us act!

In brotherly solidarity,

Niemoeller

SOURCE: W. Niemoeller, *Texte zur Geschicte des Pfarrernotbundes,* 23–26.

CONFESSION AND THE FINAL SOLUTION, 1943

Woe unto us and our nation, when the life which God has given is held in contempt and man, made in the image of god, is regarded in purely utilitarian terms; when the killing of men is justified on the grounds that they are unfit to live or that they belong to another race; when hate and callousness become widespread. For God says: "Thou shalt not kill."

. . .

Let us confess with shame: We Christians share the guilt for the contempt and perversion of the holy commandments. We have often kept our silence; we have pled too seldom, too timidly, or not at all, for the absolute validity of God's holy Commandments. . . .

SOURCE: "Twelfth Confessing Synod of the Old Prussian Church" October 17, 1943, in *Kirchliches Jahrbuch* (Gütersloh: C. Bertelsmann, 1943), 402, 404.

WALTER RAUSCHENBUSCH ON THE SOCIAL GOSPEL

IN THE CONCLUDING decades of the nineteenth century, Christian leaders became increasingly concerned about the problems caused by urbanization and extreme individualism fostered by a capitalist industrial system that seemed out of control. Bridging socialist ideals and modern theology, the social gospel offered a new interpretation of Christianity that responded creatively to labor concerns, the social order, military aggression, the status of women, and race discrimination. Walter Rauschenbusch was its leading prophet and spokesman.

THE KINGDOM OF GOD

The Kingdom of God is divine in its origin, progress, and consummation. It was initiated by Jesus Christ, in whom the prophetic spirit came to its consummation, it is sustained by the Holy Spirit, and it will be brought to its fulfillment by the power of God in his own time. The passive and active resistance of the kingdom of Evil at every stage of its advance is so great, and the human resources of the Kingdom of God so slender, that no explanation can satisfy a religious mind which does not see the power of God in its movements. The Kingdom of God, therefore, is miraculous all the way, and is the continuous revelation of the power, the righteousness, and the love of God. The establishment of a community of righteousness in mankind is just as much a saving act of God as the salvation of an individual from his natural selfishness and moral inability. The Kingdom of God, therefore, is not merely ethical, but has a rightful place in theology. This doctrine is absolutely necessary to establish that organic union between religion and morality, between theology and ethics, which is one of the characteristics of the Christian religion. When our moral actions are consciously related to the Kingdom of God they gain religious quality. Without this doctrine we shall have expositions of schemes of redemption and we shall have systems of ethics, but we shall not have a true exposition of Christianity. The first step to the reform of the Churches is the restoration of the doctrine of the Kingdom of God. . . .

The Kingdom of God is humanity organized according to the will of God. Interpreting it through the consciousness of Jesus we may affirm these convictions about the ethical relations within the Kingdom: a) Since Christ revealed the divine worth of life and personality, and since his salvation seeks the restoration and fulfillment of even the least, it follows that the Kingdom of God, at every stage of human development, tends toward a social order which will best guarantee to all personalities their freest and highest development. This involves the redemption of social life from the cramping influence of religious bigotry, from the repression of self-assertion in the relation of upper and lower classes, and from all forms of slavery in which human beings are treated as mere means to serve the ends of others. (b) Since love is the supreme law of Christ, the Kingdom of God implies a progressive reign of love in human affairs. We can see its advance wherever the free will law of love supercedes the use of force and lethal coercion as a regulative of the social order. This involves the redemption of society from political autocracies and economic oligarchies; the substitution of redemptive for vindictive penology; the abolition of constraint through hunger as part of the industrial system; and the abolition of war as the supreme expression of hate and the completest cessation of freedom. (c) The highest expression of love is the free surrender of what is truly our own, life property, and rights. A much lower but perhaps more decisive expression of love is the surrender of any opportunity to exploit men. No social group or organization can claim to be clearly within the Kingdom of God which drains others for its own ease, and resists the effort to abate this fundamental evil. This involves the redemption of society from private property in the natural resources of the earth, and from any condition in industry which makes monopoly profits possible. (d) The reign of love tends toward the progressive unity of mankind, but with the maintenance of individual liberty and the opportunity of nations to work out their own national peculiarities and ideals. . . .

The Kingdom of God is not confined within the limits of the Church and its activities. It embraces the whole of human life. It is the Christian transfiguration of the social order. The Church is one social institution alongside of the family, the industrial organization of society, and the state. The Kingdom of God is in all these, and realizes itself through them all. During the Middle Ages all society was ruled and guided by the Church. Few of us would want modern life to return to such a condition. Functions which the Church used to perform, have now far outgrown its capacities. The Church is indispensable to the religious education of humanity and to the conservation of religion, but the greatest future awaits religion in the public life of humanity.

SOURCE: Walter Rauschenbusch, *A Theology for the Social Gospel* (New York: Macmillan, 1917), 139; 142–145.

A METHODIST SOCIAL CREED

IN 1908, THE Methodist Episcopal Church in the United States put forth the statement "The Church and Social Problems," which was presented by the Methodist Federation for Social Service under the direction of Bishop Herbert Welch. It was later expanded in 1912 and 1968. The original statement was the result of the climate that sprang from the social gospel movement and was the inspiration for a similar statement adopted by the Federal Council of Churches of Christ in the United States.

OUR SOCIAL CREED

We believe in God, Creator of the world; and in Jesus Christ, the Redeemer of creation. We believe in the Holy Spirit, through whom we acknowledge God's gifts, and we repent of our sin in misusing these gifts to idolatrous ends.

We affirm the natural world as God's handiwork and dedicate ourselves to its preservation, enhancement, and faithful use by humankind.

We joyfully receive, for ourselves and others, the blessings of community, marriage, sexuality, and the family.

We commit ourselves to the rights of men, women, children, youth, and the aging to improvement of the quality of life; and to the rights and dignity of ethnic and religious minorities.

We believe in the right and duty of persons to work for the good of themselves and others, and in the protection of their welfare in so doing;

in the rights to property as a trust from God, collective bargaining, and responsible consumption; and in the elimination of economic and social distress.

We dedicate ourselves to peace throughout the world and to the rule of justice and law among nations.

We believe in the present and final triumph of God's Word in human affairs and gladly accept his commission to manifest the life the gospel in the world. Amen.

SOURCE: *The Book of Discipline of the United Methodist Church* (Nashville: The United Methodist Publishing House, 1972), 97.

FATHER JOHN RYAN ON WORKER'S RIGHTS

AT THE TURN of the twentieth century, the effects of industrialization were creating oppressive conditions for workers and families. Among Catholics in the United States, Monsignor John A. Ryan bridged the gap between theology and economic theory and advocated improved conditions for workers. His position on a just wage won the support of the National Catholic Workers Conference and interest among the administration of Franklin D. Roosevelt.

THE MINIMUM OF JUSTICE: A LIVING WAGE

The validity of needs as a partial rule of wage justice rests ultimately upon three fundamental principles regarding man's position in the universe. The first is that God created the earth for the sustenance of all His children; therefore, that all persons are equal in their inherent claims upon the bounty of nature. As it is impossible to demonstrate that any class of persons is less important than another in the eyes of God, it is logically impossible for any believer in Divine Providence to reject this proposition. The man who denies God or Providence can refuse assent to the second part of the proposition only by refusing to acknowledge the personal dignity of the human individual, and the equal dignity of all persons. Inasmuch as the human person is intrinsically sacred and morally independent, he is endowed with those inherent prerogatives, immunities, and claims we call rights. Every person is an end in himself; none is a mere instrument to the convenience or welfare of any other human being. The worth of a person is something intrinsic, derived from within, not determined or measurable by reference to any earthly object or purpose without. . . .

The second fundamental principle is that the inherent right of access to the earth is conditioned upon, and becomes actually valid through, the expenditure of useful labour. Generally speaking the fruits and potentialities of the earth do not become available to men without previous exertion. "In the sweat of thy brow thou shalt eat thy bread," is a physical, no less than a moral commandment. There are indeed exceptions: the very young, the infirm, and the possessors of a sufficient amount of property. The two former classes have claims to a livelihood through piety and charity, while the third group has at least a presumptive claim of justice to the money value of their goods. Nevertheless, the general condition is that men must work in order to live. "If a man will not work neither shall he eat." For those who refuse to comply with this condition the inherent right of access to the earth remains only hypothetical and suspended.

The two foregoing principles involve as a corollary a third principle; the men who are in present control of the opportunities of the earth are obliged to permit reasonable access to these opportunities by persons who are willing to work. In other words, possessors must so administer the common bounty of nature that non-owners will not find it unreasonably difficult to get a livelihood. To put it still in other terms, the right to subsist from the earth implies the right to access thereto on reasonable terms. When any man who is willing to work is denied the exercise of his right, he is no longer treated as the moral and juridical equal of his fellows. He is regarded as inherently inferior to them, as a mere instrument to their convenience; and those who exclude him are virtually taking the position that their rights to the common gifts of the Creator are inherently superior to his birthright. Obviously this position cannot be defended on grounds of reason. Possessors are no more justified in excluding a man from reasonable access to the goods of the earth than they would be in depriving him of the liberty to move from place to place. The community that should arbitrarily shut a man up in prison would not violate his rights more fundamentally than the community or the proprietors who shut him out from the opportunity of getting a livelihood from the bounty of the earth. In both cases the man demands and has a right to a common gift of God. His moral claim is as valid to the one good as to the other, and it is as valid to both goods as is the claim of any of his fellows.

Every man who is willing to work has, therefore, an inborn right to sustenance from the earth on reasonable terms or conditions, This cannot mean that all persons have a right to equal amounts of sustenance or income; for we have seen on a preceding page that men's needs, the primary title to property, are not equal, and that other canons and factors of distribution have to be allowed some weight in determining the division of goods and opportunities. Nevertheless, there is a certain minimum of goods to which every worker is entitled by reason of his inherent right of access to the earth. He has a right to at least a *decent* livelihood. That is, he has a right to so much of the requisites of sustenance as will enable him to live in a manner worthy of a human being. The elements of a decent livelihood may be summarily described as: food, clothing, and housing sufficient in quantity and quality to maintain the worker in normal health, in elementary comfort, and in an environment suitable to the protection of morality and religion; sufficient provision for the future to bring elementary contentment, and security against sickness, accident, and invalidity; and sufficient opportunities of recreation, social intercourse, education, and church membership to conserve health and strength, and to render possible in some degree the exercise of the higher faculties.

On what ground is it contended that a worker has a right to a decent livelihood, as this defined, rather than to a bare subsistence? On the ground that validates his right to life, marriage, or any of the other fundamental goods of human existence. On the dignity of personality . . .

Up to the present we have been considering the right of the labourer to a wage adequate to a decent livelihood for himself as an individual. In the case of an adult male, however, this is not sufficient for normal life, nor for the reasonable development of personality. The great majority of men cannot live well-balanced lives, cannot attain a reasonable degree of self-development outside the married state. Therefore, family life is among the essential needs of a normal and reasonable existence. It is not, indeed, so vitally necessary as the primary requisites of individual life, such as food, clothing, and shelter, but it is second only to these. Outside the family man cannot, as a rule, command that degree of contentment, moral strength, and moral safety which are necessary for reasonable and efficient living. It is unnecessary to labour this point further, as very few would assert that the average man can live a normal and complete human life without marriage.

Now, the support of the family falls properly upon the husband and father, not upon the wife and mother. The obligation of the father to provide a livelihood for the wife and young children is quite as definite as his obligation to maintain himself. If he has not the means to discharge this obligation he is not justified in getting married. Yet, as we have seen, marriage is essential to normal life for the great majority of men. Therefore, the material requisites of normal life for the average adult male, include provision for his family. In other words, his decent livelihood means a family livelihood. Consequently, he has a right to obtain such a livelihood on reasonable terms from the bounty of the earth. In the case of the wage earner, this right can be effectuated only through wages; therefore the adult male labourer has a right to a family living wage. If he does not get this measure of remuneration his personal dignity is violated, and he is deprived of access to goods of the earth, quite as certainly as when his wage is inadequate to personal maintenance. The difference between family needs and personal needs is a difference only of degree. The satisfaction of both is indispensable to his reasonable life.

Just as the woman worker who lives with her parents has a right to a wage sufficient to maintain her away from home, so the unmarried adult male has a right to a family living wage. If only married men get the latter wage they will be discriminated against in the matter of employment. To prevent this obviously undesirable condition, it is necessary that a family living wage be recognized as the right of all adult male workers. No other arrangement is reasonable in our present industrial system. . . .

SOURCE: John A. Ryan, *Distributive Justice: The Right and Wrong of Our Present Distribution of Wealth* (New York: Macmillan, 1922), 358–360; 373–375.

A PROTESTANT CONSENSUS ON RIGHTS

WITH THE FOUNDING in the United States of the Federal Council of Churches of Christ, social concerns had a permanent ecclesiastical home. Indeed, the Council became synonymous with the social gospel and social responsibilities of the churches. In 1908, the members produced a social creed, inspired by a previous Methodist statement. After two decades of reflection, a second, more definitive creed was issued. It encompasses many of the contemporary concerns and introduces the language of "rights."

THE SOCIAL CREED OF THE CHURCHES, 1932

The Churches shall stand for:

I. Practical application of the Christian principle of social well-being to the acquisition and use of wealth; subordination of speculation and the profit motive to the creative and cooperative spirit.

II. Social planning and control of the credit and monetary systems and economic processes for the common good.

III. The right of all to the opportunity for a self-maintenance; a wider and fairer distribution of wealth; a living wage, as a minimum, and above this a just share for the worker in the product of industry and agriculture.

IV. Safeguarding of all workers, urban and rural, against harmful conditions of labor and occupational injury and disease.

V. Social insurance against sickness, accident, want in old age and unemployment.

VI. Reduction of hours of labor as the general productivity of industry increases; release from employment at least one day in seven, with a shorter working week in prospect.

VII. Such special regulation of the conditions of work of women as shall safeguard their welfare and that of the family and community.

VIII. The right of employees and employers alike to organize for collective bargaining and social action; protection of both in the exercise of this right; the obligation of both to work for the public good; encouragement of cooperatives and other organization among farmers and other groups.

IX. Abolition of child labor; adequate provision for the protection, education, spiritual nurture and wholesome recreation of every child.

X. Protection of the family by the single standard of purity; educational preparation for marriage, home-making and parenthood.

XI. Economic justice for the farmer in legislation, financing of agriculture, transportation and the price of farm products as compared with the cost of machinery and other commodities which he must buy.

XII.   Extension of the primary cultural opportunities and social services now enjoyed by urban populations to the farm family.

XIII. Protection of the individual and society from the social, economic and moral waste of any traffic in intoxicants and habit-forming drugs.

XIV. Application of the Christian principle of redemption to the treatment of offenders; reform of penal and correctional methods and institutions, and of criminal court procedure.

XV.   Justice, opportunity and equal rights for all; mutual goodwill and cooperation among racial, economic and religious groups.

XVI. Repudiation of war, drastic reduction of armaments, participation in international agencies for the peaceable settlement of all controversies; the building of a cooperative world order.

XVII. Recognition and maintenance of the rights and responsibilities of free speech, free assembly, and a free press; the encouragement of fee communication of mind with mind as essential to the discovery of truth.

SOURCE: *Report of the Federal Council of Churches of Christ in America* (New York: Federal Council, 1932), 57.

U.S. Baptists and Religious Freedom

THE THREE MAJOR Baptist groups in the United States joined together in 1939 to issue a common statement of concern over rising totalitarian governments, encroachments upon individual liberties and the separation of church and state, and the possibility of a U.S. ambassador being appointed to the Vatican. Northern, National, and Southern Baptists issued the American Baptist Bill of Rights.

An American Baptist Bill of Rights

No issue in modern life is more urgent or more complicated than the relation of organized religion to organized society. The sudden rise of the

European dictators to power has changed fundamentally the organic law of the governments through which they exercise sovereignty, and as a result, the institutions of religion are either suppressed or made subservient to the ambitious national programs of these new totalitarian states. . . .

The conception of the dignity of the individual, as held by Baptists, is grounded in the conviction that every soul possess the capacity and the inalienable right to deal with God for himself, and to deprive any soul of his right of free access to God is to usurp the prerogatives of the individual and the function of God.

Standing as we do for the principle of voluntariness in religion, grounded upon the competency of the human soul, Baptists are essentially antagonistic to every form of religious coercion or persecution. We admit to our membership only those who give evidence that they are regenerated, but we recognize gladly that the grace of God is not limited to those who apply to us, and that our spiritual fellowship embraces all who have experienced the new birth and are walking in newness of life, by whatever name they may be called. We hold that the Church of Christ, which in the Bible is called "the Body of Christ", is not to be identified with any denomination or Church that seeks to exercise ecclesiastical authority, but includes all the regenerated whoever and wherever they are, as these are led by the Holy Spirit. This church is a body without formal organization, and therefore cannot enter into contractual relations on any basis with the State. For this reason, Baptists believe in Free Churches within a Free State. . . .

Today the tendency of government, even in democratic countries, lies in the direction of greater centralization. The philanthropic activities of the churches within the United States are being taken over by the government. The defective, the indigent, and the dependent groups of our social order have long been supported from public funds. The greatest charity agency on earth today is our Federal Government. More and more people are looking to the State to provide. As a nation we are becoming paternalistic. Efforts are now being made to place in the hands of the government the pensioning of those who are employed by the churches and the agencies that serve them: to grant to sectarian schools financial aid from tax-raised funds, and to support from public funds institutions that are established and managed by sectarian bodies . . .

We oppose the establishing of diplomatic relations with any ecclesiastical body. The extension of special courtesies by our government to any ecclesiastical official as such, and the employment of any of the branches of our national defense in connection with religious services that are held to honor any ecclesiastical leader. All such violations of principle must be resisted in their beginnings. . . .

Believing religious liberty to be not only an inalienable human right, but indispensable to human welfare, A Baptist must exercise himself to the utmost in the maintenance of absolute religious liberty for his Jewish neighbor, his Catholic neighbor, his Protestant neighbor, and for everybody else. Profoundly convinced that any deprivation of this right is a wrong to be challenged, Baptists condemn every form of compulsion in religion or restraint of the free consideration of the claims of religion. We stand for a civil state, "with full liberty in religious concernments."

SOURCE: William H. Brackney, ed., *Baptist Life and Thought 1600–1980* (Valley Forge, PA: Judson Press, 1983), 423–426.

FOUR FREEDOMS SPEECH

PRESIDENT FRANKLIN D. Roosevelt delivered his State of the Union speech to Congress on January 6, 1941. It became known as the "Four Freedoms Speech" and was the inspiration for human rights ideals following the war.

THE STATE OF THE UNION

To the Congress of the United States:

I address you, the members of the 77th Congress, at a moment unprecedented in the history of the Union. I use the word "unprecedented," because at no previous time has American security been as seriously threatened from without as it is today. . . .

What I seek to convey is the historic truth that the United States as a nation has at all times maintained opposition to any attempt to lock us in behind an ancient Chinese wall while the process of civilization went past. Today, thinking of our children and their children, we oppose enforced isolation for ourselves or for any part of the Americas. . . .

Every realist knows the democratic way of life is at this moment being directly assailed in every part of the world—assailed either by arms or secret spreading of poisonous propaganda by those who seek to destroy unity and promote discord in nations still at peace. During sixteen months this assault has blotted out the whole pattern of democratic life in an appalling number of independent nations, great and small. The assailants are still on the march, threatening other nations, great and small. . . .

A free nation has the right to expect full cooperation from all groups. A free nation has the right to look at the leaders of business, of labor, and of agriculture to take the lead in stimulating effort, not among other groups but within their own groups. The best way of dealing with the few slackers or trouble makers in our midst is, first, to shame them by patriotic example, and, if that fails, to use the sovereignty of government to save government.

As men do not live by bread alone, they do not fight by armaments alone. Those who man our defenses, and those behind them who build our defenses, must have the stamina and courage which come from an unshakable belief in the manner of life which they are defending. The mighty action which we are calling for cannot be based on a disregard of all things worth fighting for.

The Nation takes great satisfaction and much strength from the things which have been done to make its people conscious of their individual stake in the preservation of democratic life in America. Those things have toughened the fiber of our people, have renewed their faith and strengthened their devotion to the institutions we make ready to protect. Certainly this is no time to stop thinking about the social and economic problems which are the root cause of the social revolution which is today a supreme factor in the world.

There is nothing mysterious about the foundations of a healthy and strong democracy. The basic things expected by our people of their political and economic systems are simple. They are: equality of opportunity for youth and for others; jobs for those who can work; security for those who need it; the ending of special privilege for the few; the preservation of civil liberties for all; the enjoyment of the fruits of scientific progress in a wider and constantly rising standard of living.

These are simple and basic things that must never be lost sight of in the turmoil and unbelievable complexity of our modern world. The inner and abiding strength of our economic ands political systems is dependent upon the degree to which they fulfill these expectations.

Many subjects connected with our social economy call for immediate improvement. As examples: We should bring more citizens under the coverage of old age pensions and unemployment insurance. We should widen the opportunities for adequate medical care. We should plan a better system by which persons deserving or needing gainful employment may obtain it. I have called for personal sacrifice. I am assured of the willingness of almost all Americans to respond to that call. . . .

In the future days, which we seek to make secure, we look forward to a world founded upon four essential human freedoms.

The first is freedom of speech and expression—everywhere in the world.

The second is freedom of every person to worship God in his own way—everywhere in the world.

The third is freedom from want—which, translated into world terms, means economic understandings which will secure to every nation a healthy peace time life for its inhabitants—everywhere in the world.

The fourth is freedom from fear—which, translated into world terms, means a worldwide reduction of armaments to such a point and in such a thorough fashion that no neighbor will be in a position to commit an act of physical aggression against any neighbor—anywhere in the world. That is no vision of a distant millennium. It is a definite basis for a kind of world attainable in our own time and generation. That kind of world is the very antithesis of the so-called new order of tyranny which the dictators seek to create with the crash of a bomb.

To that new order we oppose the greater conception—the moral order. A good society is able to face schemes of world domination and foreign revolutions alike without fear. Since the beginning of our American history we have been engaged in change—in a perpetual peaceful revolution—a revolution which goes on steadily, quietly adjusting itself to changing conditions—without the concentration camp or the quick-lime in the ditch. The world order which we seek is the cooperation of free countries, working together in a friendly, civilized society.

This nation has placed its destiny in the hands and heads and hearts of its millions of free men and women; and its faith in freedom under the guidance of God. Freedom means the supremacy of human rights everywhere. Our support goes to those who struggle to gain those rights or keep them. Our strength is in our unity of purpose.

To that high concept there can be no end save victory.

SOURCE: B. D. Zevin, ed., *Nothing to Fear: The Selected Addresses of Franklin Delano Roosevelt 1932–1945* (Boston: Houghton Mifflin, 1946), 258–267.

THE UNITED NATIONS ACTS

AS HOSTILITIES OF World War II ended, the international community, led by the United States and Great Britain, planned for a United Nations organization. One of the prime areas to be included in the United Nations was the Commission on Human Rights, to which President Harry Truman appointed Eleanor Roosevelt as the first chair. With the able assistance of an international team that included Charles Malik of Lebanon and P. C. Chang of China, their first product was the Universal Declaration on Human Rights. It was adopted by the General Assembly of the United Nations, December 10, 1948.

THE UNIVERSAL DECLARATION OF HUMAN RIGHTS

Preamble

Whereas recognition of the inherent dignity and of the equal and inalienable rights of all members of the human family is the foundation of freedom, justice and peace in the world,

Whereas disregard and contempt for human rights have resulted in barbarous acts which have outraged the conscience of mankind, and the advent of a world in which human beings shall enjoy freedom of speech and belief and freedom from fear and want has been proclaimed as the highest aspiration of the common people,

Whereas it is essential, if man is not to be compelled to have recourse as a last resort, to rebellion against tyranny and oppression, that human rights should be protected by the rule of law,

Whereas it is essential to promote the development of friendly relations between nations,

Whereas the people of the united Nations have in the Charter reaffirmed their faith in fundamental human rights, in the dignity and worth of the human person and in the equal rights of men and women and have determined to promote social progress and better standards of life in larger freedom,

Whereas Member States have pledged themselves to achieve, in co-operation with the United Nations, the promotion of universal respect for and observance of human rights and fundamental freedoms,

Whereas a common understanding of these rights and freedoms is of the greatest importance for the full realization of this pledge,

NOW THEREFORE the GENERAL ASSEMBLY proclaims this UNIVERSAL DECLARATION OF HUMAN RIGHTS as a common standard of achievement for all peoples and all nations, to the end that every individual and every organ of society, keeping this Declaration constantly in mind, shall strive by teaching and education to promote respect for these rights and freedoms and by progressive measures, national and international, to secure their universal and effective recognition and observance, both among the peoples of Member States themselves and among the people of territories under their jurisdiction.

Article 1

All human beings are born free and equal in dignity and rights. They are endowed with reason and conscience and should act towards one another in a spirit of brother hood.

Article 2

Everyone is entitled to all the rights and freedoms set forth in this Declaration, without distinction of any kind, such as race, color, sex, language, religion, political or other opinion, national or social origin, property, birth or other status. Furthermore, no distinction shall be made on the basis of the political, jurisdictional or international status of the country or territory to which a person belongs, whether it be independent, trust, non-self-governing or under any other limitation of sovereignty.

Article 3

Everyone has the right of life, liberty and security of person.

Article 4

No one shall be held in slavery or servitude; slavery and the slave trade shall be prohibited in all their forms.

Article 5

No one shall be subjected to torture or to cruel, inhuman or degrading treatment or punishment.

Article 6

Everyone has the right to recognition everywhere as a person before the law.

Article 7

All are equal before the law and are entitled without any discrimination to equal protection of the law. All are entitled to equal protection against any discrimination in violation of this Declaration and against any incitement to such discrimination.

Article 8

Everyone has the right to an effective remedy by the competent national tribunals for acts violating the fundamental rights granted him by the constitution or by law.

Article 9

No one shall be subjected to arbitrary arrest, detention or exile.

Article 10

Everyone is entitled in full equality to a fair and public hearing by an independent and impartial tribunal, in the determination of his rights and obligations and of any criminal charge against him.

Article 11

(1) Everyone charged with a penal offense has the right to be presumed innocent until proved guilty according to law in a public trial at which he has had all the guarantees necessary for his defense.

(2) No one shall be held guilty of any penal offense on account of any act or omission which did not constitute a penal offense, under national or international law, at the time when it was committed. Nor shall a heavier penalty be imposed than the one that was applicable at the time the offense was committed.

Article 12

No one shall be subjected to arbitrary interference with his privacy, family, home or correspondence, nor to attacks upon his honor and reputation. Everyone has the right to the protection of the law against such interference or attacks.

Article 13

(1) Everyone has the right to freedom of movement and residence within the borders of each state.

(2) Everyone has the right to leave any country, including his own, and to return to his country.

Article 14

(1) Everyone has the right to seek and to enjoy in other countries asylum from persecution.

(2) This right may not be invoked in the case of prosecutions genuinely arising from nonpolitical crimes or from acts contrary to the purposes and principles of the United Nations.

Article 15

(1) Everyone has the right to a nationality.

(2) No one shall be arbitrarily deprived of his nationality nor denied the right to change his nationality.

Article 16

(1) Men and women of full age, without any limitation due to race, nationality or religion, have the right to marry and to found a family. They are entitled to equal rights as to marriage, during marriage and at its dissolution.

(2) Marriage shall be entered into only with the free and full consent of the intending spouses.

(3) The family is the natural and fundamental group unit of society and is entitled to protection by society and the State.

Article 17

(1) Everyone has the right to own property alone as well as in association with others.

(2) No one shall be arbitrarily deprived of his property.

Article 18

Everyone has the right to freedom of thought, conscience and religion; this right includes freedom to change his religion or belief, and freedom, either alone or in community with others and in public or private, to manifest his religion or belief in teaching, practice, worship and observance.

Article 19

Everyone has the right to freedom of opinion and expression; this right includes freedom to hold opinions without interference and to seek, receive and impart information and ideas through any media and regardless of frontiers.

Article 20

(1) Everyone has the right to freedom of peaceful assembly and association.

(2) No one may be compelled to belong to an association.

Article 21

(1) Everyone has the right to take part in the government of his country, directly or though freely chosen representatives.

(2) Everyone has the right of equal access to public service in his country.

(3) The will of the people shall be the basis of the authority of government; this will shall be expressed in periodic and genuine elections which shall be by universal and equal suffrage and shall be held by secret vote or by equivalent free voting procedures.

Article 22

Everyone, as a member of society, has the right to social security and is entitled to realization, through national effort and international cooperation and in accordance with the organization and resources of each State, of the economic, social and cultural rights indispensable for his dignity and the free development of his personality.

Article 23

(1) Everyone has the right to work, to free choice of employment, to just and favorable conditions of work and to protection against unemployment.

(2) Everyone, without any discrimination, has the right to equal pay for equal work.

(3) Everyone who works has the right to just and favorable remuneration insuring for himself and his family an existence worthy of human dignity, and supplemented, if necessary, by other means of social protection.

(4) Everyone has the right to form and to join trade unions for the protection of his interests.

Article 24

Everyone has the right to rest and leisure, including reasonable limitation of working hours and periodic holidays with pay.

Article 25

(1) Everyone has the right to standard of living adequate for the health and well-being of himself and of his family, including food, clothing, housing and medical care and necessary social services, and the right to security in the event of unemployment, sickness, disability, widowhood, old age or other lack of livelihood in circumstances beyond his control.

(2) Motherhood and childhood are entitled to special care and assistance. All children, whether born in or out of wedlock, shall enjoy the same social protection.

Article 26

(1) Everyone has the right to education. Education shall be free, at least in the elementary and fundamental stages. Technical and professional education shall be made generally available and higher education shall be equally accessible to all on the basis of merit.

(2) Education shall be directed to the full development of the human personality and to the strengthening of respect for human rights and fundamental freedoms. It shall promote understanding, tolerance and friendship among all nations, racial or religious groups, and shall further the activities of the United Nations for the maintenance of peace.

(3) Parents have a prior right to choose the kind of education that shall be given to their children.

Article 27

(1) Everyone has the right freely to participate in the cultural life of the community, to enjoy the arts and to share in scientific advancement and its benefits.

(2) Everyone has the right to the protection of the moral and material interests resulting from any scientific, literary or artistic production of which he is the author.

Article 28

Everyone is entitled to a social and international order in which the rights and freedoms set forth in this Declaration can be fully realized.

Article 29

(1) Everybody has duties to the community in which alone the free and full development of his personality is possible.

(2) In the exercise of his rights and freedoms, everyone shall be subject only to such limitations as are determined by law solely for the purpose of securing due recognition and respect for the rights and freedoms of others and of meeting the just requirements of morality, public order and the general welfare in a democratic society.

(3) These rights and freedoms may in no case by exercised contrary to the purposes and principles of the United Nations.

Article 30

Nothing in the Declaration may be interpreted as implying for any State, group or person any right to engage in any activity or to perform any act aimed at the destruction of any of the rights and freedoms set forth herein.

SOURCE: United Nations, 1948.

THE WORLD COUNCIL OF CHURCHES RESPONDS

ONE OF THE earliest acts of the newly formed World Council of Churches at Amsterdam in 1948 was the Declaration on Religious Liberty. It was shaped by the United Nations Universal Declaration on Human Rights and provided more Christian theological rationale. The Declaration became the Protestant and Orthodox standard on religious freedom.

A DECLARATION ON RELIGIOUS LIBERTY

An essential element in a good international order is freedom of religion. This is an implication of the Christian faith and of the worldwide nature of Christianity. Christians, therefore, view the question of religious freedom as an international problem. They are concerned that religious freedom be everywhere secured. In pleading for this freedom, they do not ask for any privilege to be granted to Christians that is denied to others. While the liberty with which Christ has set men free can neither be given nor destroyed by any government, Christians, because of that inner freedom, are both jealous for its outward expression and solicitous that all men should have freedom in religious life. The nature and destiny of man by virtue of his creation, redemption and calling, and man's activities in family, state and culture establish limits beyond which the government cannot with impunity go. The rights which Christian discipleship demands are such as are good for all men, and no nation has ever suffered by reason of granting such liberties. Accordingly:

The rights of religious freedom herein declared shall be recognized and observed for all persons without distinction as to race, color, sex, language or religion, and without imposition of disabilities by virtue of legal provisions or administrative acts.

1. Every person has the right to determine his own faith and creed.

The right to determine faith and creed involves both the process whereby a person adheres to belief and the process whereby he changes his belief. It includes the right to receive instruction and education.

This right becomes meaningful when man has the opportunity of access to information. Religious, social and political institutions have the obligation to permit the mature individual to relate himself to sources of information in such a way as to allow personal religious decision and belief.

The right to determine one's belief is limited by the right of parents to decide sources of information to which their children shall have access. In the process of reaching decisions, everyone ought to take into account his higher self-interests and the implications of his beliefs for the well being of his fellow men.

2. Every person has the right to express his religious beliefs in worship, teaching and practice, and to proclaim the implications of his beliefs for relationships in a social or political community.

The right of religious expression includes freedom of worship, both public and private; freedom to place information at the disposal of others by processes of teaching, preaching and persuasion; and freedom to pursue such activities as are dictated by conscience. It also includes freedom to express implications of belief for society and its government.

This right requires freedom from arbitrary limitation on religious expression in all means of communication, including speech, press, radio, motion pictures and art. Social and political institutions should grant immunity from discrimination and from legal disability on grounds of expressed religious conviction, at least to the point where recognized community interests are adversely affected.

Freedom of religious expression is limited by the rights of parents to determine the religious point of view to which their children shall be exposed. It is further subject to such limitations, prescribed by law, as are necessary to protect order and welfare, morals and the rights and freedoms of others. Each person must recognize the right of others to express their beliefs and must have respect for authority at all times, even when conscience forces him to take issue with the people who are in authority or with the position they advocate.

3. Every person has the right to associate with others and to organize with them for religious purposes.

This right includes freedom to form religious organizations, to seek membership in religious organizations, and to sever relationship with religious organizations.

It requires that the rights of association and organization guaranteed by a community to its members include the right of forming associations for religious purposes.

It is subject to the same limits imposed on all associations by non-discriminatory laws.

4. Every religious organization, formed or maintained by action in accordance with the rights of individual persons, has the right to determine its policies and practices for the accomplishment of its chosen purposes.

The rights which are claimed for the individual in his exercise of religious liberty become the rights of the religious organization, including the right to determine its faith and creed; to engage in religious worship, both public and private; to teach, educate, preach and persuade; to express implications of belief for society and government. To these will be added certain corporate rights which derive from the rights of individual persons, such as the right to determine the form of organization, its government and conditions of membership; to select and train its own officers, leaders and workers; to publish and circulate religious literature; to carry on service and missionary activities at home and abroad; to hold property and to collect funds; to cooperate and to unite with other religious bodies at home and in other lands, including freedom to invite or to send personnel beyond national frontiers and to give or to receive financial assistance; to use such facilities, open to all citizens or associations, as will make possible the accomplishment of religious ends.

In order that these right may be realized in social experience, the state must grant to religious organizations and their members the same rights which it grants to other organizations, including the right of self-government, of public meeting, of speech, of press and publications, of holding property, of collecting funds, of travel, of ingress and egress, and generally of administering their own affairs.

The community has the right to require obedience to non-discriminatory laws passed in the interest of public order and well-being. In the exercise of its rights, a religious organization must respect the rights of other religious organizations and must safeguard the corporate and individual rights of the entire community.

SOURCE: "Amsterdam Reports," in *Christian Century* (October 6, 1948): 1043–1045.

A Christian Government Legislates Segregation

IN 1948, the Afrikaner National Party was swept into power in South Africa. Gradually, steps were taken to realize their program, including racial segregation and increased police powers. At the heart of their program was the Group Areas Act (1950). Among the additional South African legislative acts that accompanied or followed the Group Areas Act were: Prohibition of Mixed Marriages Act (1949), Immorality Amendment (1950), Population Registration Act (1950), and the Suppression of Communism Act (1950), Prevention of Illegal Squatting Act (1951), Bantu Authorities Act (1951), Native Laws Amendment Act (1952).

THE GROUP AREAS ACT, 1950

To provide for the establishment of group areas, for the control of the acquisition of immovable property and the occupation of land and premises, and for matters incidental thereto.

(ix) 'group' means either the white group, the coloured group or the native group referred to in section *two*, and includes, to the extent required to give effect to any relevant proclamation under subsection (2) of the said section, any group of persons who have under the said section been declared to be a group;

(x) 'group area' means any area proclaimed under section *three*;

(xi) 'immovable property' includes any real right in immovable property and any right which would upon registration be such a real right and any lease or sub-lease of immovable property, (other than a lease or sub-lease of immovable property in an area which is a specified area in terms of section *eleven*), but does not include any right to any mineral (including any right to prospect for or to dig or mine any mineral) or a lease or sub-lease of any such right or a mortgage bond over immovable property, [or any other real right in immovable property excluded by the Governor-General from time to time by proclamation in the *Gazette*;] . . .

Groups for the purposes of this Act.

2.(1) For the purposes of this Act, there shall be the following groups:

(a) a white group, in which shall be included any person who in appearance, obviously is, or who is generally accepted as a white person, other than a person who although in appearance obviously a white person, is generally accepted as a coloured person, or who is in terms of sub-paragraph (ii) [or (iii)] of paragraphs (b) and (c) or of the said sub-paragraphs read with paragraph (d) of this sub-section and paragraph (a) of sub-section (2), a member of any other group;

(b) a native group, in which shall be included—

(i) any person who in fact is, or is generally accepted as a member of an aboriginal race or tribe of Africa, other than a person who is, in terms of sub-paragraph (ii) of paragraph I, a member of the coloured group; and

(ii) any woman to whichever race, tribe or class she may belong, between whom and a person who is, in terms of sub-paragraph (i), a member of [the] native group, there exists a marriage or who cohabits with such a person;

(iii) any white man between whom and a woman who is, in terms of subparagraph (i), a member of the native group, there exists a marriage or who cohabits with such a woman . . .

(c) a coloured group, in which shall be included—

(i) any person who is not a member of the white group or of the native group; and

(ii) any woman, to whichever race, tribe or class she may belong, between whom and a person who is, in terms of sub-paragraph (i), a member of the coloured group, there exists a marriage, or who cohabits with such a person; and

(iii) any white man between whom and a woman who is, in terms of sub-paragraph (i), a member of the coloured group, there exists a marriage or who co-habits with such a woman; . . .

Establishment of group areas.

3.(1) The Governor-General may, whenever it is deemed expedient, by proclamation in the *Gazette*—

(a) declare that as from a date specified in the proclamation, which shall be a date not less than one year after the date of the publication thereof, the area defined in the proclamation shall be an area for occupation by members of the group specified therein; or

(b) declare that, as from a date specified in the proclamation, the area defined in the proclamation shall be an area for ownership by members of the group specified therein. . . .

Acquisition of immovable property in group areas.

5.(1) If any group area is in terms of a proclamation under paragraph (b) of sub section (1) of section *three* a group area for ownership—

    (a) no disqualified person and no disqualified company shall, on or after the relevant date specified in the proclamation, acquire any immovable property situate within that area, whether or not in pursuance of any agreement or testamentary disposition entered into or made before that date, except under the authority of a permit; Provided that the provisions of this paragraph shall not render unlawful any acquisition of immovable property by a statutory body; . . .

  (3) A testamentary disposition or intestate succession by which any person would acquire or hold any immovable property in contravention of sub-section (1) shall, unless the beneficiary is authorized to acquire or hold such a property under permit, be deemed to be a testamentary disposition of or succession in respect of the net proceeds of such property, and it shall be the duty of the executor of the estate of the deceased to realize the property within a period of one year from the date of his death . . .

Presumptions.

35.(1) A person who in appearance obviously is a white person shall for the purposes of this Act be presumed to be a member of the white group until the contrary is proved.

  (2) A person who in fact is or is generally accepted as a member of an aboriginal race or tribe of Africa shall for the purposes of this Act be presumed to be a member of the native group until the contrary is proved.

  (3) A person who is not in appearance obviously a white person and who is not in fact or is not generally accepted as a member of an aboriginal race or tribe of Africa shall for the purposes of this Act be presumed to be a member of the coloured group until the contrary is proved.

  (4) Whenever in any proceedings under this Act, whether civil or criminal, it is alleged by or on behalf of the Minister or any officer in charge of deeds registry or in any indictment or charge that any company is a company wherein a controlling interest is held by or on behalf or in the interest of a member of any group, that

company shall be presumed to be such a company, until the contrary is proved. . . .

SOURCE: V. G. Heimstra, *Statutes of South Africa*, "Group Areas Act" (Johannesburg: Juta and Company 1957), 77, 79, 81, 87, 123, 125.

FURTHER CONCERNS ABOUT RELIGIOUS FREEDOM

IN THE LATE 1950s, growing concerns over violations of religious liberties in Asia, Africa, the Soviet Union, and China prompted a renewed declaration on religious freedom in the World Council of Churches. At the Third Assembly in New Delhi, India, the following statement was unanimously approved to be sent to the churches.

DECLARATION BY THE WORLD COUNCIL OF CHURCHES ASSEMBLY, NEW DELHI, 1961

1. MANKIND is threatened by many forces which curtail or deny freedom. There is accordingly urgent need to reinvigorate efforts to ensure that every person has opportunity for the responsible exercise of religious freedom.
2. Christians see religious liberty as a consequence of God's creative work, of his redemption of man in Christ and his calling of men into his service. God's redemptive dealing with men is not coercive. Accordingly human attempts by legal enactment or by pressure of social custom to coerce or to eliminate faith are violations of the fundamental ways of God with men. The freedom which God has given in Christ implies a free response to God's love, and the responsibility to serve fellow men at the point of deepest need.
3. Holding a distinctive Christian basis for religious liberty, we regard this right as fundamental for men everywhere.
4. We reaffirm the Declaration of Religious Liberty adopted by the World Council of Churches and the International Missionary Council in August–September 1948, and hold to its provisions. We recognize the Universal Declaration of Human Rights, proclaimed by the United Nations in December 1948, as an important instrument in promoting respect for and observance of human rights and fundamental freedoms.

5. Although freedoms of every kind are interrelated, religious liberty may be considered as a distinctive human right, which all men may exercise no matter what their faith. The article on religious freedom in the Universal Declaration is an acceptable standard, always provided that it be given a comprehensive interpretation. Everyone has the right to freedom of thought, conscience and religion; this right includes freedom to change his religion or be-lief, and freedom, either alone or in community with others and in public or private, to manifest his religion or belief in teaching, practice, worship and observance.

6. The recognition of the inherent dignity and of the equal and in-alienable rights of all members of the human family requires that the general standard here declared should be given explicit ex-pression in every aspect of society. Without seeking to be inclu-sive, we illustrate as follows:

7. Freedom of thought, conscience and belief, even considered as inner freedom, requires freedom of access to reliable information.

8. Freedom to manifest one's religion or belief, in public or in private and alone or in community with others, is essential to the ex-pression of inner freedom.

   a. It includes freedom to worship according to one's chosen form, in public or in private.

   b. It includes freedom to teach, whether by formal or informal instruction as well as preaching with a view to propagating one's faith and persuading others to accept it.

   c. It includes freedom to practice religion or belief, whether by performance of acts of mercy or by the expression in word or deed of the implications of belief in social, economic and po-litical matters, both domestic, and international.

   d. It includes freedom of observance by following religious cus-toms or by participating in religious rites in the family or in public meeting.

9. Religious liberty includes freedom to change one's religion or belief without consequent social, economic, and political disabilities. Im-plicit in this right is the right freely to maintain one's belief or disbelief without external coercion or disability.

10. The exercise of religious liberty involves other human rights. The Universal Declaration proclaims among others, the right to free-dom of peaceful assembly and association; the right to freedom of

opinion and expression including freedom to seek, receive and impart information and ideas through any media and regardless of frontiers; the prior right of parents to choose the kind of education that shall be given to either children; freedom to participate in choosing the desired form of government and in freely electing officials; freedom from the retroactive application of penal law: and freedom to leave and to return to one's own country and to seek asylum elsewhere.

11. The freedom with which Christ has set us free calls forth responsibility for the rights of others. The civil freedom which we claim in the name of Christ must be freely available for all men to exercise responsibly. It is the corresponding obligation of governments and of society to ensure the exercise of these civil rights without discrimination. It is for the churches in their own life and witness recognizing their own past failures in this regard to play their indispensable role in promoting the realization of religious liberty for all men.

Source: *Christian Century* (January 10, 1962): 59.

Pope John XXIII and *Pacem in Terris*

In 1963, Pope John XXIII issued a groundbreaking encyclical, *Pacem in Terris (Peace on Earth)* that advocated human freedom and dignity as the basis for world order and peace. The papal concern grew out of the arms race and potential of East-West conflicts, as well as the tendency among those involved in the dialogue about human rights to seek a lodgment outside religion, and specifically outside the Christian faith. The theological basis of the statement was that human rights are rooted in the creative act of God. Addressed to "all men of good will," and not just members of the Catholic Church, the encyclical signaled a new engagement of world order and contemporary global relations.

Pacem in Terris

. . . 9. Any human society, if it is to be well-ordered and productive, must lay down as a foundation this principle: that every human being is a person; his nature is endowed with intelligence and free will. By virtue of this, he has rights and duties of his own, flowing directly and simultaneously from his very nature, which are therefore universal, inviolable, and inalienable.

10. If we look upon the dignity of the humans person in the light of divinely revealed truth, we cannot help but esteem it far more highly; for men are redeemed by the blood of Jesus Christ, they are by grace the children and friends of God and heirs of eternal glory. . . .

11. Beginning Our discussion of the rights of man, We see that every man has the right to life, to bodily integrity, and to the means which are necessary and suitable for the proper development of life; these are primarily food, clothing, shelter, rest, medical care, and finally the necessary social services. Therefore, a human being also has the right to security in cases of sickness, inability to work, widowhood, old age, unemployment, or in any other case in which he is deprived of the means of subsistence through no fault of his own.

12. By the natural law every human being as the right to respect for his person, to his good reputation; the right to freedom in searching for truth and in expressing and communicating his opinions, and in pursuit of art, within the limits laid down by the moral order and the common good; and he has the right to be informed truthfully about public events.

13. The natural law also gives man the right to share in the benefits of culture, and therefore the right to a basic education and to technical and professional training in keeping with the stage of educational development in the country to which he belongs. Every effort should be made to ensure that persons be enabled, on the basis of merit, to go on to higher studies, so that, as far as possible, they may occupy posts and take on responsibilities in human society in accordance with their natural gifts and the skills they have acquired.

14. Every human being has the right to honor God according to the dictates of an upright conscience, and therefore the right to worship God privately and publicly. For, as Lactantius so clearly taught: We were created for the purpose of showing to the God Who bore us the submission we owe Him, of recognizing Him alone, and of serving Him. We are obliged and bound by this duty to God; from this religion itself receives its name. And on this point Our Predecessor of immortal memory, Leo XIII, declared: This genuine, this honorable freedom of the sons of God, which most nobly protects the dignity of the human person, is greater

than any violence or injustice; it has always been sought by the Church, and always most dear to her. This was the freedom which the apostles claimed with intrepid constancy, which the apologists defended with their writings, and which the martyrs in such numbers consecrated with their blood.

15. Human beings have the right to choose freely the state of life which they prefer, and therefore the right to establish a family, with equal rights and duties for man and woman, and also the right to follow a vocation to the priesthood or the religious life.

16. The family, grounded on marriage freely contracted, monogamous and indissoluble, should be regarded as the first and natural cell of human society. To it should be given every consideration of an economic, social, cultural, and moral nature which will strengthen its stability and facilitate the fulfillment of its specific mission.

17. Parents, however, have the prior right in the support and education of their children.

18. We now turn to the sphere of economic affairs. Human beings have the natural right to free initiative in the economic field, and the right to work.

19. Indissolubly linked with those rights is the right to working conditions in which physical health is not endangered, morals are safeguarded, and young peoples' moral development is not impaired. Women have the right to working conditions in accordance with their requirements and their duties as wives and mothers.

20. From the dignity of the human person, there also arises the right to carry on economic activities according to the degree of responsibility of which one is capable. Furthermore—and this must be specially emphasized—there is the right to a proper wage, determined according to the criteria of justice, and sufficient, therefore, in proportion to the available resources to provide the worker and his family a manner of living in keeping with the dignity of the human person. . . .

21. The right to private property, even of productive goods, also derives from the nature of man. This right, as We have elsewhere declared, is an effective aid in safeguarding the dignity of the human person and the free exercise of responsibility in all fields of endeavor. Finally, it strengthens the stability and tranquility of family life, thus contributing to the peace and prosperity of the commonwealth.

22. However, it is opportune to point out that there is a social duty essentially inherent in the right of private property.

23. From the fact that human beings are by nature social, there arises the right of assembly and association. They have also the right to give the societies of which they are members the form they consider most suitable for the aim they have in view, and to act within such societies on their initiative and on their own responsibility in order to achieve their desired objectives. . . .

25. Every human being has the right to freedom of movement and of residence within the confines of his own country; and when there are just reasons for it, the right to emigrate to other countries an take up residence there. The fact that one is a citizen of a particular state does not detract in any way from his membership in the human family as a whole, nor from his citizenship in the world community.

26. The dignity of the human person involves the right to take an active part in public affairs and to contribute one's part to the common good of the citizens. . . .

28. The natural rights with which We have been dealing are, however, inseparably connected, in the very person who is their subject, with just as many respective duties; and rights as well as duties find their source, their sustenance, and their inviolability in the natural law which grants or enjoins them.

29. For example, the right of every man to life is correlative with the duty to preserve it. . . .

37. The moral order which prevails in society is by nature moral. Grounded as it is in truth, it must function according to the norms of justice, it should be inspired and perfected by mutual love, and finally it should be brought to an ever more refined and human balance in freedom.

38. Now, an order of this kind, whose principles are universal, absolute, and unchangeable, has its ultimate source in the one true God, Who is personal and transcends human nature. Inasmuch as God is the first Truth and the highest Good, he alone is that deepest source from which human society can draw its vitality, if that society is to be well-ordered, beneficial, and in keeping with human dignity. . . .

SOURCE: "Pacem in Terris," in *Catholic Social Thought: The Basic Historical Documents*, eds. D. J. O'Brien and T. A. Shannon (Maryknoll, NY: Orbis Books, 1992), 131–162.

Vatican II and *Dignitatis Humanae*

In 1965, at the conclusion of Vatican II, Pope Paul VI issued one of the most far-reaching proclamations in the history of Catholicism. *Dignitatis Humanae*, the Declaration on Human Freedom, was a quantum leap beyond the *Syllabus of Errors* in the nineteenth century and reflected both the United Nations' Universal Declaration of Human Rights and Pope John XXIII's *Pacem in Terris*.

Declaration on Religious Freedom on the Right of the Person and of Communities to Social and Civil Freedom in Matters Religious

A sense of the dignity of the human person has been impressing itself more and more deeply on the consciousness of contemporary man. And the demand is increasingly made that men should act on their own judgment, enjoying and making use of a responsible freedom, not driven by coercion but motivated by a sense of duty. The demand is also made that constitutional limits should be set to the powers of government, in order that there may be no encroachment on the rightful freedom of the person and of associations.

This demand for freedom in human society chiefly regards the quest for the values proper to the human spirit. It regards, in the first place, the free exercise of religion in society.

This Vatican Synod takes careful note of those desires in the minds of men. It proposes to declare them to be greatly in accord with truth and justice. To this end, it searches into the sacred tradition and doctrine of the Church—the treasury out of which the Church continually brings forth new things that are in harmony with the things that are old.

First, this sacred Synod professes its belief that God himself has made known to mankind the way in which men are to serve him, and thus be saved in Christ and come to blessedness. We believe that this one true religion subsists in the catholic and apostolic Church, to which the Lord Jesus committed the duty of spreading it abroad among all men. . . .

The sacred Synod likewise professes its belief that it is upon the human conscience that these obligations fall and exert their binding force. The truth cannot impose itself except by virtue of its own truth, as it makes its entrance into the mind at once quietly and with power. Religious freedom, in turn, which men demand as necessary to fulfill their duty to worship God, has to do with immunity from coercion in civil society. Therefore, it leaves untouched the traditional Catholic doctrine on the moral duty of men and societies toward the true religion and toward the one Church of Christ.

Over and above all this, in taking up the matter of religious freedom this sacred Synod intends to develop the doctrine of recent Popes on the inviolable rights of the human person and on the constitutional order of society.

2. This Vatican Synod declares that the human person has a right to religious freedom. This freedom means that all men are to be immune from coercion on the part of individuals or of social groups, and of any human power, in such wise that in matters religious no one is to be forced to act in a manner contrary to his own beliefs. Nor is anyone to be restrained from acting in accordance with his own beliefs, whether privately or publicly, whether alone or in association with others, within due limits.

The Synod further declares that the right to religious freedom has its foundation in the very dignity of the human person, as this dignity is known through the revealed Word of God and by reason itself. This right of the human person to religious freedom is to be recognized in the constitutional law whereby society is governed. Thus it is to become a civil right.

It is in accordance with their dignity as persons—that is, beings endowed with reason and free will and therefore privileged to bear personal responsibility—that all men should be at once impelled by nature and also bound by a moral obligation to seek the truth, especially religious truth. They are also bound to adhere to the truth, once it is known, and to order their whole lives in accord with the demands of truth.

However, men cannot discharge these obligations in a manner in keeping with their own nature unless they enjoy immunity from external coercion as well as psychological freedom. Therefore, the right to religious freedom has its foundation, not in the subjective disposition of the person, but in his very nature. In consequence, the right to this immunity continues to exist even in those who do not live up to their obligation of seeking the truth and adhering to it. Nor is the exercise of this right to be impeded, provided that the just requirements of public order are observed.

3. Further light is shed on the subject if one considers that the highest

norm of human life is the divine law—eternal, objective, and universal—whereby God orders, directs, and governs the entire universe and all the ways of the human community, by a plan conceived in wisdom and love. Man has been made by God to participate in this law, with the result that, under the gentle disposition of divine Providence, he can come to perceive ever increasingly the unchanging truth. Hence every man has the duty, and therefore the right, to seek the truth in matters religious, in order that he may with prudence form for himself right and true judgments of conscience, with the use of all suitable means.

Truth, however, is to be sought after in a manner proper to the dignity of the human person and his social nature. The inquiry is to be free, carried on with the aid of teaching or instruction, communication, and dialogue. In the course of these, men explain to one another the truth they have discovered, or think they have discovered, in order thus to assist one another in the quest for truth. Moreover, as the truth is discovered, it is by a personal assent that men are to adhere to it.

On his part, man perceives and acknowledges the imperatives of the divine law through the mediation of conscience. In all his activity a man is bound to follow his conscience faithfully, in order that he may come to God, for whom he was created. It follows that he is not to be forced to act in a manner contrary to his conscience. Nor, on the other hand, is he to be restrained from acting in accordance with his conscience, especially in matters religious.

For, of its very nature, the exercise of religion consists before all else in those internal, voluntary, and free acts whereby man sets the course of his life directly toward God. No merely human power can either command or prohibit acts of this kind.

However, the social nature of man itself requires that he should give external expression to his internal acts of religion; that he should participate with others in matters religious; that he should profess his religion in community. Injury, therefore, is done to the human person and to the very order established by God for human life, if the free exercise of religion is denied in society when the just requirements of public order do not so require.

There is a further consideration. The religious acts whereby men, in private and in public and out of a sense of personal conviction, direct their lives to God transcend by their very nature the order of terrestrial and temporal affairs. Government, therefore, ought indeed to take account of the religious life of the people and show it favor, since the function of government is to make provision for the common welfare. However, it would clearly transgress the limits set to its power were it to presume to direct or inhibit acts that are religious.

4. The freedom or immunity from coercion in matters religious which is the endowment of persons as individuals is also to be recognized as their right when they act in community. Religious bodies are a requirement of the social nature both of man and of religion itself.

Provided the just requirements of public order are observed, religious bodies rightfully claim freedom in order that they may govern themselves according to their own norms, honor the Supreme Being in public worship, assist their members in the practice of religious life, strengthen them by instruction, and promote institutions in which they may join together for the purpose of ordering their own lives in accordance with their religious principles.

Religious bodies also have the right not to be hindered, either by legal measures or by administrative action on the part of government, in the selection, training, appointment, and transferal of their own ministers, in communicating with religious authorities and communities abroad, in erecting buildings for religious purpose, and in the acquisition and use of suitable funds or properties.

Religious bodies also have the right not to be hindered in their public teaching and witness to their faith, whether by the spoken or the written word. However, in spreading religious faith and in introducing religious practices, everyone ought at all times to refrain from any manner of action which might seem to carry a hint of coercion or of a kind of persuasion that would be dishonorable or unworthy, especially when dealing with poor or uneducated people. Such a manner of action would have to be considered an abuse of one's own right and a violation of the right of others.

In addition, it comes within the meaning of religious freedom that religious bodies should not be prohibited from freely undertaking to show the special value of their doctrine in what concerns the organization of society and the inspiration of the whole of human activity. Finally, the social nature of man and the very nature of religion afford the foundation of the right of men freely to hold meetings and to establish educational, cultural, charitable, and social organizations, under the impulse of their own religious sense.

5. Since the family is a society in its own original right, it has the right freely to live its own domestic religious life under the guidance of parents.

Parents, moreover, have the right to determine, in accordance with their own religious beliefs, the kind of religious education that their children are to receive.

Government, in consequence, must acknowledge the right of parents to make a genuinely free choice of schools and of other means of education. The use of this freedom of choice is not to be made a reason for imposing unjust burdens on parents, whether directly or indirectly. Besides, the rights of parents are violated if their children are forced to attend lessons or instruction which are not in agreement with their religious beliefs. The same is true if a single system of education, from which all religious formation is excluded, is imposed upon all.

6. The common welfare of society consists in the entirety of those conditions of social life under which men enjoy the possibility of achieving their own perfection in a certain fullness of measure and also with some relative ease. Hence this welfare consists chiefly in the protection of the rights, and in the performance of duties, of the human person. Therefore, the care of the right to religious freedom devolves upon the people as a whole, upon social groups, upon government, and upon the Church and other religious Communities, in virtue of the duty of all toward the common welfare, and in the manner proper to each.

The protection and promotion of the inviolable rights of man ranks among the essential duties of government. Therefore, government is to assume the safeguard of the religious freedom of all its citizens, in an effective manner, by just laws and by other appropriate means. Government is also to help create conditions favorable to the fostering of religious life, in order that the people may be truly enabled to exercise their religious rights and to fulfill their religious duties, and also in order that society itself may profit by the moral qualities of justice and peace which have their origin in men's faithfulness to God and to His holy will.

If, in view of peculiar circumstances obtaining among certain peoples, special legal recognition is given in the constitutional order of society to one religious body, it is at the same time imperative that the right of all citizens and religious bodies to religious freedom should be recognized and made effective in practice.

Finally, government is to see to it that the equality of citizens before the law, which is itself an element of the common welfare, is never violated for religious reasons whether openly or covertly. Nor is there to be discrimination among citizens.

It follows that a wrong is done when government imposes upon its people, by force or fear or other means, the profession or repudiation of any religion, or when it hinders men from joining or leaving a religious body. All the more is it a violation of the will of God and of the sacred rights of the person and the family of nations, when force is brought to bear in any way in order to destroy or repress religion, either in the whole of mankind or in a particular country or in a specific community.

7. The right to religious freedom is exercised in human society; hence its exercise is subject to certain regulatory norms. In the use of all freedoms, the moral principle of personal and social responsibility is to be observed. In the exercise of their rights, individual men and social groups are bound by the moral law to have respect both for the rights of others and for their own duties toward others and for the common welfare of all. Men are to deal with their fellows in justice and civility.

Furthermore, society has the right to defend itself against possible abuses committed on pretext of freedom of religion. It is the special duty of government to provide this protection. However, government is not to act in arbitrary fashion or in any unfair spirit of partisanship. Its action is to be controlled by juridical norms which are in conformity with the objective moral order.

These norms arise out of the need for effective safeguard of the rights of all citizens and for peaceful settlement of conflicts of rights. They flow from the need for an adequate care of genuine public peace, which comes about when men live together in good order and in true justice. They come, finally out of the need for a proper guardianship of public morality. These matters constitute the basic component of the common welfare: they are what is meant by public order.

For the rest, the usages of society are to be the usages of freedom in their full range. These require that the freedom of man be respected as far as possible, and curtailed only when and in so far as necessary.

8. Many pressures are brought to bear upon men of our day, to the point where the danger arises lest they lose the possibility of acting on their own judgment. On the other hand, not a few can be found who seem inclined to use the name of freedom as the pretext for refusing to submit to authority and for making light of the duty of obedience.

Therefore, this Vatican Synod urges everyone, especially those who are charged with the task of educating others, to do their utmost to form men who will respect the moral order and be obedient to lawful authority. Let them form men too who will be lovers of true freedom—men, in other words, who will come to decisions on their own judgment and in the light of truth, govern their activities with a sense of responsibility, and strive after what is true and right, willing always to join with others in cooperative effort.

Religious freedom, therefore, ought to have this further purpose and aim, namely, that men may come to act with greater responsibility in fulfilling their duties in community life.

SOURCE: Walter M. Abbott, S. J., ed., *The Documents of Vatican II, In a New and Definitive Translation, with Commentaries and Notes By Catholic, Protestant, and Orthodox Authorities* (New York: Herder and Herder, 1989), 675–688.

DECLARATION OF CHRISTIAN FREEDOM

AT A SYMPOSIUM held at Catholic University in 1968, Roman Catholic leaders met to discuss the question of whether the North American Catholic Church was faithful to its own teachings as called for in the papal declaration, *Gaudium et Spies*. The Report of the Symposium was far-reaching and is included here. No other ecclesiastical body of Christians has indicated such a self-critical and searching process.

SYMPOSIUM ON "DECLARATION OF CHRISTIAN FREEDOMS" CATHOLIC UNIVERSITY (WASHINGTON), 1968

1. The right to freedom in the search for truth, without fear of administrative sanctions.
2. The right to freedom in expressing personal beliefs and opinions as they appear to the individual, including freedom of communication and publication.
3. The right of individuals to access to objective information, in particular about the internal and external operations of the Church.
4. The right to develop the unique potentialities and personality traits proper to the individual without fear of repression by the Christian community or Church authorities.
5. The right of the Christian to work out his salvation in response

to the unique challenges offered by the age and society in which he lives.

6. The rights of persons employed by, or engaged in the service of, the Church to conditions of work consonant with human dignity as well as their right to professional practices comparable to those in the society at large.

7. All members of the Church have the right to freedom of assembly and of association.

8. All members of the Church have the right to participate, according to their gift from the Spirit, in the teaching, government, and sanctification of the Church.

9. All members of the Church are entitled to all the rights and freedoms of Christians without discrimination on the basis of race, colour, sex, birth, language, political opinion, or national or social origin.

10. All members of the Church have a right to effective remedies for the redress of grievances and the vindication of their rights.

11. In all proceedings in which one of the parties may suffer substantial disadvantage, the procedure must be fair and impartial, with an opportunity for submission to boards of mediation and arbitration.

12. In all procedures, administrative or judicial, in which penalties may be imposed, the accused shall not be deprived of any right, office or communion with the Church except by due process of law; said due process should include, but not be limited to, the right not to be a witness against oneself; the right to a speedy and public trial; the right to be informed in advance of the specific charge against him; the right to confront the witnesses against him; the right to have the assistance of experts and of counsel for his defense; and a right of appeal.

SOURCE: James Coriden, ed., "Towards a Declaration of Christian Rights," Consensus Paper included in *The Case for Freedom: Human Rights in the Church* (Washington, DC: Corpus, 1969), 5–14.

EVANGELICALS AND HUMAN RIGHTS

THE CHICAGO DECLARATION of Evangelical Social Concern was passed on November 25, 1973, in Chicago, Illinois. Fifty-three persons acknowledged injustices and violations of human rights, particularly in the United States. It was principally the work of Ronald Sider, Paul Henry, and Nancy Hardesty. No reference is made to the Universal Declaration, nor to any preexisting theological rationale for human rights. Tacit mention is made of God's identification with the poor, a recognition of the growing claims of liberation theology.

THE CHICAGO DECLARATION

As evangelical Christians committed to the Lord Jesus Christ and the full authority of the Word of God, we affirm that God lays total claim upon the lives of his people. We cannot, therefore, separate our lives from the situation in which God has placed us in the United States and the world.

We confess that we have not acknowledged the complete claim of God on our lives.

We acknowledge that God requires love. But we gave not demonstrated the love of God to those suffering social abuses.

We acknowledge that God requires justice. But we have not proclaimed or demonstrated his justice to an unjust American society. Although the Lord calls us to defend the social and economic rights of the poor and oppressed, we have mostly remained silent. We deplore the historic involvement of the church in America with racism and the conspicuous responsibility of the evangelical community for perpetuating the personal attitudes and institutional structures that have divided the body of Christ along color lines. Further, we have failed to condemn the exploitation of racism at home and abroad by our economic system.

We affirm that God abounds in mercy and that he forgives all who repent and turn from their sins. So we call our fellow evangelical Christians to demonstrate repentance in a Christian discipleship that confronts the social and political injustice of our nation.

We must attack the materialism of our culture and the maldistribution of the nation's wealth and services. We recognize that as a nation we play a crucial role in the imbalance and injustice of international trade and development. Before God and a billion hungry neighbors, we must rethink our values regarding our present standard of living and promote a more just acquisition of and distribution of the world's resources.

We acknowledge our Christian responsibilities of citizenship. Therefore, we must challenge the misplaced trust of the nation in economic and military might—a proud trust that promotes a national pathology of war and violence which victimizes our neighbors at home and abroad. We must resist the temptation to make the nation and its institutions objects of near-religious loyalty.

We acknowledge that we have encouraged men to prideful domination and women to irresponsible passivity. So we call both men and women to mutual submission and active discipleship.

We proclaim no new gospel, but the Gospel of our Lord Jesus Christ who, through the power of the Holy Spirit, frees people from sin so that they might praise God through works of righteousness.

By this declaration, we endorse no political ideology or party, but call our nation's leaders and people to that righteousness which exalts a nation.

We make this declaration in the biblical hope that Christ is coming to consummate the kingdom and we accept his claim on our total discipleship until he comes.

SOURCE: Philadelphia: Evangelicals for Social Action, November 25, 1973.

LIBERATION THEOLOGY AND HUMAN RIGHTS

AS THE EXTREME poverty of Latin America mounted in the 1950s and 1960s and went largely unanswered in the church, a bold attempt was made to address issues from a reinterpretation of the gospel. This new approach, labeled "liberation theology," formally appeared at the Second Latin American Bishops Conference at Medellin, Colombia, and has characterized the Latin American scene and profoundly influenced both liberal and evangelical thinkers alike. Among its most widely read proponents is Gustavo Gutierrez, author of *A Theology of Liberation* (1973).

THE GOSPEL AS LIBERATION FOR THE POOR

Taking Sides.

Evangelization, or the proclamation of the good news, is the proclamation of Christ's liberation. It is a total liberation, which goes straight to the root of all injustice and exploitation, straight to the root of the breach in friendship and love. But it is a liberation that dare not be interpreted "spiritually," "spiritualistically,"—though there is a strong penchant for such interpretation in certain Christian circles. Love and its antithesis, sin, are historical realties. They are experienced and lived in concrete circumstances. Hence it is that the Bible speaks of liberation and justice as opposed to slavery and the humiliation of the poor.

The gift of the status of child of God is experienced only in historical contexts. It is in making our neighbors into sisters and brothers that we receive this gift, for it is a gift not of word but of work. This is what it means to experience the Father's love and to bear him witness. The proclamation of a God who loves all human beings in equal fashion must be enfleshed, incarnated, in history—must become history.

The proclamation of this liberating love in the midst of a society characterized by injustice and the exploitation of one social class by another social class is what will make this emergent history something challenging and filled with conflict. This is how we bring to pass the truth of God at the very heart of a society in which social classes confront one another with hostility. For we shall be taking sides with the poor, with the populous classes, with the ethnic groups others scorn, with cultures that are marginalized. It is from here that we must strive to live and proclaim the gospel of the love of God. Its proclamation to the exploited, to the laborers and *campesinos* of our lands, will lead them to perceive that their situation is contrary to the will of God who makes himself known in events of liberation. It will help them come to a consciousness of the profound injustice of their situation.

Unmasking Misuse of the Gospel.

It must not be forgotten that the Bible has been read and communicated from the viewpoint of the dominating sectors and classes, abetted by a good part of exegesis that is thought of as "scientific." In this way what is "Christian" has been forced to play a role, within the dominant ideology, that affirms and consolidates a society divided into classes. The masses will arrive at an authentic political consciousness only in direct participation in the popular struggles for liberation.

In the immensity and complexity of the social process that must crush a system of oppression and lead to a classless society, ideological struggle too has an important place. Hence it is that the communication of the message as reread from the point of view of the poor and oppressed, and from the point of view of militant cooperation with them in their struggles, will have the function of unmasking all intent and effort to make the gospel play the role of justifying a situation at odds with what the Bible calls "justice and right". . . .

Today we clearly see that what was a movement for liberty in some parts of the world, when seen from the other side of the world, from beneath, from the popular classes, only meant new and more refined forms of exploitation of the very poorest—of the wretched of the earth. For them, the attainment of freedom can only be the result of a process of liberation from the spoliation and oppression being carried on in the name of "modern liberties and democracy." Here faith is lived by the poor of this world. Here the theological reflection seeking self-expression has no intention of being a palliative for these sufferings and refuses integration into the dominant theology. Here theology is ever more conscious of what separates it from the dominant theologies, conservative or progressive.

SOURCE: Gustavo Gutierrez, *The Power of the Poor in History: Selected Writings,* trans. Robert R. Barr (Maryknoll, NY: Orbis Books, 1983), 18; 186. Used by permission of the publisher.

A U.S. RESPONSE TO SOUTH AFRICAN APARTHEID

IN 1977, THE Reverend Leon H. Sullivan, pastor of Zion Baptist Church in Philadelphia, wrote a set of action principles as a response to the apartheid conditions he witnessed in South Africa in 1974. These principles were later adopted by a number of U.S. corporations and religious organizations.

THE SULLIVAN PRINCIPLES

Each of the firms endorsing the Statement of Principles have affiliates in the Republic of South Africa and support the following principles:

1. Non-segregation of the races in all eating, comfort, and work facilities.
2. Equal and fair employment practices for all employees.

3. Equal pay for all employees doing equal or comparable work for the same period of time.
4. Initiation of and development of training programs that will prepare in substantial numbers Blacks and other non-whites for supervisory, administrative, clerical and technical jobs.
5. Increasing the number of Blacks and other non-whites in management and supervisory positions.
6. Improving the quality of employees' lives outside the work environment in such areas as housing, transportation, schooling, recreation, and health facilities.

We agree to further implement these principles. Where implementation requires a modification of existing South African working conditions, we will seek such modification through appropriate channels.

We believe that the implementation of the foregoing principles is consistent with respect for human dignity and will contribute greatly to the general economic welfare of all the people of the Republic of South Africa.

SOURCE: Leon H. Sullivan, "The Sullivan Principles" (minutes of the General Board of the American Baptist Churches in the U.S.A., December 7–9, 1981), 16.

A RADICAL CHALLENGE TO THE CHURCH IN SOUTH AFRICA

BETWEEN 1960 AND the later 1980s, a number of church groups issued statements critical of apartheid. The most radical statement of all was the Kairos Document published in September 1985. Its origin was at the Institute for Contextual Theology in Johannesburg and several black pastors and theologians participated in the process. The Dominican theologian Albert Nolan was a principal author. One hundred fifty pastors, theologians, and laypersons, black and white, signed the document, which evolved as a kind of confessional statement addressed to both the churches and the state.

THE KAIROS DOCUMENT

The Moment of Truth

The time has come. The moment of truth has arrived. South Africa has been plunged into a crisis that is shaking the foundations and there is every indication that the crisis has only just begun and that it will deepen and become even more threatening in the months to come. It is the KAIROS or moment of truth not only for apartheid but also for the Church.

We as a group of theologians have been trying to understand the theological significance of this moment in our history. It is serious, very serious. For very many Christians in South Africa this is the KAIROS, the moment of grace and opportunity, the favourable time in which God issues a challenge to decisive action. It is a dangerous time because, if this opportunity is missed and allowed to pass by, the loss for the Church, for the Gospel and for all the people of South Africa will be immeasurable. Jesus wept over Jerusalem. He wept over the tragedy of the destruction of the city and the massacre of the people that was imminent, "and all because you did not recognize your opportunity (KAIROS) when God offered it" (Lk 19:44).

A crisis is a judgment that brings out the best in some people and the worst in others. A crisis is a moment of truth that shows us up for what we really are. There will be no place to hide and no way of pretending to be what we are not in fact. At this moment in South Africa the Church is about to be shown up for what it really is and no cover-up will be possible.

What the present crisis shows up, although many of us have known it all along, is that *the Church is divided*. More and more people are now saying that there are in fact two Churches in South Africa—a White Church and a Black Church. Even within the same denomination there are in fact two Churches. In the life and death conflict between different social forces that has come to a head in South Africa today, there are Christians (or at least people who profess to be Christians) on both sides of the conflict—and some who are trying to sit on the fence!

Does this prove that Christian faith has no real meaning or relevance for our times? Does it show that the Bible can be used for any purpose at all? Such problems would be critical enough for the Church in any circumstances, but when we also come to see that the conflict in South Africa is between the oppressor and the oppressed, the crisis for the

Church as an institution becomes much more acute. Both oppressor and oppressed claim loyalty to the same Church. They are both baptised in the same baptism and participate together in the breaking of the same bread, the same body and blood of Christ. There we sit in the same Church while outside Christian policemen and soldiers are beating up and killing Christian children or torturing Christian prisoners to death while yet other Christians stand by and weakly plead for peace.

The Church is divided and its day of judgment has come.

The moment of truth has compelled us to analyse more carefully the different theologies in our Churches and to speak out more clearly and boldly about the real significance of these theologies. We have been able to isolate three theologies and we have chosen to call them 'State Theology', 'Church Theology', and 'Prophetic Theology'. In our thorough-going criticism of the first and second theologies we do not wish to mince our words. The situation is too critical for that.

Critique of State Theology

The South African apartheid State has a theology of its own and we have chosen to call it 'State Theology'. 'State Theology' is simply the theological justification of the status quo with its racism, capitalism and totalitarianism. It blesses injustice, canonises the will of the powerful and reduces the poor to passivity, obedience and apathy.

How does 'State Theology' do this? It does it by misusing theological concepts and biblical texts for its own political purposes. In this document we would like to draw your attention to four key examples of how this is done in South Africa. The first would be the use of Roman 13:1–7 to give an absolute and 'divine' authority to the State. The second would be the use of the idea of 'Law and Order' to determine and control what the people may be permitted to regard as just and unjust. The third would be the use of the word 'communist' to brand anyone who rejects 'State Theology'. And finally there is the use that is made of the name of God. . . .

2.2 Law and Order

The State makes use of the concept of law and order to maintain the status quo which it depicts as 'normal'. But this *law* is the unjust and discriminatory laws of apartheid and this *order* is the organised and insti-tutionalised disorder of oppression. Anyone who wishes to change this law and this order is made to feel that they are lawless and disorderly. In other words they are made to feel guilty of sin. . . .

2.4   The God of the State

The State in its oppression of the people makes use again and again of the name of God. Military chaplains use it to encourage the South African Defence Force, police chaplains use it to strengthen policemen and cabinet ministers use it in their propaganda speeches. But perhaps the most revealing of all is the blasphemous use of God's holy name in the preamble to the new apartheid constitution.

> In humble submission to Almighty God, who controls the destinies of nations and the history of peoples; who gathered our forebears together from many lands and gave them this their own; who has guided them from generation to generation; who has wondrously delivered them from the dangers that beset them.

This god is an idol. It is as mischievous, sinister and evil as any of the idols that the prophets of Israel had to contend with. Here we have a god who is historically on the side of the white settlers, who dispossesses black people of their land and who gives the major part of the land to his "chosen people". . . .

Critique of 'Church Theology'

We have analysed the statements that are made from time to time by the so-called 'English-speaking' Churches. We have looked at what Church leaders tend to say in their speeches and press statements about the apartheid regime and the present crisis. What we found running through all these pronouncements is a series of inter-related theological assumptions. These we have chosen to call 'Church Theology'. We are well aware of the fact that this theology does *not* express the faith of the majority of Christians in South Africa today who form the greater part of most of our Churches. Nevertheless the opinions expressed by Church leaders are regarded in the media and generally in our society as the official opinions of the Churches. We have therefore chosen to call these opinions 'Church Theology'. The crisis in which we find ourselves today compels us to question this theology, to question its assumptions, its implications and its practicality.

In a limited, guarded and cautious way this theology is critical of apartheid. Its criticism, however, is superficial and counter-productive because instead of engaging in an in-depth analysis of the signs of our times, it relies upon a few stock ideas derived from Christian tradition and then uncritically and repeatedly applies them to our situation. The stock ideas used by almost all these Church leaders that we would like to examine here are: reconciliation (peace), justice and nonviolence.

3.1   Reconciliation

'Church Theology' takes 'reconciliation' as the key to problem resolution. It talks about the need for reconciliation between white and black, or between all South Africans. 'Church Theology' often describes the Christian stance in the following way: "We must be fair. We must listen to both sides of the story. If the two sides can only meet to talk and negotiate they will sort out their differences and misunderstandings, and the conflict will be resolved". On the face of it this may sound very Christian. But is it?

The fallacy here is that 'reconciliation' has been made into an absolute principle that must be applied in all cases of conflict or dissension. But not all cases of conflict are the same. We can imagine a private quarrel between two people or two groups whose differences are based upon misunderstandings and to reconcile the two sides. But there are other conflicts in which one side is right and the other wrong. There are conflicts where one side is a fully armed and violent oppressor while the other side is defenceless and oppressed. There are conflicts that can only be described as the struggle between justice and injustice, good and evil, God and the devil. To speak of reconciling these two is not only a mistaken application of the Christian idea of reconciliation, it is a total betrayal of all that Christian faith has ever meant. Nowhere in the Bible or in Christian tradition has it ever been suggested that we ought to try to reconcile good and evil, God and the devil. We are supposed to do away with evil, injustice, oppression and sin—not come to terms with it. We are supposed to oppose, confront and reject the devil and not try to sup with the devil.

In our situation in South Africa today it would be totally unChristian to plead for reconciliation and peace before the present injustices have been removed. Any such plea plays into the hands of the oppressor by trying to persuade those of us who are oppressed to accept our oppression and to become reconciled to the intolerable crimes that are committed against us. That is not Christian reconciliation, it is sin. It is asking us to become accomplices in our own oppression, to become servants of the devil. No reconciliation is possible in South Africa *without justice*. . . .

3.3 Non-violence

The stance of 'Church Theology' on non-violence, expressed as a blanket condemnation of all that is *called* violence, has not only been unable to curb the violence of our situation, it has actually, although unwittingly, been a major contributing factor in the recent escalation of State violence. Here again non-violence has been made to an absolute principle that applies to anything anyone *calls* violence without regard for who is using it, which side they are on or what purpose they may have in mind. In our situation, this is simply counter-productive.

The problem for the Church here is the way the word violence is being used in the propaganda of the State. The State and the media have chosen to call violence what some people do in the townships as they struggle for their liberation, i.e. throwing stones, burning cars and buildings and sometimes killing collaborators. But this *excludes* the structural, institutional and unrepentant violence of the State and especially the oppressive and naked violence of the police and the army. These things are not counted as violence. And even when they are acknowledged to be 'excessive', they are called 'misconduct' or even 'atrocities' but never violence. Thus the phrase 'violence in the townships' comes to mean what the young people are doing and not what the police are doing or what apartheid in general is doing to people. If one calls for nonviolence in such circumstances one appears to be criticising the resistance of the people while justifying or at least overlooking the violence of the police and the State. This is how it is understood not only by the State and its supporters but also by the people who are struggling for their freedom. Violence, especially in our circumstances, is a loaded word. . . .

Towards a Prophetic Theology

Our present KAIROS calls for a response from Christians that is biblical, spiritual, pastoral, and, above all, prophetic. It is not enough in these circumstances to repeat generalised Christian principles. We need a bold and incisive response that is prophetic because it speaks to the particular circumstances of this crisis, a response that does not give the impression of sitting on the fence but is clearly and unambiguously taking a stand.

4.1 Social Analysis

The first task of a prophetic theology for our times would be an attempt at social analysis or what Jesus would call "reading the signs of the times" (Mt 16:3) or "interpreting the KAIROS" (Lk 12:56). It is not possible to do this in any detail in this document but we must start with at least the broad outlines of an analysis of the conflict in which we find ourselves.

It would be quite wrong to see the present conflict as simply a racial war. The racial component is there, but we are not dealing with two equal races or nations each with its own selfish group interests. The situation we are dealing with here is one of oppression. The conflict is between an oppressor and the oppressed. The conflict is between two irreconcilable *causes* or *interests* in which the one is just and the other is unjust.

On the one hand we have the interests of those who benefit from the status quo and who are determined to maintain it at any cost, even at the cost of millions of lives. It is in their interests to introduce a number of reforms in order to ensure that the system is not radically changed and that they can continue to benefit from it as they have done in the past. They benefit from the system because it favours them and enables them to accumulate a great deal of wealth and to maintain an exceptionally high standard of living. And they want to make sure that it stays that way even if some adjustments are needed.

On the other hand we have those who do not benefit in any way from the system the way it is now. They are treated as mere labour units, paid starvation wages, separated from their families by migratory labour, moved about like cattle and dumped in homelands to starve—and all for the benefit of a privileged minority. They have no say in the system and are supposed to be grateful for the concessions that are offered to them like crumbs. It is not in their interests to allow this system to continue even in some 'reformed' or 'revised' form. They are no longer prepared to be crushed, oppressed and exploited. They are determined to change the system radically so that it no longer benefits only the privileged few. And they are willing to do this even at the cost of their own lives. What they want is justice for all.

This is our situation of civil war or revolution. The one side is committed to maintaining the system at all costs and the other side is committed to changing it at all costs. There are two conflicting projects here and no compromise is possible. Either we have full and equal justice for all or we don't.

The Bible has a great deal to say about this kind of conflict, about a world that is divided into oppressors and oppressed. . . .

Challenge to Action

5.1   God Sides with the Oppressed

To say that the Church must now take sides unequivocally and consistently with the poor and the oppressed is to overlook the fact that the majority of Christians in South Africa have already done so. By far the greater part of the Church in South Africa *is* poor and oppressed. Of course it cannot be taken for granted that everyone who is oppressed has taken up their own cause and is struggling for their own liberation. Nor can it be assumed that all oppressed Christians are fully aware of the fact that their cause is God's cause. Nevertheless it remains true that the Church is already on the side of the oppressed because that is where the majority of its members are to be found. This fact needs to be appropriated and confirmed by the Church as a whole.

At the beginning of this document it was pointed out that the present crisis has highlighted the divisions in the Church. We are a divided Church precisely because not all the members of our Churches have taken sides against oppression. In other words not all Christians have united themselves with God "who is always on the side of the oppressed" (Ps 103:6). As far as the present crisis is concerned, there is only one way forward to Church unity, and that is for those Christians who find themselves on the side of the oppressor or sitting on the fence to cross over to the other side to be united in faith and action with those who are oppressed. Unity and reconciliation within the Church itself is only possible around God and Jesus Christ who are to be found on the side of the poor and the oppressed.

If this is what the Church must become, if this is what the Church as a whole must have as its project, how then are we to translate it into concrete and effective action?

5.2   Participation in the Struggle

Christians, if they are not doing so already, must quite simply participate in the struggle for liberation and for a just society. The campaigns of the people, from consumer boycotts to stayaways, need to be supported and encouraged by the Church. Criticism will sometimes be necessary but encouragement and support will also be necessary. In other words the present crisis challenges the whole Church to move beyond a mere 'ambulance ministry' to a ministry of involvement and participation.

5.3 Transforming Church Activities

The Church has its own specific activities: Sunday services, communion services, baptisms, Sunday school, funerals and so forth. It also has its specific way of expressing its faith and its commitment, i.e. in the form of confessions of faith. All of these activities must be re-shaped to be more fully consistent with a prophetic faith related to the KAIROS that God is offering us today. The evil forces we speak of in baptism must be named. We know what these evil forces are in South Africa today. The unity and sharing we profess in our communion services or Masses must be named. It is the solidarity of the people inviting all to join it the struggle for God's peace in South Africa. The repentance we preach must be named. It is repentance for our share of the guilt for the suffering and oppression in our country.

Much of what we do in our Church services has lost its relevance to the poor and the oppressed. Our services and sacraments have been appropriated to serve the need of the individual for comfort and security. Now these same Church activities must be reappropriated to serve the real religious needs of all the people and to further the liberating mission of God and the Church in the world.

5.4 Special Campaigns

Over and above its regular activities the Church would need to have special programmes, projects and campaigns because of the special needs of the struggle for liberation in South Africa today. But there is a very important caution here. The Church must avoid becoming a 'Third Force', a force between the oppressor and the oppressed. The Church's programmes and campaigns must not duplicate what the people's organisations are already doing and, even more seriously, the Church must not confuse the issue by having programmes that run counter to the struggles of those political organisations that truly represent the grievances and demands of the people. Consultation, co-ordination and co-operation will be needed. We all have the same goals even when we differ about the final significance of what we are struggling for.

5.5 Civil Disobedience

Once it is established that the present regime has no moral legitimacy and is in fact a tyrannical regime certain things follow for the Church and its activities. In the first place *the Church cannot collaborate with tyranny*. It cannot or should not do anything that appears to give legitimacy to a morally illegitimate regime. Secondly, the Church should not only pray for a change of government, it should also mobilise its members in every parish to begin to think and work and plan for a change of government in South Africa. We must begin to look ahead and begin working now with firm hope and faith for a better future. And finally the moral illegitimacy of the apartheid regime means that the Church will have to be involved at times in *civil disobedience*. A Church that takes its responsibilities seriously in these circumstances will sometimes have to confront and to disobey the State in order to obey God.

5.6 Moral Guidance

The people look to the Church, especially in the midst of our present crisis, for moral guidance. In order to provide this the Church must first make its stand absolutely clear and never tire of explaining and dialoguing about it. It must then help people to understand their rights and their duties. There must be no misunderstanding about the *moral duty* of all who are oppressed to resist oppression and to struggle for liberation and justice. The Church will also find that at times it does need to curb excesses and to appeal to the consciences of those who act thoughtlessly and wildly.

But the Church of Jesus Christ is not called to be a bastion of caution and moderation. The Church should challenge, inspire and motivate people. It has a message of the cross that inspires us to make sacrifices for justice and liberation. It has a message of hope that challenges us to wake up and to act with hope and confidence. The Church must preach this message not only in words and sermons and statements but also through its actions, programmes, campaigns and divine services.

SOURCE: Institute for Contextual Theology (Johannesburg), *The Kairos Document* (Geneva: World Council of Churches, 1985), 47–51.

AN EVANGELICAL ORGANIZATION RESPONDS TO POVERTY

FOLLOWING HIS MISSIONARY involvement in China and Korea after World War II, the Reverend Bob Pierce* rallied support for refugees and orphans in an evangelical Christian organization he founded in 1950, World Vision International. It became the leading exponent of evangelical concern for issues similar to human rights and has evolved as the foremost relief organization of any kind, worldwide. Currently, it supports programs in over twenty-five hundred projects of "transformational development, emergency relief, justice, strategic initiatives, and witness for Jesus Christ, without regard for race, religion, or ideology."

Core Values

The World Vision Partnership shares a common understanding bound together by six core values. These core values are the fundamental and guiding principles that determine World Vision's actions. The core values are our aim, a challenge that we seek to live and work to . . .

We are Christian

We acknowledge one God: Father, Son and Holy Spirit. In Jesus the love, mercy and grace of God are made known to us and all people.

We seek to follow Jesus—in his identification with the poor, the powerless, the afflicted, the oppressed, and the marginalised; in his special concern for children; in his respect for the dignity bestowed equally on women and men; in his challenge to unjust attitudes and systems; in his call to share resources with each other; in his love for all people without discrimination or conditions; in his offer of new life through faith in him.

We hear his call to servant hood, and to humility.

We maintain our Christian identity while being sensitive to the diverse contexts in which we express that identity.

We are committed to the poor

We are called to serve the neediest people of the earth; to relieve their suffering and to promote the transformation of their wellbeing.

We stand in solidarity in a common search for justice. We seek to understand the situation of the poor and work alongside them.

We seek to facilitate an engagement between the poor and the affluent that opens both to transformation.

We respect the poor as active participants, not passive recipients, in this relationship. They are people from whom others may learn and receive, as well as give. The need for transformation is common to all.

Together we share a quest for justice, peace, reconciliation, and healing in a broken world.

We value people. We regard all people as created and loved by God. We give priority to people before money, structures, systems and other institutional machinery. We act in ways that respect the dignity, uniqueness and intrinsic worth of every person—the poor, the donors, our staff and their families, boards, and volunteers.

We celebrate the richness of diversity in human personality, culture and contribution.

We are stewards

The resources at our disposal are not our own. They are a trust from God through donors on behalf of the poor. We speak and act honestly. We are open and factual in our dealings with donors, project communities, governments and the public at large.

We demand of ourselves high standards of professional competence and financial accountability.

We are stewards of God's creation. We care for the earth and act in ways that will restore and protect the environment. We ensure that our development activities are ecologically sound.

We are partners

We are partners with the poor and with donors in a shared ministry.

We are members of an international World Vision partnership that transcends legal, structural, and cultural boundaries.

We pursue relationships with all churches and desire mutual participation in ministry.

We maintain a cooperative stance and a spirit of openness towards other humanitarian organisations.

We are responsive

We are responsive to life-threatening emergencies where our involvement is needed and appropriate. We are willing to take intelligent risks and act quickly.

We do this from a foundation of experience and sensitivity to what the situation requires. We also recognise that even in the midst of crisis the destitute have a contribution to make.

We are responsive in a different sense where deep seated and often complex economic and social deprivation calls for sustainable, long-term development.

SOURCE: "Who is World Vision?" www.wvi.org (January 24, 2003).

WORLD EVANGELICALS UNITE

FOLLOWING THE WORLD Congress on Evangelism in Lausanne that brought together the international evangelical community in 1974, a Second International Congress met in Manila, The Philippines, in July 1989. The participants carried earlier definitions further to include social concern implications of the gospel, particularly in light of the human rights declarations in Protestant and Catholic circles and The Philippines' record on human rights. The motion passed by an overwhelming majority of the forty-three hundred delegates present from 170 nations, "for study, reflection, and comment." It is considered a definitive evangelical statement on issues including human rights.

THE MANILA MANIFESTO

1. We affirm our continuing commitment to the Lausanne Covenant as the basis of our cooperation in the Lausanne movement.

2. We affirm that in the Scriptures of the Old and New Testaments God has given us an authoritative disclosure of his character and will, his redemptive acts and their meaning, and his mandate for mission.

3. We affirm that the biblical gospel is God's enduring message to our world, and we determine to defend, proclaim and embody it.

4. We affirm that human beings, though created in the image of God, are sinful and guilty, and lost without Christ, and that this truth is a necessary preliminary to the gospel.

5. We affirm that the Jesus of history and the Christ of glory are the same person, and that this Jesus Christ is absolutely unique, for he alone is God incarnate, our sin-bearer, the conqueror of death and the coming judge.

6. We affirm that on the cross Jesus Christ took our place, bore our

sins and died our death; and that for this reason alone God freely forgives those who are brought to repentance and faith.

7. We affirm that other religions and ideologies are not alternative paths to God, and that human spirituality, if unredeemed by Christ, leads not to God but to judgment, for Christ is the only way.

8. We affirm that we must demonstrate God's love visibly by caring for those who are deprived of justice, dignity, food and shelter.

9. We affirm that the proclamation of God's kingdom of justice and peace demands the denunciation of all injustice and oppression, both personal and structural; we will not shrink from this prophetic witness.

10. We affirm that the Holy Spirit's witness to Christ is indispensable to evangelism, and that without this supernatural work neither new birth nor new life is possible.

11. We affirm that spiritual warfare demands spiritual weapons, and that we must both preach the word in the power of the Spirit, and pray constantly that we may enter into Christ's victory over the principalities and powers of evil.

12. We affirm that God has committed to the whole church and every member of it the task of making Christ known throughout the world; we long to see all lay and ordained persons mobilized and trained for this task.

13. We affirm that we who claim to be members of the Body of Christ must transcend within our fellowship the barriers of race, gender and class.

14. We affirm that the gifts of the Spirit are distributed to all God's people, women and men, and that their partnership in evangelization must be welcomed for the common good.

15. We affirm that we who proclaim the gospel must exemplify it in a life of holiness and love; otherwise our testimony loses its credibility.

16. We affirm that every Christian congregation must turn itself outward to its local community in evangelistic witness and compassionate service.

17. We affirm the urgent need for churches, mission agencies and other Christian organizations to cooperate in evangelism and social action, repudiating competition and avoiding duplication.

18. We affirm our duty to study the society in which we live, in order to understand its structures, values and needs, and so develop an appropriate strategy of mission.

19. We affirm that world evangelization is urgent and that the reaching of unreached peoples is possible. So we resolve during the last decade of

the twentieth century to give ourselves to these tasks with fresh determination.

20. We affirm our solidarity with those who suffer for the gospel, and will seek to prepare ourselves for the same possibility. We will also work for religious and political freedom everywhere.

21. We affirm that God is calling the whole church to take the whole gospel to the whole world. So we determine to proclaim it faithfully, urgently and sacrificially until he comes.

A. The Whole Gospel

The gospel is the good news of God's salvation from the power of evil, the establishment of his eternal kingdom and his final victory over everything which defies his purpose. In his love God purposed to do this before the world began and effected his liberating plan over sin, death and judgment through the death of our Lord Jesus Christ. It is Christ who makes us free, and unites us in his redeemed fellowship. (Col 2:15; 1. Co 15: 24–28; Eph. 1:4; Col. 1:19; Tit. 2:14)

1. Our Human Predicament

We are committed to preaching the whole gospel, that is, the biblical gospel in its fullness. In order to do so, we have to understand why beings need it.

Men and women have an intrinsic dignity and worth, because they were created in God's likeness to know, love and serve him. But now through sin every part of their humanness have been distorted. Human beings have become self-centered, self-serving rebels, who do not love God or their neighbour as they should. In consequence, they are alienated both from their Creator and from the rest of his creation, which is the basic cause of the pain, disorientation and loneliness which so many people suffer today. Sin also frequently erupts in anti-social behavior, in violent exploitation of others, and in a depletion of the earth's resources of which God has made men and women his stewards. Humanity is guilty, without excuse, and on the broad road which leads to destruction.

Although God's image in human beings has been corrupted, they are still capable of loving relationships, noble deeds and beautiful art. Yet even the finest human achievement is fatally flawed and cannot possibly fit anybody to enter God's presence. Men and women are also spiritual beings, but spiritual practice and self-help techniques can at the most alleviate felt needs; they cannot address the solemn realities of sin, guilt and judgment. Neither human religion, nor human righteousness, nor sociopolitical programs can save people. Self-salvation of every kind is impossible. Left to themselves, human beings are lost forever.

So we repudiate false gospels which deny human sin, divine judgment, the deity and incarnation of Jesus Christ, and the necessity of the cross and resurrection. We also reject half-gospels, which minimize sin and confuse God's grace with human self-effort. We confess that we ourselves have sometimes trivialized the gospel. But we determine in our evangelism to remember God's radical diagnosis and his equally radical remedy. (Ac. 2:27; Ge. 1:26,27; Ro. 3:9–18; 2 Ti. 3:2–4; Ge. 3:17–24; Ro. 1:29–31; Ge. 1:26, 28; 2:15; Ro. 1:20; 2:1; 3:19; Mt. 7:13; Mt. 5:46; 7:11; 1 Ti. 6:16; Ac. 17:22–31; Ro. 3:20; Eph. 2:1–3; Gal. 1:6–9; 2 Co. 11:2–4; 1 Jn. 2:22, 23; 4:1–3; 1 Co. 15:3,4; Jer. 6:14; 8:11)

2. Good News for Today

We rejoice that the living God did not abandon us to our lostness and despair. In his love he came after us in Jesus Christ to rescue and remake us. So the good news focuses on the historic person of Jesus, who came proclaiming the kingdom of God and living a life of humble service, who died for us, becoming sin and a curse in our place, and whom God vindicated by raising him from the dead. To those who repent and believe in Christ, God grants a share in the new creation. He gives us new life, which includes the forgiveness of our sins and the indwelling, transforming power of his Spirit. He welcomes us into his new community, which consists of people of all races, nations and cultures. And he promises that one day we will enter his new world, in which evil will be abolished, nature will be redeemed, and God will reign forever.

This good news must be boldly proclaimed, wherever possible, in church and in public halls, on radio and television, and in the open air, because it is God's power for salvation and we are under obligation to make it known. In our preaching we must faithfully declare the truth which God has revealed in the Bible and struggle to relate it to our own context.

We also affirm that apologetics, namely "the defence and confirmation of the gospel", is integral to the biblical understanding of mission and essential for effective witness in the modern world. Paul "reasoned" with people out of the Scriptures, with a view to "persuading" them of the truth of the gospel. So must we. In fact, all Christians should be ready to give a reason for the hope that is in them.

We have again been confronted with Luke's emphasis that the gospel is good news for the poor and have asked ourselves what this means to the majority of the world's population who are destitute, suffering or oppressed. We have been reminded that the law, the prophets and the wisdom books, all the teaching and ministry of Jesus, all stress God's concern for the materially poor and our consequent duty to defend and care for them. Scripture also refers to the spiritually poor who look to God alone for mercy. The gospel comes as good news to both. The spiritually poor, who, whatever their economic circumstances, humble themselves before God, receive by faith the free gift of salvation. There is no other way for anybody to enter the Kingdom of God. The materially poor and powerless find in addition a new dignity as God's children, and the love of brothers and sisters who struggle with them for their liberation from everything which demeans or oppresses them.

We repent of any neglect of God's truth in Scripture and determine both to proclaim and to defend it. We also repent where we have been indifferent to the plight of the poor, and where we have shown preference for the rich, and we determine to follow Jesus in preaching good news to all people by both word and deed. (*Eph. 22:4, Lk. 15; 19;10; Ac. 8:35; Mk. 1:14, 15; 2 Co. 5:21; Gal. 3:13; Ac. 2:23,24; 2 Co. 5:17; Ac. 2: 38,39; Eph. 2:11–19; Rev. 21:1–5; 22:1–5; Eph. 6:19,20; 2 Ti. 4:2; Ro. 1:14–16; Jer. 23:28; Php. 1:7; Ac. 18:4; 19:8–9; 2 Co. 5:11; 1 Pe. 3:15; Lk. 4:18; 6:20; 7:22; Dt. 15:7–11; Am. 2:6,7; Zec. 7:8–10; Pr. 21:13; Zep. 3:12; Mt. 5:3; Mk. 10:15; 1 Jn. 3:1; Ac. 2:44,45; 4:32–35*) . . .

4. The Gospel and Social Responsibility

The authentic gospel must become visible in the transformed lives of men and women. As we proclaim the love of God we must be involved in loving service, as we preach the Kingdom of God we must be committed to its demands of justice and peace. Evangelism is primary because our chief concern is with the gospel, that all people may have the opportunity to accept Jesus Christ as Lord and Saviour. Yet Jesus not only proclaimed the Kingdom of God, he also demonstrated its arrival by works of mercy and power. We are called today to a similar integration of words and deeds. In a spirit of humility we are to preach and teach, minister to the sick, feed the hungry, care for prisoners, help the disadvantaged and handicapped, and deliver the oppressed. While we acknowledge the diversity of spiritual gifts, callings and contexts, we also affirm that good news and good works are inseparable.

The proclamation of God's kingdom necessarily demands the prophetic denunciation of all that is incompatible with it. Among the evils we deplore are destructive violence, including institutionalized violence, political corruption, all forms of exploitation of people and of the earth, the undermining of the family, abortion on demand, the drug traffic, and the abuse of human rights. In our concern for the poor, we are distressed by the burden of debt in the two-thirds world. We are also outraged by the inhuman conditions in which millions live, who bear God's image as we do.

Our continuing commitment to social action is not a confusion of the kingdom of God with a Christianized society. It is, rather, a recognition that the biblical gospel has inescapable social implications. True mission should always be incarnational. It necessitates entering humbly into other people's worlds, identifying with their social reality, their sorrow and suffering, and their struggles for justice against oppressive powers. This cannot be done without personal sacrifices.

We repent that the narrowness of our concerns and vision has often kept us from proclaiming the lordship of Jesus Christ over all of life, private and public, local and global. We determine to obey his command to "seek first the kingdom of God and his righteousness." *(1 Th. 1:6–10; 1 Jn. 3:17; Ro. 14:17; Ro. 10:14; Mt. 12:28; 1 Jn. 3:18; Mt. 25:34–46; Ac. 6:1–4; Ro. 12:4–8; Mt. 5:16, Jer. 22:1–5; 11–17; 23:5–6; Am. 1:1–2,8; Is. 59; Lev. 25; Job 24:1–12; Eph. 2:8–10; Jn. 17:18; 20:21; Php. 2: 5–8; Ac. 10:36; Mt. 6:33)* . . .

Some of us are members of churches which belong to the World Council of Churches and believe that a positive yet critical participation in its work is our Christian duty. Others among us have no link with the World Council. All of us urge the World Council of Churches to adopt a consistent biblical understanding of evangelism. We confess our own share of responsibility for the brokenness of the Body of Christ, which is a major stumbling-block to world evangelization. We determine to go on seeking that unity in truth for which Christ prayed. We are persuaded that the right way forward towards closer cooperation is frank and patient dialogue on the basis of the Bible, with all who share our concerns. To this we gladly commit ourselves. . . .

12. Difficult Situations

Jesus plainly told his followers to expect opposition. "If they persecuted me," he said, "they will persecute you also." He even told them to rejoice over persecution, and reminded them that the condition of fruitfulness was death.

These predictions, that Christian suffering is inevitable and productive, have come true in every age, including our own. There have been many thousands of martyrs. Today the situation is much the same. We earnestly hope that glasnost and perestroika will lead to complete religious freedom in the Soviet Union and other Eastern bloc nations, and that Islamic and Hindu countries will become more open to the gospel. We deplore the recent brutal suppression of China's democratic movement, and we pray that it will not bring further suffering to the Christians. On the whole, however, it seems that ancient religions are becoming less tolerant, expatriates less welcome, and the world less friendly to the gospel.

In this situation we wish to make three statements to governments which are reconsidering their attitude to Christian believers.

First, Christians are loyal citizens, who seek the welfare of their nation. They pray for its leaders, and pay their taxes. Of course, those who have confessed Jesus as Lord cannot also call other authorities Lord, and if commanded to do so, or to do anything which God forbids, must disobey. But they are conscientious citizens. They also contribute to their country's well-being by the stability of their marriages and their homes, their honesty in business, their hard work and their voluntary activity in the service of the handicapped and needy. Just governments have nothing to fear from Christians. Secondly, Christians renounce unworthy methods of evangelism. Though the nature of our faith requires us to share the gospel with others, our practice is to make an open and honest statement of it, which leaves the hearers entirely free to make up their own minds about it. We wish to be sensitive to those of other faiths, and we reject any approach that seeks to force conversion on them.

Thirdly, Christians earnestly desire freedom of religion for all people, not just freedom for Christianity. In predominantly Christian countries, Christians are at the forefront of those who demand freedom for religious minorities. In predominantly non-Christian countries, therefore, Christians are asking for themselves no more than they demand for others in similar circumstances. The freedom to "profess, practice and propagate" religion, as defined in the Universal Declaration of Human Rights, could and should surely be a reciprocally granted right.

We greatly regret any unworthy witness of which followers of Jesus may have been guilty. We determine to give no unnecessary offence in anything, lest the name of Christ be dishonored. However, the offence of the cross we cannot avoid. For the sake of Christ crucified we pray that we may be ready, by his grace, to suffer and event to die. Martyrdom is a form of witness which Christ has promised especially to honor. (*Jn. 15: 20; Mt. 5:12; Jn. 12:24; Jer. 29:7; 1 Ti. 2:1,2; Ro. 13:6,7; Ac. 4:19; 5: 29; 2 Co. 4:1,2; 2 Co. 6:3; 1 Co. 1:18,23; 2:2; Php. 1:29; Rev. 2:13; 6:9–11; 20:4*)

SOURCE: Lausanne Committee for World Evangelization, "The Manila Manifesto," 1989.

FROM RIGHTS TO RESPONSIBILITIES

THE MOST SIGNIFICANT shift of the last decades of the twentieth century discussions of human rights has involved the new terminology of "human responsibilities." Spurred on by the theological instigation of Reformed theologian Jürgen Moltmann and Catholic/ecumenical theologian Hans Küng, this has now become the interest of a growing global community of politicians ethicists and religious leaders. The InterAction Council was founded in 1983 by Takeo Fukuda, former Prime Minister of Japan. A series of meetings of world leaders was held from 1987 to 1997 closely following events and declarations of the United Nations. Finally the Council adopted a "Universal Declaration of Human Responsibilities" at Noordwijk and passed the document on to the Secretary General of the United Nations, Kofi Annan.

A UNIVERSAL DECLARATION OF HUMAN RESPONSIBILITIES

Preamble
Whereas recognition of the inherent dignity and of the equal and inalienable rights of all members of the human family is the foundation of freedom, justice and peace in the world and implies obligations or responsibilities,

whereas the exclusive insistence on rights can result in conflict, division, and endless dispute, and the neglect of human responsibilities can lead to lawlessness and chaos, *whereas* the rule of law and the promotion of human rights depend on the readiness of men and women to act justly,

whereas global problems demand global solutions which can only be achieved through ideas, values, and norms respected by all cultures and societies,

whereas all people, to the best of their knowledge and ability, have a responsibility to foster a better social order, both at home and globally, a goal which cannot be achieved by laws, prescriptions, and conventions alone,

whereas human aspirations for progress and improvement can only be realized by agreed values and standards applying to all people and institutions at all times,

Now, therefore,

The General Assembly

proclaims this Universal Declaration of Human Responsibilities as a common standard for all peoples and all nations, to the end that every individual and every organ of society, keeping this Declaration constantly in mind, shall contribute to the advancement of communities and to the enlightenment of all their members. We, the peoples of the world, thus renew and reinforce commitments already proclaimed in the Universal Declaration of Human Rights: namely, the full acceptance of the dignity of all people; their inalienable freedom and equality, and their solidarity with one another. Awareness and acceptance of these responsibilities should be taught and promoted throughout the world.

Fundamental Principles for Humanity

Article 1

Every person, regardless of gender, ethnic origin, social status, political opinion, language, age, nationality, or religion, has a responsibility to treat **all people in a humane way.**

Article 2

No person should lend support to any form of inhumane behaviour, but all people have a responsibility to strive for the dignity and self-esteem of all others.

Article 3

No person, no group or organization, no state, no army or police stands above good and evil; all are subject to ethical standards. Everyone has a responsibility to promote good and to avoid evil in all things.

Article 4

All people, endowed with reason and conscience, must accept a responsibility to each and all, to families, and communities, to races, nations, and religions in a spirit of solidarity: **what you do not wish to be done to yourself, do not do to others**.

Non-Violence and Respect for Life

Article 5

Every person has a responsibility to **respect life**. No one has the right to injure, to torture or to kill another human person. This does not exclude the right of justified self-defence of individuals or communities.

Article 6

Disputes between states, groups or individuals should be resolved without violence. No government should tolerate or participate in acts of genocide or terrorism, nor should it abuse women, children, or any other civilians as instruments of war. Every citizen and public official has a responsibility to act in a peaceful, non-violent way.

Article 7

Every person is infinitely precious and must be protected unconditionally. The animals and the natural environment also demand protection. All people have a responsibility to protect the air, water and soil of the earth for the sake of present inhabitants and future generations.

Article 8

Every person has a responsibility to behave with **integrity, honesty and fairness**. No person or group should rob or arbitrarily deprive any other person or group or their property.

Article 9

All people, given the necessary tools, have a responsibility to make serious efforts to overcome poverty, malnutrition, ignorance, and inequality.

They should promote sustainable development all over the world in order to assure dignity, freedom, security and justice for all people.

Article 10

All people have a responsibility to develop their talents through diligent endeavour; they should have equal access to education and to meaningful work. Everyone should lend support to the needy, the disadvantaged, the disabled and to the victims of discrimination.

Article 11

All property and wealth must be used responsibly in accordance with justice and for the advancement of the human race. Economic and political power must not be handled as an instrument of domination, but in the service of economic justice and of the social order.

Truthfulness and Tolerance

Article 12

Every person has a responsibility to **speak and act truthfully**. No one, however high or mighty, should speak lies. The right to privacy and to personal and professional confidentiality is to be respected. No one is obliged to tell all the truth to everyone all the time.

Article 13

No politicians, public servants, business leaders, scientists, writers or artists are exempt from general ethical standards, nor are physicians, lawyers and other professionals who have special duties to clients. Professional and other codes of ethics should reflect the priority of general standards such as those of truthfulness and fairness.

Article 14

The freedom of the media to inform the public and to criticize institutions of society and governmental actions, which is essential for a just society, must be used with responsibility and discretion. Freedom of the media carries a special responsibility for accurate and truthful reporting. Sensational reporting that degrades the human person or dignity must at all times be avoided.

Article 15

While religious freedom must be guaranteed, the representatives of religions have a special responsibility to avoid expressions of prejudice and acts of discrimination toward those of different beliefs. They should not incite or legitimize hatred, fanaticism and religious wars, but should foster tolerance and mutual respect between all people.

Mutual Respect and Partnership

Article 16

All men and all women have a **responsibility to show respect** to one another **and understanding** in their partnership. No one should subject another person to sexual exploitation or dependence. Rather, sexual partners should accept the responsibility of caring for each other's well-being.

Article 17

In all its cultural and religious varieties, marriage requires love, loyalty and forgiveness and should aim at guaranteeing security and mutual support.

Article 18

Sensible family planning is the responsibility of every couple. The relationship between parents and children should reflect mutual love, respect, appreciation and concern. No parents or other adults should exploit, abuse or maltreat children.

Conclusion

Article 19

Nothing in this Declaration may be interpreted as implying for any state, group or person any right to engage in any activity or to perform any act aimed at the destruction of any of the responsibilities, rights and freedom set forth in this Declaration and in the Universal Declaration of Human Rights of 1948.

SOURCE: Hans Küng and Helmut Schmidt, eds., *A Global Ethic and Global Responsibilities: Two Declarations* (London: SCM Press, 1998), 6–32.

BIOGRAPHICAL SKETCHES OF HUMAN RIGHTS LEADERS IN THE CHRISTIAN TRADITION

Backus, Isaac (1724–1806)

American Baptist minister and political theorist. Self-taught, Backus experienced a conversion in 1741 and shortly thereafter he began to preach among the Separates, a group of congregations in New England that supported the Great Awakening. He was ordained and served a church at Titicut, Massachusetts, in 1747. He came under the influence of Baptist principles and converted to that movement in 1755. In 1756, he organized the Middleborough, Massachusetts, First Baptist Church, which he served for fifty years. Backus became an opponent of infant baptism and religious taxation to support ministers, two hallmarks of New England Congregationalism. He began to publish tracts on the subject of religious liberty and joined petition movements for separation of church and state and disestablishment directed in 1754 at the Massachusetts Legislature and in 1774 the Continental Congress. In 1779, he supported a bill of rights for the Massachusetts Constitution and he spoke out against slave trade in the Massachusetts debate on the ratification of the federal constitution in 1788. Long an advocate of religious liberty in the Lockean tradition, Backus was a leader in ending establishment in Massachusetts. **Works:** *The Difference Between the Bond-Woman and the Free* (1756); *An Appeal to the Public for Religious Liberty* (1773); *History of New England Baptists* (1777; 1784). **Suggested Readings:** Alvah Hovey, *A Memoir of the Life and Times of the Rev. Isaac Backus, A.M.* (Boston: 1858); Thomas B. Maston, *Isaac Backus: Pioneer* *of Religious Liberty* (Rochester, NY: 1962); William G. McLoughlin, ed., *The Diary of Isaac Backus*, 3 vols. (Providence, RI: 1979).

Benezet, Anthony (1713–1784)

Quaker educator and social reformer. The son of Huguenots, Benezet joined the Society of Friends in London and in 1731 immigrated to Philadelphia, where he became a merchant. Sensing little fulfillment in that work, he turned to teaching and became an advocate of the education of youth. He published spelling books and took a special interest in disadvantaged youth. In 1770, he opened a school for freed blacks in his home. In the 1750s, Benezet developed abolitionist views and published important tracts on the evils of the slave trade and the keeping of slaves. He was a leading voice among the Society of Friends in creating an abolitionist position and his works greatly impressed a variety of leaders including Granville Sharp, John Wesley, and Thomas Clarkson. His work was widely circulated in England and France during the nineteenth century. Benezet also wrote on the plight of the Acadian refugees, temperance, peace, poor relief, and the fair treatment of Native Americans. He willed his estate to his school for black children in Philadelphia. **Works:** *Observations on the Inslaving, Importing, and Purchasing of Negroes* (1759); *Thoughts on the Nature of War and Its Repugnancy to the Christian Life.* **Suggested Readings:** Nancy Slocum Hornick, "Anthony Benezet: Eighteenth Century Social Critic, Educator, and Abolitionist" (unpublished PhD diss., University of Maryland, 1974); George S. Brookes, *Friend Anthony Benezet* (Philadelphia: 1937).

Boff, Leonardo (1938–)

Brazilian Franciscan priest and liberationist. Boff was born in Concordia, Brazil and ordained in the Franciscan Order in 1964. He studied at universities in Brazil at Petroplis and Curitiba, and at Munich in Germany. Mentored by Gustavo Gutierrez, Boff wrote the book *Charism and Power* in 1981 in which he tied the insights of liberation theology not only to society, but to the church as well. He was, for instance, critical of human rights abuses within the Catholic Church. His former theological teacher in Brazil, Bonaventura Kloppenburg, reviewed the book negatively, causing widespread disfavor for Boff. In May 1985, Cardinal Ratzinger of the Sacred Congregation for the Doctrine of the Faith in

Rome summoned Boff to the Vatican and "silenced" him from his teaching and editorial responsibilities. Ten months later on Easter Day 1986, the "silencing" was lifted after Pope John Paul II had conferred with Brazilian bishops and agreed to cast liberation thought in a more favorable light. Worldwide Christians came to view Boff as a kind of modern human rights symbol of freedom of thought within the Christian tradition. Boff has continued to write and lecture as Professor of Systematic Theology at the Franciscan Institute in Petropolis and editor of *Ecclesiastica Brasiliera*. He also advises ecclesial base communities in Latin America. **Works:** *Jesus Christ, Liberator* (1971); *Church, Charism, and Power* (1981); *Trinity, Society, and Liberation* (1987). **Suggested Readings:** Jose Miquez-Bonino, *Faces of Jesus: Latin American Christologies* (Maryknoll, NY: Orbis Books, 1984); Harvey G. Cox, *The Silencing of Leonardo Boff: The Vatican and the Future of World Christianity* (Oak Park, IL: 1988); David J. Hillman, *Ecotheology: Voices from the South and North* (Geneva World Council of Churches, 1994).

Bojaxhiu, Agnes Gonxha, "Mother Theresa" (1910–1997)

Catholic nun, charity worker, and social activist. Born in Albania and raised in a middle-class family, Bojaxhiu entered the Sisters of Loreto and studied English in Ireland. She taught school in Calcutta and with Episcopal permission she left the Lureto Convent in 1948 and went to Matizhil (also Motijhil, meaning "Pearl Lake"), a nearby slum area in the eastern industrial district of Calcutta where she found the "poorest of the poor." She organized dispensaries and outdoor schools where she fed, clothed, and instructed poor children. She enlisted women of her former students and they became the "Missionaries of Charity." In 1950, this order received papal approval. In 1952, "Mother Theresa" founded a hospice for the dying and a leper colony in 1957. Later, AIDS victims were added to the concern of the Sisters. She was awarded the first Pope John XXIII Peace Prize in 1971 and the Nobel Peace Prize in 1979. She was elected every year until 1997 to be the major superior of her order and traveled worldwide in support of human rights and the basic needs of the desperately poor and infirmed. **Works:** *Words to Love By* (New York: 1983); *My Life for the Poor* (San Francisco: 1985); *A Simple Path* (New York: 1995). **Suggested Readings:** B. L. Marthaler, "Mother Theresa" *Catholic Encyclopedia*, vol. X (2003), 15–16; C. Feldman,

Mother Theresa: Love Stays. (New York: 1998); Malcolm Muggeridge, *Something Beautiful for God* (San Francisco: 1998).

Bonhoeffer, Dietrich (1906–1945)

German theologian, ethicist, and martyr. Bonhoeffer was born in Germany in Breslau, the son of a physician and university lecturer. In her youth, Mrs. Bonhoeffer had spent time at Herrnhut, home of the Moravian Pietists. Early in life, he determined on a career in ministry and he studied in Germany at Tübingen with Adolph Schlatter, and later at Berlin where he completed a doctoral thesis under Reinhold Seeberg. Three influences that helped to define the young Bonhoeffer were his fascination with Roman Catholicism, the theological work of Karl Barth, and the historical method of Adolph von Harnack. He served a pastorate in the German Colony in Barcelona in 1928 and then returned to Berlin to prepare for his habilitation thesis. From 1930–1933 he traveled for study at Union Theological Seminary in New York and within Europe among an elite ecumenical circle that included W. A. Visser't Hooft and George K. A. Bell, bishop of Chichester. As he took up lecturing in theology at Berlin, he was confronted with the rise of National Socialism. Increasingly, Bonhoeffer became concerned about the Jewish situation and the pressure placed upon the State Church to adopt an Aryan policy. He was also troubled over the attempts of the Nazi Party to influence and later control the German church as the Reich Church Government. In 1934, he joined those who drafted the Barmen Declaration and moved to shape the Confessing Church in Germany, in essence an "opposition" church to the Third Reich. When regional "preacher's seminaries" were organized in the Confessing Church, in 1935 he joined the faculty and became director of an Old Prussian Council of Brethren seminary at Finkenwald where he designed the entire curriculum. For a time his lectures attracted numbers of students. Gradually, however, Bonhoeffer's circle of colleagues were silenced and the seminaries were closed in 1940. With the first deportation of Jews in 1940, he took the advice of friends in Switzerland, Sweden, and the United States and concluded that, like Christ, he must identify with his country and bear its suffering, whatever that might entail. Following the attempted assassination plot against Hitler in 1943, he was arrested and charged with "subversion of the armed forces" and treason against his country. Imprisoned at Tegel Prison with Josef Mueller and Hans von

Dohnanyi, Bonhoeffer continued to write and fight his case legally. While his own role in the plot against Hitler was small, his participation in the opposition and his wide reputation placed a premium on his head. He was given over to the Gestapo in 1944 and sent to Buchenwald Concentration Camp in February 1945. Transferred to Floessenburg, he was executed during the night of April 9. His impact upon Christian ethics has been long term, advocating a biblical and Christological basis for human rights if such rights are to be acceptable to the Christian Church. **Works:** *Sanctorum Communio* (Berlin: 1930); *Act and Being* (Berlin: 1931); *Cost of Discipleship* (Berlin: 1937). **Suggested Readings:** Mary Bosanquet, *The Life and Death of Dietrich Bonhoeffer* (New York: 1968); Eberhard Bethge, *Dietrich Bonhoeffer: Man of Vision, Man of Courage* (New York: 1970); Keith W. Clements, *What Freedom? The Persistent Challenge of Dietrich Bonhoeffer* (Bristol: 1990); Michael Westmoreland-White, "Contributions to Human Rights in Dietrich Bonhoeffer's Ethics," *Journal of Church and State* (Winter 1997): 67–83.

Brunner, Emil (1889–1966)

Reformed theologian. Brunner was educated at the universities of Zurich and Berlin, receiving his doctorate in theology from Zurich. He completed post-graduate work at Union Theological Seminary in New York. He was pastor of a Reformed congregation in Switzerland, after which he assumed the chair in Systematic and Practical Theology at the University of Zurich. Brunner attracted scores of students to his seminars, where he discarded the reigning liberal theology in favor of re-grounding the Christian faith in the revelation of God in Christ. Along with Karl Barth and Reinhold Niebuhr, he virtually defined "Neo–Orthodox" theology. His crowning appointment was in postwar Japan as visiting Professor of Christianity and Ethics at International Christian University in Tokyo. Brunner made an influential Reformed contribution to a Christian theology of human rights in his book, *Christianity and Civilization*, in which he argued for a definition of rights that applied to all humans as part of the dignity of God's creation. Rights, he held, were derived from God and pertained solely to humans. **Works:** *Christianity and Civilization* (New York: 1948); *The Christian Doctrine of Redemption*; *Revelation and Reason*; *Eternal Hope*. **Suggested Readings:** Paul K. Jewitt, *Emil Brunner: An Introduction to the Man and His Thought* (Downer's Grove, IL: 1961); J. Edward Humphrey, *Emil Brunner* (Waco, TX: 1976);

Dale Moody, "An Introduction to Emil Brunner," *Review and Expositor* (July 1947).

Burgess, David S. (1917–)

United Church of Christ human rights activist. Reared in China where his parents were YMCA workers, Burgess was educated at Oberlin College and Union Theological Seminary in New York. He became a chaplain for the Congregational Christian Churches to the Southern Tenant Farmers Union in 1944. In that role, Burgess fought for the rights of poor blacks against oppression of industrial canners and local landowners. Later, in Missouri, he fought to save the housing projects of sharecroppers in the Delmo Projects. Subsequently, he served as a labor union organizer and a political manager. After a term of service in India, Burgess became the Indonesia chief of the United States Agency for International Development (USAID) where he organized the first generation of Peace Corps workers. In 1966, he left the Foreign Service for a position in Thailand with UNICEF, concentrating on poor children and mothers from three Southeast Asian nations, and later as a fund-raiser for the U.S. office of UNICEF. Burgess concluded his career as an urban pastor in two parishes with the United Church of Christ in Newark, New Jersey. There he built positive relations between races and he helped the congregations to address various neighborhood problems. During his tenure in Newark, he was executive director of Metropolitan Ecumenical Ministry following the race riots of 1967. Improvement of housing, schools, and neighborhood development composed Burgess's agenda, which he fostered through ecumenical relationships. **Works:** "Wake Up Theologians" *Christian Century*, (December 4, 1946); *Fighting for Social Justice: The Life Story of David Burgess* (Detroit: 2000). **Suggested Reading:** H. L. Mitchell, *Mean Things Happening in the Land* (Montclair, NJ: 1970).

Calvert, Cecilius, Second Lord Baltimore (1605–1675)

Colonial planter and founder of Maryland. Born in Kent County, England, the son of George Calvert, First Lord Baltimore, Calvert attended Trinity College in Oxford, but took no degree. Initially a conforming Anglican, he announced his conversion to Roman Catholicism before 1624. He took the name Cecilius when he was confirmed in the Catholic faith. He inherited his father's estate and dream to start a colony in North America. In 1632, he took charge of his father's charter from Charles I to colonize Maryland, but was prevented from traveling to America himself. The charter gave him feudal proprietary privileges and he worked through several governors to manage his enterprise. From the beginning, he avoided conflicts over religious matters, recognizing the advantages to toleration. In two important early cases he ruled in favor of Protestants, demonstrating his commitment to balanced administration. Bitter quarrels erupted in the young colony's history and Calvert moved strategically to avert major strife. He ensured the rights of Catholics in the colony by an oath each officer took not to interfere with any Christian's free exercise of religion. In 1649, he sent the Maryland Legislature a draft of An Act Concerning Religion. The Legislature passed the Act, after much debate and the Act became the first legal guarantee of Christian's rights to worship free of molestation from government authorities. Although the Act was rescinded in 1654, Baltimore's dream of governing a religiously pluralistic society with toleration lasted until 1688 when Protestants enforced intolerant practices against Catholics. **Works:** Richard J. Cox, *A Guide to the Microfilm Edition of the Calvert Papers* (Baltimore: 1973). **Suggested Reading:** John D. Krugler, "Lord Baltimore, Roman Catholics, and Toleration: Religious Policy During the Early Catholic Years, 1632–1649," *Catholic Historical Review* 65 (January 1979): 49–75.

Carter, James Earl, Jr. (1924–)

Thirty-ninth U.S. president and Baptist leader. He was educated at the United States Naval Academy and served seven years in the U.S. Navy. He then pursued a career in peanut agriculture. In 1962, he entered state politics in Georgia and was elected governor. In 1974, he was elected president on the Democratic ticket. Carter's one-term presidency was marked by close attention to Christian principles and human rights. He appointed a record number of women and minorities to government positions and was a model of racial equality. His foreign affairs policies were dictated by human rights. His posture with respect to other nations was set by their conformity to international human rights standards. In the Middle East, he secured the Camp David Accord between Egypt and Israel, he brought full recognition to China, and he completed a strategic arms limitation treaty with the Soviet Union. In 1977, President Carter signed the Human Rights Agreement, hoping for Senate ratification that never occurred. Throughout his presidency, he openly attended church and taught a Sunday School class at First Baptist, Washington, D.C. Following his term in office, Carter became active in international projects, observing democratic processes and advocating human rights in various crisis situations. At home, he was active in Habitat for Humanity and democratic decision making as his own Southern Baptist denomination absorbed a takeover by fundamentalists. In 2002, Carter was awarded the Nobel Prize for Peace in recognition of his record in human rights advocacy. The Carter-Menil Human Rights Award was established in 1986 to honor individuals or organizations that promote human rights. **Works:** *Keeping Faith: Memoirs of a President* (New York: 1982); *The Blood of Abraham* (Boston: 1985); *Talking Peace: A Vision for the Next Generation* (New York: 1993). **Suggested Readings:** Peter Meyer, *James Earl Carter: The Man and the Myth.* (Kansas City: 1978); Burton I. Kaufman, *The Presidency of James Earl Carter, Jr.* (Lawrence, KS: 1993).

Clarke, John (1609–1676)

Baptist clergyman and colonial leader in Rhode Island. Clarke was possibly educated at Cambridge University and received training in medicine. Immigrating to Boston in 1637, he became a supporter of Anne Hutchinson in the Antinomian Controversy and shortly thereafter left the colony to settle at Newport, Rhode Island. Clarke became pastor of a congregation in Newport and adopted Baptist views after 1644. In 1648, his church became the second Baptist congregation in America, after a church in Providence. During an evangelical pastoral call in Lynn, Massachusetts, in 1651, he and two colleagues, Obadiah Holmes and John Crandall, were imprisoned. He became a vocal critic of intolerant attitudes in Massachusetts and published *Ill Newes from New England; or A Narrative of New England's Persecution. Wherein is Declared that While Old England is Becoming New, New England Is Become Old* (1652). He returned to London to be an agent for the colony, and in 1661, he led the fight to obtain a charter for Rhode Island. The charter, issued in 1663, called for religious liberty in broad terms similar to those expressed by Thomas Helwys. Clarke returned to his pastorate at Newport where he again faced controversy over Sabbatarian issues. He steadfastly resisted a highly confessional style of ecclesiology. **Works:** *Ill Newes from New England* (London: 1652). **Suggested Readings:** Wilbur

Nelson, *The Hero of Aquidneck: A Life of Dr. John Clarke* (1938); Sydney James, *John Clarke and His Legacies: Religion and Law in Colonial Rhode Island 1638–1750* (University Park, PA: 1999).

Dawson, Joseph Martin (1879–1973)

Baptist clergyman and public affairs executive. Dawson was educated at Baylor University and served churches in central Texas. He served as executive director of the Baptist Joint Committee on Public Affairs from 1946 to 1953. He represented Baptists at the founding of the United Nations in San Francisco in 1945 and advocated a declaration of religious liberty for the U.N. charter. Dawson was an ecumenical leader in a denominational tradition that stressed individualism and local church autonomy. He was a member of the Religious Liberty Committee of the National Council of Churches, a board member of the American Civil Liberties Union, and a founder of Protestants and Other Americans United for the Separation of Church and State (POAU). Baylor University named its Church State Institute in his honor in 1957. **Works:** J. M. Dawson, *America's Way in Church, State, and Society* (1953); *A Thousand Months to Remember: An Autobiography* (1964). **Suggested Readings:** James E. Wood, Jr., "The Legacy of Joseph Martin Dawson: 1879–1973," *Journal of Church and State* (1973); "Dawson, Joseph Martin" in *Encyclopedia of Southern Baptists*, vol. IV (Nashville: Baptist Sunday School Board, 1982): 2181.

Douglas, Thomas Clement (1904–1986)

Canadian Baptist minister, social reformer, and political leader. Douglas was born in Scotland and studied for the Baptist ministry at Brandon College. He was pastor at Weyburn, Saskatchewan, 1931–1933. He became acquainted with Dores R. Sharpe, a student of Walter Rauschenbusch and the social gospel. During the Great Depression, Douglas developed programs to alleviate poverty and unemployment as a member of the Federal House of Commons and later in the Province of Saskatchewan as premier for seventeen years. First associated with the Canadian Commonwealth Federation (CCF) and, after 1961, the New Democratic Party (NDP), he advocated many social improvements including collective bargaining, minimum wages, social welfare, and rural electrification. His greatest achievement was his plan for a national health-care system, realized in the 1960s. **Works:** *Essays on the Left: In*

Honour of T. C. Douglas (Toronto: 1971); *Making of a Socialist: Recollections of T. C. Douglas* (Edmonton: 1982). **Suggested Readings:** Robert Tyre, *Douglas in Saskatchewan: The Story of a Socialist Experiment* (Vancouver: 1962); Davis French, *Tommy Douglas* (Toronto: 1975); Thomas H. McLeod, *Tommy Douglas: The Road to Jerusalem* (Edmonton: 1987).

Dussel, Enrique (1934–)

Latin American ethicist. Dussel was born in Argentina and took degrees in theology and church history. A lecturer in ethics and church history in Mexico, he is president of the CEHILA project, the Study Commission on Church History of Latin America. He is a founder of the Ecumenical Association of Third World Theologians and the author of numerous liberationist works on the history of the church in Latin America. More than any other writer, Dussel has amassed data and interpretation on the plight of the poor and their role in the development of Christian Latin America. **Works:** *Ethics and the Theology of Liberation* (1978); *History of the Church in Latin America 1492–1992* (Maryknoll, NY: 1992). **Suggested Readings:** Michael D. Barber, *Ethical Hermeneutics: Rationality in Enrique Dussel's Philosophy of Liberation* (New York: 1997); Linda Alcoff, *Thinking from the Underside of History: Enrique Dussel's Philosophy of Liberation* (London: 2000).

Eddy, Thomas (1758–1827)

Quaker merchant and social reformer. Eddy made his fortune in the tobacco trade of the revolutionary era and turned to Quakerism about 1779 in New York. A Tory by political sentiment, he was imprisoned in a Monmouth County jail, and this sensitized him to the inhumane conditions of those incarcerated. He and Philip Schuyler joined forces through the Philadelphia Society for Alleviating the Miseries of Public Prisons and influenced the New York Assembly to modify its penal laws. Eddy designed the Newgate Prison in Greenwich Village and later superintended the project himself. Much influenced by the British reformer, John Howard, he advocated single prison cells and sanitary, humane treatment for insane patients. He thought that alcohol and gambling were principal causes for modest crimes and lobbied to have prisoners guilty of more serious offenses handled separately from minor offenders. He also opposed the death penalty. **Works:** *An Account of the*

State Prison or Penitentiary House in the City of New York (New York: 1801); *An Account of the New-York Hospital* (New York: 1811). **Suggested Readings:** Samuel L. Knapp, *Life of Thomas Eddy* (New York: 1834); Hugh Barbour, et al., eds., *Quaker Crosscurrents: Three Hundred Years of Friends in the New York Yearly Meetings* (Syracuse, NY: 1995).

Francis of Assisi (c.1182–1226)

Catholic friar and spiritual leader. The son of a textile merchant, Francesco di Pietro di Bernardone received a liberal arts education, with a knowledge of Latin and French. He was imprisoned during a conflict between Assisi and Perugia after which he was seriously ill. About 1205, he had a religious conversion and set upon rebuilding the church in Assisi. Hearing a sermon on the mission of the gospel, he renounced his family relationships and took an oath of poverty in 1209. His lifestyle attracted several followers and he drew up a form of life for his "brothers." Pope Innocent III approved the document and the brothers became a penitential movement based in the valley below Assisi. Francis made several tours in the Middle East, Dalmatia, and Spain. During the Fifth Crusade, he attempted to convert the sultan of Egypt. The Friars Minor became under his leadership a worldwide order devoted to preaching and the alleviation of human suffering. He is remembered as an apostle of peace and one who extolled the beauty of creation. In 1979, Pope John Paul II proclaimed St. Francis to be the patron saint of ecology. **Works:** R. Armstrong, J. Hellman, and W. Short, eds., *Francis of Assisi: Early Documents*. 3 vols. **Suggested Reading:** R. Mansell, *St Francis of Assisi* (Chicago: 1988).

Fuller, Millard (1935–)

United Church of Christ humanitarian leader and activist. Raised in eastern Alabama, Fuller was majored in economics at Auburn University and later earned a law degree at the University of Alabama. Upon graduation, Fuller and a partner started a direct mail and publishing business that made him a millionaire. Lacking fulfillment in his life, Ferguson and his wife, Linda, visited Koinonia Farm and were mentored by Clarence Jordan. In 1968, the Fullers moved permanently to Koinonia Farm and, with Jordan, developed a project called Partnership Housing and Fund for Humanity. From 1973 to 1976, the couple began a mission for the Disciples of Christ in Mbandaka, Zaire, in which they worked on improving housing. In 1976, upon returning to Koinonia Farm, the Fullers organized Habitat for Humanity, a partnership of Christians dedicated to eradicating poverty housing from the face of the earth through construction projects in which private donations financed the homes and volunteers donated labor. Between 1976 and 1991, Habitat built ten thousand homes, and Fuller moved to become one of the top housing construction executives in the United States. All the while, he and his family still lived in a simple house without air conditioning in a low-income area of Americus, Georgia. In 1983, former president Jimmy Carter and his wife Rosalynn joined forces with Habitat in fund-raising and actual construction work. **Works:** *No More Shacks: The Daring Vision of Habitat for Humanity* (Waco, TX: 1986); *Love in the Mortar Joints: The Story of Habitat for Humanity* (Clinton, NJ: 1980); *Theology of the Hammer* (Macon, GA: 1994). **Suggested Readings:** Frye Gaillard, *If I Were a Carpenter: Twenty Years of Habitat for Humanity* (Winston-Salem, NC: 1996); Jerome P. Baggett, *Habitat for Humanity: Building Private Homes, Building Public Religion* (Philadelphia: 2001); "Millard Fuller" in *Current Biography Yearbook*, 1995, 196–201.

Garrison, William Lloyd (1805–1879)

Publisher and rights activist. Young William was raised in abject poverty and was much influenced by his mother's Baptist piety. At an early age, he was apprenticed to a newspaper publisher and opened his own paper at Newburyport, Massachusetts, in 1818. His publishing efforts languished in part because of his acerbic tongue. During the 1820s, he fell in with Benjamin Lundy, a Quaker activist, and Garrison became a convinced abolitionist. His circle soon included other prominent antislave enthusiasts like Arthur and Lewis Tappan of New York. In 1831, Garrison began publication of the *Liberator*, the paper that won him national attention for reform advocacy. The following year he helped organize the New England Antislavery Society and exhibited an immediatist position that he pursued with religious fervor. He soon led in the creation of the American Antislavery Society in 1833 and traveled to England to link up with British abolitionists. Upon his return to the United States, he was widely acclaimed as a reformer opposing colonization, all positions in defense of slavery, any attitude of racial superiority, and, due to his association with the Grimke sisters, women's rights.

He lost touch with organized religion which he disdained, referring to scripture as "superstition." "Garrisonianism" came to be associated with extreme reform and was shunned by moderates. Garrison was bypassed by the political process and spent the remainder of his career in publishing and advocating rights for former slaves. **Works:** *Thoughts on Slavery* (Boston: 1832); *Declaration of Sentiments of the American Antislavery Society* (New York: 1833); Wallace Merrill, ed., *The Letters of William Lloyd Garrison 1805–1879* (Cambridge, MA: 1979). **Suggested Readings:** Dwight L. Dumond, *Antislavery: The Crusade for Freedom in America* (New York: 1961); John L. Thomas, *The Liberator, William Lloyd Garrison, A Biography* (Boston: 1963); James B. Stewart, *William Lloyd Garrison and the Challenge of Emancipation* (Arlington Heights, IL: 1992).

Gladden, Solomon Washington (1836–1918)

Congregational minister and social reformer. Gladden was raised in a rural Puritan community and educated at Williams College. As a pastor of congregations in Brooklyn, New York; North Adams, Massachusetts; and Columbus, Ohio, he observed the disparities between wealthy factory owners and poorer laboring classes. Opposing socialism, he preached a doctrine that the law of love should govern human relationships. Conciliatory in presenting his views, he was deeply influential among the Congregationalist churches. The author of thirty books and more articles, he advocated racial justice, organization of labor, protection of workers, unemployment insurance, and distribution of profits. He served on many boards of the National Council of Congregational Churches and was its moderator in 1904. **Works:** *Working People and Their Employers* (Boston: 1876); *Social Salvation* (Boston: 1902); *The Church in Modern Life* (New York: 1908). **Suggested Readings:** Jacob H. Dorn, *Washington Gladden: Prophet of the Social Gospel* (Columbus, OH: 1966); Richard Knudten, *The Systematic Thought of Washington Gladden* (New York: 1968).

Grimke, Sarah Moore (1792–1873); Angelina Emily (1805–1879)

Sisters, American abolitionists, and advocates of women's rights, both were born to a prominent planter in Charleston, South Carolina. They were educated in the fine arts by private tutors. At an early age, both girls observed slavery and were repulsed by the degrading treatment of persons of color. Angelina refused the sacrament of confirmation because the Episcopal Church tolerated slavery. In 1819, Sarah went to Philadelphia with her father on a business trip and mingled among the Quaker community. Angelina joined her in 1829, but the two sisters soon concluded that the Quakers treatment of freed blacks was lukewarm. Angelina wrote a letter to William Lloyd Garrison, editor of the *Liberator*, offering him support and a new perspective on slaveholding. Garrison published the letter and this caused a furor. In 1836, Angelina wrote *An Appeal to the Women of the South* and the next year targeted the women of the Free States. Angelina thus became the first white Southern woman to be linked with abolitionism. Sarah likewise joined the cause and the two began to appear on the platform of the American Antislavery Society. Their popularity with New England audiences produced protests from male supporters who feared the enhanced role for women. In 1838, Angelina married Theodore Dwight Weld, and their wedding resulted in her expulsion from the Society of Friends. Sarah, unmarried, went to live with the Welds. The sisters achieved great notoriety, notably supplying material to Harriet Beecher Stowe for her book, *Uncle Tom's Cabin* (1852). In the 1850s, the sisters retired from abolitionism and moved into education, first teaching at schools in New Jersey, then in Massachusetts. In their later years as faculty members at a school in Hyde Park, Massachusetts, they collaborated on projects in women's education and often boarded emancipated black children. **Works:** *An Appeal to Women of the South* (New York: 1836); *An Appeal to Women of the Nominally Free States* (New York: 1837); *American Slavery As It Is: Testimony of a Thousand Witnesses* (New York: 1839; rpr. 1968); Larry Ceplair, ed., *The Public Years of Sarah and Angelina Grimke* (New York: 1989). **Suggested Readings:** Theodore Dwight Weld, *In Memory of Angelina Grimke Weld* (New York: 1880); Gilbert H. Barnes and Dwight L. Dumond, eds., *Letters of Theodore Dwight Weld, Angelina Grimke, and Sarah Grimke 1822–1844* (Gloucester, MA: 1965); Gerda Lerner, *The Grimke Sisters: Pioneers for Women's Rights and Abolition* (Boston: 1967); Catherine DuPre Lumpkin, *The Emancipation of Angelina Grimke* (Chapel Hill, NC: 1974); Pamela R. Durso, *The Power of Woman: The Life and Writings of Sarah Moore Grimke* (Macon, GA: 2004).

Gutierrez, Gustavo (1928–)

Catholic theologian and liberationist. Born in Peru, Gutierrez studied medicine and philosophy at Peruvian universities before moving to the Catholic University at Louvain, Belgium, where he presented a thesis on the thought of Sigmund Freud. Later he did a theology degree at the University of Lyons, preparing a second thesis on religious liberty. He was ordained a priest in 1959. Gutierrez became National Adviser to the National Union of Catholic Students and Professor of Theology and Social Sciences in the Catholic University of Lima, Peru. Beginning with his participation in CELAM II (Consejo Episcopal Latinoamericano) in 1968, he became one of the leading liberation theologians of the Christian tradition. In 1973, he founded in Lima the Centro Bartolome de las Casas, an urban focus on poverty. **Works:** *Le Pastoral de la Iglesia latinoamericana* (Montevideo, Uruguay: 1968); *Teologia de la Liberacion (Theology of Liberation)* (1988); *La Fuerza historica de los pobres (The Power of the Poor in History)* (1979). **Suggested Readings:** Robert M. Brown, *Gustavo Gutierrez* (Atlanta: 1980); Curt Cadorette, *From the Heart of the People: The Theology of Gustavo Gutierrez* (Oak Park, IL: 1988); Rosino Gibellini, *Frontiers of Theology in Latin America* (Maryknoll, NY: 1979); Jeffrey S. Siker, *Scripture and Ethics: Twentieth Century Portraits.* (New York: 1997); Marc H. Ellis, *The Future of Liberation Theology: Essays in Honor of Gustavo Gutierrez* (Maryknoll, NY: 1989).

Helwys, Thomas (1550–1616)

English lawyer, Baptist clergyman, and political writer. Helwys was educated at Grey's Inn and practiced law in Nottinghamshire, England. He owned a considerable house at Broxtowe Hall. About 1606, he joined a Separatist conventicle that John Smyth led. The group emigrated to Amsterdam under pressure from the government. Helwys broke with Smyth over Smyth's desire to join the group to the Waterlander Mennonites, and Helwys and a faction returned to England. About 1611, he founded at Spitalfields near London the first Baptist congregation on English soil. In 1612, he published *A Short Declaration of The Mistery of Iniquity* in which he called for complete religious freedom for all subjects of the king. This has been called the finest argument for religious liberty in the English language. It resulted in imprisonment for Helwys who seems to have died at Newgate about 1616. **Works:** Thomas Helwys, *A*

Declaration of The Mistery of Iniquity (London: 1612); Thomas Helwys, *A Proof That God's Decree Is Not the Cause of Any Man's Sin or Condemnation* (London: 1611). **Suggested Readings:** Thomas Crosby, *A History of the English Baptists*, Vol. I (London: 1738); Barrington R. White, *The English Baptists of the Seventeenth Century* (Didcot, UK: Baptist Historical Society, 1996); Richard Groves, ed., *A Short Declaration of the Mystery of Iniquity: Classics of Religious Liberty 1* (Macon, GA: 1998).

Hubmaier, Balthasar (1480?–1528)

Swiss theologian. Hubmaier was educated at the University of Freiburg and came under the tutelage of the Catholic scholar, John Eck. He followed Eck to Ingolstadt, Germany, where Hubmaier was granted a doctorate in theology. At that university, he taught theology and he served as a popular preacher in the city's largest church. In 1515–1516, he was administrative head of the university. The next year, without explanation, he went to Regensburg, Germany, as cathedral preacher. There he was involved in an anti-Jewish incident that led to the destruction of a synagogue. He became a preaching attraction at a chapel on the site, reputedly the location of miracles in the name of the Blessed Virgin. In 1520, he went to Waldshut near Zurich. He encountered Huldrych Zwingli and Oecolampadius in Basel and became identified with religious reform. He moved a final time to Nikolsburg and wrote numerous tracts on reformation themes. Hubmaier advocated believer's baptism and religious toleration. He was apprehended in 1528 by church authorities and burned at the stake for his views. **Works:** George D. Davidson, ed. and trans., *The Writings of Balthasar Hubmaier*. 3 vols. (Goshen, IN: 1939); Wayne Pipkin and John H. Yoder, eds., *Balthasar Hubmaier: Theologian of Anabaptism* (Scottdale: 1989). **Suggested Readings:** Henry C. Vedder, *Balthasar Hubmaier: The Leader of the Anabaptists* (New York: 1905); Carl Sachsse, *Balthasar Hubmaier als Theologe* (Berlin: 1914); Torsten Bergsten, *Balthasar Hubmaier: Seine Stellung zu Reformation und Taufertum* (Kassel, Germany: 1961).

Humphrey, John Peters (1905–1995)

Canadian law professor and human rights advocate. Born in New Brunswick, Canada, Humphrey lost both parents in childhood and was severely burned, resulting in the loss of an arm. He was educated at Mt. Allison University, McGill University, and the University of Paris. Called to the Montreal Bar in 1929, Humphrey practiced law in the firm of Wainwright, Elder, and McDougall, 1930–1936. He then joined the Faculty of Law at McGill University where he specialized in Roman law. Later in his career, he taught at the law schools of the University of Toronto and University of Western Ontario and was a fellow at the University of Paris. In 1946, Humphrey was selected to direct the new U.N. Secretariat Human Rights Division, a post he held until 1966. He was invited by Human Rights Commission chair Eleanor Roosevelt to draft the Universal Declaration on Human Rights, joined by Charles Malik and P. C. Chang. His original draft included forty-eight articles, which he reduced to thirty. Humphrey served on several key U.N. conferences or committees, including Freedom of Information, Refugees, Status of Stateless Persons, and Slavery. He was widely sought for advice on famine, Vietnam, the status of women, and Canadian reparations after World War II; he was also an organizer of Amnesty International. Returning to teaching international law, Humphrey received numerous awards in human rights and honorary degrees, including the U.N. Human Rights Award and the Order of Canada. In 1988, the John Humphrey Annual Lectureship in Human Rights was inaugurated in his honor at McGill University, and, in 2000, the John Humphrey Centre for Peace and Human Rights was established in Edmonton, Alberta. **Works:** *The Inter-American System: A Canadian View* (1942); with R. St. J. MacDonald, *The Practice of Freedom: Canadian Essays on Human Rights and Fundamental Freedoms* (Toronto: 1979); *Human Rights and the United Nations: A Great Adventure* (Dobbs Ferry, NY: 1983); *No Distant Millennium* (1989); A. J. Hobbins, ed., *On the Edge of Greatness: The Diaries of John Humphrey, First Director of the United Nations Division of Human Rights* (Montreal: 1994). **Suggested Readings:** *International Who's Who, 1998* (Jacksonville, NC: 1999): 728; "John Peters Humphrey: A Crusader for Human Rights" in *Towards Global Human Rights*, ed. Patricia Morales. Tillburg (The Netherlands, 1996); "Eleanor Roosevelt, John Humphrey and Canadian Opposition to the Universal Declaration of Human Rights: Looking Back on the 50th Anniversary," *International Journal* 53 (Spring 1998): 325–342; "John Peters Humphrey and the Genesis of the Universal Declaration of Human Rights" *Journal of Oriental Studies* IX (1999): 24–41.

Judson, Adoniram (1788–1850)

American Congregationalist and later Baptist missionary to Burma. Son of a prominent New England Congregationalist pastor, Judson was educated at Brown University and Andover Theological Seminary. In 1812, he and a group of young missionary enthusiasts offered themselves to the newly formed American Board of Commissioners for Foreign Missions and were sent to India. En route to India, Judson and his wife, Ann, became convinced of Baptist principles. Finding a hostile response from British interests, the Judsons transferred to Burma, previously an un-evangelized field. Judson suffered torturous imprisonment during the Burmese civil war in 1824 and nearly died. Thereafter, he commenced preaching stations at Ava and Rangoon accompanied by school teaching and overseeing a printing concern. His advocacy of religious freedom was influential in public policy toward foreigners in Burma and led to an openness to Christianity. In his letters to the supporting Baptist Board for Foreign Missions, he strongly advocated that candidates for missionary service must learn the history of the cultures and their languages before arrival on the field to achieve maximum effectiveness. Judson's wives, Ann Hasseltine, Sarah Boardman, and Emily Chubbock, set new patterns fore American womanhood as they broke rules of missionary decorum and submissive spousal roles for leadership as missionaries in their own rights. **Works:** Francis Wayland, *Memoir of the Rev. Adoniram Judson* 2 vols. (Boston: 1853). **Suggested Readings:** Courtney Anderson, *To the Golden Shore: The Life of Adoniram Judson* (Boston: 1956); Joan Jacobs Brumberg, *Mission for Life: The Dramatic Story of the Family of Adoniram Judson* (New York: 1981).

King, Martin Luther, Jr. (1929–1968)

The son of a leading black Baptist minister in Atlanta, Martin was educated at Morehouse College and Crozer Theological Seminary and earned a doctorate from Boston University. Instead of a teaching career at a prominent black college, he sought a pastoral ministry and served Dexter Avenue Baptist Church in Montgomery, Alabama, 1954–1959. King was much influenced by the nonviolent tactics of Mahatma Gandhi and came to apply them to racial desegregation across the American South. He organized the Southern Christian Leadership Conference with Ralph Abernathy, was active in the National Association for the

Advancement of Colored People, and led important civil rights marches in 1962, 1963, and 1965. His speech, "I have a Dream," delivered on the steps of the Lincoln Memorial in Washington, D.C., in 1963, became one of the most famous statements of racial equality in American history. King made an enormous impact upon public opinion through his boycotts and electrifying speeches and drew international attention to his cause. In 1964, he was awarded the Nobel Prize for Peace. During the buildup of American military presence in Vietnam under President Lyndon Johnson, King came to oppose the war and drew harsh criticism. While attending a rally in Memphis, Tennessee, in 1968, he was assassinated by a sniper. **Works:** Clayborne Carson, ed., *The Papers of Martin Luther King, Jr.* (Berkeley: 1992); James Melvin Washington, ed., *Testament of Hope: The Essential Writings of Martin Luther King, Jr.* (San Francisco: 1986). **Suggested Readings:** David Lewis, *King: A Biography* (Urbana, IL: 1978); John J. Ansbro, *Martin Luther King, Jr.: The Making of a Mind* (Maryknoll, NY: 1982); Stephen Oates, *Let The Trumpet Sound: The Life of Martin Luther King, Jr.* (New York: 1982); Richard Lischer, *The Preacher King: Martin Luther King, Jr. and the Word that Moved America* (New York: 1995).

Knibb, William (1803–1845)

English Baptist missionary and abolitionist. Knibb was the son of a tradesman and received only a grammar school education before entering the printing business. He was baptized by the eminent Baptist minister, John Ryland, at Broadmead Church in Bristol. Ryland and Broadmead were known for their evangelical concerns. Knibb volunteered for missionary service in Jamaica with the Baptist Missionary Society. There he taught school in Kingston and later preached at Savannah la Mar and Montego Bay. He saw the treatment and plight of the slave population and wrote widely in protest. He took his case to members of the British Parliament and was the moving force behind Thomas Fowell Buxton's motion to end slavery in the colonies. The planters in Jamaica violently opposed him and his chapel was destroyed. During his twenty-one years on the island, Knibb worked to build institutions and improve the quality of life for indigenous Jamaicans. **Works:** *Colonial Slavery: A Defense of the Baptist Missionaries from the Charge of Inciting the Late Rebellion in Jamaica* (London: 1830); *Rev. William Knibb's Speech at Exeter Hall May 22, 1840* (London: 1834); *The*

Spiritual Prospects of Africa (London: 1834). **Suggested Readings:** John M. Cramp, *A Brief Memoir of William Knibb, Late Missionary in Jamaica* (Montreal: 1846); J. Howard Hinton, *Life of William Knibb* (London: 1847); Mary E. Smith, *William Knibb: Missionary in Jamaica, A Memoir* (London: 1896); Ernest Payne, *The Great Succession: Leaders of the Baptist Missionary Society During the Nineteenth Century* (London: 1938).

Küng, Hans (1928–)

Catholic and later ecumenical theologian. Küng was born in Switzerland and educated in Rome at the German College and the Gregorian University. He also studied in Berlin, Paris, London, and Amsterdam. Ordained a parish priest in 1955, Küng became professor of theology in the Catholic faculty at the University of Tübingen in 1960. He was supportive of the directions of Vatican II and actively pursued ecumenical conversations with theologians in the Reformed tradition because he sensed basic similarities with the Catholic Church. Moving far beyond orthodox Catholic positions, however, Küng had major questions about the papacy as a true pastoral role and about the church's teaching on birth control. Holding to the value of historical context, he came to question the infallibility of scripture. In 1975, he was admonished about his lack of orthodoxy. Refusing to recant, he was deposed from his office as a Roman Catholic teacher. Küng continued in the role of ecumenical theologian at Tübingen and began a publishing career that took him in new directions. His interpretation of scripture has been called "Christological centrism," holding Jesus as an ultimate example of Christian ethics. He has ventured into serious dialogue with other world religions and written extensively in support of a universal global ethics. Küng was a theological consultant to the World's Parliament of Religions in 1993 and to the InterAction Council's proposals. **Works:** *Council, Reformation, and Reunion* (1961); *Infallible* (Garden City, NY: 1972); *On Being a Christian* (Garden City, NY: 1978); *Christianity and World Religions* (1986); *Ethics of World Religions* (1993). **Suggested Readings:** C. M. LaCugna, *The Theological Method of Hans Küng* (Chico, CA: 1982); R. Nowell, *A Passion for Truth: Hans Küng and His Theology* (New York: 1989); Leonard Swidler, *Consensus in Theology: Küng in Conflict* (Philadelphia: 1980).

Las Casas, Bartolomé (1474–1566)

Spanish Dominican missionary and author, known as the "Apostle to the Indians." Las Casas was the son of a merchant who had accompanied

Christopher Columbus on his second voyage. Bartolomé himself went to Central America in 1502 and was ordained there. His experiences in Cuba led him to advocate reform of the colonial system, especially the notorious encomienda system. In 1523, thwarted by lack of interest in his proposals, he became a Dominican friar. As a member of that Order, he engaged in missions in Nicaragua and Guatemala and he played a significant part in the writing of the New Laws of 1542–1543. He returned to America in 1544 to try to actualize the New Laws, but failed except in the Dominican mission at Vera Paz. His crusade to end the enslavement of the Indians reached its zenith at Valladolid in 1550 in a debate with Juan Gines de Sepulveda. This resulted in a thorough revision of colonial policy and a ban on enslavement and brutalization of the Indians. His writings ranged from doctrinal subjects to a history of the Indian peoples of Central America. His negative treatment of the abuses of the Spanish colonial system in large part created the Black Legend that still colors unfavorably the Spanish conquest. **Works:** H. R. Wagner and H. R. Parish, *The Life and Writings of Bartolomé de las Casas* (Albuquerque, NM: 1967). **Suggested Readings:** Lewis Hanke, *The Spanish Struggle for Justice in the Conquest of America* (Philadelphia: 1993); Gustavo Guitierrez, *Las Casas: In Search of the Poor of Jesus Christ* (Philadelphia: 1949).

Leland, John (1754–1841)

Baptist clergyman and advocate of religious liberty. Born and raised in colonial Connecticut, Leland was a product of the evangelistic preaching of Elhanan Winchester. He was self-taught and ordained to the Baptist ministry in 1786. His pastoral work included churches at Mount Poney, Virginia, and Cheshire, Massachusetts, and itinerant ministries in the southern states. Leland was a rationalistic Pietist who revered the common man. He adopted extreme individualistic views on religious experience and held no creed to be valid for disciplinary purposes. He equated congregational polity with democracy and opposed all forms of favoritism for the church. Leland was also disinclined toward religious organizations above the local congregation and he wrote against Sabbath-keeping laws. He held religion to be completely free and voluntary and likely was influential in Virginia on the thinking of Thomas Jefferson and James Madison. **Works:** Louise F. Greene, ed., *The Writings of the Late Elder John Leland, Including Some Events in His Life* (New York: 1845); **Suggested Readings:** L. H. Butterfield, *Elder John Leland,*

Jeffersonian Itinerant (Worcester, MA: 1953); Edwin S. Gaustad, "The Backus-Leland Tradition," *Foundations* 2:2 (April 1959): 131–152.

Malik, Charles (1906–1987)

Lebanese Orthodox rights activist. Malik was educated at the University of Beirut and worked for the Rockefeller Foundation in Cairo. Later he was a graduate student at Harvard University where he earned a master's degree, and then he earned a doctorate at the University of Freiburg. From 1937–1945 Malik taught at the American University in Beirut. He was named the first minister from Lebanon to the United States in 1945 and the next year he was appointed a delegate to the Conference on Organization of the United Nations. A rapporteur for the Third Committee of the General Assembly dealing with social and humanitarian rights, he was a natural choice for appointment to the Commission on Human Rights in 1947. Malik was a principal writer of the Universal Declaration on Human Rights and he chaired the ratification process with great skills, exhibiting fairness and yet convictions of his own. His major contribution to the discussion was on the right to change one's belief, because he held that the essence of religious freedom is the right to become, not the right to be. In 1958–1959, he was president of the U.N. General Assembly. A Greek Orthodox layman, Malik became a popular figure among American evangelicals, lecturing on anticommunist themes for Campus Crusade for Christ and delivering the dedication address at the Billy Graham Center at Wheaton College. In 1981, he became the first holder of the Jacques Maritain Chair in Philosophy at Catholic University of America. **Works:** O. Frederick Nolde, *Toward Worldwide Christianity* (New York: 1946); *The Wonder of Being*; *A Christian Critique of the University* (Downer's Grove, IL: 1982). **Suggested Readings:** "Noted Diplomat Dies," Obituary, *Christianity Today* 32:2 (February 5, 1988); Obituary of Charles H. Malik, *New York Times*, December 29, 1987.

Maritain, Jacques (1882–1973)

Raised in Paris and educated at the College Sorbonne, his first teaching position was with the College Stanislaus in 1910. Following World War II, Maritain served as French ambassador to the Vatican and, in 1948, he moved to Princeton University where he remained until he retired in 1956. Maritain was enamored of the thought of Thomas Aquinas and this dominated his methodology and writing throughout his career. Most importantly for the issues of human rights, Maritain emphasized the distinction between individuals and persons. Personhood involves inherent spiritual values and freedoms, and society must promote greater personhood, he thought. Maritain introduced what has come to be known as the modern "proof" for the existence of God, namely that the realization of human finitude directs humans to seek the ground of all being, namely God's eternal Being. This became important grist for discussion of a core theological principle in human rights foundations. **Works:** *Approaches to God: Person and the Common Good.* "The Rights of Man," in Maurice Cranston, *What Are Human Rights?* (London: 1973). **Suggested Readings:** J. M. Dunnaway, *Jacques Maritain*; C. A. Fecher, *The Philosophy of Jacques Maritain.*

Moltmann, Jürgen (1926–)

Reformed Church theologian. Moltmann was born in Hamburg, Germany, and received degrees from Goettingen. During World War II, he was a German prisoner of war in a British camp and experienced a shattering of his Christian perspective. While in graduate studies, he was deeply influenced by Karl Barth's thought. He has taught theology at Kirchliche Hochschule Wuppertal (1958–1963) and the University of Bonn (1963–1967) and currently teaches at the University of Tübingen (1967–) in systematic theology. President of the Gesellschaft fur Evangelische Theologie, he has written widely on the theological foundation for human rights. Moltmann's great work, *A Theology of Hope*, emphasized the apocalypse of the promised future and he argued that there was much for Christians to overcome in the meantime. His work shifted in the 1980s toward human rights and ecotheology that involved not only human beings, but nonhuman parts of the creation. **Works:** *Der Mensch (Man)* (1973); *Der gekreuzigte Gott (The Crucified God)* (1985); *Zukunft der Schopfung (The Future of Creation)* (1979); *Gerechtigkeit schafft Zukunft (Creating a Just Future)* (1989). **Suggested Readings:** M. D. Meeks, *Origin of the Theology of Hope* (Philadephia: 1974); A. J. Conyers, *God, Hope, and History: Jürgen Moltmann and the Christian Concept of History* (Macon, GA: 1988).

Montgomery, Helen Barrett (1861–1934)

American Baptist leader and social reformer. Montgomery was educated at Wellesley College and became a schoolteacher in Philadelphia. Married to a Rochester, New York, industrialist, William A. Montgomery, Helen had opportunity to travel widely in the interest of women's work and missions. She was also active in Rochester as a promoter of public education and women's concerns, helping to establish a women's division at the University of Rochester. A thoroughgoing ecumenist, in 1910 she toured Europe and Asia for the International Jubilee of Women's Missions, advocating women's education and the emancipation of women. Among American Baptists, she was one of the organizers of the national woman's missionary society and was the first female president of her denomination, the Northern Baptist Convention, 1921–1922. **Works:** *Western Women in Eastern Lands* (1910); *From Jerusalem to Jerusalem* (1929); *From Campus to World Citizenship* (1940). **Suggested Readings:** R. Pierce Beaver, *All Loves Excelling: American Protestant Women in Mission* (Grand Rapids, MI: 1968); William H. Brackney, "Helen Barrett Montgomery and Lucy W. Peabody," in Gerald H. Anderson, *Mission Legacies* (Grand Rapids, MI: 1994); "Helen Barrett Montgomery" *Encyclopedia of New York State* (Syracuse, NY: 2004).

Murray, John Courtney (1904–1967)

American Catholic theologian and advocate of religious liberty. Murray was educated at Boston College and Woodstock (Md.) Seminary and received a doctorate at Gregorian University in Rome. An ordained priest, he taught in the Philippines from 1927 to 1930 and then as professor of theology at Woodstock from 1937 to 1967. He was editor of *Theological Studies* from 1941 to 1967. Murray understood the international crises the church faced in the war years, as well as the rising interest in the separation of church and state, and he pushed the Catholic Church away from its doctrine of a religious understanding of the state. He came to be a leading advocate of religious liberty, holding a position, against stiff opposition within the church, that the duty of a state was to ensure freedom. Importantly, he was a principal advisor to Vatican II 1963–1965, the primary author of *Dignitatis Humanae* (1965). **Works:** *Foreign Policy and the Free Society* (New York: 1958); *The Problem of Religious Freedom* (Westminster, MD: 1965). **Suggested Readings:** Thomas Love, *John Courtney Murray's Contemporary Church-State Theory* (Garden City, NY: 1965); Donald Pelotte, *John Courtney Murray: Theologian in Conflict* (New York: 1975); J. Leon Hopper, *The Ethics of Dis-*

course: The Social Philosophy of John Courtney Murray (Washington, DC: 1986).

Muste, Abraham John (1885–1967)

Quaker human rights activist. Born in Holland and educated at Hope College, Muste studied to become a Dutch Reformed pastor. He was transformed by reading the work of Rufus Jones and turned aside a teaching career and a pastorate in New York City. He joined the Friends in Providence, Rhode Island, and led a nonviolent strike among textile workers in Lawrence, Massachusetts, in 1919. In 1936, he became a pacifist and worked in the Labor Temple in New York City for the Presbyterians. The next year he became the staff leader for the Fellowship of Reconciliation in Nyack, New York. For the remainder of his career, he trained young black leaders in nonviolence and conscientious objectors in resisting the draft during the Cold War. Muste led a march from San Francisco to Moscow for peace and was opposed to nuclear testing in Nevada in the 1950s. He won national attention for refusing to pay income taxes as a peace statement and he visited the leaders of North Vietnam in 1967. **Works:** *Labor: Between the Devil and the Deep Blue Sea* (Katonah, NY: 1929); *Pacifism and Aggression* (New York: 1936). **Suggested Readings:** JoAnn Robinson, *The Traveler from Zierkzee: The Religious, Intellectual, and Political Development of A. J. Muste from 1885 to 1940* (Baltimore, MD: 1972); William G. Batz, *Revolution and Peace: The Christian Pacifism of A. J. Muste (1885–1967)* (New York: 1974); Nat Hentoff, *Peace Agitator: The Story of A. J. Muste* (New York: 1982).

Navarre, Henry of (Henry IV of France) (1553–1610)

A direct descendant of Louis IX, Navarre was baptized in the Catholic faith, but upon his mother's direction, he was instructed in the Calvinist (Reformed) faith. He was placed in the service of Admiral Colignay, the leader of the Protestant cause, in 1568. Henry joined the Huguenots about that time. Civil war broke out in 1672, culminating in the St. Bartholomew's Eve Massacre and widespread religious strife. Henry of Navarre fought for supremacy in France against Henry III and Henry Guise and ultimately proclaimed himself sovereign in 1589. Politically astute and aware that he represented a Protestant minority of about 10 percent, Henry IV became a Catholic and supported the aims of the church in France. Once his reign was secure, however, he declared the Edict of Nantes in 1598 to reassure Protestants of his goodwill. National union was achieved, and Protestant churches expanded across France, as well as schools to instruct Protestant children. The edict was the most far-reaching statement of religious toleration in European history to its day. **Suggested Readings:** P. F. Willert, *Henry of Navarre and the Huguenots in France* (New York: 1893); Stanley Leathers, "Henry IV of France," in *Cambridge Modern History* (Cambridge: 1904); Edmund H. Dickerman, "The Conversion of Henry IV," *Catholic Historical Review* 68 (1977): 1–13; "Henry IV," in *Dictionnaire de Biographie Francais* Fascicule C (1987): 934–939; "Henry IV," in *Great Lives From History*, vol. 2, *Renaissance to 1900* (Pasadena, CA: 1989), 1040–1044.

Nolde, O. Frederick (1899–1972)

American Lutheran professor and ecumenical leader. Nolde was educated at Muhlenburg College and took the B. D. degree at Lutheran Theological Seminary in Philadelphia. Later he earned a doctorate at the University of Pennsylvania. He taught in the field of religious education at Lutheran Seminary and was dean of their graduate studies, as well as at the University of Pennsylvania 1929–1943. He first became active in ecumenical relations with the Federal Council of Churches as a member of the Department of International Justice and Goodwill in 1928. Later, he was an advocate for reconciliation on the basis of justice after World War II and the Committee on Human Rights of the Commission to Study the Organization of Peace in 1939. During the war, Nolde served as executive secretary of the Joint Committee on Religious Liberty (1944), and it was his article "Possible Function of the Commission on Human Rights" in 1946 that led to the agenda for the projected U.N. Commission on Human Rights. He was a Federal Council of Churches of Christ representative to the U.N. Charter Conference in San Francisco and among a small group that laid plans for the Amsterdam meetings in 1948. Nolde was a representative of the Church Council on International Affairs to the meetings of the U.N. Commission on Human Rights in 1947–1948 and is credited with much of the phraseology in support of the "right to change one's religion." An active member of the United Lutheran Church in America, he urged his church to support the United Nations in 1945–1946. He later served as

Associate General Secretary of the World Council of Churches, and Vice Chair of the Carnegie Endowment for Peace. **Works:** *Christian World Action* (Philadelphia: 1942); *Christian Messages to the Peoples of the World* (New York: 1943); *Power for Peace* (Philadelphia: 1946). **Suggested Readings:** "O. Frederick Nolde" *Current Biography* (1947), 470–472; Obituary of O. Frederick Nolde, *New York Times*, June 19, 1972.

Penn, William (1644–1718)

Quaker leader and American colonial planter. Penn was the son of the illustrious British Naval Admiral William Penn and was educated by a private tutor and later at Christ Church, Oxford. He studied law at Lincoln's Inn and served in the military in Ireland. In 1667, he became a Quaker under the influence of George Fox. He established himself as a country gentleman in Sussex and aided the Quaker cause by advocacy and as an itinerant preacher. James the Duke of York was a family friend, and as King James II, he acquiesced to Penn's pleas on behalf of imprisoned Quakers, liberating twelve hundred from prison. Penn also petitioned Parliament for a Quaker relief clause. In 1680, Penn obtained a charter for a colony in America and he moved swiftly to organize his plan and settle the patent. His plan of government provided that all modes of religious worship compatible with monotheism and Christian morality were to be tolerated in "Pennsylvania." In one of his published essays on the future of Europe, he advocated an international organization. Penn continued to his death to advocate particularly the rights of Quakers and generally religious toleration for Christians. **Works:** *Essay Towards the Present and Future Peace of Europe* (1693); Mary Dunn, ed., *Papers of William Penn* (Philadelphia: 1981–1987). **Suggested Reading:** *Witness of William Penn* (New York: 1957).

Pierce, Robert Willard "Bob" (1914–1978)

Missionary and relief organizer. Pierce attended Pasadena College and was related to fundamentalist Baptists at the beginning of his career. Under assignment of the Church of the Nazarene, he went to conduct evangelism and missionary work in China and later Korea. Pierce developed an interest in Korean orphans and refugees and rallied friends to form World Vision International in 1950. His oft-repeated statement, "Let my heart be broken with the things that break the heart of God," helped many to respond to what became the largest Christian relief organization in the world. After his service as president (1950–1967), Pierce started Samaritan's Purse, another relief agency. **Works:** *The Untold Story* (Grand Rapids, MI: 1951); *Exploring Mission in the Local Church* (Grand Rapids, MI: 1964); *Orphans of the Present: Stories that Will Touch Your Heart* (Grand Rapids, MI: 1964). **Suggested Readings:** John R. Hamilton, "An Historical Study of Bob Pierce and World Vision's Development of the Social Action Film" (unpublished PhD dissertation, University of Southern California, 1980); Marilee Pierce Dunker, *Man of Vision, Woman of Prayer* (Grand Rapids, MI: 1980); "Robert Pierce," *Biographical Dictionary of Christian Missions*, 535–536.

Rauschenbusch, Walter (1860–1918)

Baptist minister and theological educator. Rauschenbusch was the son of a prominent German American Baptist pastor, August Rauschenbusch. Educated at the University of Rochester, the Gymnasium at Gutersloeh, and Rochester Theological Seminary, he embarked upon a pastoral ministry in Hell's Kitchen, New York City, in 1886. While in the city, he observed the deplorable conditions of life and work and conferred with social reformers like Jacob Riis, Henry George, and Richard Ely. The result was the development of a "social gospel" that Rauschenbush described as "the righteous reign of God in human affairs." He was called to teach in the German program and then to a chair in church history in Rochester Theological Seminary where he spent the bulk of his career writing and teaching. His close friendship with Augustus H. Strong protected him from very harsh critics who charged that he had lost his zeal for the evangelical tradition. Rauschenbusch persevered, however, in his work with the Brotherhood of the Kingdom and through students. His influence was felt in the reordering of Baptist life in the Northern Baptist Convention to account for a social dimension to the gospel and in his influence upon thinkers such as Howard Thurman and Mordecai W. Johnson in the emerging black tradition. **Works:** *Christianity and the Social Crisis* (New York: 1907); *A Theology for the Social Gospel* (New York: 1917). **Suggested Readings:** Dores R. Sharpe, *Walter Rauschenbusch* (New York: 1942); Paul J. Minus, *Walter Rauschenbusch* (New York: 1988); Winthrop S. Hudson, *Walter Rauschenbusch* (Maryknoll, NY: 1984).

Roncalli, Angelo Giuseppe, Pope John XXIII (1881–1963)

Italian Catholic theologian, diplomat and Roman pontiff. Roncalli was educated at Bergamo, Italy and graduated with a doctorate from S. Apollinare Institute in Rome. He taught church history in Bergamo and served as a chaplain in World War I. In 1921, he was appointed national director of the Congregation for the Propagation of the Faith, and then Pius XI launched him on a diplomatic career. He served in Bulgaria, Turkey, Greece, and France. In the East, he developed friendships with Orthodox leaders. During the German occupation of Greece, Roncalli tried to relieve the distress of Jews and prevent their deportation. In France, he negotiated the problem of bishops accused of complicity with the Vichy government. Later he worked on educational strategies for German ordinands who were prisoners of war. He was a principal advisor to Rene Cassin, a drafter of the Universal Declaration on Human Rights, and the first permanent observer for the Holy See at UNESCO. He was elected pope and rather than become a caretaker at age 77, he opened new vistas for the church. He made international appointments to the College of Cardinals and revised canon law. His great achievement, the convoking of Vatican II, was a watershed in the history of Christianity. Pope John's encyclical, *Pacem in Terris* (1963), was the foundation of a new Catholic understanding of human rights and the core of a later Declaration on Religious Freedom. **Works:** *Gli atti della visita apostolica di s Carlo Borromeo a Bergamo* (Florence: 1936); *Mons. G. M. Radini-Tedeschi, vescovo di Bergamo* (Rome: 1963). **Suggested Readings:** E.E.Y. Hales, *Pope John and His Revolution* (London: 1965); P. B. Johnson, *Pope John XXIII* (London: 1975); P. Hebblethwaite, *John XXII: Pope of the Council* (London: 1985).

Roosevelt, Anna Eleanor (1884–1962)

American first lady and social reformer, she was married to President Franklin D. Roosevelt. Educated at the primary and secondary school levels, early in life she found satisfaction in benevolent work, notably with children. She joined the National Consumer's League that championed health and safety standards and worked with immigrants at the Rivington St. Settlement House in New York City. In 1905, she married Franklin Roosevelt and followed his career through government service in the Department of the Navy, as governor of New York, and as president. During World War I, for instance, she worked with Navy Relief and operated a Red Cross Canteen. In the 1920s, she worked for the League of Women Voters and the Women's Trade Union League, where she supported a five-day workweek and an end to child labor. Mrs. Roosevelt also publicly supported the League of Nations. When her husband developed permanent paralysis, she became his chief advocate and presence beyond the governor's mansion and White House. A behind-the-scenes architect of the New Deal, she lent support to model communities, civil rights for black Americans, and relief for displaced war families. In FDR's second and third terms, Eleanor rose to national attention, writing a weekly newspaper column and traveling extensively. In 1939, she resigned from the Daughters of the American Revolution in protest of their denial of their concert hall in Washington, D.C., to black singer Marian Anderson. In 1948, she helped form the Americans for Democratic Action and campaigned for desegregated federal housing. President Harry Truman tapped Mrs. Roosevelt as a major player in the development of the United Nations and she was elected chair of the Human Rights Commission. This brought forth what she called her greatest achievement: the U.N. Declaration on Human Rights (1948). A lifelong Episcopalian, Eleanor believed in principles of universal brotherhood, interracial cooperation, ecumenical and interfaith endeavor, and government responsibility for the weak. **Works:** "What Religion Means to Me" *Forum* (December 1932): 322–324; *This Is My Story* (New York: 1937); *On My Own* (New York: 1958); Rochelle Chadakoff, ed., *Eleanor Roosevelt's "My Day": Her Acclaimed Column 1936–45* (1989). **Suggested Readings:** Joseph P. Lash, *Eleanor and Franklin* (London: 1971); Lois Scharf, *Eleanor Roosevelt: First Lady of American Liberalism* (Boston: 1987); Allida M. Black, *Casting Her Own Shadow: Eleanor Roosevelt and the Shaping of Postwar Liberalism* (New York: 1996).

Rustin, Bayard (1912–1987)

Quaker human rights activist. The grandson of slaves, Rustin was educated at Wilberforce College and Cheney State University, and he also studied at City College in New York and the London School of Economics. One of his first positions was as race relations secretary with the Fellowship of Reconciliation for twelve years under the tutelage of A. J. Muste. He joined the New York Yearly Meeting of Friends and devoted his life to nonviolence and social justice. After the beginning of World

War II, he went to the West Coast and worked among the Japanese internment camps. With A. Phillip Randolph, Rustin planned a nationwide mass march on Washington to address segregation in war industries. The march was called off when President Roosevelt signed legislation ending discrimination in war industries. In 1942, he was a founder of the Congress on Racial Equality (CORE) and he traveled widely in the South in protest against Jim Crow laws and chain gangs. He assisted Martin Luther King, Jr., in organizing the 1963 March on Washington and forming the Southern Christian Leadership Conference. Late in his career, he started Project South Africa to link proponents of nonviolence against apartheid. In the 1980s, Rustin also became involved in advocating the plight of Cambodian refugees. **Works:** *Have We Reached the End of the Second Reconstruction?* (Bloomington, IN: 1976); Nanette Dobrosky, ed., *Bayard Rustin Papers* (Frederick, MD: 1988). **Suggested Readings:** E. Vann Woodward, *Civil Rights: The Movement Re-examined* (New York: 1967); Nancy D. Kates, *Brother Outsider: The Life of Bayard Rustin* (Burlington, VT: 2002).

Ryan, John Augustine (1869–1945)

Catholic theologian and social reformer. He was educated at St. Thomas College and St. Paul's Seminary in Minnesota, after which he earned an S.T.D. at Catholic University of America. His teaching career began at St. Paul's Seminary in moral theology and for twenty-five years he taught political science and moral philosophy at Catholic University, 1915–1939. Ryan bridged the intellectual chasm between theology and economics at a time when the United States was transformed into an industrial economy. His applied theories led to two major public policy advocacies: wage protection for workers and economic justice in the industrial order. Ryan organized Catholic social opinion in the National Catholic Welfare Conference, which he helped to direct through the years of the Depression and World War II. He was a popular lecturer and joined many associations that Catholics had previously shunned like the American Civil Liberties Union and the Federal Council of Churches of Christ in the United States. During the Depression, he openly supported Franklin Roosevelt's economic recovery program and influenced the American Catholic Bishops' statements on social concerns. **Works:** *A Living Wage: Its Ethical and Economic Aspects* (New York: 1906); *Distributive Justice: The Right and Wrong of Our Present*

Distribution of Wealth (New York: 1916); *Declining Liberty and Other Papers* (New York: 1927). **Suggested Readings:** Patrick W. Carey, "John A. Ryan," *The Roman Catholics* (Westport, CT: 1993), 302–303; Patrick Gearty, *The Economic Thought of Monsignor John A. Ryan* (Washington, DC: 1953); Francis L. Broderick, *The Right Reverend New Dealer: John A. Ryan* (New York: 1963).

Stassen, Harold (1907–2001)

Politician and activist. Stassen graduated from the University of Minnesota and its law school and practiced law in St. Paul. A Republican, he was elected to local offices and to governor of Minnesota in 1938. As governor, he led in labor legislation that would eventually be a model for the national Taft-Hartley Law. In 1943, he went on active duty in the Naval Reserve and assisted Admiral William Halsey in the Pacific in the American POW return. In 1945, President Roosevelt named him a delegate to the San Francisco conference that gave birth to the United Nations. Thereafter, Stassen served in disarmament roles and in foreign aid administration in the Eisenhower administration, where he favored an end to nuclear weapons. He served as president of the University of Pennsylvania 1947–1953. Altogether, he ran for the U.S. presidency eight times. A lifelong Baptist, he was president of the American Baptist Convention in 1963–1964, during which he was an ambassador for religious liberty and improved relations among Baptists East and West. Later in his career, Stassen participated in the National Council of Churches and the National Conference of Christians and Jews. In the 1970s, he was associated with the U.S. Inter-religious Committee on Peace. **Works:** *The United Nations Charter* (New York: 1945); *Where I Stand!* (Garden City, NY: 1947); *Man Was Meant to Be Free: Selected Statements 1940–1951* (Garden City, NY: 1951); Eisenhower, *Turning the World Toward Peace* (St. Paul, MN: 1990). **Suggested Readings:** *Nomination of Harold E. Stassen to Be Director for Mutual Security, January 21, 1953* (Washington, DC: 1953); *Current Biography* (May 1948); Obituary of Harold Stassen, *New York Times* (March 5, 2001): 6; 2001 *Current Biography Yearbook*, 643.

Sullivan, Leon (1922–2001)

American black Baptist minister and social reformer. He was educated at West Virginia State University and Union Theological Seminary in

New York. He also studied sociology at Columbia University. Sullivan interned at Abyssinian Baptist Church in New York City under Adam Clayton Powell, Jr., later serving as pastor of First Baptist Church, South Orange, New Jersey. In 1950, he became pastor at Zion Baptist Church on North Broad Street in Philadelphia and led it to national and international prominence. From his youth he was an activist, advocating racial equality in West Virginia. In 1974, after a visit to South Africa, during which he was abusively treated by police, he took special interest in the appalling conditions of apartheid and began a crusade to awaken American politicians in changing that system. His "Sullivan Principles" included desegregation, fair employment practices, and appointment of black managers. Sullivan called upon churches and corporations to disinvest in South African businesses until the regime changed. His role as a board member of General Motors Corporation created several opportunities for extension of his principles. In Philadelphia, he organized Opportunities Industrialization Center and Progress Aerospace Enterprises. In the 1990s, he worked with United Nations General Secretary Kofi Annan to push forward a global version of the Sullivan Principles, and he devised a program to bridge the gap between African and African American leaders. **Works:** *A Welfare Program That Works* (Philadelphia: 1971); *Philosophy of a Giant: Quotations* (Philadelphia: 1973); *The Sullivan Statement of Principles* (Philadelphia: 1974). **Suggested Readings:** *Leon Sullivan and the United States Congress: The Legislative History of Opportunities Industrialization Centers of America* (Philadelphia: 1978); J. Deotis Roberts, *A Theological Commentary on the Sullivan Principles* (Philadelphia: 1980); Ossie Davis, *A Principled Man: Rev. Leon Sullivan* (London: 1984); Kathleen S. Hasselblad, "The United States Foreign Policy with South Africa: Leon Sullivan and the Sullivan Principles 1948–1980" (Master's thesis, Pacific Lutheran Seminary, 1994).

Thurman, Howard (1899–1981)

American clergyman. Thurman was educated at Morehouse College, Columbia University, and Rochester Theological Seminary where he was influenced by Walter Rauschenbusch and George Cross. A denial of his application to Newton Theological Institution gave Thurman a lifelong antagonism to racial discrimination. He was appointed chaplain at Howard University where he took an interest in world religions and looked for common streams of spirituality. Later he served as chaplain at Boston

University, where he encountered the young Martin Luther King, Jr. In 1943, he formed the Church for the Fellowship of All Peoples in San Francisco, California, a unique interracial experiment in congregational life. Thurman traveled and lectured on topics of human rights, always emphasizing the inherent dignity of all persons before God. Deeply cha-grined by the poor relationship between Christianity and other world religions, he built upon the principle of reconciliation. Nonviolence was essential to his understanding as was openness to other people's views. **Works:** *With Head and Heart: The Autobiography of Howard Thurman* (New York: 1979); *For the Inward Journey: Writings of Howard Thurman* (San Diego, CA: 1984). **Suggested Readings:** Luther E. Smith, *Howard Thurman, The Mystic as Social Prophet* (Washington, DC: 1981); Henry J. Young, *God and Human Freedom: A Festschrift in Honor of Howard Thurman* (Richmond, IN: 1983); Elizabeth Yates, *Howard Thurman: Portrait of a Practical Dreamer* (New York: 1964).

Tutu, Desmond (1931–)

South African Anglican bishop and civil rights activist. The son of a Methodist schoolteacher, Tutu contracted tuberculosis at fourteen and was hospitalized for twenty months in a Catholic hospital. During this period, he was visited continuously by Trevor Huddleston, an anti-apartheid activist and source of inspiration. Originally intending to study medicine, he turned to school teaching and theological studies. In 1957, he entered the Anglican ministry and was ordained in 1961. From 1962 to 1967, he lived in England as a student at Kings College, University of London and as a staff worker for the World Council of Churches. Returning to South Africa, he taught at the Universities of Botswana, Lesotho, and Swaziland. In 1975, he was appointed dean of Johannes-burg and bishop of Lesotho in 1976, the first black in either role. He resigned the episcopacy to become general secretary of the South Afri-can Council of Churches to take up issues of justice. In 1979, his pass-port was withdrawn temporarily and he participated in a major protest march in 1980 in Johannesburg. Throughout the 1980s, Tutu became a tireless advocate of antiapartheid and stood firmly against the Botha government's oppressive police tactics. No other clergyman was as in-fluential in ending apartheid as Bishop Tutu. Since the political tran-sition in South Africa, Tutu has lectured and traveled on behalf of human rights around the world. The bishop was awarded the Nobel Prize for Peace in 1986. **Works:** *Crying in the Wilderness: The Struggle for Justice in South Africa* (Grand Rapids, MI: 1982); *The Nobel Prize Lecture: Desmond M. Tutu* (New York: 1986); *The Words of Desmond Tutu* (New York: 1989). **Suggested Readings:** Shirley DuBoulay, *Tutu: Voice of the Voiceless* (Grand Rapids, MI: 1988); Michael Battle, *Reconciliation: The Ubuntu Theology of Desmond Tutu* (Cleveland, OH: 1997); Jose Ramos-Horta, *The Art of Peace: Nobel Peace Laureates Discuss Human Rights, Conflict, and Reconciliation* (Ithaca, NY: 2000).

Williams, Roger (1603–1683)

English, and later American, clergyman and colonial planter. Likely educated at Cambridge University, Williams entered the ministry and developed Puritan and later Separatist views. He immigrated to Massachusetts Bay Colony in 1630 and became a teacher in the Puritan church at Salem. He incurred the hostility of Bay leaders over what he thought was their authoritarian policies and he was banished in 1638. He and a small group settled in Narragansett Country where they concluded a treaty with the Indians and planted the colony of Rhode Island. His friendship with the Indians led to colonial success in the Pequot War. It was Williams's policy of religious toleration that led to the prevailing sentiment in Rhode Island a generation before their charter guaranteed religious freedom. Williams was a Baptist in 1638–1639 but thereafter was not an active church member and considered himself a "Seeker." Williams was a principal advocate of a colonial charter for the Colony of Rhode Island. **Works:** *A Key Into the Language of America* (London: 1633); *The Bloudy Tenent of Persecution* (London: 1644); *The Bloudy Tenent of Persecution Yet More Bloudy* (London: 1652). **Suggested Readings:** Samuel H. Brockunier, *The Irrepressible Democrat: Roger Williams* (New York: 1940); W. Clark Gilpin, *The Millenarian Piety of Roger Williams* (Chicago: 1979); Edwin S. Gaustad, *Liberty of Conscience: Roger Williams in America* (Grand Rapids, MI: 1991).

Wojtyla, Karol, Pope John Paul II (1920–)

Polish Catholic theologian, bishop, and Roman Catholic pontiff. Wojtyla was educated at the Jagiellonian University in Krakow where he studied Polish language and literature and was occupied in poetry and drama. He worked for a time in factories and was called to the priesthood in 1942. He graduated from the university with distinction in theology and later from the Pontifical University in Rome with a doc-torate in theology. He served as professor of ethics at the University of Lublin and won national distinction in the field. He was elevated to the episcopacy in 1958, the arch-episcopacy in 1963, and the cardinalate in 1967. He traveled extensively in the church and wrote several important papers on theological topics and human rights. His work was of primary importance to Pope Paul VI in creating *Humanae Vitae*. Wojtyla worked tirelessly for his primate, Stefan Wyszynski, to secure legal status for the church in Poland. In 1978, he succeeded John Paul I and as pope has promulgated several statements on human rights. He has supported and implemented Vatican II and he has issued a call for a new economic order based upon the rights of workers and the dignity of labor. A con-servative theologically, John Paul II has continued to support priestly celibacy and he is opposed to liberation theology because of its assump-tion of class conflict. **Works:** *Cruzando el Umbral de la Esperanza* (Bar-celona: 1995); *La Fe Segun San uan de la Cruz* (Madrid: 1997); *Mi Vision del Hombre: Hacia una Nueva Etica* (Madrid: 1998). **Suggested Readings:** Mieczyslaw Malinski, *Pope John Paul II, the Life of Karol Wojtyla* (New York: 1979); Wladyslaw Strozewski, *Servo Veritatis: Materialy Sesji Naukowej Poswieconej Mysli Karola Wojtyly* (Krakow: 1988); Samuel Gregg, *Challenging the Modern World: Karol Wojtyla/John Paul II and the Development of Catholic Social Teaching* (Lanham, MD: 1999); Jaroslav Kupczak, *Destined for Liberty: The Human Person in the Philosophy of Karol Wojtyla/John Paul II* (Washington, DC: 2000).

Woolman, John (1720–1772)

Quaker merchant and social reformer. Self-educated, Woolman became a merchant and then a tailor in west New Jersey. Finding his trade unfulfilling, he took up a relationship with the Society of Friends and traveled widely as a minister. About 1746, during his travels, he became an abolitionist. At one point he made an extensive trip of about fifteen hundred miles through the Middle Colonies and the South, observing in his journal the circumstances of slave keeping among the Friends. This led to his producing *Some Considerations on the Keeping of Negroes* (1754). The next year, he published a tract against war in the midst of the Seven Years War. For the next few years, he traveled the eastern coast colonies and visited England, counseling against slavery. His influence with the Philadelphia Yearly Meeting led to their adopting a resolution against slavery, one of the most important stances of any religious group in the American colonies. In other works, Woolman wrote in support of Native Americans, especially concerned about their involvement in liquor traffic. Woolman's journal was published, revealing his lifelong moral concerns; it influenced generations of social reformers in the United States and Britain. William Ellery Channing called the journal the sweetest and purest autobiography in the English language. **Works:** *Journal of John Woolman* (Chicago: 1950); *Some Considerations on the Keeping of Negroes* (1754). **Suggested Readings:** Janet Whitney, *John Woolman: American Quaker* (1942); Edwin H. Cady, *John Woolman* (1965); Paul Rosenblatt, *John Woolman* (1969).

NOTES |

Introduction

1. Rhoda E. Howard, *Human Rights and the Search for Community* (Boulder, CO: Westview Press, 1995), 37.

2. Michael J. Perry, *The Idea of Human Rights: Four Enquiries* (New York: Oxford University Press, 1998), 41.

3. Max L. Stackhouse, *Creeds, Society, and Human Rights: A Study in Three Cultures* (Grand Rapids, MI: Eerdmans, 1984), 21.

4. For a useful survey of the development of Christianity, see W.H.C. Frend, *The Rise of Christianity* (Philadelphia: Fortress Press, 1984) and Williston Walker, Richard A. Norris, David W. Lotz and Robert T. Handy, *A History of The Christian Church*, 4th ed. (New York: Charles Scribner's Sons, 1985).

5. A. John Simmons, *The Lockean Theory of Rights* (Princeton: Princeton University Press, 1992), 173.

Chapter 1. Christian Theological Foundations of Human Rights

1. Thorwald Lorenzen, "Towards a Theology of Human Rights," *Review and Expositor* 97 (2000): 51.

2. Wolfgang Huber, "Human Rights: A Concept and Its History," in *The Church and the Rights of Man*, eds. Alois Müller and Norbert Greinacher (New York: The Seabury Press, 1979), 8–9.

3. This is a term that my author-colleague, Peter Haas, uses in the volume, *The Jewish Tradition*. It is roughly co-equal with the Greco-Roman era.

4. Karl Barth, *Church Dogmatics*, 5 vols, trans. G. T. Thomson (Edinburgh: T and T Clark, 1958), I, 183.

5. *Life in All Its Fullness: The Word of God and Human Rights* (Washington, DC: Baptist Joint Committee and American Bible Society, 1992), 39.

6. James Limburg, "Human Rights in the Old Testament," in *The Church and the Rights of Man*, eds. Alois Müller and Norbert Greinacher (New York: Seabury Press, 1979), 22–23, 25.

7. Ron O'Grady, *Bread and Freedom: Understanding and Acting on Human Rights* (Geneva: World Council of Churches, 1979), 72–73.

8. Josef Blank, "The Justice of God as the Humanisation of Man—The Problem of Human Rights in the New Testament," in *The Church and the Rights of Man*, eds. Alois Müller and Norbert Greinacher (New York: Seabury Press, 1979), 30–35.

9. Ibid., 30–31.

10. Stackhouse, *Creeds, Society, and Human Rights: A Study in Three Cultures*, 38–49.

11. Ibid., 58–64.

12. Ibid., 65–76.

13. Albert Gelin, *The Concept of Man in the Bible*, trans. D. Murphy (London: Chapman, 1968), 193ff.

14. Jan Milic Lochman, "Ideology or Theology of Human Rights? The Problematic Nature of the Concept of Human Rights Today" in Albert Gelin, *The Concept of Man*, 17–18.

15. *Baptist World Congress, Celebrating Christ's Presence Through the Spirit: Official Reports of the Fourteenth World Congress Toronto, Canada July 8–13 1980* (Nashville: Broadman Press, 1981), 77.

16. Emil Brunner, *Christianity and Civilization* (London: Nisbet, 1947–1948), 108.

17. Jürgen Moltmann, "Christian Faith and Human Rights" in Falconer, *Understanding Human Rights* (Dublin: Irish School of Ecumenics, 1980), 193ff.

18. Albert C. Knudsen, *The Principles of Christian Ethics* (New York: Abington Cokesbury, 1943), 39.

19. This was Brunner's point in post-World War II thinking: *Christianity and Civilization*, 121.

20. Robert A. Evans and Alice Fraser Evans, *Human Rights: A Dialogue Between The First and Third Worlds* (Maryknoll, NY: Orbis Books, 1984), 8–12.

21. James M. Gustafson, *Theology and Christian Ethics* (Philadelphia: The Pilgrim Press, 1974), 263–266.

22. Hans Küng, "Towards a World Ethic of World Religions," in *The Ethics of World Religions and Human Rights* (London: SCM Press, 1990), 116.

23. Cf. the survey in James E. Wood, Jr., "Baptists and Human Rights" (paper presented to Baptist World Alliance Commission on Human Rights, 1997), 3–5.

24. Roger Williams, *The Bloudy Tenent of Persecution for Cause of Conscience* (London: 1644; Macon, GA: Mercer University Press, 2001).

25. Lorenzen, "Towards a Theology of Human Rights," 54–56.

26. Ibid., 59.

27. *Theological Perspectives on Human Rights: Report on an LWF Consultation on Human Rights Geneva June 29–July 3, 1976* (Geneva: Lutheran World Federation, 1977), 27–32.

28. Lochman, "Ideology or Theology of Human Rights?" 16.

29. Huber, "Human Rights: A Concept and Its History," in *The Church and the Rights of Man,* 7–9.

30. Dietrich Bonhoeffer, *Ethics, Part I,* ed. Eberhard Bethge, trans. Neville Horton Smith (New York: Macmillan, 1955), 64–70.

31. Ibid., 125–138; 289–292.

32. Michael L. Westmoreland-White, "Contributions to Human Rights in Dietrich Bonhoeffer's Ethics," *Journal of Church and State* 39:1 (Winter 1997): 67.

33. Jan Lochman, "Human Rights from a Christian Perspective," in *A Christian Declaration on Human Rights: Theological Studies of the World Alliance of Reformed Churches,* ed. Allen O. Miller (Grand Rapids, MI: Eerdmans, 1977), 21.

34. Ibid., 44–45.

35. Emil Brunner, *Christianity and Civilization: The Gifford Lectures Delivered at the University of St. Andrews 1947* (New York: Charles Scribner's Sons, 1948), 23.

36. Ibid., 117–118.

37. On this point, see his "Original Study Paper: A Theological Basis of Human Rights and of the Liberation of Human Beings" (1971).

38. Jürgen Moltmann, *Creating a Just Future* (London: SCM Press, 1989), 38–39.

39. Moltmann, "Human Rights, the Rights of Humanity, and the Rights of Nature," in *The Ethics of World Religions and Human Rights,* eds. Hans Küng and Jürgen Moltmann (London: SCM Press, 1990), 126–127.

40. Jürgen Moltmann, *The Experiment Hope,* trans. M. Douglas Meeks (Philadelphia: Fortress Press, 1975), 7; "Human Rights, the Rights of Humanity and the Rights of Nature" in *Ethics of World Religions and Human Rights,* eds. Hans Küng and Jürgen Moltmann (London: SCM Press, 1990), 123–129.

41. The relational aspect of theological interpretation is amplified in John MacIntyre, *Faith, Theology and Imagination* (Edinburgh: Hansel Press, 1987) and Donel Murray, "The Theological Basis for Human Rights" *Irish Theological Quarterly* 56:2 (1990), 81–101.

42. David Hollenbach, *Justice, Peace, and Human Rights: American Catholic Social Ethics in a Pluralistic World* (New York: Crossroad, 1988), 88–95.

43. Gustavo Gutierrez, *The Power of the Poor in History: Selected Writings* (Maryknoll, NY: Orbis Books, 1979), 16.

44. Ibid., 18, 21.

45. Jan Sorbrino, "The Crucified Peoples: Yahweh's Suffering Servant Today," in Leonardo Boff and Virgil Elizondo, *Voice of the Victims* (London: SCM Press, 1991), 122–123.

46. Pablo Richard, "1492: The Violence of God and the Future of Christianity," in Boff and Elizondo, *Voice of the Victims,* 65, 211.

47. The Institute for Contextual Theology, founded in Johannesburg in 1981, was the source of the Kairos Document. See Peter Walshe, "Christianity and the Anti-

Apartheid Struggle: The Prophetic Voice within Divided Churches," in *Christianity in South Africa: A Political, Social, and Cultural History*, eds. Richard Elphick and Rodney Davenport (Berkeley: University of California Press, 1997), 392.

48. Daniel Vidal, "Examining the European Commission's Theses," in Miller, *Christian Declaration*, 42–45.

49. Hans Küng, "Towards a World Ethic of World Religions: Fundamental Questions of Present Day Ethics in a Global Context," in *The Ethics of World Religions and Human Rights*, eds. Hans Küng and Jürgen Moltmann (London: SCM Press, 1990), 112.

50. Küng, "Towards a World Ethic," 114.

51. Ibid., 115.

52. Ibid., 116.

53. Part of the declaration is quoted in Küng, "Towards a World Ethic," 118–119.

54. Carl F. H. Henry, *God, Revelation and Authority V: The God Who Stands and Stays, Part I* (Waco, TX: Word Books, 1982), 422.

55. Ibid., *God, Revelation and Authority IV: The God Who Speaks and Shows* (Waco, TX: Word Books, 1976), 588.

56. Ibid., *The God Who Stands and Stays, Part I*, Vol. V: 198; *The God Who Stands and Stays, Part II*, Vol. VI: 426, 607.

57. Ibid., Vol. V: 382; Vol. VI: 426. The previous theologian was a Baptist, William Newton Clarke.

58. Ibid., Vol. VI: 318.

59. Ibid., Vol. IV: 512–514.

60. Ibid., Vol. VI: 436.

61. Ronald J. Sider, *Rich Christians in an Age of Hunger* (New York: Paulist Press, 1977), 72, 209.

62. Ibid., 209.

63. Vinay Samuel and Chris Sugden, "Theology of Development: A Guide to the Debate," in *Evangelicals and Development: Towards a Theology of Social Change* (Philadelphia: The Westminster Press, 1981), 19.

64. John R. W. Stott, *Human Rights and Human Wrongs: Major Issues for a New Century* (Grand Rapids, MI: Baker Books, 1999), 170.

65. Ibid., 172.

66. See Christopher J. H. Wright, *Human Rights: A Study in Biblical Themes* (Cambridge: Grove Books, 1979), 16.

67. Ibid., 178.

68. Hans Küng and Helmut Schmidt, eds., *A Global Ethic and Global Responsibilities: Two Declarations* (London: SCM, 1998), 12, 14.

69. Ibid., 16–24.

70. John Clement, ed., *Human Rights and the Churches: New Challenges* (Geneva: World Council of Churches, 1998), 26.

71. Jürgen Moltmann, "A Definitive Study Paper: A Christian Declaration on Human Rights," in Miller, *Christian Declaration on Human Rights*, 130.

Chapter 2. Organized Christianity and Obstacles to Human Rights

1. Desmond Tutu, preface to *Religious Human Rights in Global Perspective: Religious Perspectives*, ed. John Witte, Jr. and Johan D. van der Vyver (The Hague: Martinus Nijhoff, 1996), xiv.

2. Walter Nigg, *The Heretics* (New York: Dorset Press, 1962), 11–15.

3. Irenaeus, *Against Heresies*, IV, Preface.

4. Ibid., III, xxv.

5. "Quantum praedecessores" issued by Eugenius III, quoted in Hallam, *Chronicles of the Crusades: Eye-Witness Accounts of the Wars Between Christianity and Islam* (Godalming, UK: Bramley Books, 1997), 1149–1150.

6. Jonathan Riley-Smith, *The Crusades: A Short History* (New Haven: Yale University Press, 1987), xxviii.

7. Ibid., 93.

8. From the "Annals of Marbach" in *Chronicles of the Crusades: Eye-Witness Accounts of the Wars Between Christianity and Islam*, ed. Elizabeth Hallam (Godalming, UK: Bramley Books, 1997), 242–243.

9. Nigg, *The Heretics*, 224–225.

10. Darcy Ribeiro, "The Latin American People" in *1492–1992: The Voice of the Victims*, eds. Leonardo Boff and Virgil Elizondo (London: SCM Press, 1990), 15.

11. Enrique Dussel, "The Real Motives for the Conquest" in *1492–1992*, 30.

12. Quoted in Lewis Hanke, *Aristotle and the American Indians: A Study in Race Prejudice in the Modern World* (Bloomington: Indiana University Press, 1959), 16.

13. Ibid., 17.

14. On the reduction process, see Margarita Duran Estrago, "The Reductions" in Enrique Dussel, *Church in Latin America 1492–1992* (Maryknoll, NY: Orbis Books, 1992), 351, 358.

15. The immediate context was the revocation of the Edict of Nantes in 1685.

16. Laennec Hurbon, "The Church and Afro-American Slavery" in Dussel, *Church in Latin America*, 367, 368, 371–372.

17. Roland Bainton, *Here I Stand: A Life of Martin Luther* (Nashville, TN: Abingdon Press, 1950), 376–377.

18. Quoted in Hans J. Hillerbrand, ed., *The Reformation: A Narrative History Related by Contemporary Observers and Participants* (New York: Harper and Row, 1964), 225.

19. *Huldrych Zwingli Writings*, Vol. I., trans. E. J. Furcha (Allison Park: Pickwick Publications, 1984), 280.

20. Calvin preferred beheading because it was more humane. Alister E. McGrath, *A Life of John Calvin: A Study in the Shaping of Western Culture* (Oxford: Blackwell, 1990), 114–120, indicates Calvin was overruled by a city council that at the time was disenchanted with him.

21. G. R. Potter, *Zwingli* (Cambridge: Cambridge University Press, 1976), 400, 413.

22. Thieleman J. van Braght, *Martyrs Mirror: The Story of Fifteen Centuries of Christian*

Martyrdom from the Time of Christ to A.D. 1660 (Scottdale, PA: Herald Press, 1950), 445, 465.

23. *Chronicle of the Hutterian Brethren* (Rifton, NY: Plough Publishing House, 1987), 574.

24. The great irony was the marriage of Charles I to Henrietta Maria who was Catholic and had chapels built in the royal palaces.

25. W. K. Jordan, *The Development of Religious Toleration In England, from the Convention of the Long Parliament to the Restoration, 1640–1660* (repr. Gloucester, MA: Peter Smith, 1938), 112, 134, 146.

26. John R. H. Moorman, *A History of the Church in England* (London: Adam and Charles Black, 1953), 252–253.

27. Relief for Quakers who refused to take oaths was further provided for in "An Act that the Solemn Affirmation and Declaration of the People Called Quakers Shall Be Accepted Instead of an Oath in the Usual Form" (1696). Reproduced in *English Historical Documents 1660–1714*, ed. Andrew Browning (New York: Oxford University Press, 1953), 404.

28. "An Act for Exempting Their Majesties' Protestant Subjects Dissenting from the Church of England From the Penalties of Certain Laws" in *English Historical Documents 1660–1714*, 400–403.

29. Thomas Jefferson Wertenbaker, *The Puritan Oligarchy: The Founding of American Civilization* (New York: Grosset and Dunlap, 1947), 279.

30. Elizabeth Isichei, *A History of Christianity in Africa: From Antiquity to the Present* (Grand Rapids, MI: Eerdmans, 1995), 71, 194.

31. Winthrop S. Jordan, *White Over Black: American Attitudes Toward the Negro 1550–1812* (Chapel Hill: University of North Carolina Press, 1968), 94.

32. Isichei, *Christianity in Africa*, 72.

33. "Fuller to Wayland, Letter V" in *Domestic Slavery Considered as a Scriptural Institution; in Correspondence Between The Rev. Richard Fuller of Beaufort, S.C., and The Rev. Francis Wayland of Providence, R.I.* (New York: Lewis Colby, 1845), 198.

34. William G. McLoughlin, *Cherokees and Missionaries 1789–1839* (New Haven: Yale University Press, 1984), 79. He shows that Cherokees "wanted education, not Christianity; teachers not preachers. And they got them." (53).

35. Ibid., 299, 331–332.

36. The authoritative source on this movement is Ray Allen Billington, *The Protestant Crusade 1800–1860: A Study in the Origins of American Nativism* (Chicago: Quadrangle Paperbacks, 1938), 32–76.

37. J. R. Miller, *Shingwauk's Vision: A History of Native Residential Schools* (Toronto: University of Toronto Press, 1996), 54–55.

38. For the responses to the crisis, see Anglican Church of Canada's "Apology to Native People" and "Stewards of a Legacy: Residential Schools, the Anglican Church, and Canada" in *Anglican News Service*, August 8, 1993; March 1999; and "United Church Response to the Government Announcement Related to Residential Schools Settlement" in *Bulletin of the United Church of Canada*, October 29, 2001.

39. Jean-Pierre Bastian, "Protestantism in Latin America" in *The Church in Latin America 1492–1992*, ed. Enrique Dussel (Maryknoll, NY: Orbis Books, 1992), 336–337.

40. Peter Matheson, ed., *The Third Reich and the Christian Churches* (Grand Rapids, MI: Eerdmans, 1981), 72–73.

41. For a balanced discussion of the religious dimensions of the Irish situation, consult John Fulton, *The Tragedy of Belief: Division, Politics, and Religion in Oreland* (Oxford: Clarendon Press, 1991), esp. 89–130.

42. Johann Kinghorn, "Modernization and Apartheid: The Afrikaner Churches" in Elphick and Davenport, *Christianity in South Africa*, 143.

43. Ger Duijzings, *Religion and the Politics of Identity in Kosovo* (New York: Columbia University Press, 2000), 30.

44. Paul Mojzes, *The Yugoslavian Inferno: Ethnoreligious Warfare in the Balkans* (New York: Continuum Press, 1995), 126.

45. Lukas Vischer, "The Ecumenical Movement and the Roman Catholic Church" in *The Ecumenical Advance: A History of the Ecumenical Movement Vol. II, 1948–1968*, ed. Harold E. Fey (Geneva: World Council of Churches, 1970), 319.

Chapter 3. Religious Liberty—The Cornerstone of Human Rights

1. Roger Williams, *The Danger of a Hireling Ministry* (London: 1652) quoted in *American Christianity: An Historical Interpretation with Representative Documents*, Vol. I, eds. H. Shelton Smith, Robert T. Handy, and Lefferts A. Loetscher (New York: Charles Scribner's Sons, 1960), 160.

2. David Hollenbach, S. J., "A Communitarian Reconstruction of Human Rights: Contributions from Catholic Tradition" in *Catholicism and Liberalism: Contributions to American Public Philosophy*, eds. R. Bruce Douglass and David Hollenbach (Cambridge: Cambridge University Press, 1994), 142.

3. *Translations and Reprints from the Original Sources of European History*, Vol. IV (Philadelphia: University of Pennsylvania Press, 1897), 28–30.

4. W. K. Jordan, *The Development of Religious Toleration in England, From the Beginning of the English Reformation to the Death of Queen Elizabeth* (Gloucester, MA: Peter Smith, 1965), 31.

5. Balthasar Hubmaier, "On Heretics and Those Who Burn Them" in *Balthasar Hubmaier: Theologian of Anabaptism*, trans. and eds. H. Wayne Pipkin and John H. Yoder (Scottdale, PA: Herald Press, 1989), 66.

6. Menno Simons, *Christian Baptism 1539* in *The Complete Writings of Menno Simons c.1496–1561*, trans. Leonard Verduin and ed. John C. Wenger (Scottdale, PA: Herald Press, 1984), 286.

7. John Hooper, *A Brief and Clear Confession*, Article 78 in *Later Writings of Bishop Hooper, Together with His Letters and other Pieces*, ed. Charles Nevinson (Cambridge: Cambridge University Press, 1852).

8. *Confession of Faith Put Forth by the Elders and Brethren of Many Congregations of*

Christians (baptized upon Profession of their Faith) in London and the Country (London: 1677), art. xxi, par. 2.

9. Richard Walsh and William Lloyd Fox, eds., *Maryland: A History, 1632–1974* (Baltimore: Maryland Historical Society, 1974), 12–13.

10. Quoted in Anson Phelps Stokes, *Church and State in the United States*, Vol. I (New York: Harper Brothers, 1950), 205.

11. Ibid., 207.

12. Mary Maples Dunn, *William Penn: Politics and Conscience* (Princeton, NJ: Princeton University Press, 1967), 67. His 1675 tract, *England's Present Interest Discovered with Honour to the Prince, and Safety to the People* (London: s.n., 1675) developed the contract theory of rights inherent in government.

13. William Penn, *England's Present Interest*, 23–28; *A Discourse of the General Rule of Faith and Practice and Judge of Controversie* (London: T. Sowle, 1699), 158–159.

14. Ibid., 70–71.

15. Noel B. Gerson, *The Edict of Nantes* (New York: Grosset and Dunlap, 1969), 149–151.

16. Quoted in Stokes, 419.

17. See Edwin S. Gaustad, "The Backus Leland Tradition," *Foundations* 2, no. 2 (April 1959): 146–150.

18. The story is told in Courtney Anderson, *To the Golden Shore: The Life of Adoniram Judson* (Boston: Little, Brown, 1956), 239, 250.

19. Kenneth Scott Latourette, *The Great Century in Northern Africa and Asia A.D. 1800–A.D. 1914* (New York: Harper & Brothers, 1944), 257–258.

20. Ibid., 374–375.

21. William H. Brackney, ed., *Baptist Life and Thought 1600–1980: A Sourcebook* (Valley Forge, PA: Judson Press, 1983), 423–426.

22. O. Frederick Nolde, "Ecumenical Action in International Affairs" in *The Ecumenical Advance: A History of the Ecumenical Movement 1948–1968*, ed. Harold E. Fey (Geneva: World Council of Churches, 1970), 270–271.

23. Stackhouse, *Creeds, Society, and Human Rights*, 44.

24. For a discussion of the religious liberty developments, see "Human Rights and Religious Liberty," *The New Delhi Report* (Geneva: World Council of Churches, 1961), 276–279.

25. For an excellent short survey, see Leonard Swidler, "Human Rights: A Historical Overview" in *The Ethics of World Religions and Human Rights*, eds. Hans Küng and Jürgen Moltmann (London: SCM Press, 1990), 21ff.

26. On the "Declaration on Religious Freedom" see John Courtney Murray, "The Declaration on Religious Freedom" in *Moral Theology: War, Poverty, Freedom: The Christian Response* (Mahwah, NJ: Paulist Press, 1966), 3–17.

27. Charles Wackneheim, "The Theological Meaning of the Rights of Man" in *The Church and the Rights of Man*, 51.

28. "Declaration on Religious Freedom" in *Documents of Vatican II*, ed. Walter M. Abbott (New York: Herder and Herder, 1989), 675.

29. Ibid., 685.

30. Lukas Vischer, "Religious Freedom and the World Council of Churches" in *Religious Freedom* (New York: Paulist Press, 1966), 63.

31. See the discussion in Pietro Pavan, "The Right to Religious Freedom in the Concilliar Declaration" in *Religious Freedom*, 37–45.

Chapter 4. The Social Concerns of Christianity

1. Quoted in Edwin S. Gaustad, *Liberty of Conscience: Roger Williams in America* (Grand Rapids, MI: Eerdmans, 1991), 30–31.

2. A good summary of Catholic heritage is Thomas Bokenkotter, *A Concise History of the Catholic Church* (New York: Doubleday: 1900), 134–137.

3. Rufus Jones, *The Quakers in the American Colonies* (New York: W. W. Norton, 1966), 516–520.

4. Minutes of the General Committee of the United Baptist Churches of Virginia, quoted in *Baptist Life and Thought: A Sourcebook*, ed. William Brackney (Valley Forge, PA: Judson Press, 1983), 143.

5. For an excellent summary of Quaker activities in this era, see *Quaker Crosscurrents: Three Hundred Years of Friends in the New York Yearly Meetings*, ed. Hugh Barbour, et al. (Syracuse, NY: Syracuse University Press, 1995), 79–90.

6. "Moral Considerations" in *Colonial Ecclesiastical Establishment: Being a Brief View of the State of the Colonies of Great Britain, and of Her Asiatic Empire, In Respect to Religious Instruction*, by Claudius Buchanan (London: Cadell and Davies, 1813), 121–126.

7. See Leon O. Hynson, "Wesley's 'Thoughts Upon Slavery': A Declaration of Human Rights" in *Methodist History* 33, no. 1 (October 1994): 47–49.

8. Donald W. Dayton, *Discovering an Evangelical Heritage* (New York: Harper and Row, 1976), 1–99.

9. See William H. Brackney, *Religious Antimasonry: The Genesis of a Political Party 1826–1830* (Ann Arbor, MI: University Microfilms, 1976), 1–30.

10. Dayton, *Evangelical Heritage*, 135.

11. Joan Jacobs Brumberg, *Mission for Life: The Dramatic Story of the Wives of Adoniram Judson* (New York: The Free Press, 1980).

12. Quoted in Alice Felt Tyler, *Freedom's Ferment: Phases of American Social History from the Colonial Period to the Outbreak of the Civil War* (New York: Harper Torchbooks, 1962), 405.

13. Sheridan Gilley, "The Church of England in the Nineteenth Century" in *A History of Religion in Britain: Practice and Belief from Pre-Roman Times to the Present* (Oxford: Blackwell, 1994), 295.

14. William H. Brackney, *Christian Voluntarism in Britain and North America: A Bibliography and Critical Assessment* (Westport, CT: Greenwood Press, 1995), 43–54.

15. A comprehensive listing is found in Brackney, *Christian Voluntarism*, Appendix A.

16. Robert Baird, *Religion in the United States of America* (repr. New York: Arno Press, 1969), 288; 410.

17. Among the better primers on the social gospel is Charles Howard Hopkins, *The Rise of the Social Gospel in American Protestantism 1865–1915* (New Haven: Yale University Press, 1940).

18. Hopkins, *Social Gospel in American Protestantism*, 109.

19. Raymond W. Albright, *A History of the Protestant Episcopal Church* (New York: Macmillan, 1964), 312–316.

20. Quoted in Albright, *A History of the Protestant Episcopal Church*, 215.

21. John A. Hutchison, *We Are Not Divided: A Critical and Historical Study of the Federal Council of Churches of Christ in America* (New York: Roundtable Press, 1941), 97–104.

22. Gregory Baum, "Canadian Socialism and the Christian Church" in *Christianity and Socialism*, eds. Johann-Baptist Metz and Jean-Pierre Jossua (New York: Seabury Press, 1977), 17.

23. Ibid., 20–21.

24. Robert Moats Miller, *American Protestantism and Social Issues 1919–1939* (Chapel Hill: University of North Carolina Press, 1958), 134–135.

25. Ibid., 298.

26. See the citations in Miller, *American Protestantism*, 306–311.

27. L. DeAne Lagerquist, *The Lutherans* (Westport, CT: Greenwood Press, 1999), 142–143.

28. Robert Pritchard, *A History of the Episcopal Church* (Harrisburg, PA: Morehouse Publishing, 1991), 260–264; William H. Brackney, "A Baptist Witness for Peace" in *Baptist Life and Thought* (Valley Forge, PA: Judson Press, 1998), 450–453.

29. John Tracy Ellis, *American Catholicism* (Chicago: University of Chicago Press, 1969), 142–143.

30. See R. Paul Ramsay, "Modern Papal Social Teachings" in *The Heritage of Christian Thought: Essays in Honor of Robert Lowry Calhoun*, eds. Robert E. Cushman and Egil Grislis (New York: Harper and Row, 1966), 220–238.

31. E. H. McKinley, *Marching to Glory: The History of The Salvation Army in the United States, 1880–1992* (Grand Rapids, MI: Eerdmans, 1995), 299–315.

32. Ibid., 299.

33. On the Lausanne movement, see William H. Brackney, *Christian Voluntarism: Theology and Praxis* (Grand Rapids, MI: Eerdmans, 1997), 88–89.

34. "The Manila Manifesto," Lausanne Committee for World Evangelization, www.gospelcom.net/lcwe/statements/manila.html (Jan. 14, 2003).

35. Adrian Hastings, *A History of English Christianity 1920–2000* (London: SCM Press, 1970), 179ff.

36. See Alan Suggate's essay, "The Christian Churches in England Since 1945: Ecumenism and Social Concern" in *History of Religion in Great Britain*, 467–487 and in Hastings, *History of English Christianity*, 429, 573.

Chapter 5. Christian Responses to the United Nations Declarations

1. The Life and Work Movement was one of three predecessors to the World Council of Churches. It held meetings at Stockholm (1925) and Oxford (1937).

2. One sentence of this oft-quoted speech is found in Egon Schwelb, *Human Rights and the International Community: The Roots and Growth of the Universal Declaration of Human Rights, 1948–1963* (Chicago: Quadrangle Books, 1964), 25.

3. The best administrative summary of the history of the U.N. Commission on Human Rights is Howard Tolley, Jr., *The U.N. Commission on Human Rights* (Boulder, CO: Westview Press, 1987), 8–13. Major structural changes occurred in 1954, 1967, and 1980.

4. As recalled in John P. Humphrey, *Human Rights and the United Nations: A Great Adventure* (Dobbs Ferry, NY: Transitional Publishers, 1984), 40–45.

5. This "tripartite" handling of standards and responses was first suggested by P. C. Chang of China and became standard operating process.

6. Based upon the arrangement of Tolley, *U.N. Commission on Human Rights*, ix–x.

7. Quoted in O. Frederick Nolde, *Free and Equal: Human Rights in Ecumenical Perspective* (Geneva: World Council of Churches, 1968), 10–13.

8. O. Frederick Nolde, "The United Nations Acts for Human Rights." Release by the World Council of Churches, CCIA Archives.

9. "Human Rights Bill Is Voted by United Nations Committee: Mrs. Roosevelt Acclaims It as a Moral and Spiritual Milestone for the World," *New York Herald Tribune*, December 7, 1948.

10. The Roman Catholic Church is a full member of the Faith and Order Commission.

11. O. Frederick Nolde, "Ecumenical Action in International Affairs" in *A History of the Ecumenical Movement: The Ecumenical Advance*, Vol. II, ed. Harold E. Fey (Geneva: World Council of Churches, 1970), 271–272.

12. John Clement, ed., *Human Rights and the Churches: New Challenges* (Geneva: World Council of Churches, 1998), 10–22.

13. Ibid., 120–121.

14. Charles Wackenheim, "The Theological Meaning of the Rights of Man" in *The Church and the Rights of Man*, eds. Alois Müller and Norbert Greinacher (New York: Seabury Press, 1979), 51.

15. Thomas Aquinas, *Summa Theologica*, II–II, 66 art. 2.

16. Richard Evans Brown, "Theological Interpretations of Human Rights: An Analysis of Recent Roman Catholic Papal Encyclicals and the Ethics of Jürgen Moltmann" (unpublished PhD diss., University of Virginia, 1994), 98.

17. Peter Riga, *Peace on Earth: A Commentary on Pope John's Encyclical* (London: Herder and Herder, 1964), 200–205, 208.

18. Georges Crespy, "The Image of Man According to Vatican II and Uppsala 1968" in *Humanism and Christianity*, ed. Claude Geffre (London: Herder and Herder, 1973), 108–109.

19. On the developments of Vatican II, see *The Documents of Vatican II, With Notes and Comments by Catholic, Protestant, and Orthodox Authorities*, ed. Walter M. Abbott, S. J. (New York: Guild Press, 1966).

20. Quoted in David M. Byers, ed. *Justice in the Marketplace: Collected Statements of the Vatican and the U.S. Catholic Bishops on Economic Policy, 1891–1984* (Washington, DC: United States Catholic Conference, 1985), 22.

21. "Religious Liberty and Human Rights" in *Nations and Religions*, ed. Leonard Swidler (Philadelphia: Ecumenical Press, 1986), 22.

22. Knut Walf, "Gospel, Church Law and Human Rights: Foundations and Deficiencies" in *Ethics of World Religions and Human Rights* (London: SCM Press, 1990), 38–39.

23. Peter A. Sulyok, "The Fullness of Life: The Vision of Micah and the Golden Rule" in *Church and Society: The Journal of "Just" Thoughts* (March/April 1998): 11.

24. Robert F. Smylie, "Human Rights and Justice: Presbyterian Public Policy 1935–1950, In Which the Presbyterian Church's Voice on Human Rights Is Developed and Heard," *Church and Society* (March/April 1998): 28–35.

25. J. William T. Youngs, *The Congregationalists* (Westport, CT: Greenwood Press, 1990), 174–178; 184.

26. Jan M. Lochman, "Human Rights from a Christian Perspective" in *A Christian Declaration on Human Rights: Theological Studies of the World Alliance of Reformed Churches*, ed. Allen O. Miller (Grand Rapids, MI: Eerdmans, 1977), 21–23.

27. Ibid., 18.

28. Liberato C. Batista, "Bishops Affirm the Universal Declaration of Human Rights," *Christian Social Action* (June 1998): 35.

29. Liberato C. Bautista, "The United Nations Ministry of the General Board of Church and Society of the United Methodist Church," *Christian Social Action* (October 1999), 31–33.

30. Quoted in Brackney, *Baptist Life and Thought*, 426.

31. Quoted in Ernest A. Payne, *The Baptist Union: A Short History* (London: Carey Kingsgate Press, 1959), 290.

32. A useful summary of the BWA participation in human rights concerns is James E. Wood, Jr., "Baptists and Human Rights" (unpublished BWA paper in files, 1997), esp. 9–12. Wood was the second director of the Baptist Joint Committee on Public Affairs and spent two decades with the J. M. Dawson Institute for Church State Studies at Baylor University.

33. Martin Luther King, Jr., "The Ethical Demands for Integration" in *A Testament of Hope: The Essential Writings of Martin Luther King, Jr.*, ed. James Melvin Washington (San Francisco: Harper and Row, 1986), 122.

34. Martin Luther King, Jr., "See the Promised Land" in *A Testament of Hope*, 280.

35. James H. Cone, *A Black Theology of Liberation* (Maryknoll, NY: Orbis Books, 1986), v.

36. See, for instance, J. Deotis Roberts, *Black Theology in Dialogue* (Philadelphia: Westminster Press, 1987), 106.

37. Peter Walsh, "Christianity and the Anti-Apartheid Struggle: The Prophetic Voice within Divided Churches" in *Christianity in South Africa: A Political, Social, and Cultural History*, eds. Richard Elphick and Rodney Davonport (Berkeley: University of California Press, 1997), 388.

38. See Willis H. Logan, ed., *The Kairos Covenant: Standing With South African Christians* (New York: Friendship Press, 1988), 146–149. Related to the Kairos Covenant

were inmates at Sing Sing Prison who were also enrolled at New York Theological Seminary and made a statement in solidarity with South Africa.

39. I am indebted here to Robert Traer's book, *Faith in Human Rights*, chapter 4, for his survey of the world church through the 1980s.

40. Hastings, *History of English Christianity*, 655–659.

41. Mortimer Arias, "Ministries of Hope in Latin America," *International Review of Missions* 71 (January 1982): 6.

42. Küng and Schmidt, eds., *Global Ethic and Global Responsibilities*, 85–87.

43. Ibid., 88–100.

44. See Arvind Sharma, "Towards a Declaration of Human Rights by the World's Religions" in *Human Rights and Responsibilities in the World's Religions*, eds. Joseph Runzo, Nancy Martin, and Arnold Sharma (Oxford: Oneworld, 2003).

Chapter 6. The Future of Christianity and Human Rights

1. Louis Henkin, "Human Rights: Reappraisal and Readjustment" in *Essays on Human Rights: Contemporary Issues and Jewish Perspectives*, ed. David Sidorsky (Philadelphia: The Jewish Publication Society of America, 1979), 68–71.

2. James E. Wood, Jr., "An Apologia for Religious Human Rights" in *Essays on Human Rights*, 457.

3. I use the term "stumbling block" deliberately. In the Christian tradition, Jesus Christ is described as a stumbling block to those who do not believe (I Peter 2:8). The metaphor is used no less than eight times in the New Testament.

4. Martin E. Marty, "Religious Dimensions of Human Rights," in *Religious Human Rights in Global Perspective: Religious Perspectives*, eds. John Witte, Jr., and Johann D. van der Vyver (The Hague: Martinus Nijhoof, 1996), 7.

5. Ibid. See Marty's discussion of this point.

6. A. J. Conyers, *The Long Truce: How Toleration Made the World Safe for Power and Profit* (Dallas: Spence Publishing, 2001), 217–219.

7. John Witte, introduction to *The Long Truce*, xxx–xxxv.

8. The phrase was first coined by George Dangerfield, *The Strange Death of Liberal England* (1936) and it spun off more recent works like Dwight D. Murphey, *Liberal Thought in Modern America* (1987) and H. W. Brands, *The Strange Death of American Liberalism* (2001). Among the first church historians to note this was Winthrop S. Hudson in *Religion in America: An Historical Account of the Development of American Religious Life* (New York: Scribner's, 1973), 412–415. Hudson speaks of the "mainline" becoming the "old line" and "Protestant disarray." See also Robert Handy's analysis in *A History of the Churches in the United States and Canada* (New York: Oxford University Press, 1974), 422–423, where he writes of a decline of Christendom and a "post-Christian era."

9. Consult the *Yearbook of the American Baptist Churches in the USA*, 1990–2002.

10. James E. Wood, "An Apologia for Religious Human Rights," in *Religious Human Rights*, 482.

11. Martin E. Marty, "Religious Dimensions of Human Rights" in *Religious Human Rights*, 12.

12. *Book of Discipline of the United Methodist Church 2000*, General Conference of the United Methodist Church (Nashville: Methodist Publishing House, 2000), 165.

13. Desmond Tutu, preface to *Religious Human Rights*, xvi.

Chapter 7. Sources Illustrative of Human Rights in the Christian Tradition

1. Later in the treatise, Luther magnified his point: "First that their synagogues be burned down, and that all who are able toss in sulphur and pitch; it would be good if someone could also throw in some hellfire. That would demonstrate to God our serious resolve and be evidence to all the world that it was in ignorance that we tolerated such houses, in which the Jews have reviled God, our dear Creator and Father, and his Son most shamefully up till now, but that we have now given them their due reward." (p. 285)

ANNOTATED BIBLIOGRAPHY |

Theological Foundations

Arias, Mortimer. "The Emerging Theology of Life in Latin America." *Apuntes* 6:2 (1986): 30ff. Ecumenical theologian summarizes recent developments in Latin America.

Banana, Canaan. "The Biblical Basis for Liberation Struggles." *International Review of Missions* 68 (October 1979): 417–423.

Berkouwer, G. C. *Man: The Image of God.* Grand Rapids, MI: Eerdmans, 1962. A prominent conservative Reformed theologian defines the *imago dei* in his tradition.

Bonhoeffer, Dietrich. *Ethics, Part I.* Edited by Eberhard Bethge. Translated by Neville Horton Smith. New York: Macmillan, 1955. In retrospect, one of the seminal ethics of the century; it continues to be debated.

Bonino, Jose Miguez. "Whose Human Rights?" *International Review of Missions* LXVI: 263 (July 1977): 220–224. Leading liberation theologian offers analysis of various approaches to human rights.

Brunner, Emil. *Christianity and Civilisation: The Gifford Lectures Delivered at the University of St. Andrews, 1947.* New York: Charles Scribner's Sons, 1948. This is Brunner's classic definition of human rights, among the most influential statements in the Reformed tradition.

Carr, Burgess. "Biblical and Theological Basis for the Struggle for Human Rights." *The Ecumenical Review* 27 (April 1975): 117–123.

Cronin, Kieran. *Rights and Christian Ethics.* Cambridge: Cambridge University Press, 1992. Excellent discussion of rights terminology; models of rights; and rights, power, and covenant. Especially useful is her discussion of various interpretations of the *imago dei.* Describes models of image, covenant, freedom, and power.

Dayton, Donald, ed. *Five Sermons and a Tract By Luther Lee.* Chicago: Holrad House, 1975. Theological perspective from an American Wesleyan Methodist.

De Gruchy, John W. *Bonhoeffer for a New Day: Theology in a Time of Transition.* Grand Rapids, MI: Eerdmans, 1997. See especially N. Barney Pityana's article, "The Ethics of Responsibility: Human Rights in South Africa."

Dunn, Mary M. *William Penn: Politics and Conscience.* Princeton: Princeton University Press, 1967. Covers Penn's variation on the theme of religious toleration and how he was closer to Puritans and Anglicans than Baptists.

Esbeck, Carl H. *Religious Beliefs, Human Rights, and the Moral Foundation of Western Democracy.* Columbia: University of Missouri Press, 1986.

Evans, Robert A., and Alice F. Evans. *Human Rights: A Dialogue Between the First and Third Worlds.* Maryknoll, NY: Orbis Books, 1984. A useful introduction to the problems of human rights, identifying different perspectives on the issues. The authors were active in introducing North American Christians to human rights topics by use of the case method of learning.

Frenz, Helmut. "Divine Rights and Human Rights." *Church and Society* 69 (November 1978): 54–60.

Gustafson, James M. *Theology and Christian Ethics.* Philadelphia: The Pilgrim Press, 1974. A prominent representative ethicist raises questions about the process by which ethical decisions, like the agenda of human rights, are made.

Henkin, Alice, ed. *Human Dignity: The Internationalization of Human Rights.* New York: Aspen Institute for Humanistic Studies, 1979.

Jenkins, David. "Human Rights in Christian Perspective." *Study Encounter*. Geneva: World Council of Churches, 1974.

———. "Theological Inquiry Concerning Human Rights." *The Ecumenical Review* 27 (April 1975): 97–103.

Justicia et Pax: The Church and Human Rights. Rome: Pontifical Commission, 1974. Useful, succinct summary of Catholic development of human rights doctrines.

Krusche, Guenter. "Human Rights in a Theological Perspective." *Lutheran World* (1977): 59–65. Prominent Lutheran theologian examines theological issues.

Küng, Hans, and Moltmann, Jürgen, eds. *The Ethics of World Religions and Human Rights*. Philadelphia: Trinity Press International, 1990. A series of most-useful essays that detail the interface of Islam, Christianity, Judaism, Hinduism, and Buddhism and the issues presented by human rights. Küng and Moltmann both have essays, as does Leonard Swidler on an overview of human rights, especially of the Catholic heritage.

Maritain, Jacques. "The Rights of Man." In *What Are Human Rights?* Edited by Maurice Cranston. London: Bodley Head, 1973. Noted Roman Catholic philosopher-theologian who revisited the thought of Thomas Aquinas and created a theological basis in the 1950s for human rights.

Moltmann, Jürgen. *On Human Dignity: Political Theology and Ethics*. Translated by Douglas Meeks. Philadelphia: Fortress Press, 1984. Exceedingly important text for recent transition to environment and global ethical perspectives.

Montgomery, John Warwick. *Human Rights and Human Dignity*. Grand Rapids, MI: Zondervan, 1986. American fundamentalist lawyer builds case for human rights from a biblical perspective.

Müller, Alois, and Greinacher, Norbert, eds. *The Church and The Rights of Man*. New York: Seabury Press, 1979. This most enlightening volume contains three helpful essays, "Human Rights on the Old Testament" (James Limburg), "The Justice of God as the Humanisation of Man—the Problem of Human Rights in the New Testament" (Josef Blank), and "The Theological Meaning of the Rights of Man" (Charles Wackenheim).

Muzaffar, Chandra. *Rights, Religion, and Reform: Enhancing Human Dignity Through Spiritual and Moral Transformation*. London: Routledge, Curzon, 2002.

Nelson, J. Robert. "Human Rights in Creation and Redemption: A Protestant View." In *Human Rights in Religious Traditions*. Edited by Arlene Swidler. New York: Pilgrim Press, 1982.

Niebuhr, Reinhold. *The Nature and Destiny of Man*. New York: Scribners, 1949. A Reformed and Neo-orthodox treatment of the doctrine of man.

Otto, Rudolph. *The Idea of the Holy: An Inquiry into the Non-Rational Factor of the Idea of the Divine and Its Relation to the Rational*. New York: Oxford University Press, 1950. Otto is useful in discussing the nature of moral obligation and the divine elements in human nature.

Perry, Michael J. "The Idea of Human Rights: Is the Idea of Human Rights Ineliminably Religious?" In *Problems and Conflicts Between Law and Morality in a Free Society*. Edited by James E. Wood, Jr. and Derek Davis (Waco, TX: 1994): J. M. Dawson Institute, 55–116.

Power, Jonathan. *Against Oblivion: Amnesty International's Fight for Human Rights* London: Fontana Books, 1981. The story of Amnesty International and its advocacy of human rights.

Reuver, Marc, ed. *Human Rights: A Challenge to Theology*. Rome: CCIA International, 1983. An excellent series of essays that illustrate how various regions and traditions have developed theological responses to human rights issues.

Simmons, A. John. *The Lockean Theory of Rights*. Princeton: Princeton University Press, 1992. Simmons gives sharp definition to the rights discussion of John Locke. He separates out six possible categories of natural rights. Very helpful in defining the philosophic background to human rights. Three implications are deduced from this narrative. First, human beings are special, superior parts of the creation. Second, rights help humans to focus on outcomes. Third, rights bring discretion to the moral life.

Sundman, Per. *Human Rights, Justification, and Christian Ethics*. Uppsala, Sweden: Uppsala University Press, 1996. Swedish Lutheran theologian works on the problems, philosophical and theological, of human rights discourse.

Todt, Heinz-Eduard. "Theological Reflections on the Foundations of Human Rights." *Lutheran World* (1977): 45–58. Key treatment of theological foundations from Lutheran perspective.

Tutu, Desmond. Preface to *Religious Human Rights*. Edited by John Witte. The Hague: Nijhoff, 1996, ix–xvi. Influential essay on human rights.

Weingartner, Erich, and Marilyn Weingartner, eds. *Human Rights Is More Than Human Rights: A Primer for Churches on Security and Cooperation in Europe*. Rome: IDOC International, 1977.

Wingren, Gustaf. "Human Rights: A Theological Analysis." *The Ecumenical Review* 27 (April 1975): 124–127.

Witte, John, and Johan D. van der Vyver, eds. *Religious Human Rights in Global Perspectives-Religious Perspectives*. The Hague: Matinus Nijhoff, 1996. See especially the articles by Martin Marty, "Religious Rights: An Historical Perspective" and James E. Wood, Jr., "Religion and Human Rights: A Theological Apologetic."

World Alliance of Reformed Churches. *Theological Basis of Human Rights*. Geneva: World Alliance of Reformed Churches, 1976. The official statement with useful rationale summarizing the Reformed position.

Social Concerns of Christianity

Albright, Raymond W. *A History of the Protestant Episcopal Church*. New York: Macmillan, 1964. Contains a helpful chapter on social activism and transatlantic relations.

Allen, Richard. *The Social Passion: Religion and Social Reform in Canada*. Toronto: University of Toronto Press, 1971. The standard authority on the social gospel in Canada.

Baum, Gregory. "Canadian Socialism and the Christian Church." In *Christianity and Socialism*. Edited by Johann-Baptist Metz and Jean-Pierre Jossua. New York: Seabury Press, 1977.

Blaggett, Jerome P. *Habitat for Humanity Building Private Homes, Building*

Public Religion. Philadelphia: Temple University Press, 2001. Recent analysis of Habitat with useful sociological chapter on voluntarism.

Booty, John. "Stephen Bayne's Perspective on the Church and the Civil Rights Movement, 1967–1970." *Anglican and Episcopal History* 64:3 (September 1995): 353–370. Stephen Bayne was the first vice president of the church's Executive Council and director of its overseas work. He was a leader in the desegregation of the church.

Cunningham, Gerald. "But Did You Free the Boy? Church Action for Safe and Just Communities." *Church and Society* 87 (March/April 1997): 101–108. Justice and violence alternatives from a Disciples perspective.

Dayton, Donald. *Discovering An Evangelical Heritage*. New York: Harper and Row, 1976. A historiographically pacesetting book that recovers the social concerns of the evangelical community in the Second Great Awakening. Particular emphasis upon Wesleyan contributions.

Eckardt, A. Roy. "Anti-Isrealism, Antisemitism and the Quakers." *Christianity and Crisis: A Christian Journal of Opinion* 31 (September 20, 1971): 180–186. The Quaker search for the role of "honest broker" in the debates over Israel and the Palestinians of the 1970s.

Edds, William Harold. "Disciples and Their Major Social Issue." *College of the Bible Quarterly* 41 (July 1964): 20–25. Ownership of the race issue in the Disciples of Christ (Christian Church).

Evangelical Witness in South Africa. Dobson: Concerned Evangelicals, 1986.

Fey, Harold E. "Disciples on Civil Rights." *Christian Century* 80 (October 30, 1963): 1326–1327. Brief survey of Disciples of Christ (Christian Church) and civil rights.

Fuller, Millard, with Diane Scott. *No More Shacks: The Daring Story of Habitat for Humanity*. Waco, TX: Word Books, 1986. The compelling saga of America's foremost self-help project in the words of the founder.

Hopkins, Charles Howard. *The Rise of the Social Gospel in American Protestantism 1865–1915*. New Haven, CT: Yale University Press, 1940.

Standard mid-century text upon which most scholarship of Protestant social activism is based.

Howes, Graham. "Urban Problems and Policy: An Anglican Case Study." *Social Compass* 45:1 (1998): 43–55. Examines the Church of England's response to urban problems and draws heavily upon the nineteenth century.

Hutchison, John A. *We Are Not Divided: A Critical and Historical Study of The Federal Council of Churches of Christ in America*. New York: Roundtable Press, 1941. The authoritative history of the Council that connects the Social Gospel and the federation movement. Contains useful original sources.

Hutchinson, Roger. "The Fellowship for a Christian Social Order." ThD dissertation, Victoria University, 1975. Detailed work on a major Canadian social activist organization from the turn of the twentieth century.

Jennings, Judith. "Mid-Eighteenth Century British Quakerism and the Response to the Problem of Slavery." *Quaker History* 66 (September 1977): 23–40. An insightful look at the British slave trade with the colonies and the Quaker response.

Kollar, Rene. "Anglican Brotherhoods and Urban Social Work." *Churchman* 101:2 (June 1987): 140–145. The frustrating story of the emergence of Anglican inner-city work in Britain.

Lagerquist, L. DeAne. *The Lutherans*. Westport, CT: Greenwood Press, 1999. Recent general Lutheran history that notes social activism and organization.

Lewis, Harold T. "Racial Concerns in the Episcopal Church Since 1973." *Anglican and Episcopal History* 67:4 (December 1998): 467–479. The saga of the development of black Episcopalians under the influence of human rights and the civil rights movement.

Liebenburg, Gillian A. W. "Cautious and Conservative: Anglican Social Policy in New Brunswick, 1906–1918." *Journal of the Canadian Church Historical Society* 41 (1999): 27–55. Accompanying the thrust of the social gospel, under the leadership of Anglican bishop John Andrew Richardson, the church adopted a variety of moral and social reforms that transformed its identity in the province of New Brunswick.

McKinley, E. H. *Marching to Zion: The History of the Salvation Army in the United States, 1880–1992*. Grand Rapids, MI: Eerdmans, 1995. Presents the story of a major evangelical approach to Christian social concerns.

Metz, Johann-Baptist, and Jean-Pierre Jossua. *Christianity and Socialism*. New York: Seabury Press, 1977. Contains several essays on the Catholic response to various forms of socialism in theory and practice within five regions. The most useful is Gregory Baum's essay, "Canadian Socialism and the Christian Church."

Miller, Robert Moats. *American Protestantism and Social Issues, 1919–1939*. Chapel Hill: University of North Carolina Press, 1958. A follow-up study, chronologically after the social gospel literature, of the social conscience of American Christianity.

Moody, Joseph N., ed. *Church and Society: Catholic Social and Political Thought and Movements 1789–1950*. New York: Arts Press, 1953. A comprehensive survey of American Catholic involvement in social concerns and movements. Contains documents not found easily elsewhere.

Nkwoka, A. O. "The Church and Polygamy in Africa: The 1988 Lambeth Conference Resolution." *Africa Theological Journal* 19:2 (1990): 139–154. A look at clashing social realities with profound implications for Christianity and human rights.

Oliver, John. "J. Walter Malone: *The American Friend* and an Evangelical Quaker's Social Agenda." *Quaker History* 80: 4 (Fall 1991): 63–84. A social analysis of Malone's influential newspaper in comparison with the views of Rufus Jones.

Olsen, Gerald W. "From Parish to Palace: Working-Class Influences on Anglican Temperance Movements, 1835–1914." *Journal of Ecclesiastical History* 40:2 (April 1989): 239–252.

Pranis, Kay. "From Vision to Action: Some Principles of Restorative Justice." *Church and Society* (March/April 1997): 32–42. A progressive United Methodist view on the rights and care of prisoners.

Pritchard, Robert. *A History of the Episcopal Church*. Harrisburg, PA: Morehouse Publishing, 1991. Standard history of Episcopal Church, noting social concerns organizations.

Spencer, Carole D. "Evangelism, Feminism, and Social Reform: The Quaker Woman Minister and the Holiness Revival." *Quaker History* 80:3 (September 1991): 24–48. The impact of the holiness movement upon Quaker ideas of social reform and the advance of women in ministry.

Tutu, Desmond. *Crying in the Wilderness: The Struggle for Justice in South Africa*. Grand Rapids, MI: Eerdmans, 1982. Tutu's own words declare his lifelong struggle for human rights.

Tyler, Alice Felt. *Freedom's Ferment: Phases of American Social History from the Colonial Period to the Outbreak of the Civil War*. New York: Harper and Row, 1944. An old standard that accurately categorizes and traces the reform movement of the antebellum period in the United States.

Washburn, Wilcomb E. *The Indian in America*. New York: Harper Torchbooks, 1975. A survey of the Indian tribes at the onset of English colonization. Part of a series written from an American colonial perspective.

Woolverton, John F. "Evangelical Protestantism and Alcoholism 1933–1962: Episcopalian Samuel Shoemaker, The Oxford Group and Alcoholics Anonymous." *Historical Magazine of the Protestant Episcopal Church* 52 (March 1983): 53–65. A survey of a prominent Episcopalian's involvement in Alcoholics Anonymous.

Wyatt-Brown, Bertram. *Lewis Tappan and the Evangelical War Against Slavery*. New York: Atheneum, 1971. Essentially a biography of Tappan, it stresses the contribution of evangelical Protestants to the crusade against slavery.

Religious Liberty

Buckley, Thomas E. "Church and State in Massachusetts Bay: A Case Study of Baptist Dissent, 1651." *Journal of Church and State* 23:2 (Spring 1981): 309–322. The story of Baptist response to grievous establishment politics in the case of Obadiah Holmes.

Canon Law. *Religious Freedom. Concilium: Theology in an Age of Renewal*. New York: Paulist Press, 1966. Post-Vatican III Catholic analysis.

Curran, Charles E. "Religious Freedom and Human Rights in the World and the Church: A Christian Perspective." In *Religious Liberty and Human Rights in Nations and Religions*. Edited by Leonard Swidler. Philadelphia: Ecumenical Press, Temple University, 1986.

Dalberg-Acton, John Emerich Edward. "The History of Freedom in Christianity." In *Essays in the History of Liberty: Selected Writings of Lord Acton*. Vol. 1. Edited by J. Rufus Fears. Indianapolis: Liberty Fund, 1985. The classic historical treatment of the topic in a new edition with a helpful introduction.

Gaustad, Edwin S. "The Backus Leland Tradition." *Foundations* 2:2 (April, 1959): 131–152. Baptist historian creates a classic fusion of Isaac Backus and John Leland into a common libertarian Enlightenment understanding of separation of church and state.

———. *Liberty of Conscience: Roger Williams in America*. Grand Rapids, MI: Eerdmans, 1991. Recent scholarly study of Williams, extolling his libertarian thought.

Gerson, Noel B. *The Edict of Nantes*. New York: Grosset and Dunlap, 1969. Useful, succinct history of the edict, with text.

Hanley, Thomas O'Brien. "Church and State in the Maryland Ordinance of 1639." *Church History* (December 1957): 325–341. Important study of the neglected Maryland colonial statute.

Jordan, W. K. *The Development of Religious Toleration in England*. 4 vols. Gloucester, MA: Peter Smith, 1938. Multivolume work, still the most comprehensive discussion of toleration in the English political culture.

Lasson, Kenneth. "Free Exercise in the Free State: Maryland's Role in Religious Liberty and the First Amendment." *Journal of Church and State* 31:3 (Autumn 1989): 419–449.

Miller, Allen O. *A Christian Declaration on Human Rights: Theological Studies of the World Alliance of Reformed Churches*. Grand Rapids, MI: Eerdmans, 1977.

Murray, John Courtney. *Religious Liberty: An End and A Beginning: The Declaration on Religious Freedom*. New York: Macmillan, 1966. Eight papers by prominent theologians, Catholic and Protestant, from a conference on religious freedom in 1966. Edited and contributed to by the leading theologian of Vatican II.

Nobles, Bryant R. "John Clarke's Political Teachings: Historical Developments." *Foundations* 14:4 (October 1971): 318–324.

Selement, George. "John Clarke and the Struggle for Separation of Church and State." *Foundations* 15:2 (April 1972): 111–126.

Stokes, Anson Phelps. *Church and State in the United States.* 3 vols. New York: Harper Brothers, 1950. Old, standard compilation of key documents pertaining to religious liberty in the United States.

White, Barrie. "Early Baptist Arguments for Religious Freedom: Their Overlooked Agenda." *Baptist History and Heritage* 24:4 (October 1989): 3–10.

Christian Obstacles to Human Rights

Abraham, Garth. *The Catholic Church and Apartheid: The Response of the Catholic Church in South Africa to the First Decade of National Party Rule 1948–1957.* Johannesburg, South Africa: Ravan, 1989.

Beuken, Wim, and Karl-Josef Kuschel, eds. *Religion as a Source of Violence.* London: SCM Press, 1997.

Boff, Leonardo, and Virgil Elizondo, eds. *1492–1992: The Voice of the Victims.* London: SCM Press, 1990. Excellent set of essays from a Third World (mostly Latin American) perspective on the conquest of the Americas.

Brands, H. W. *The Strange Death of American Liberalism.* New Haven, CT: Yale University Press, 2001. Argues that the end of the Cold War ushered in a new era of American distrust of government and an end to many federal programs to address social ills.

DeGruchy, John W. *The Church Struggle in South Africa.* Grand Rapids, MI: Eerdmans, 1986. Most useful survey of the struggle against apartheid in South Africa, by one who was an observer.

Dussel, Enrique, ed. *The Church in Latin America 1492–1992.* Maryknoll, NY: Orbis Books, 1992. A valuable set of essays produced by the

CEHILA project that focuses upon the church of the poor in Latin America. Especially useful essays include "The Church and Emergent Nation States" (Enrique Dussel); "Protestantism in Latin America" (Jean-Pierre Bastian); "The Reductions" (Margarita Duran Estrago); "The Church and Afro-American Slavery" (Laennec Hiurbon); "The Church and Defense of Human Rights" (Jose Comblin).

Ferguson, John. *Pelagius: A Historical and Theological Study*. Cambridge, MA: W. Heffner, 1956. An older but informative work that places Pelagius in the context of theological unrest of the fourth century and details his difficulties with Jerome and others in the Middle East.

Fulton, John. *The Tragedy of Belief: Division, Politics, and Religion in Ireland*. Oxford: Clarendon Press, 1991. Excellent contemporary analysis of Catholic Nationalism, Protestant Loyalism, and the religious factor in Irish politics and statecraft.

Jennings, Francis. *The Invasion of America: Indians, Colonialism, and the Cant of Conquest*. New York: W. W. Norton, 1975. Traces conquest themes and the impact of European conquest upon indigenous peoples.

Kinghorn, Johann. *Die NG Kerk en Apartheid*. Johannesburg, South Africa: Macmillan, 1986. Contemporary study of the Afrikaner Church on apartheid.

McLoughlin, William G. *Cherokees and Missionaries, 1789–1839*. New Haven, CT: Yale University Press, 1984. A thorough interpretation, using documents from both government and denominational archives, of the Cherokee question. McLoughlin concludes it was a triumph of racism and ethnocentrism over the aboriginal culture.

Rees, B. R. *Pelagius: A Reluctant Heretic*. Rochester, NY: Boydell Press, 1998. Excellent analysis of the Pelagian controversy, including a time line of events.

Walshe, Peter. *The Rise of African Nationalism in South Africa*. Berkeley: University of California Press, 1971. Traces one of the powerful organizations to bring down apartheid.

Worsnip, Michael E. *Between Two Fires: The Anglican Church and Apartheid*. Pietermaritzburg: University of Natal Press, 1991.

Organized Christianity and Human Rights

Abrams, Elliott. *The Influence of Faith: Religious Groups and U.S. Foreign Policy*. Lanham, MD: Rowman and Littlefield, 2001. Former U.S. undersecretary of state perspective on the influence of religion.

Baum, Gregory. "The Catholic Foundation of Human Rights." *The Ecumenist* (1979).

Burns, J. H. "The Rights of Man Since the Reformation: An Historical Survey." In *An Introduction to the Study of Human Rights*. Edited by Francis A. Vallat. London: University of London, 1972.

"Declaration of Korean Theologians." *East Asian Journal of Theology* 3:2 (October 1985): 290–292.

Dipboye, Carolyn Cook. "The Roman Catholic Church and the Political Struggle for Human Rights in Latin America, 1868–1980." *Journal of Church and State* 24 (1982): 497–524. An excellent survey of the critical era in the region and the growth of indigenous Roman Catholic action toward human rights recognition.

Gremillion, Joseph, ed. *The Gospel of Peace and Justice: Catholic Social Teaching Since Pope John*. Maryknoll, NY: Orbis Books, 1976. Includes not only human rights matters, but a wide variety of social encyclicals.

Harakas, Stanley S. "Human Rights: An Eastern Orthodox Perspective." In *Human Rights in Religious Traditions*. Edited by Arlene Swidler. New York: Pilgrim Press, 1982. Concise, well-written summary of the Orthodox Church's teachings.

Hollenbach, David. *Justice, Peace, and Human Rights: American Catholic Social Ethics in a Pluralistic Context*. New York: Crossroad, 1988. Major theological essay by a Jesuit on the meaning of human rights post-Vatican II and its origins.

Humphrey, John P. *Human Rights and the United Nations: A Great Adventure*. Dobbs Ferry, NY: Transnational Publishers, 1984. A thematic, personal history of the early years of U.N. history.

John, Clement, ed. *Human Rights and The Churches: New Challenges: A Compilation of Reports of International and Regional Consultations organized by the Commission of the Churches on International Affairs*

(October 1994–June 1998). Geneva: World Council of Churches, 1998.

Kairos Theologians. *The Kairos Document: Challenge to the Church: A Theological Comment on the Political Crisis in South Africa.* Grand Rapids, MI: Eerdmans, 1986. The full text of the most influential of the transformative declarations with an introduction by South African theologian, John W. De Gruchy.

Kuriakose, K. K. *Human Rights and Christians in India 1947–1980.* Master's thesis, Graduate Theological Union, 1982. One of the few summaries of the human rights positions and work in the Indian Christian community.

Langan, John. "Human Rights in Roman Catholicism." In *Human Rights in Religious Traditions.* Edited by Arlene Swidler. New York: Pilgrim Press, 1982. Very strong, concise summary of the topic.

Lemoux, Penny. *Cry of the People: United States Involvement in the Rise of Fascism, Torture and Murder and the Persecution of the Catholic Church in Latin America.* Garden City, NY: Doubleday, 1980.

Logan, Willis H. *The Kairos Covenant: Standing with South African Christians.* New York: Friendship Press, 1988. Contains interpretive essays on the Kairos Document and its acceptance among a worldwide community, including Cornel West and Richard Mouw.

Miller, Allen O., ed. *Christian Declaration on Human Rights.* Grand Rapids, MI: Eerdmans, 1977. The official papers and declarations of the World Alliance of Reformed Churches with respect to their seven-year study of human rights. Contains essays by Jürgen Moltmann, Daniel Migliore, James Cone, and Douglas J. Hall.

Nolde, Frederick O. *Free and Equal: Human Rights in Ecumenical Perspective.* Geneva: World Council of Churches, 1968. On the twentieth anniversary of the Universal Declaration of Human Rights, one of the participants reflected on the role of organized Christians upon the process. An insightful statement on the importance of the Christian community is given by Charles Malik, rapporteur to the United Nations.

Norman, Edward. *Christianity and the World Order.* Oxford: Oxford University Press, 1979. A useful wide-ranging essay on the ecumenical Christian community and issues of rights.

O'Grady, Ron. *Bread and Freedom: Understanding and Acting on Human Rights*. Geneva: World Council of Churches, 1979. A New Zealand Churches of Christ advocate for human rights. Helpful summary of historical and theological developments, with special emphasis upon Asia.

Riga, Peter. *Peace on Earth: A Commentary on Pope John's Encyclical*. London: Herder and Herder, 1964.

Traer, Robert. *Faith in Human Rights: Support in Religious Traditions for a Global Struggle*. Washington, DC: Georgetown University Press, 1991. The best available survey of the religious dimension of human rights. Strong on the Christian tradition and especially the U.N. declarations and various responses.

Tutu, Desmond. *Crying in the Wilderness: The Struggle for Human Rights in South Africa*. Grand Rapids, MI: Eerdmans, 1982. A useful collection of Tutu's writings spanning his career.

Wako, Amos. "Human Rights in Africa Today." In *Political Trends in Africa: Development, Arms Race, Human Rights*. Geneva: CCIA, 1982. Covers the issues and struggle for human rights in Africa.

The United Nations and Human Rights

Cassin, Rene. *La Declaration universelle et la Mise en oeuvre des Droit de l'Homme*. Leyden, Holland: Academy of International Law, 1951. The history of the Declaration from the perspective of one of the members of the drafting committee.

Doherty, Earl. "John Peters Humphrey, Unsung Canadian Hero: Celebrating the 50th Anniversary of the Universal Declaration of Human Rights and the Canadian Who Was at the Center of Its Creation." *Humanist In Canada* 31:4 (Winter 1998): 26–27. A reminder of the silent author of the Universal Declaration.

Encyclopedia of the United Nations and International Agreements. 4 vols. Edited by Edmund Jan Osmanczyk and Anthony Mango. New York: Routledge, 1975, 1980, 2003. A comprehensive reference tool that includes articles on each of the declarations and conventions. Periodically updated.

Evans, Archibald A. *Worker's Rights Are Human Rights*. Rome: IDOC International, 1981. An examination of the application of human rights to the workplace. Important documentation for the formulation of policy.

Lillich, Richard B. *The Human Rights of Aliens in Contemporary International Law*. Manchester, England: Manchester University Press, 1984.

Morsink, J. *The Universal Declaration of Human Rights: Origins, Drafting, and Intent*. Philadelphia: University of Pennsylvania Press, 2000.

Mower, A. Glenn. *The United States, The United Nations and Human Rights: The Eleanor Roosevelt and Jimmy Carter Eras*. Westport, CT: Greenwood Press, 1979.

Nickel, James. *Making Sense of Human Rights: Philosophical Reflections on the Universal Declaration of Human Rights*. Berkeley: University of California Press, 1987. A significant analysis from a philosophical perspective.

Robinson, Nehemiah. *The Universal Declaration of Human Rights*. New York: Institute of Jewish Affairs, 1958. A legal history of the declaration.

Schwelb, Egon. *Human Rights and the International Community: The Roots and Growth of the Universal Declaration of Human Rights, 1948–1963*. Chicago: Quadrangle Books, 1964. A Jewish lawyer's reflection on the development of the declaration. Contains helpful background references.

Tolley, Howard. *The U.N. Commission on Human Rights*. Boulder, CO: Westview Press, 1987. Traces the recent history of the commission as it investigates human rights violations.

Van Dyke, Vernon. *Human Rights, the United States and World Community*. London: Oxford University Press, 1970. An important essay on the development of U.S. human rights policy and the role of the United States.

Wagner, Teresa, ed. *Fifty Years After the Declaration: The United Nations' Record on Human Rights*. Lanham, MD: University Press of America, 2001.

INDEX

About the Author

WILLIAM H. BRACKNEY is Professor in and Chair of the Department of Religion at Baylor University. His books include *The Baptists* (Greenwood, 1988), *Christian Voluntarism in Britain and North America* (Greenwood, 1992), *Christian Voluntarism: Theology and Praxis* (1997), *Pilgrim Pathways* (1998), and *Historical Dictionary of the Baptists* (1999).